NEW W...

1980s TV in Britain

edited by Rodney Marshall

ACKNOWLEDGEMENTS

I would like to thank every one of the writers who has contributed to this book...

Edward Kellett explores *The Bill*, during its earliest years: how it combined some of the energy of *The Sweeney* and the social realism of *Z Cars*, yet forged its own unique 'middle path', both reflecting the changes taking place in the real-life police force and the production changes within the series itself.

Cailin Thomas examines how *Inspector Morse* revolutionised the British crime series by introducing the two-hour format and how it reinterpreted the character created by novelist Colin Dexter.

JZ Ferguson looks at *Cuffy* as an example of how a gentle social comedy can make acute observations about a changing world, including values which cannot be measured in financial terms.

Madeleine Langham explores the history of women in the British police and the ways in which fictional Maggie Forbes (*The Gentle Touch*) represents a ground-breaking figure in British television.

Chris Wood is a graphic designer who offers us an insider's guide through the evolution of main titles sequences as technology evolved.

Paul Watts re-appraises Chris Boucher's visionary hybrid, the short-lived *Star Cops*, a series which arguably should have become a long-running landmark BBC show, but which suffered from creative conflict and was buried by the corporation on BBC2 in a death-knell time slot: 8.30 pm during the summer holidays.

Lucy Smith places *The Comic Strip Presents* within the context of both the new wave of 'alternative comedy' and a decade of social, political and cultural change, examining how the mini films reflected and satirised the times.

Ian Payn journeys into what he calls 'Lovejoy World', exploring how the production team sanitised the lead character as portrayed in the novels, and why he feels that the series offered a distinctively different type of television escapism, or 'Comfort TV'.

Al Samujh explores how *Hammer House of Horror* represents a dramatic departure (and last hurrah) for the ITC company – normally associated with clean-cut action-adventure – which funded it, but which also set a new benchmark for TV anthology horror as a genre.

Joanne Knowles explores *Auf Wiedersehen, Pet* as a condition-of-England series, a comedy-drama, a hybrid which allowed the writers to 'balance out the bleaker aspects of 1980s social situations with a lighter perspective'. Jo centres on the seven (deracinated) protagonists' sense of nostalgia both for another *time* and *place* – a working-class England where jobs were easier to find and where a man's role (as the 'patriarch breadwinner') seemed easier to define and achieve.

Andrew Lane explores the odd 'shared universe' of *Strangers*, *Bulman* and *The Paradise Club*, centring on the impact of Murray Smith's left-field approach to writing: creating stories which are 'anchored in reality' – in terms of social and political change, pop music etc – yet frequently contain quirky, comedic, bizarre and even surreal elements.

Richard Marson explores a 'golden age' of BBC children's television which, following directly on from the 1970s evolution/revolution, continued to provide younger viewers with 'emotionally intelligent drama'. His recent interviews with both Colin Cant and Anna Home enrich his own insights.

Tomas Marshall explores *Alice* (*Něco z Alenky*), filmmaker Jan Švankmajer's darkly surreal live-action/stop-motion fantasy which was part-financed by Channel 4, a film which challenged both adult viewers' expectations of the Wonderland subject matter and their preconceptions of animation as being exclusively a child's medium.

Trevor Knight's chapter on 'Nuclear TV' explores several US and British productions but is (understandably) dominated by his examination of the outstanding *Edge of Darkness*. He argues that it is the daring "blend" which makes this drama series special: political thriller, murder mystery, conspiracy drama, mythological fantasy, ghost story, and character study of grief. Trevor explores *Doctor Who*'s complicated and rocky 'road to nowhere' in the 80s, including the wider context of internal battles within the BBC and the Corporation's clashes with the government.

Morris Bright has written a loving 'appreciation' of *Rumpole of the Bailey*, a series which helped inspire a personal and professional lifetime dedicated to television and film drama, and the studios where the magic of moving pictures is created.

I look at two Granada series – *Travelling Man* and *Floodtide* – as shows whose topical, drug-related narratives were shaped by location managers finding intriguing settings which then inspired the plots. My exploration of *Bergerac*'s initial run centres on how a winning formula for a series can be partly the result of reassembling the key parts from a previously successful one, *Shoestring*. I re-examine how Channel 4's black barber shop sitcom *Desmond's* provided insights into a marginalised Black Britain, aimed specifically at white viewers.

Finally, **Mike Pegler** offers us a grand tour of the popular shows on British television – both US imports and home-made programmes – exploring the power which terrestrial TV had, either to reinforce or question the Establishment.

PREFACE

Social commentators tend to break time periods up into chunks, reviewing post-war history in bite-size decades, much as we have done in this book and its two predecessors. There is a danger, of course, in exploring any decade in isolation. For one thing, radical change can occur during a ten-year period, meaning that an umbrella term such as the 'Roaring Twenties' or 'Swinging Sixties' can be meaningless, unhelpful or misleading; for another, we need to explore any decade in the knowledge of what came before. Nor, I might add, do television series always respect decade divides...

When it comes to Britain in the 1980s, we have a third potential problem. No other post-war decade has been dominated in terms of politics by a single figure. This can result in a temptation to review all political, economic and social change or conflict solely in Margaret Thatcher's shadow. We become in danger of 'Thatcher fixation'. In terms of television drama, this obsession has even led to decontextualized misassumptions and misconceptions. Let us take two contrasting examples: *Minder* (1979-94) and *Boys from the Blackstuff* (1982). The charismatic conman Arthur Daley is often labelled as an on-screen projection of Thatcher's free-market philosophy. The problem with this reading is that the character was created before Britain's first female PM came to power. Equally, Alan Bleasdale's dramas are frequently labelled as anti-Thatcherite, something which the playwright himself has sought to correct:

"The irony about the way that *Boys from the Blackstuff* was perceived is that it was seen as a righteous and violent attack on Thatcher's Britain. The irony being that I wrote four of the five episodes before Thatcher came to power." [1]

Bleasdale's anger was directed at a more general 'state of the nation' and the devastating socio-economic effects of long-term unemployment in a deindustrialised Britain. As for Leon Griffith's

Arthur Daley, he too is a product of a more general 'sign of the times' context, one in which Britain was gradually moving from an industrial nation heavily reliant on state ownership to a post-industrial entrepreneurial economy. It is important, therefore, that when we explore 1980s television drama we do so with eyes wide open, able to see where writers *were* directly responding to the ever-increasing social, cultural and economic effects of the policies of Thatcherism, and, conversely, where dramas were either reflecting more general longer-term change or voicing concerns about specific, worrying malaises in British society, such as the objectification of women, the misuse of HIV/AIDS as a tool for discrimination, or the representation of black people and other minority groups in the media.

Most social historians reviewing the decade agree that − in the distinct absence of articulate and powerful opposition in the House of Commons − it was often in the fields of music, film and television drama that we found what we might call 'dissident voices'. Some of these were, of course, directly responding to Thatcherism and a growing public sense of an emerging 'greed culture'. Government policies clearly shaped some of British television's comedy and drama during the 1980s. Examples include Harry Enfield's Loadsamoney character, Rik Mayall's Alan B'Stard MP, Ben Elton's satirical comedy acts on *Saturday Live*, and Phil Redmond's soap *Brookside*.

The decade began with Britain agreeing to buy Trident missiles from the US, an opinion poll suggesting that 40% of the population feared that nuclear war was a distinct possibility, while *Panorama* transmitted excerpts from leaked Public Information films which the Government planned to broadcast if an attack was deemed to be imminent. This genuine public fear would be brilliantly tapped into by Troy Kennedy Martin's landmark BBC drama *Edge of Darkness* mid-decade, a remarkable series which is explored at length in our book.

Alan Bleasdale's social drama *The Black Stuff* was shown on television in a year where the closure of steelworks led to one place in County Durham being described as a 'ghost town', which would become the title of a chart-topping pop song the following year. [2]

Both Maggie Forbes (*The Gentle Touch*) and Jean Darblay (*Juliet Bravo*) emerged as fictional female police chiefs in 1980, at a time when a male-dominated real-life police force was failing to catch a serial killer despite a trail of evidence, leaving women increasingly angry and frustrated by what many perceived as a society in which females were still treated as second class citizens: instructed to stay indoors while a killer was on the loose, blamed by a number of male judges (for hitchhiking) in rape cases, objects of a forensic male gaze as page 3 'pin-ups'. While both *The Gentle Touch* and *Juliet Bravo* were created by male writers, these landmark shows fulfilled two vital needs: modernising the police series in terms of placing strong female characters at the heart of the narrative – Britain was lagging decades behind the US in this respect – and offering aspirational figures, particularly for female viewers.

In terms of women writers, the decade would see Julie Welch (*Those Glory Glory Days* 1983); Lynda La Plante (*Widows* 1983-85); Fay Weldon (*The Life and Loves of a She-Devil* 1986); [3] and Carla Lane (*Butterflies* 1978-83 and *Bread* 1986-91) making waves, part of a growing number of females having an impact in what was still a male-dominated industry. Female writers and performers like Victoria Wood, Dawn French and Jennifer Saunders were also gatecrashing the domain of satirical comedy, including French & Saunders collaborating on the infamous, never broadcast *Back to Normal with Eddie Monsoon* (*The Comic Strip Presents...*)

Black Britain was something rarely explored on television in terms of drama. Trix Worrell would emerge in the 1980s as a key figure in terms of responding to both the continuing absence of racial minorities foregrounded on the small screen and the worrying marginalisation or even misrepresentation of the black community in the mainstream press. The hard-hitting yet soulful *Just Like Mohicans* (1985) was a ground-breaking one-off drama, while the popularity of *Desmond's* (1989-94) with white viewers demonstrated how important television can be in terms of social glue, connecting disparate people and challenging stereotypes. Arguably, only Channel 4 would have had the bravery and vision to commission the sitcom, as its creator acknowledged.

The arrival of Channel 4 in the autumn of 1982 may not have had a similar impact – in terms of popular culture – as that of ITV back in 1955. Nevertheless, its film production arm helped fund many innovative feature-length dramas, including made-for-television movies which were both critically acclaimed and popular, such as Jack Rosenthal's *P'tang, Yang, Kipperbang* (1982) and Hanif Kureishi and Stephen Fears' *My Beautiful Laundrette* (1985). [4] Within two years, they were investing in a third of the feature films being made in the UK, in addition to several left-field overseas movies such as Wim Wenders' metaphorical road movie *Paris, Texas* (1984) and the dark surrealism of Jan Švankmajer's *Alice* (1988).

Channel 4's opening evening's offerings – *Brookside*, *The Comic Strip Presents …Five Go Mad in Dorset* and Stephen Frears' *Walter* – suggested that it would be a welcome addition to the alternative voices which were emerging in what many perceived as an increasingly deeply divided society. Part of Channel 4's ethos was to provide a platform both for new writers and small production companies. It swiftly became a key player in a countercultural movement which included pop musicians. Alwyn Turner observes:

"Their voices were seldom acknowledged by the Thatcher governments, but even so their impact was felt and – perhaps more than the official opposition – it was often these cultural dissidents who kept alive the idea that there was indeed an alternative to Thatcherism. Certainly they provided a running commentary on the era that was hard to ignore." [5]

It is important that any book exploring 1980s television does not give the false impression that all four terrestrial channels were filling their schedules with what Turner terms 'cultural dissidents'. If I had to pick out arguably the two most significant fictional characters in the decade's TV in terms of their impact on popular culture, neither would count as politically subversive. At least, not on the surface. [6] Leon Griffith's Arthur Daley (George Cole) in *Minder* and John Sullivan's Derek 'Del Boy' Trotter (David Jason) in *Only Fools and Horses* became two of the most loved television characters of the decade. The popularity of both Arthur and Del Boy exemplifies the power that television still had in terms of society, with expressions such as "Er indoors" a "nice little earner", "lovely jubbly" and the priceless misuse of "mange tout" being used in school playgrounds, offices and pubs alike.

Nor does 'innovative drama' necessarily apply exclusively to scripted content. It can refer to experimentation with a traditional genre or format. Several series explored in this book are 'hybrid' shows, including *Star Cops* (sci-fi crime), and *Auf Wiedersehen, Pet* (comedy-drama). The 1980s decade was, arguably, blurring the traditional genre boundaries. In terms of format, *Inspector Morse* (1987-2000) challenged both the network and the viewer with a two-hour crime drama. Would audiences be willing to follow a highbrow, non-action-based police/crime show lasting twice as long? The popularity of *Morse* is unquestionably proof positive that if you provide viewers with a quality product, even incorporating complex plots, there will be a sizeable audience for it. Today, that 'Morse format' has become standard practice for several dramas. [7] If Zenith and Central were taking something of a leap of faith with *Morse*, then the BBC appeared to be 'modernising' itself in several ways...

The creation of a primetime soap, *EastEnders* (1985-), can be seen as representing the corporation's attempts to rival the mass audience appeal of *Coronation Street* (1960-). While *Howards' Way* (1985-90) shares connective tissue with *The Brothers* (1972-76), as

9

it gradually evolved from drama into soap it too reflected the BBC's desire to adopt a more populist approach, in this case a glossy rival to American soap dramas. Crime dramas such as *Shoestring* (1979-80) and *Bergerac* (1981-91) were following in the footsteps of *Target* (1977-78) as all-film productions, no doubt as a reaction to the popularity of Euston Films' output for Thames TV.

In terms of children's drama, Phil Redmond's *Grange Hill* (1978-2008) continued to break away from the middle-class bubble or preserve of many previous BBC series, as did *Byker Grove* (1989-2006) from the end of the 1980s. Both tackled a wide range of hard-hitting social themes, something unthinkable before the mid to late-1970s. Time-travelling/historical series such as *Shadow of the Stone* (1987) and *Moondial* (1988) continued the tradition of thought-provoking fantasy drama. Tyne Tees TV's *Barriers* (1981-82) was an intriguing example of a slow-paced, adventure/ mystery series which treated teenagers as maturing viewers.

The 1980s timeline which accompanies this book (pages 21-29) offers readers a reminder of some of the major political, social and cultural events which helped to shape the decade. Inevitably, these include conflicts – Falklands, Miners' Strike, mainland bombings, the continuing Troubles in Northern Ireland; technological developments such as the launching of the Sinclair home computer at the beginning of the decade, the mobile phone mid-decade and the invention of the World Wide Web at the end; mass gatherings such as 30,000 women creating a human chain at Greenham and 72,000 attending Live Aid at Wembley [8]. Events elsewhere which sent global shockwaves included the Chernobyl nuclear disaster and the Tiananmen Square protests and massacre. The 1980s began with *Another Brick in the Wall* (Part 2) at Number 1 in the charts and ended with the Berlin Wall coming down.

While *Coronation Street* and *EastEnders* were breaking ratings records, it is only fair to observe in this preface that many of the sitcoms, soaps and crime series which attracted high viewing figures or critical acclaim during the decade were US imports. Both *Dallas* (1978-91) and *Dynasty* (1981-89) offered UK audiences the American Dream in all its nightmarish glossy glory. The storyline surrounding "Who shot JR?" in 1980 captured the attention of both the British popular press and millions of UK viewers.

The popularity of sitcoms like M*A*S*H (1972-83), *Soap* (1977-81), *Taxi* (1978-82), *Cheers* (1982-93) and *The Golden Girls* (1985-92) is a reminder that – as a (dangerous) generalisation – American humour crosses the Atlantic more successfully than the British variety. This growing trend would continue into the 90s, with shows like *Frasier* (1993-2004) and *Friends* (1994-2004).

Meanwhile, several US crime series were demonstrating how you could revolutionise a well-established genre. *Hill Street Blues* (1981-87) was a landmark series in many ways: the method of filming, including the use of hand-held cameras; its multiple, overlapping plots; its exploration of urban decay and an underclass often ignored by American television series; its daring blend of drama and comedy.

While arguably less experimental, the 'MTV cops' of *Miami Vice* (1984-89) nevertheless offered UK viewers something new again, with the series' cinematography and choice of music connecting to the New Wave post-punk pop culture. Both shows were offering us something distinctively different from British tv crime fiction. In addition, for many British viewers, particularly in the depths of a grey winter, watching *Miami Vice* provided the added escapist attraction of sunshine, sea, palm trees or even the fabulous Art Deco beach-front architecture. [9] I guess that the closest domestic equivalent would have been the much-loved and long-running Jersey-based *Bergerac*.

Whether it is US imports or home-grown products, the variety of drama available to UK television viewers across the four channels was impressive. Some of that drama contained challenging, gritty material, but the schedules also offered both savage and gentler satire, or even pure escapist entertainment, such as *Lovejoy*. The wide choice available also applied to *how* and *when* people decided to watch their favourite shows. No need to rush back from the office or pub as was the case back in the 1960s or 70s. The increasing popularity of the video recorder was changing the way many of us watched programmes, while the arrival of satellite television would begin to dilute the market. Nevertheless, the concept of television as a 'shared experience' was still alive, and there remained plenty of good reasons to stay in and submerge yourself in the new waves.

Mike Pegler's endpiece chapter offers a fascinating journey through popular 80s TV – both the US imports and the UK shows. He explores, amongst other genres, both contemporary and costume drama, soaps and sitcoms. I have placed it as the book's final essay, but it is not a conclusion, more an intriguing overview on both the decade and the power of television. You could immediately flick to it now and treat it as an extended introduction or leave it until the end and read it as a last tour of the 80s. Either way, it is a piece which is bound to spark debate.

© Rodney Marshall
January 2024

1. Interview with Alan Bleasdale, available on *YouTube*, VHS Gold, March 2020.
2. The Pet Shop Boys were one of the many pop bands offering musical commentary on the state-of-the-nation, including *Opportunities (Let's Make Lots of Money)* "a satire of 80s excess", and *Shopping*, "a withering portrait of London consumerism between the Big Bang and Black Monday, so shrewdly drawn you could imagine a City boy of the era banging the wheel of his Ferrari and bellowing along, oblivious to its real intent." Equally significant was their poignant AIDS-related elegy *Your Funny Uncle* (1988).

(Guardian, 24/01/2020) As they would continue to do so in the decades after the 1980s, Pet Shop Boys demonstrated their ability to produce popular sounds while responding to social change, be it 'yuppie satires' or ballads about the cultural effects of HIV/AIDS. Other songs worth exploring from their 1980s repertoire would include *Suburbia* (1986) and *It's A Sin* (1987).

3. While Weldon did not write the screenplay, the television drama remained largely faithful to her experimental novel.

4. Originally made for Channel 4, the critical acclaim which *My Beautiful Laundrette* received at the Edinburgh Film Festival led to it being acquired by Orion and given a cinema distribution. It even received an Oscar nomination. Initially, the plan was for Channel 4 Films to invest in twenty films every year, to be screened in their *Film on Four* slot. This original vision of films made exclusively for television broadcast was partly a result of the three-year 'holdback' rule between cinematic release and initial television screening. Channel 4 played its part in getting this rule changed for low-budget films. It would soon be responsible for part-funding some landmark British films, including the aforementioned *My Beautiful Laundrette* and *Mona Lisa*. Channel 4 worked alongside companies such as Goldcrest Films, Working Title Films and Merchant Ivory. Mike Leigh: "*Film on Four* saved the British film industry. This is a non-negotiable, historical fact of life and anybody who suggests that this isn't the case is simply either suffering from some kind of ignorance or has got some terrible chip." (Admittedly, trying to determine what constitutes a 'TV movie' and what is a 'cinema venture' can be a nightmare, as the boundaries became blurred during the 1980s with Channel 4's arrival.)

5. Alwyn W Turner, 'Eighties: This is the dawning of a New Era', *Rejoice! Rejoice! Britain in the 1980s*, p. xxi.

6. As Mike Pegler will argue in his absorbing Endpiece, as viewers we can love them both, yet still be aware of an underlying satire about 'entrepreneurial Britain'.
7. Here in the UK, we were used to US 'TV movies' offering us a longer crime format, as in *Columbo*.
8. The multi-venue event saw 89,000 attend in Philadelphia. Estimates put the global audience at almost two billion.
9. *Magnum, PI* (1980-88) fulfilled a similar function in terms of escapist sunshine, while constantly making its viewers second guess what to expect each week, from genuinely dark storylines, through Vietnam flashbacks, dream narratives, ghost stories, to almost slapstick comedic plots.

"Pop music, comedy, fiction: all felt moved to remark upon political developments, normally from a hostile position...it was often these cultural dissidents who kept alive the idea that there was indeed an alternative to Thatcherism. Certainly they provided a running commentary on the era that was hard to ignore."
Alwyn W Turner, *Rejoice! Rejoice! Britain in the 1980s*)

"It was as though she [Thatcher] had unlocked a Pandora's box and released forces into society over which she had little or no control. She called for a return to thrift and good housekeeping, and presided over a massive increase in credit card and mortgage indebtedness...she wished to reverse the effects of 1960s permissiveness and found herself in a country where drug taking had become almost the norm amongst young people, where condoms were promoted by government ministers and where home video recorders and satellite television made pornography ever more available."
(**Alwyn W Turner**, *Rejoice! Rejoice! Britain in the 1980s*)

"Channel 4 was set up on the ethos of actually having multi-racial production companies etc. and trying to champion various new voices."
(**Trix Worrell**, BFI Q&A, 08/02/2019)

"I know I'll never grow up because I still have that childish feeling that "it isn't fair!" When I think that...I go to the typewriter and fight back."
(**Alan Bleasdale**)

"More change and more conflict were crammed into the 1980s, particularly the first half of the decade, than any other decade in the second half of the twentieth century. Out of political chaos, Britain arrived at a settlement that lasted, for better or worse. The way we live now follows directly from the tumultuous events of the 1980s."

(**Andy McSmith**, *No Such Thing As Society: A History of Britain in the 1980s*)

"Weren't we just a generation still fascinated with the magic lantern in the corner of the front room, which offered us escape?" (**Peter Kay**, *T.V.: Big Adventures on the Small Screen*)

1980s TIMELINE

1980 Pink Floyd's *Another Brick in the Wall (Part II)* is No 1
1980 Alan Bleasdale's *The Black Stuff* play broadcast (January 2nd)
1980 *Shillingbury Tales* first broadcast; feature-length pilot (Jan 6th)
1980 Sinclair ZX80 home computer launched (January 29th)
1980 Political satire sitcom *Yes Minister* first broadcast (Feb 25th)
1980 Drama series *Fox* first broadcast (March 10th)
1980 *Panorama* broadcast excerpts of nuclear PI films (March)
1980 Opinion poll suggests 40% think nuclear war is likely (April)
1980 Riot in St Paul's area of Bristol (April 2nd)
1980 *The Gentle Touch* first broadcast (April 11th)
1980 First official case in the US of the AIDS epidemic (April 24th)
1980 Iranian embassy siege in London (April 30th)
1980 Rubik's Cube released internationally (May)
1980 Government pamphlet *Protect and Survive* published (May)
1980 Britain agrees to buy Trident missiles from USA (July 15th)
1980 UB40 release debut album *Signing Off* (August 29th)
1980 *Juliet Bravo* first broadcast (August 30th)
1980 *World in Action* exposes UK pop chart-rigging (August)
1980 *Hammer House of Horror* anthology first broadcast (Sept)
1980 Iran-Iraq War commences (September 22nd)
1980 Closure of steelworks in Consett; 'murder of a town' (Sept)
1980 Housing Act allows tenants to buy a council property (Oct 3rd)
1980 PMs' 'The Lady's Not for Turning' speech (October 10th)
1980 H-Block prisoners go on hunger strike in N. Ireland (Oct 27th)
1980 Michael Foot voted in as Labour leader (November 10th)
1980 NFFC film *Babylon* film released (November)
1980 John Lennon is murdered in New York (December 8th)
1980 *Magnum, PI* debuts in US (December 11th)
1980 WAVAW stage protests about 'Page 3 girls' (December 12th)
1980 Detective series *Shoestring* comes to its end (December 21st)
1980 Political thriller *The Secret Servant* published
1980 Use of barcodes spreads with introduction at WH Smith

1980 289 police officers working full time on 'Ripper hunt'

1980 Modern art series *The Shock of the New* broadcast

1981 Lennon's *Imagine* re-enters the charts following his death

1981 Tyne Tees children's drama *Barriers* begins (January 4th)

1981 TV series *The Hitchhiker's Guide to the Galaxy* begins (Jan 5th)

1981 Peter Sutcliffe charged with 13 murders (January 5th)

1981 ABC launch *Dynasty* as a soap rival to *Dallas* (Jan 12th)

1981 Phil Collins' *In the Air Tonight* released (January)

1981 Phil Collins releases *Face Value* album (February 13th)

1981 '13 dead and nothing said' demo/march, New Cross (Mar 2nd)

1981 4th Time Lord Tom Baker leaves *Doctor Who* (Mar 21st)

1981 Social Democratic Party founded (March 26th)

1981 *Chariots of Fire* released (March 30th)

1981 Brixton riot/uprising begins (April 10th)

1981 Scottish romcom *Gregory's Girl* released (April 23rd)

1981 Police drama *The Chinese Detective* debuts (April 30th)

1981 Bobby Sands dies after 66 days on hunger strike (May 5th)

1981 *Stand and Deliver* (Adam and the Ants) at Number 1 (May 9th)

1981 183m Nat West Tower skyscraper opened (June 11th)

1981 Debut album *Duran Duran* released (June 15th)

1981 Southall riot after Asian youths attacked by skinheads (July 3rd)

1981 Arrest of Leroy Cooper leads to Toxteth riots (July 3rd)

1981 The Specials' *Ghost Town* at Number 1 (July 11th)

1981 Prince Charles and Lady Diana Spencer marry (July 29th)

1981 24-hour music channel MTV launched (August 1st)

1981 Greenham Women camp outside cruise missile base (Sept 5th)

1981 Soft Cell's *Tainted Love* at Number 1 (September 5th)

1981 Sitcom *Only Fools and Horses...* debuts (September 8th)

1981 Tebbit makes remark about cycling to seek work (Oct)

1981 The Human League album *Dare* released (October 16th)

1981 Crime drama *Bergerac* debuts (October 18th)

1981 *A Fine Romance* debuts (November 1st)

1981 The Human League's *Don't You Want Me* tops charts (Dec)

1981 Ken Livingstone becomes the leader of the GLC

1981 110 non-white officers out of 24,000 in Metropolitan Police

1981 Salman Rushdie's *Midnight's Children* wins the Booker Prize

1981 London Docklands Development Corporation (LDDC) created

1981 Rupert Murdoch's News International buys up *The Times*

1982 5th Time Lord Peter Davison joins *Doctor Who* (Jan 4th)

1982 Period drama *Shine on, Harvey Moon* begins (January 8th)

1982 GLC County Hall signpost monthly unemployment figures (Jan)

1982 Sitcom *Whoops Apocalypse* first broadcast (March 14th)

1982 Undeclared *Falklands War* begins (April 2nd)

1982 Sci-fi anthology *Play for Tomorrow* begins (April 13th)

1982 Techno-thriller *Bird of Prey* serial begins (April 22nd)

1982 McCartney/Wonder's *Ebony and Ivory* at Number 1 (April 24th)

1982 Controversial sinking of the Belgrano outside TEZ (May 2nd)

1982 Pat Barker's *Union Street* published (May 13th)

1982 *Rocky III* released in the US (May 28th)

1982 Duran Duran album *Rio* released (May)

1982 Lebanon War or 'invasion' commences (June 6th)

1982 Argentina surrenders in the Falklands war zone (June 14th)

1982 Gay Men's Health Crisis founded in NYC (June 30th)

1982 Thatcher uses term 'Falklands Factor' as rallying call (July 3rd)

1982 Terrence Higgins dies from an AIDS-related illness (July 4th)

1982 Hyde Park & Regent's Park bombings kill eleven (July 20th)

1982 Archbishop of Canterbury 'War is a sign of human failure' (Jul)

1982 The term AIDS is proposed to replace GRID (July 27th)

1982 Heavily criticised *Who Dares Wins* is released (August 26th)

1982 *The Draughtsman's Contract* released (September 4th)

1982 Culture Club single *Do You Really Want to Hurt Me?* (Sept 6th)

1982 BBC spy series *Smiley's People* begins (September 20th)

1982 *Boys from the Blackstuff* drama series begins (October 10th)

1982 Crime drama *Strangers* ends its run (October 20th)

1982 Channel 4 begins transmission (November 2nd)

1982 Phil Redmond's soap opera *Brookside* broadcast (Nov 2nd)

1982 *The Comic Strip Presents...* debuts (November 2nd)

1982 Television drama *Walter* broadcast on C4 launch night

1982 *P'tang, Yang, Kipperbang* broadcast (November 3rd)

1982 Music programme *The Tube* is launched (November 5th)

1982 'Anarchic' sitcom *The Young Ones* debuts (November 9th)

1982 *Saturday Night Thriller* anthology series starts (Nov 13th)

1982 Michael Jackson's *Thriller* is released (November 29th)
1982 Period biographical *Gandhi* released (November 30th)
1982 30,000 women create human chain at Greenham (Dec 12th)
1982 Chris Mullin's *A Very British Coup* published
1983 Sitcom *No Problem!* first broadcast (Jan 7th)
1983 TV-am launched (February 1st)
1983 *The Professionals* series comes to an end (February 6th)
1983 Scottish comedy-drama *Local Hero* released (February 17th)
1983 Spandau Ballet release *True* album (March 4th)
1983 Michael Jackson's *Billie Jean* at Number 1 (March 5th)
1983 Bernard Cribbins sitcom *Cuffy* first airs (March 13th)
1983 *Widows* crime drama first broadcast (March 16th)
1983 Ian MacGregor moves from British Steel to the NCB (March)
1983 Comedy sketch series *Alfresco* first broadcast (May 1st)
1983 *Sweet Dreams (Are Made of This)* is released (May 1983)
1983 *The Ploughman's Lunch* released (May)
1983 *Mail on Sunday* refers to a 'gay plague' (May)
1983 UK General Election won by Conservative Party (June 9th)
1983 Period sitcom *The Black Adder* first broadcast (June 15th)
1983 *Red Monarch* first broadcast (June 16th)
1983 Pilot for what became *The Bill* is broadcast (August 16th)
1983 *Lytton's Diary* drama series begins (August 30th)
1983 Mini-series *Killer* introduces Taggart (September 6th)
1983 Neil Kinnock elected leader of the Labour Party (October 2nd)
1983 Comedy-drama *Auf Wiedersehen, Pet* debuts (November 11th)
1983 *Those Glory Glory Days* released (Nov 17th)
1983 US TV film *The Day After* 100 million + viewers (Nov 20th)
1983 The Flying Pickets top the charts at Christmas
1983 Channel 4 launch *Opinions*, a one person talk show
1984 CND membership rises from 4,500 (1979) to 100,000
1984 BBC bans Frankie Goes to Hollywood's *Relax* (January 13th)
1984 *The Living Planet* first broadcast (Jan 19th)
1984 Frankie Goes to Hollywood's *Relax* Number 1 (Jan 28th)
1984 *Panorama*'s 'Maggie's Militant Tendency' broadcast (January)
1984 Satirical puppet show *Spitting Image* debuts (February 26th)
1984 *Free Nelson Mandela* single released (March 5th)

1984 NUM Miners' Strike begins at Cortonwood (March 6th)
1984 6th Time Lord Colin Baker joins *Doctor Who* (Mar 22nd)
1984 BBC *Missing from Home* serial begins (March 29th)
1984 Pet Shop Boys release *West End Girls* (April 9th)
1984 Libyan embassy siege in London (April 17th)
1984 Period drama *Robin of Sherwood* debuts (April 28th)
1984 *Paris, Texas* released (May 19th)
1984 Bronski Beat release *Smalltown Boy* (May 25th)
1984 Opening of the new Thames Barrier (May)
1984 FGTH's *Two Tribes* at Number 1 (June 16th)
1984 Virgin Atlantic's first scheduled flight (June 22nd)
1984 *Mitch* series begins broadcast (August 31st)
1984 *Hammer House of Mystery and Suspense* begins (Sept 5th)
1984 *The Tripods* first series begins broadcast (Sept 15th)
1984 *Miami Vice* debuts in US (September 16th)
1984 Apocalyptic TV war drama *Threads* broadcast (Sept 23rd)
1984 Grand Hotel Brighton bombing kills four (October 12th)
1984 Comedy-drama *Big Deal* debuts (October 14th)
1984 *The Bill* is first broadcast (October 16th)
1984 BBC reports on 'biblical' famine in Ethiopia (October 24th)
1984 *The Terminator* released (October 26th)
1984 *Welcome to the Pleasuredome* album (October 29th)
1984 *The Killing Fields* released (November 2nd)
1984 *Travelling Man* first mini-series begins (November 7th)
1984 Alison Moyet releases *Alf* album (November 9th)
1984 *Do They Know It's Christmas?* recorded (November 25th)
1984 New Labour MP Chris Smith 'comes out' (November)
1984 Half of British Telecom on sale to public as shares (Nov)
1984 Band Aid's *Do They Know It's Christmas?* Number 1 (Dec 15th)
1984 BBC's *Miss Marple* first broadcast (December 26th)
1984 Pat Barker's *Blow Your House Down* published
1984 Translation of *The Unbearable Lightness of Being* published
1984 Dubpoet Linton Kwesi Johnson releases *Making History* album
1984 An estimated 50,000 regular users of heroin in the UK
1984 Beatrix Campbell's *Wigan Pier Revisited* published
1984 London Underground bans smoking on trains

1984 Robert Maxwell buys Mirror Group Newspapers
1985 *A Woman of Substance* drama serial debuts (January 2nd)
1985 *Dempsey and Makepeace* begins (January 11th)
1985 Sketch show *Victoria Wood: As Seen on TV* (Jan 11th)
1985 Battery-powered C5 given green light for road use (Jan 11th)
1985 *Saturday Night Live* variety show debut (January 12th)
1985 *Blott on the Landscape* begins on BBC2 (February 6th)
1985 Soap *EastEnders* begins on BBC1 (February 9th)
1985 Smiths' album *Meat is Murder* released (Feb 11th)
1985 NUM Miners' Strike ends (March 3rd)
1985 *Oranges Are Not The Only Fruit* published (March 21st)
1985 *Just Like Mohicans* first broadcast on C4 (March 21st)
1985 American-Italian *A.D.* mini-series released (March 31st)
1985 *C.A.T.S. Eyes* first broadcast (April 12th)
1985 *Home to Roost* first broadcast (April 19th)
1985 Larry Kramer's *The Normal Heart* debuts in NYC (April 21st)
1985 Valley Parade fire in Bradford kills fifty-six (May 11th)
1985 Dire Straits *Brothers in Arms* album released (May 17th)
1985 Heysel Stadium disaster results in 39 deaths (May 29th)
1985 Crime drama spin-off *Bulman* first broadcast (June 5th)
1985 Scottish detective series *Taggart* debuts (July 2nd)
1985 *Back to the Future* released (July 3rd)
1985 Unseeded 17-year-old Boris Becker wins Wimbledon (July 7th)
1985 Live Aid benefit concerts in London and US (July 13th)
1985 Edward Bond's trilogy *The War Plays* at Barbican (July 25th)
1985 *The War Game* 60s pseudo-documentary broadcast (July 31st)
1985 Thames crime series *King and Castle* begins (August 20th)
1985 *Howards' Way* first broadcast (September 1st)
1985 *Travelling Man* second mini-series begins (September 3rd)
1985 *My Beautiful Laundrette* released (September)
1985 Mandelson appointed Labour's Director of Communications
1985 Police officer killed in Broadwater Farm estate (October 6th)
1985 Sitcom *Girls on Top* begins (October 23rd)
1985 *Edge of Darkness* political thriller serial begins (November 4th)
1985 Political thriller *Defence of the Realm* released (Nov 21st)
1985 *Letter to Brezhnev* released (November)

1985 Comic Relief is launched (December 25th)
1985 Merchant-Ivory film *A Room With A View* released (Dec)
1985 The number of bank ATMs doubles in three years
1985 First commercially available mobile phones in UK
1985 Number of UK people living in poverty rises to 2.64m
1986 Unemployment tops 3m, 12.5% of working population (Jan)
1986 *The Lost Language of Cranes* is published (January 1st)
1986 *Blackadder II* debuts (January 9th)
1986 First series of *Lovejoy* begins (January 10th)
1986 Pet Shop Boys' *West End Girls* at Number 1 (January 11th)
1986 Period drama *Bluebell* begins broadcast (January 12th)
1986 ITV drama *Boon* begins (January 14th)
1986 54-week Wapping print union strike starts (January 24th)
1986 Government admit BSE outbreak; 178 will die (March 20th)
1986 Bombing of West Berlin disco popular with US (April 5th)
1986 US air strikes of Libya (April 15th)
1986 Shops Bill to relax Sunday trading is rejected (April 15th)
1986 Chernobyl nuclear power plant disaster (April 26th)
1986 Carla Lane's sitcom *Bread* first broadcast (May 1st)
1986 *A Very Peculiar Practice* first broadcast (May 21st)
1986 Neo-noir *Mona Lisa* released (June)
1986 Derek Jarman's *Caravaggio* released (August 29th)
1986 *The Monocled Mutineer* begins broadcast (August 31st)
1986 Detective series *Call Me Mister* begins (September 5th)
1986 Medical drama *Casualty* debuts (September 6th)
1986 *Paradise Postponed* debuts on TV (September 15th)
1986 *The Independent* newspaper is launched (October 7th)
1986 Four-part drama *The Life and Loves of a She-Devil* (Oct 8th)
1986 Animated film *When the Wind Blows* released (Oct 24th)
1986 Big Bang in the City of London (October 27th)
1986 London Orbital Motorway (M25) completed (October 29th)
1986 Dennis Potter's *The Singing Detective* begins (November 16th)
1986 *EastEnders* 30.15m record audience for a TV drama (Dec 25th)
1986 Comedy film *Whoops Apocalypse* released
1986 Talawa Theatre Company founded for black artists
1986 European Premiere of *The Normal Heart* at the Royal Court

1987 *Inspector Morse* first broadcast (January 6th)
1987 Police procedural *Rockliffe's Babies* debuts (January 9th)
1987 Ealing vicarage burglary/rape case scandal (February)
1987 Zeebrugge ferry capsizes killing 188 (March 6th)
1987 HIV/AIDS drama *Intimate Contact* broadcast (March)
1987 *Personal Services* released (April 3rd)
1987 *Prick Up Your Ears* released (April 17th)
1987 Martin Amis' *Einstein's Monsters* published (April 30th)
1987 Channel 4 launch late night discussion *After Dark* (May 1st)
1987 *Rita, Sue and Bob Too* released (May 29th)
1987 UK General Election won by Conservative Party (June 11th)
1987 Four members of Labour Party Black Sections become MPs
1987 *Floodtide* first mini-series begins (June 14th)
1987 *It's A Sin* (Pet Shop Boys) at Number 1 (July 4th)
1987 Sci-fi drama series *Star Cops* begins broadcast, BBC 2 (July 6th)
1987 Period comedy-drama *Wish You Were Here* released (July)
1987 Hungerford massacre leaves 17 dead (August 19th)
1987 Jarman's arthouse film *The Last of England* released (August)
1987 7th Time Lord Sylvester McCoy joins *Doctor Who* (Sept 7th)
1987 Sitcom *The New Statesman* debuts (September 13th)
1987 *Blackadder the Third* debuts (September 17th)
1987 *A Month in the Country* released (September 27th)
1987 Black Monday sees shares collapse (October 19th)
1987 Thatcher in *Women's Own*: 'no such thing' as society (Oct)
1987 Remembrance Day bomb kills eleven in Enniskillen (Nov 8th)
1987 London Underground fire at Kings Cross; 31 killed (Nov 18th)
1987 Oliver Stone's *Wall Street* is released (December 11th)
1987 Michael Cashman provides the first gay kiss in a UK soap
1987 Caryl Churchill's *Serious Money* play first staged
1988 *Floodtide* second mini-series begins (January 8th)
1988 Sci-fi sitcom *Red Dwarf* debuts on BBC 2 (February 15th)
1988 *The Swimming-Pool Library* is published (February 22nd)
1988 Comic Strip present *The Strike* (Feb 28th)
1988 Social & Liberal Democrats form; Paddy Ashdown leader (Mar)
1988 *Tracy Chapman* album released (April 5th)
1988 *Theme from S'Express* at Number 1 (April 30th)

1988 *For Queen and Country* released (May 17th)
1988 Clause/Section 28 is enacted (May 24th)
1988 BBC broadcast 'political' play *Tumbledown* (May 30th)
1988 Political serial *A Very British Coup* begins (June 19th)
1988 Piper Alpha oil-rig explosion claims 167 lives (July 6th)
1988 Salman Rushdie's *The Satanic Verses* is published (Sept 26th)
1988 Pan Am Flight 103 blown up over Scotland (December 21st)
1988 Property prices rise by a third in one year
1988 Construction begins on Canary Wharf project
1988 David Lodge's novel *Nice Work* is published
1989 Ben Elton environmental comedy *Stark* published (January 1st)
1989 C4 black barbershop sitcom *Desmond's* debuts (January 5th)
1989 Satellite company Sky start broadcasting (February 5th)
1989 *The Firm* drama highlights football hooliganism (Feb 26th)
1989 Ayatollah Khomeini issues Rushdie fatwa (February)
1989 Community Charge/Poll Tax introduced in Scotland (April 1st)
1989 Hillsborough stadium disaster sees 96 killed (April 15th)
1989 Tiananmen Square protests begin (April 15th)
1989 Stonewall charity formed in response to Section 28 (May 24th)
1989 Black Box's *Ride on Time* at Number 1 (September 9th)
1989 *The Paradise Club* first broadcast (September 19th)
1989 *Blackadder Goes Forth* debuts (September 28th)
1989 *Jeffrey Bernard is Unwell* opens in Brighton (September)
1989 Tracy Chapman releases *Crossroads* album (October 3rd)
1989 *Nice Work* first broadcast on BBC2 (October 4th)
1989 Sitcom *Birds of a Feather* debuts (October 16th)
1989 *Blackadder* final episode *Goodbyeee* broadcast (Nov 2nd)
1989 The night the Berlin Wall 'came down' (November 9th)
1989 *Back to the Future Part II* released (November 22nd)
1989 The 'final' episode of *Doctor Who* is broadcast (Dec 6th)
1989 C4 show censored 6-part version of *Alice* in 1.40 pm timeslot
1989 Peter Mayle's *A Year in Provence* is published
1989 British consumers owe an estimated £304 billion
1989 Tim Berners-Lee invents the World Wide Web at CERN
1990 Uncut version of *Alice* shown on C4 at midnight (Jan 1st)

CONTENTS

TRIALS, TRIBULATIONS AND TRANSITION: TITLE SEQUENCE DESIGN IN THE 1980s

It had become obvious that things needed to change…

I had been creative director for less than six months and the senior studio artist was refusing point blank to use the new typesetting equipment and insisted on sticking to laboriously applied Letraset. The whole department was becoming atrophied. Jobs were failing. It ended in his dismissal. The union (my union too) took the company (and me) to an industrial tribunal for firing him. However, the tribunal's conclusion was that we were right to do so.

Its decision was that the whole industry was changing and those of us working in it were expected to change and adapt with it. This was 1981. That need to change and adapt was imperative, and it shaped the whole direction of our work in the 1980s.

Our work was creating title sequences for television productions made on film. The disciplines for programmes made on videotape and those made on film at that time were still quite different but throughout the decade the two would move much closer. Today they are almost the same.

The essential difference then was that on video you could immediately see what you were getting, whereas on film you had to wait for what you had done to return from the processing laboratory to see if you had got what you intended. In the early 1980s, film offered more physical flexibility than video, meaning that drama for television could be less studio-bound. The procedures adopted were those of the cinema; the programme would be made as a film, but it would be shown on television. A programme distributed on film would need the titles and credits that appeared at the top and tail of it to be shot on film as well.

Once upon a time, title sequences were expected to act as no more than a frontispiece for the content that followed: many older movies actually use the opening pages of a book as a device for imparting information deemed necessary as the audience settled into what was to follow: the company making the movie, what the movie was called, who was in it and who were the important big-wigs who contributed to making it come about. Rather than the dull flap of pages being turned, specially composed or adapted music would accompany the visuals to set the emotional level of the story about to be told. The images and the music set out to engage the viewer. Together, they formed in sight and sound an overture to the film the audience had elected to see.

For television, the demands of a title sequence are slightly greater. In a cinema, the audience has already shelled out for a ticket and sits comfortably in the dark, waiting for a return on their investment. Due to its domestic setting, television is different. By the time a programme starts, the television and any subscriptions required to watch it will have already been paid for and there is no obligation for its audience to watch anything in particular. The production makers want the audience to watch their programme, so there needs to be a call to attention: hence the TV title sequence.

In the 1970s, while the designers of the 80s were learning their craft at Art School, I recall being part of a raging argument which took place between film lecturers as well as students about the importance of a soundtrack to a television title sequence. Those that thought the soundtrack was not important did not become TV title designers; those who did, did.

Music can be heard throughout the house; visuals are only accessible if you are in the room. You can't watch the living room television though the kitchen wall. Therefore, visuals with a soundtrack are the two essential components of a title sequence. Some sequences will be a perfect balance of the two; in others, either may predominate. Yet in all cases, title sequences need to be unique in the way they present and package the particular programme that follows.

At the start of the 80s, home video recording was a pipe dream for most people and streaming did not exist, so it was imperative for viewers to catch the programme from the moment its transmission began. The title sequence had an important part or role to play.

In the earliest days of television, straightforwardness was essential, and a simple caption sequence and musical theme could be expected to do the job. But that time was now passing and advertising was becoming more significant to daily life. A greater range of products was becoming available, and the public became exposed to increasingly varied methods of them being promoted. Television titles needed to follow suit. Programmes became something the audience was expected to consume.

America, at the forefront of design and packaging, led the way. The glamour and style of US title sequences impressed audiences around the world. The 'Enterprise' at warp speed, Raymond Burr's bulky form collapsing to the floor or a map burning away to reveal the Cartwright family meant *Star Trek*, *Ironside* or *Bonanza* was about to begin, three examples of thousands of keenly anticipated invitations to view. Lew Grade's ITC in the UK had been following the trend since the 60s. Yet, unless you were actually sitting in front of your television set, the call to attention was inevitably not their lush visuals but the indisputably recognisable theme tunes that accompanied them.

Surprisingly, even in the enlightened 80s, the need for cohesion between designer and composer was regularly overlooked. Music would be composed to fit completed visuals, or visuals designed to fit finished music, often without any contact between the creator of either. For example, *Hammer House of Horror* (1980) did not have the budget for me to animate the lettering out from the barbed tendrils I initially intended, but the production provided a series of eerie backgrounds, so we superimposed a spooky mist across the landscape, and I went to town on the menacing typography. It was the tremendous Roger Webb theme which brought everything together perfectly: haunting, threatening, mysterious; it suited the subject matter to a tee.

Having a piece of music appropriate to the subject matter is imperative. Occasionally a contemporary hit or piece of classical music considered to be empathetic will be selected by the production team, and the designer will be tasked to illustrate it. If a particular piece is not available, a sound-alike can be sourced, either from a composer or the endless catalogues of production music libraries. If not, something bespoke and original will be commissioned.

The subtleties of creating a piece apposite to the programme's content or period may be praiseworthy but, remember, in the context of a television title sequence its prime task is to 'catch the ear'. Is the elegance of Ray Ogden's opening sequence to the BBC drama series *Tenko* (1981) enhanced by James Harpham's theme music? Does the calm, oriental style of the abstracted images and the iconic title lettering fit with the threatening and disturbing orchestration of the music? Is this a case of counterpoint rather than complement and if the former, is the counterpoint intentional? If so, it more than adequately sets the scene for the following programme. Yet would the theme music alone attract you to the screen? Is it a memorable 'call to attention'?

Many opening sequences use a series of straightforward shots of the characters and locations about to appear in the following episode. Over this, captions will be superimposed. This is fine if the stars and the venue are the hook for attracting attention. A certain amount of embellishment - packaging it imaginatively - can make the sequence even more of a draw. Yet the style and elegance of many more elaborate title sequences often conceal the agony of their gestation, and the fact that some have been completed at all is occasionally a miracle.

Once a filmed series is into production, the editing staff will be busy inheriting the previous day's footage and cutting it into some semblance of how the script (and all the parties investing in the production since the script was commissioned) envisaged the completed episode to look. They are concerned about telling that particular episode's story and won't want to be bothered with what, at that moment, appears to be the ephemera of titles, end credits and part titles: the packaging the programme comes in. All that can come later.

Except that it can't. If the spirit of the show needs to be encapsulated at the start of every episode - as in programmes such as *Minder* - facilities need to be provided to the title designer, and the several minutes of information intended to drop in seamlessly at the start and end of (and scattered throughout) that pristine new episode all need to be made in advance. It will take time.

Worse, for the independent title designer, the hideous and all too familiar spectre of a budget already over-running starts to raise its ugly head. That budget notionally allocated for all those 'effortless' visuals lovingly storyboarded several months ago has been eaten away by the unseen - or, rather, 'incorrectly anticipated' - excesses of studio and location production. The twin evils of less time and less money regularly stack up to thwart the ambitions of the titles designer. Elaboration will be the first victim of overspend.

Which is why the simple elegance of white out of black title sequences such as those in *Inspector Morse* (1987) might be a better option. A haunting musical motif (that 'call to attention' again) and a well-paced, typographically attractive sequence of captions may be all that is needed, evocative of the tasteful typography on the cover and frontispieces of editions of a classic novel. We don't need to see fast cut, dramatically angled vignettes of John Thaw disgusted by the latest outrage on the streets of Oxford, wrestling with his inner demons over a pint of Wadsworth's 6X or trying to forget the vicissitudes of the world as he slumps on his unprepossessing sofa, immersing himself in Wagner. There are two hours for us to discover all this. *Inspector Morse* is a big show, and its time span lets the audience discover all these things by deliberation, its considered pace and structure.

ITV had an advantage back in the 80s in that, because it was a network, many of its programmes were produced by its constituent companies and, as a result, were branded with the station logo or ident at the start. Most of these came with highly recognisable musical stings - think of the Thames skyline, the slinking Tube lines of London Weekend or the gilt statuette of the Anglia knight. Hearing the few notes accompanying them would prompt an immediate viewer's reaction to the screen: *The Bill*, *Game For A Laugh* or *Tales Of The Unexpected* was about to begin.

This opening delay offered an opportunity for British television to adopt a technique regularly seen on programmes imported from the United States. That opening ident had called attention to the programme: was it really essential for titles to follow immediately?

American television devours programme material and frenzied efforts are made by operators to keep viewers hooked on their particular station or network output. A programme will end and another immediately follow, butted up, often without even a station break or trail. A unique and tantalising opening sequence is considered imperative in capturing the interest of viewers potentially worn out by the constant consumption of thousands of potentially similar shows. This need not be the title sequence, yet a 'hook' is essential. We need to see some action, and it is only after that, the tantalising prospect of an exciting programme coming up, that the titles follow. For the US audience it is after the titles when the screen is festooned with the commercials and the other presentation ephemera UK audiences have come to expect at the top and tail of programmes.

That American influence was starting to have some effect on the way the openings of programmes were constructed in the United Kingdom. In many film series of the 1980s and later, the programme starts with a minute (or more) of a location being established and a player in the forthcoming story depicted experiencing some significant event. Intrigue is established and the scene is set for the story to begin. That minute or so is called the 'cold start'.

In the 80s the cold start was becoming more regularly adopted in British television. Hence, in the case of *Inspector Morse*, a bucolic tracking shot through the coppices of the Isis might lead to the bedraggled corpse of this week's victim being found in the undergrowth. The hook has been cast. It is at this point that the revelatory process is interrupted by a cut to the titles. The screen is suddenly black; simple lettering and a haunting musical theme is introduced, giving us time to pause and think, to appraise what has happened and where the story might be going. Or to nip out and quickly put the kettle on, because we are intrigued: this is all looking rather promising...

However, in the 80s white out of black captions were still an exception, and imaginative designers were more than capable of identifying incidental elements in the programme story that could be extracted and developed as a device to carry an effective and attractive title sequence.

For example, take the silvan expanses of Hampstead Heath, bedecked with weather-beaten benches, their paint peeling from exposure through years of sun and rain. Look closely and you might see an innocuous chalk mark, a clandestine invitation to a furtive rendezvous, a small and enigmatic part of the tradecraft that supports the story in *Smiley's People* (1982). This is a simple and intriguing motif, and it formed an ideal visual basis for a title sequence. The camera in Stewart Austin's glorious 1982 sequence lovingly caresses the flaking textures of a bench on which a chalk line reveals from nowhere. It is the background texture for the opening titles as Patrick Gowers' profound and haunting orchestral theme lures us into an atmosphere which is languid, ominous and deliberately restrained...until a final resolve as the chalk is suddenly blasted to pieces. Shocking - but isn't that what the story is all about? Isn't that why we are all watching, waiting for something sensational to occur? The scene is set.

Or look at the elegantly simple aerial journey of Alan Jeapes' title sequence for *Eastenders* (1985) as the camera spirals up, out and above the Isle of Dogs to a delightful and remarkably memorable musical theme. Redolent of the evocative tunes organ grinders once plied back in the day on so many London street corners, Simon May's modern adaptation of an almost mechanical melody has to be one of British television's most successful 'calls to attention'.

This considered pace and structure of a successful title sequence preempts its programme. Fun and games follow bright and breezy graphics; menace and gloom follow the opposite. Action means things moving quickly. Terry Griffiths' *Dempsey & Makepeace* (1985) titles do their job admirably. Alan Parker's thundering music, nonstop stunt action, the protagonists treading a narrow line as they transgress the limits of the law; fights, explosions, car chases, gun play, a hunk of a hero and the foxiest ever heroine teasing us with the never-answered question 'Will they? Won't they?' throughout, all flawlessly packaged into 46 seconds. If you have never seen the show before, it will tell you precisely what you are about to get: if you have, then it reminds you of all the excitement it brought you last time.

A title sequence I was closely involved with was *Minder* and it is worth examining the processes that went into the creation of both the opening and closing title sequences. Made by Euston Films, *Minder* was initially launched at the very end of 1979, and it occupied our screens for over a decade.

The live action opening titles depict Terry McCann (Dennis Waterman) in the throes of buying a car from Arthur Daley (George Cole), a transaction which neatly encapsulates the relationship between the two characters in a tight and effective sequence. That live action freeze frame as an uncertain Terry decides whether to go ahead with the transaction - and possibly anything else that might involve being with Arthur - is the appropriate moment to wipe on Bob Ellis's attractive hand-drawn script main title logo.

The rest of the sequence shows Terry concluding the deal with Arthur and the images are used as backgrounds for the other introductory credits. Intercut with this live action are stills illustrating snapshots of Terry's past life: boxing, a criminal record, and a night out on the razz with Arthur. By the time the sequence ends, we know the two protagonists intimately, where they are, what happened in the past and the basis of the relationship between the two of them. Arthur is weighing up what he can get away with, with Terry; Terry perhaps isn't too sure about Arthur, but it looks like he may as well give things a go...and isn't that *Minder* in a nutshell?

The *Minder* end credits, despite what might have just happened in the previous 50 minutes, depict Arthur and Terry's ostensibly care-free lives carrying on as normal. The sequence consists of a selection of stills of them out and about in the London in which their escapades take place: the back streets of Fitzrovia (that wonky lamp post in Newman Passage was there for decades: the original lantern is now mounted on the nearby wall); on the riverfront at Hammersmith; outside a West London police station and at one of the several locations of the Winchester Club (this one at Chalk Farm Tube station), all of which reflect the neighbourhoods in which the protagonists operate. With hindsight, I have always thought that the photograph used as a background to the producer's credit, with Arthur and Terry in Leicester Square, queers the pitch somewhat. In the series, very little of the show's action actually takes place in this most recognisable part of 'Up West', where the marquee at the Leicester Square Theatre is displaying *Butch and Sundance - The Early Years*. Although the inclusion of an image relating to loveable outlaws appearing behind our roguish heroes may have been considered a fortuitous coincidence by the producers at the time, *The Early Years* was not a notably successful film and this image weakens and very much dates a credit sequence which ended up running for the best part of a decade.

For Euston Films I also designed and produced the titles for *Prospects* (1986), a comedy drama series for Channel 4 set in East London. The Isle of Dogs had recently been earmarked for the massive development that was to become London Docklands and *Prospects* followed two young, likely entrepreneurs wanting to turn their aspirations into gold. Location was pivotal to the plot, and so it would be for the title sequence. Swathes of derelict dockland were being cleared for development.

My concept was based on a scene typical to the time and place: a derelict site, ready for demolition with just another graffitied wall ready to be cleared. Yet I surmised that if the graphic tag on the wall was the series' title the whole premise of the show could be portrayed seamlessly by establishing the location in its current, dilapidated state and then swinging a wrecker's ball through the wall to reveal a new horizon, the distant towers of the City of London and the allure of wealth: 'prospects'.

The idea was enthusiastically received by the production team. A suitable brick wall was found adjacent to the waterfront at Limehouse Pier which, once demolished, would offer a view along the Thames to the City of London. A street art-style logo more elaborate than, but in the style of, a typical graffiti 'tag' was devised and painted up on the wall.

The nature of filming anything involving destruction is unique - it is a one-off occasion and must work first time, otherwise a new location, together with a complete and expensive rebuild, will be required. Elaborate planning is essential.

On the day of the shoot, the giant crane with the wreckers' ball needed to practise. The ball had to hit the wall in the centre of the logo 'Prospects' in order for the main camera to depict the word being smashed, the wall collapse and the towers of the City be revealed on the distant horizon. Rehearsal took place and the crane driver swivelled the ball through an arc several times to get the correct position, always stopping short so as to not hit the wall before we went for the take. Unfortunately, all the concerns I had regarding centrifugal force went unheeded: if the ball was travelling further round to actually hit the wall, and hence at greater speed, the angle of the arc would be slightly higher and the ball further out. It would therefore hit the wall at the beginning of the word, rather than in the centre. People in the East End demolition industry tend to be quite forthright so my argument went unheeded: confident this would not be the case, the crane driver stuck to his guns when we went for the take.

The master shot was square on to the logo with half a dozen other cameras set up as back-up, many to cover the event in slow motion, positioned at key angles to record the sequence. The cue was given to turn over, and action was called to start the crane. Around swung the wrecker's ball and, sure enough, it smashed into the wall with all the drama we wanted - but not in the right place.

Unfortunately, and as I had predicted, it only knocked out the first three letters.

The cameras filmed the dust settling until my call came to cut: a ponderous silence descended over the entire crew. Half the wall stood untouched: on it remained the lettering 'spects'.

"I reckon that's what that crane driver needs…" muttered some wag standing by the catering vehicle. "No, no," I found myself replying, "We can use it, we can use it…"

And we did. By covering the destruction of the wall with a multi-camera shoot, we had provided ourselves with a selection of angles which captured all the drama of the old and shabby past being knocked aside, plus one master shot which (fortunately) did provide a shot of the City of London, no longer obscured, shimmering away in the distance. I would have liked to have told the story from one simple angle, but the shots all cut together into quite an effective montage sequence and the whole concept of the titles was subsequently conveyed successfully.

Our company, National Screen, in addition to being commissioned to creating opening and credit sequences for independent production companies, regularly undertook the technical work of producing title sequences on behalf of designers at various television companies. In many instances, we were simply provided with the elements to create the sequence in the form of artwork or pre-shot footage, with full timings and camera instructions. The latter were known as dope sheets ('dope' after 'information' rather than any opinion of the person tasked with responding to them) and could vary from simple 'fit at the bottom of frame and hold for six seconds' to elaborate multi-pass sequences incorporating aerial image, bi-pack matte runs, back projection, tracking cameras, model shoots, rotating and panning artwork, slit-scan time exposure and multi-faceted star filters, all of which had to be choreographed precisely to be frame-accurate.

Granada brought in *Jewel in The Crown*, *The Adventures of Sherlock Holmes* and *World In Action*; the BBC *Shoestring* and *Bergerac*. Work for Yorkshire Television included Arthur C. Clarke's Mysterious World and Diane Dunn's sumptuously elegant titles for the *Biederbecke* series. In 1985 Scottish TV brought in *Taggart*, and whereas most title sequences were turned around without a problem, this particular one became a real headache.

'Less is more' is a pretty reliable rule of thumb when it comes to almost all aspects of good visual design, because not only will too much over-egg the viewer's cake, but it will also be a pain for the production company to create. The plans for *Taggart* were far too complicated. The initial opening titles included time-lapse cloud footage, solarised landscapes, hand-drawn pencilled rotoscoping (along the lines of the A-Ha 'Take On Me' video of the time), chrome lettering complete with star flourish...and all together, it proved just too much. To the extent that the only way to finish assembling the job was by video editing, and because the unions at STV wouldn't accept video for a film production (even though the film was transferred to video for transmission) a whole new nest of worms was entered into. The project went way over budget.

Note, however, that it was now 1985, and the means of resolving the technical problems were identified as foregoing film and completing the work on video.

There was a moment in an early 1970s episode of *Monty Python's Flying Circus* when, after a cut between a studio scene and one filmed on location, Michael Palin's character says, "Oh, look! We're now on film". The glaring pin-sharpness of the studio shots had been suddenly replaced by soft, dull and poorly graded 16mm filmed exteriors. Even in the 1980s, viewers were constantly expected to ignore and be undistracted by such awkward changes in picture quality. A couple of decades later, that cut would be seamless but back then it stood out like a sore thumb.

It is important to look at the physical parameters that typically bound title designers back at the start of the 1980s. Time, money and technical constraints made their job very different to today.

For credit captions on video productions, studio cameras pointed at music stands on which black cards, printed with white lettering were placed. Camera 1 would show the first caption; cut to camera 2 and the second caption; a floor assistant would change to caption 3 on camera 1, cut back to camera 1 etc., etc. The lettering image would be mixed or keyed over a background and, probably timed to the beat of the music, the sequence would be established. Simple stuff. Greater control - and avoiding the hassle of tying up studio cameras - would be obtained by preparing the captions on photographic transparencies and feeding them into the vision mixer from a special slide projector. Or a camera would point at a roller caption. Electronic caption generators were still very much in their infancy.

Of course, the caption card method, together with some mischievous imagination ("Why don't we pan the captions in and out of shot?") led to such memorable gems as the wonderfully inconsistent end credit sequences for *Crossroads* (and *Acorn Antiques*).

The rule of thumb adopted over this period was that lettering should be no less than 36pt height on a 12" wide field - the 'field' being the 4:3 aspect ratio of the TV screen. Anything smaller would be difficult to read and could become corrupted due to fluctuation in the relatively small number of horizontal lines making up the picture. Choice of font was equally important.

Because film was transferred to video for transmission, the same typographic size constraints applied. For example, once the production line for *Minder* had been established, it became a straightforward task for us at National Screen to organise the weekly changes to front and end credits. What became apparent to me during the first series was that - bearing in mind the 36pt/12" field rule - the initial choice of typeface was causing problems because it was too wide on screen. Trying to squeeze a credit such as 'Stephen Tompkinson as Detective Constable Park' onto one line in that font was asking for trouble. From Series Two, a condensed version of the same font became flavour of the day. (Notice also how Glynn Edwards' barman Dave's credit grows in proportion to his role as the series continues).

One simple but extremely expedient device used in the credit sequences of *Minder* and many other filmed series is the inclusion of a few text-free frames at the start of the still images used as backgrounds for a credit caption. In fact, it was usual to create a full 'textless' sequence simply so alternate credits could be inserted each week. Clean backgrounds also offered the opportunity to superimpose the same information in a foreign language: readily (or rapidly) available foreign language versions would make international sales of filmed series both attractive and lucrative. Once the custom of transferring film sequences to video became standard practice, rather than spending days waiting for film opticals to be delivered, altering credit sequences became nothing more than a simple video edit.

No matter what the wording was, the task of every television graphic designer back in the time was to adapt their work to the limitations imposed by 'definition', 'aspect ratio', 'cut-off' and 'safe-areas'. We had to compensate for the medium's imperfections which, although the boffins in their sandals, suits and screwdrivers were working hard to overcome, still demanded compromise.

Up until 1950, British television was transmitted at the ratio of 5:4. Cathode ray tubes used in domestic televisions prior to that date were little more than adapted versions of WWII radar screens. As such they were pretty crude, to the extent that one day in 1954 (and without a word to the licence-fee paying public) the BBC changed the British television aspect ratio from 5:4 to 4:3, ostensibly bringing television to the same aspect ratio as the film industry, without any new or adapted equipment being required. The BBC also reckoned that, because valves heated up so arbitrarily during the course of an evening's viewing anyway, continual variance in aspect ratio was endemic: viewers were used to it, and no one would notice an overnight change in aspect ratio. And they didn't.

Shortcomings in domestic TV receiver manufacture back then meant that screens on certain receivers were more distorted than others or, worse, could be partially obscured by the cabinet or mask which framed the tube. For this reason, TV graphic designers had to ensure that any information was always placed in a position where all the viewing public could see it. 'Cut-off' had to be avoided, and designers were provided with guides and equipment to ensure the graphics they were creating would appear within a 'safe area'.

Unlike the High-Definition screens of today, throughout the second half of the twentieth century the television image was made of constantly scanning lines of varying brightness, colour being rendered through a screen of tiny dots. Of the 625 lines on the UK TV system only 576 were visible; inherited material from the American system had even fewer of them, it ran at a different rate and the picture quality loss on their conversion to the UK standard was significant. Film at least was film, however it ended up being shown.

This was the 1980s and video was still frustratingly crude. Too much white would burn out. Flashing, especially flashing red, could cause epileptic fits. Edges of lettering would tear and flicker - the dreaded 'anti-aliasing'. Different colours appeared as the same tone in monochrome (the giant results board in the second 1976 BBC General Election studio had to be remade at the last minute because Conservative Blue and Labour Red came out as exactly the same grey in black and white). Many domestic sets still used valves and all of them rendered an image slightly different to each other. It was a minefield.

It was, therefore, sometimes a blessing to get to the end of the show. British television had decided to adopt the film industry standard of dating copyright years indistinctly. The much more impressive 'MCMLXXXVIII' would be used rather than '1988', inferring that the programme might have been made to the same criteria as those of the money-laden cinema industry. However, everyone secretly knew it would be harder for the viewer to determine if what they were watching was old or, perish the thought, a repeat if they couldn't read the year in which it was made. (That said, repeats were immensely rarer on the three or four channels of the early and mid-1980s than they are in the multichannel conglomeration of today). Probably for the same reason - i.e. 'the audience doesn't need to know this' - any other copyright details also broke the no-smaller-than-36pt rule.

The recipe was one for inconsistency, which is why at the time I had elected to work on film. Film, despite being measured horizontally in metric (35mm) and vertically in imperial (3-foot dissolves, 100-foot reels), was a constant. Even if you did have to send it away overnight to see if everything had worked.

Most of National Screen's work was for the cinema industry, and we knew that, when it came to running movies on television, the vast canvas of the Cinemascope format (an aspect ratio of 2.35:1 or thereabouts) meant that opulent titles such as those of Maurice Binder's James Bond sequences (which we produced) would have to be either squashed sideways compressing them ridiculously tall and thin (making 007 twelve feet tall) or 'letterboxed' to render any typography minute and unreadable. Fritz Lang once described Cinemascope as only good 'for snakes and funerals'. A dreadful remedy for television was 'pan-and-scan', which physically shifted the film painfully slowly left and right in the telecine machine. Involving the physical insertion of metal pegs into sprocket holes, it was impossible to time accurately and could be guaranteed to show either the wrong half of the screen at any pivotal moment or, more usually, two unidentifiable noses in conversation. When the demand was there, studios stretched the budget to design and provide TV networks (and airlines) with bespoke 5:4 versions that viewers could actually make sense of on a television screen, but this didn't happen often.

Yet technical advances were being made. As the decade passed, computer graphics were finally starting to deliver the desired effects. With higher resolutions, all that nasty anti-aliasing as lower resolution edges of the image tore on movement could be rectified. Keying levels had become more sophisticated. Still far from ideal, the effects of well-designed computer graphics could eventually be rendered to 625-line resolution videotape at an acceptable standard.

An example would be Michael Graham-Smith's stylish titles for *Life and Loves of A She-Devil* (1986), which utilised computer graphics to animate what would otherwise have been a nightmare to construct with film opticals. Melding images of the protagonists are depicted within the frame of a slowly tumbling golden pentacle, to an intriguing vocal music track (possibly of note, being one of the few Dennis Waterman programmes in which he appears but doesn't sing the theme song). It is a clean, modern and attractive sequence.

Once the issue of transferring an image from computer to film had been resolved, big, mechanical film post-production equipment quickly became redundant. Initially, computer processing took time yet, what a few years earlier would involve an overnight wait for something which might have worked to come back from the laboratory, it was now a matter of minutes before the end result could be seen. Non-linear editing offered risk-free experimentation. Committing to rostrum camerawork and film opticals became unnecessary. Sequences could be produced effortlessly, without the need for physical artwork. Schedules shrank because processes could be accelerated.

By the time UK television adopted a digital wide-screen ratio of 16:9 in 2001, graphic designers were breathing comfortably again. On the implementation of full digital, their working parameters of broadcast colour, clarity and definition were standardised. Improvement continues. Techniques taking weeks or costing thousands of pounds an hour back in 1980 can be done instantly today on a phone. That tribunal had been right. The whole industry did change. And we had changed and adapted with it. [1]

© Chris Wood

1. Editor: ironically, despite all the technical advances, I find that few television series today offer me the same satisfaction in terms of titles sequences as the classic, iconic ones from the 1960s-80s. This particularly applies to the 'call to attention' theme tune. I'm thinking of composers such as Edwin Astley, Ron Grainer, Laurie Johnson, Roger Webb, George Fenton...

PIGS IN THE MIDDLE: *THE BILL* PRESERVES THE BALANCE

The Bill's arrival on TV screens in October 1984 came at something of a tipping point for British drama. The demise of the BBC's long-running single drama strand, *Play for Today*, just two months earlier represented the end of that view of TV as broadcast theatre that dated back to the 1950s. With the move towards shooting 'prestige drama' on film, the play itself became an increasingly rare commodity. The drama series was becoming the dominant form; and, as ever, the cop show was the dominant series, having acted as a Trojan horse for the new approach some ten years earlier. Euston Films, one of the first companies to advocate shooting entirely on film rather than relying on studio videotape, scored a major breakthrough with *The Sweeney*. Its success proved that it was possible to capture footage quickly and efficiently with film crews shooting out and about on the real streets of London. That kinetic energy can be traced through to the early days of *The Bill*, which adopted its own style of guerrilla shooting. So too can the rise of the anti-hero: the efforts of Regan and Carter to overcome bureaucracy and get the job done, by fair means or foul, give way to subsequent Euston hits like *Minder* and *Widows* in which our sympathies rest with the lawbreakers, not lawmakers. The time was ripe for a police series with its feet on the ground, putting officers out into the real world and painting them in the same mixed shades as those they deal with. However, at the same time one can see the influence of studio-bound drama, picking apart issues through densely knit dialogue, a tradition which was still alive and kicking in the 1980s. *The Bill* was revolutionary in part because it was willing to take the best from different sources: not only treading a middle path in its attitude to the police, but placing equal weight on both visual flair and social comment.

For a long time, every police series that followed *Dixon of Dock Green* was billed as a departure from 'the George Dixon approach': an image of cosy, reassuring paternalism that enjoyed a greater shelf life than the series itself. A fuller and fairer picture is difficult to unearth in a show that has had 400 of its 432 episodes junked. *Dixon* was itself an innovation, an attempt to show the real life of the street copper, not the cases of murder and intrigue pursued by X of the Yard that kept the British B-picture healthily supplied with material. But an innovative programme always risks becoming old hat if it sticks around long enough; this process is visible in both the edgy new kid on the block, *Z Cars*, and latterly in *The Bill*. Policing changed as society changed, and through those transformative decades of the 1960s and 70s, the frailties of the police as an organisation became more visible. If television gets more critical of the boys in blue, it is also increasingly critical – and realistic – about the times in which they operate. *The Bill*'s creator Geoff McQueen got his writing breakthrough on the first new cop show of the 80s, *The Gentle Touch*: LWT's London-set procedural following the trials and tribulations of DI Maggie Forbes. The series' opening minutes, in which Maggie's lower-ranked police husband Ray launches into a vicious rant about the job, feel like an overdue attempt by TV to acknowledge its real brutality. "Not your job; not even my job. Just *the bloody* job!" He picks up a photo of them as young, hopeful recruits and declares it "a lifetime ago." No longer bobbies or coppers, "we're the Fuzz...the filth...pigs...fascist swine!" His own dad was killed at Normandy fighting fascists, "and for what? To make a land fit for heroes? The rockers, muggers, and punks, and freeloaders, and all the rest of the gang!"

Forbes rages about the Great Train Robbers being turned into folk heroes, and the peaceful demos, "exercising their democratic rights ...I mean what about our rights? Sometimes we're fighting for our bloody lives out there, Maggie!" Most of all he dreads football duty, a once-coveted role. "I mean they're not kids...they're animals. But don't you lose your bottle and retaliate when somebody spits in your face and puts the boot in on one of your mates. You remember Sid, Sid Wallace? He lost an eye – defending somebody's democratic rights. Half blind at twenty-six. But that wasn't on the telly. Funny how they never seem to have the cameras down the hospital after a demo. Watching *our* lads getting their stitches put in for 'em! Pig in the middle, that's me...pig in the middle." Planning to leave the force, Ray is gunned down only minutes later trying to prevent a robbery while off duty, symbolising the growing dangers in society both in and out of uniform. Those dangers may have had added piquancy for veteran scriptwriter Brian Finch, given that his son Paul became a young police recruit in the 1980s and later turned to his own crime writing, including two episodes of *The Bill* in 2000/2001. That gives an extra dimension to the struggles of the central character, Maggie, left to bring up her teenage son alone while coping with the demands of work.

This living room rant takes place firmly in the domestic sphere: a three-walled studio set on which the drama plays out, in the stage tradition of TV. It's no coincidence that, in filling in that fourth wall, *The Bill* simultaneously removes the home/work divide that was a common part of the police series. The intent to take personal lives out of the equation is visible in Geoff McQueen's earliest ideas. *Woodentop*, the single play broadcast by Thames in 1983 as part of its *Storyboard* anthology that laid the ground for *The Bill*, was one of a planned trilogy of plays, each focused on a different rank of the police force. The USP is the notion of spending a day at work with someone: following them into the office, through the travails of a shift, and leaving at the same time as them. The ultimate accolade would be for a viewer to tune in and think they had stumbled on a documentary, an illusion that would be dispelled at once by scenes of domestic tiffing. One can also see in that trilogy a desire to convey the total breadth of people's experiences, from top brass to raw recruits. It's no surprise that the latter, in the form of rookie PC Jimmy Carver, is what gets the nod; the trials and tribulations of the new boy are the best way into a strange world. By confining itself to working hours, *The Bill* is able to let the demands of policing speak for themselves. The rigours of the job are hurled at the officers and us, shown rather than told. Nowhere is that better illustrated than in the pilot, in which Carver and his shepherdess June Ackland deal first with nuisance teenagers and then with the death of an old woman at home. The blackened, rotting arm that flops out of its sludgy bath water for only a second, leading into the ad break, illustrates what normality looks like for the police. The odd, grotesque corners of life that the rest of us don't see have to be tidied away by somebody.

The attempt to create a single, unified world is hamstrung at first by the dichotomy in how most TV was made. *Woodentop* occurs partly in a real world of sun-kissed pavements and seething traffic, and partly in a world of interior sets filmed at Teddington Studios. Very quickly, however, that division is a thing of the past. When Sgt. Bob Cryer arrives for work at the start of *The Bill* proper, the camera is fixed to the back seat of his car as it is enveloped by the building in which he lives most of his life. In a later episode he and another officer are followed out on patrol, straight from a corridor into a real street, passing by real people. Sun Hill is a three-sixty-degree space in which cast and crew have to make room for one another. Moreover, the camera has no God-like perspective on the action. It is constantly moving between rooms, hurrying behind people's backs, trying to keep up with a rhythm that is second nature to its subjects. The hunt goes on behind the typewriter as well as the lens. *The Bill* is constantly experimenting, picking up what works and running with it. The show's *raison d'etre* is an ideal reached only gradually. In its first series it is not bound by its subsequent Golden Rule, of showing every event from the perspective of the police; both small cutaways and large chunks of story are taken over by crooks or victims. Nor is it an ensemble piece balancing the lives of uniform and detectives. The show might be named *Galloway*, such is the prominence of its fearsome Detective Inspector. Exuding a burning intensity throughout, John Salthouse is often treated as the lead and could easily have been it. Told that Carver has info on a case, the DI orders him recalled from leave at once: "Do you want him in in uniform or civvies?" "In his bloody Yfronts for all I care, just *get him here*, what's all that about?" In the mould of Jack Regan, Roy Galloway is another grizzled workaholic who goes through a painful divorce, only seeing his daughter on trips out to the zoo: "You know me, I love looking at things behind bars."

Yet here too the mould is broken. Salthouse, like his co-star Eric Richard, was far from a household name; the two were seasoned performers in theatre and its televised counterpart, the aforementioned *Play for Today*. Familiar telly faces were another obstacle to the realism the production team aimed for, hence the show was cast for relative obscurity. It was also cast young, an aspect of the police that *Woodentop*'s director Peter Cregeen wanted to put on screen for the first time, and Galloway is a major break with the older men who had occupied his role in previous series. If the hapless Carver symbolises the innocence of youth, then Roy of the Overtime is the result of its fast-learning curve. This is a thirty-something who has seen it all, which says plenty for the fatiguing world he is part of. "Must be easier ways of earning a crust," he growls at one point, as he considers chucking the job in. The tide of work that beats at his door is notable for the near-total absence of murder, TV crime's first resort. Here it's a once a year event, and treated with little of the reverence we might expect. First the apparent murder of safecracker Alfie Mullins in *Death of a Cracksman* is found to be an argument gone wrong. Then towards the end of Series 2, Galloway has to give his sergeant Ted Roach a lecture on his responsibilities before he will pursue the murder of a down-and-out. Ted does his homework and unearths a full picture, "except who did it. I think we're pissing in the wind with this one." "Still, did our best," the DI remarks, casually closing the book; it's important to keep up appearances. The picture is even more inconclusive in Series 3's *Missing, Presumed Dead*, when the signs of a gangland shooting eventually produce a victim, but no body, and a suspect who is now long gone. Howdunnit, not whodunnit, is *The Bill*'s watchword.

Gradually more roles are built up in both CID and in uniform, filling out not just the lower ranks but the upper too. The show becomes a proper team effort in which every character has something to contribute. What *The Bill* does so well with its officers is to give each one a hinterland and then push them beyond it, to uncomfortable places where a hidden side emerges. Bob Cryer, father of the station, has been around the block so many times that he knows it all, acting as everyone's first port of call. And yet, in attempting to enforce the law 'the right way', he is responsible for deaths in both an hour-long and an early half-hour episode. Viv Martella, good time girl of the relief, appears to get through life with a wink and a smile but ends up enduring brutal situations that challenge her wobbly belief that she, as a woman, can make it on the frontline with the blokes. Taff Edwards, initially a cheerful soul, devolves into the Eeyore of the Valleys, growing disenchanted with the police and with 'Captain Bob', who pursues him relentlessly for slacking off. But we also see well-meaning attempts to help that somehow end up mangled and unappreciated. "I *do* give a damn!" he shouts at Cryer as he gets attached to the problems of an escaped psychiatric patient, identifying with an outsider. Most startlingly of all, the man at the heart of the project, Jim Carver, betrays his do-gooding ideals when apprenticed to CID and put on a case involving racist attacks. "I don't think I like Asians," he admits to Galloway in embarrassment. "I don't know, I've tried, when I was on the beat I used to force myself to talk to them, go into their shops..." All of these characters learn that they are a different person in extremis – and that is the realm police officers inhabit more than most.

Undoubtedly the most important figure in *The Bill*'s early days is Barry Appleton, ex-Flying Squad and Special Branch officer, who had retired from the force and tried in vain to establish a writing career before being hired as the show's technical adviser. Like so many programmes launched with high hopes and huge efforts, *The Bill* was a decent idea sorely in need of scripts. Often this can result in thin, identikit offerings that simply feed the production machine, rather than leading it. But, tasked with writing virtually all the first series and much of the next two, Appleton builds up the world of Sun Hill as though born to it. His existing police contacts gave the actors a chance to research the people they would be bringing to life. But just as importantly, the issues of policing in the 1980s are analysed by a man who had been there for the past decades of declining image and changing expectations. The preceding fifteen years, in which wide-ranging corruption had been exposed in both the Met and City of London police, cast a shadow that is never forgotten. From the beginning it is visible in the sleazy Tommy Burnside, later rechristened Frank. "How that bastard ever got past Countryman I'll never know," says his mortal enemy Cryer, referring to the real-life operation that used provincial coppers to try and root out London's bad apples, with limited results. When Appleton puts Galloway on the scent of two different porn rackets during Series 1, he acknowledges that some members of the force had been trying to throw off that scent for over a decade. The movie director who, when arrested, suggests that they could "pop into my bank" on the way to Sun Hill hints at a well-established arrangement; the top shelf mag swiped by the blokey Dave Litten before he pops into the toilets highlights the receptive market that the porn barons are dealing with.

The gangland killing in *Missing, Presumed Dead* illustrates the wider damage of the Countryman era. It turns out to be the execution of a supergrass, the kind the police had relied on to build cases against corrupt officers and the crooks they were in bed with. His widow reminds Galloway that the last time she saw her husband, before he had to go into exile in Spain, "You and your mates were standing at the back of the Bailey laughing your bollocks off! Blowing the whistle on everyone who could put a finger on him? It's the people left behind that suffer, that's what you people tend to forget. Treated like a leper by all your friends!" The DI tries to beg a favour off her, having got a little too close last time: "Boasting to your mates down at the nick how you made love to your snout?" The blurriness of the dividing line is emphasised further when Galloway visits the new crime boss who controls the area, Harry Stobbs, fully aware he ordered the killing but unable to prove it. Stobbs was put in the frame by the testimony of that supergrass: "Standing in the dock at the Old Bailey, charged with four counts of robbery I didn't commit, solely on the word of a man like Mr Corrigan? Made me a very bitter man." "You paid off a lot of people." "I'm a great believer in British justice." "On my firm," Galloway points out bitterly. But in the age of the yuppie, the villains have realised there is more mileage in going 'legit' than in charging around with sawn-offs. Installed in a plush office with a secretary fetching him coffee, Stobbs is more in tune with the present day than Galloway. The irony of criminals moving faster with the times than the police is a typically sharp observation for *The Bill* to pounce on. Warned not to play the Godfather, Stobbs insists, "I'm talking about my duty as a public-spirited citizen. Where would we be without the law? Without justice?" "Bullshit. What you and I call justice are two different things."

Appleton's work can be seen as another kind of tipping point, drawing from two different schools of television writing. In the ITC adventure series of the 1960s and 70s, kidnappings, espionage and general derring-do were the order of the day: colourful escapism with scant glimpses of emotional depth, and no lasting effect on the stoic hero. Conversely, modern TV is awash with gloomy dramas about the devastating impact of a missing child, but offers little in the way of fun to sweeten the pill. Appleton treads the perfect line, of adventure grounded in realism, proving that there doesn't need to be an either/or. *The Drugs Raid* uncovers a pipeline from West Africa, run using diplomatic cover. Listening to smug officials patting themselves on the back about international co-operation to stamp out the trade, Galloway is more concerned with the inside man he sent in from the local community, who has died from a stab wound. "Out there, there are parents at their wits' end, unable to do anything. And I've got to sit here, listening to you talking about this job as if it's an embarrassment to some foreign embassy!" The view of an exotic global crime has more potency when it comes from those dealing with its local effects: the car crime, the burglaries, the overdoses "dumped outside the hospital gates!" Likewise, in Series 2's *Ringer*, a massive pile-up caused by a defective Porsche leads to a hunt for the gang that supplied it. The raid on their lair is one of the best action sequences seen on TV, more elaborate than the final bust of the drug dealers in *The French Connection*. Yet what leads up to it is the business of the enquiry, including scenes of uniform breaking the news of half a dozen deaths to the victims' relatives. The resulting sorrow and pain, visible in the messengers too, illustrate the full cost of the crime; in addition, it adds satisfaction to the takedown of the villains. This is what can be achieved by taking a holistic view of police work, not just crime-fighting.

The arrival of *The Bill*'s other key author Christopher Russell in Series 2 signals an increase in both comedy and politics, natural bedfellows in real life but rarely blended on the screen. The runaway porker at the start of *This Little Pig* is only stage one in a series of ordeals for its larger cousins. First come anti-fur protesters dragged into custody, their dulcet tones drifting out of the cells: "All things wise and wonderful, the fur trade killed them all..." Then Cryer has to supply two PCs as muscle for a Home Office bust of a sweatshop employing migrant labour. "I've got to take men off real police work for this, and I'm stretched enough as it is." "Why do we have to get this bastard job eh?" sulks Carver. "Cheaper to use us, innit?" explains his colleague Pete Muswell, always on the lookout for overtime, and trying to arrange a covert second job to pay for his next holiday. Finally, when June spots a man wanted on an outstanding warrant who has just tied the knot, Sun Hill ends up hosting his wedding reception. "Last time I was in here was when we got done for that lead, do you remember?" the best man asks the bloke behind him, who quickly replies, "No." But these entertaining snippets are build-up to the pivotal scene, in which Cryer and Galloway meet Chief Superintendent Brownlow and are told that overtime is now off the table, save for the most "serious" of crimes. Furious that he will have to ditch a burglary victim – "We don't bother, right? She goes to the bottom of the pile and she stays there" – the DI sums up Brownlow's logic on a leaner, more cost-effective service: "We're deliberately not solving crime now, in order to solve it in the year 2000." Later in the pub, the two men reflect on a new life of accountancy. Cryer points out Muswell and his recent, lucrative work up north, putting down the miner's strike: "See chummy over there? He's cost effective. Five thousand quid for policing a picket line." Money is always available for the right causes.

One can see the two strands of the police drama, the visceral energy of *The Sweeney* and the social realism of *Z Cars*, dovetail perfectly in this episode. The Outside Broadcast department of Thames, charged with handling the show, feared that it was unachievable but was spurred into action when Peter Cregeen cleverly suggested the job may go to their rivals in film instead. Despite the enormous difficulties of trailing heavy cameras and cables everywhere, the shooting is fluid and continuous, following people into real shops and factories. With the camerawork on the move, so too is the story, breaking down events, and issues, into small chunks. The picture of a police force buffeted on all sides, co-opted for dirty jobs and always pressed for resources, is built up without any need for long, static reflections on the subject – an inevitable feature of prior series made in that hybrid film/VT style, which, even if only on a subconscious level, divided the story into 'action' and 'acting'. Here the final argument between Galloway and Cryer – "Change your vote next time, that's what I mean!" – is delivered in a pub heaving with wedding guests, who neither know nor care about their troubles. Life is always moving and always chaotic; *The Bill* conveys this in the way it brings issues to the surface and then submerges them again before anyone can provide a satisfying answer. The very title, *This Little Pig*, displays an irreverence to its subject that fits the concurrent decline of the police's standing. But dig deeper into the material and you find an empathy and understanding for its subject; these people are nobody's heroes, but they're hardly in a heroic world.

With speed and economy of shooting comes the density of storytelling that distinguished *The Bill*. This is a programme in which a single line, or a single look, is vested with huge meaning. When June Ackland manages to detach herself from the babbling Reg Hollis in a corridor, the venomous stare she gives Cryer needs no elaboration. The much-cited 'documentary feel' of the early *Bill* is about more than just the visual style; it's also about recognising that not everything on screen has to be driven into the ground. Small, gnomic asides hint at backstory or attitudes that are never referred to again. An elderly couple brought in for housebreaking in *The Sweet Smell of Failure* provide plenty of comedy in the charge room. "You're a real gent, you are," the old woman coos at Galloway, as Cryer and Ackland try to contain the giggles. "Let me whisper in your shell, like." She pleads with him not to pursue "old Fred over there", as it was her idea: "He's all I've got." Then she gives the DI a useful tip-off on another crime. He agrees to speak for them to the judge, and put in a word for the old man, "like I was his dad." Suddenly we cut to the yard, where Galloway sits in his car, staring out of the window. "Everything all right, sir?" asks June. "I don't like nicking old people," he mutters, almost inaudibly. "It's disturbing...it brings back bad memories, I suppose." We are left to infer the rest for ourselves. Galloway provides another tiny morsel for thought in *Suspects*, when, investigating an armed robbery, he drives to the London Docks to see a snout. Instead, he encounters a kid on a bike, who declares that his brother "got stitched up by the Bill; got six months for doing up a Paki in a newsagents." "Was he at it?" "Oh, yeah." "Well," the DI concludes, throwing his cigar in the water, "there you go." This useful reminder to them both, that most villains are habitual, makes Galloway realise that the man he has in custody for the robbery doesn't fit this particular Bill.

In its pursuit of small moments, the show often buries its most significant messages below the line. When Sun Hill's first black officer, Abe Lyttelton, is introduced in Series 2, the reaction from bigot, mercenary and all-round wrong 'un Pete Muswell – "'Scuse me," he belches, before getting up and walking out of the canteen –

is supposed to represent the racism Abe is dealing with in the force. But the following day, when he arrives for work in his civvies, the front desk is in turmoil thanks to a pair of electricians who have hit a wire and cut off the power. Geoff McQueen paints a picture of aggro that he had probably caused himself in his time, given that his work as a painter and decorator in a police station gave him the initial idea for *Woodentop*. That initial play showcased the babbling overlap of dialogue that *The Bill* continued with in its attempt to capture the hue and cry of daily life, and it proves its worth here. As Cryer strolls in and says hello to everyone, in the foreground a suspicious Sgt. Peters can be heard asking Abe, "What's your number?" before he lets him in. No hardcore bigot, he is so accustomed to the hostility between the Met Police and the black community that he can't believe 'one of them' is really 'one of us'. Brownlow has already warned a somewhat offended Cryer that Lyttelton's third posting in as many years must have a different outcome: "I want this station to succeed where all the others have failed." That brief gesture from Peters is a hint that the problems are not just from upfront prejudice, but from subtler, more ingrained forms of it. The assumptions of the well-meaning can be as damaging as those from outright enemies.

The storytelling range of *The Bill* gets wider with each successive year. Geoff McQueen's Series 3 opener *The New Order of Things* illustrates how far the show has come in richness and complexity in a short time. Across fifty minutes he balances five plotlines, three on heavyweight subjects of the day: legal appeals against police wrongdoing, the AIDS crisis and the continued fallout from the miners' strike. The latter, in particular, showcases the even-handed approach of the programme to a bitterly divisive topic. A man arrested outside the station for carrying an iron bar is waiting in the hope of doing over Muswell, who gave his kid brother a gaping, and ultimately fatal, head injury on the picket lines. This issue strikes close to home for one PC, the happy go lucky Nick Shaw, who tries to build a rapport with the prisoner as "we're from same part of world." Instead, after a disgusted look from his fellow Yorkshireman for putting on the stripes of the enemy, he has to sit through a diatribe about how they behaved. "They brought in hard bastards from all over the country to bash the lads back to work. They call themselves coppers, they're nowt but a bunch of legalised thugs: Thatcher's bleeding brownshirts...The bastards were using bloody great clubs as big as pit props." But Nick responds with the view from the other side: "I could show you some things, used against us, that would make your hair stand on end...You think as coppers we liked it? Listen: there were some lads that went from here, that came back crying mate! You don't know owt about it, you've been bloody brainwashed like most back home, you make me sick! Yeah, all right, maybe there were a few headcase coppers who were more than keen, but for most we hated it!"

This attempt at revenge is served too cold, for Muswell has by now left the force – and that in itself symbolises a pivoting of the show's concerns. The money-grabbing Mus is one of those young coppers on the make who were attracted to the job by the pay rises the Thatcher government gave to the police. But the hard-edged approach to law and order gave way during the 1980s to a focus on crime management: running a cost-effective business, serving the customers, acting in partnership with other agencies. *The Bill* launched in the same year as the Police and Criminal Evidence Act, a landmark piece of legislation that has governed police powers ever since and dictated the show's agenda for much of its life. The new orthodoxy imposed on Sun Hill, forced to handle its prisoners with kid gloves, is a shot in the arm for the programme at the start of Series 3. Suddenly there is an inbuilt source of conflict, around which varying attitudes can be clustered. 'PACE says', PACE bloody says?" the ever-fiery Ted Roach erupts. "Why should that bastard have eight hours' kip, I've only had three!" When he gets back from court hoping to speak to his man, he finds that his much-loathed opposite number Tom Penny has stuck rigidly to the rulebook. "Couldn't you have waited another half an hour?" "Fifty-three minutes, to be precise," tuts Penny, glancing at his watch as he emerges from an empty cell. "I'm not here for your convenience.

You had no evidence on McClafferty anyway, he's just one of the tired old lags you pull in every time. You want to start thinking with your brains mate, instead of your balls..." Tom is only saved from a punch in the gob by the arrival of a colleague with a supply of tampons. "Don't use them all at once," Ted advises his enemy as he stalks off. Somewhere between these two extremes of thought is the mild-mannered Alec Peters, who has his own gripes with the new system: "PACE is a pain in the neck. The only thing I don't have to write down now is how often a prisoner farts."

This changing picture gave the programme all the material it needed to adapt to the formidable challenge of being made all year round, when it was remodelled as a series of twice a week half-hours in 1988. Tellingly, the indispensable figure of the early days, Galloway, is the only one not to continue into the new era and yet it thrives regardless. A different kind of moody inspector takes his place, as the sinister Frank Burnside is promoted from his cameo role as a DS to DI. Burnside is the best example of the ambiguous line the show treads with the police. Cryer is told that he was "a very important part" of the aforementioned Countryman, but there is no further elaboration on this, leaving plenty of rumour to fill the void. "Do you think for one moment the brass aren't clued in to your reputation?" asks Bob. "And do you think for one moment that I give a toss?" replies his defiant adversary.

When Burnside is set up on charges of corruption by a vengeful ex-colleague, he is in genuine despair as he pleads his innocence: "This man has framed me because he wrongly believes I copped some money from a job of his years ago..." He is reprieved at the last moment, but he can never fully escape his image. When the irritatingly ethical Jim Carver berates him for trying to force a confession from an innocent man, Burnside hits back at once: "I do not fit people up, and I do *not* break the law! If detective work is too much for your sensitive soul, I suggest you retrain as a ballet dancer!" He is furious not just at the accusation, but at the emphatic denial he is forced to issue; the last thing he wants is to go on the record, one way or the other. Or, as he laughs at Jim during an argument in another episode, when the latter asks if he wants the truth: "From a detective?"

Every time *The Bill* returned to the screen in its early years it was Geoff McQueen who kicked off the new run, and his half-hour episodes act as a standard bearer for the format. *Stop and Search* packs no less than three storylines into twenty-four minutes: a complaint about police harassment from a black man stopped multiple times, the hopes and ambitions of an engaged pair of special constables, and the confession of a man to killing his wife thirty years ago. Moreover, the last of these is dumped on a new character, DC Alfred 'Tosh' Lines, who hits the screen as a fully-rounded figure – in every sense – despite the number of plots being juggled around him. "Even the old woman calls me Tosh!" he explains as he ambles into the building, plastic bag in hand. "You don't surprise me," comments Roach. Sent out on this thankless job with the new recruit, Jim throws his toys out of the pram. But Tosh handles it with due diligence and is convinced by the husband's story – especially his torment at being haunted by his wife's ghost. And then, come the conclusion, Burnside voices a sentiment rarely heard from a committed TV cop: "After thirty years? Who cares?"

Such a blunt ending demonstrates why the show wasn't stymied by a half-hour format: it is unafraid of dead ends, both literal and metaphorical. The number of episodes that finish unfinished, with villains still at large and questions unanswered, is no weakness but further reinforcement of the show's house style. What we are seeing is only a glimpse of police work, not a gift-wrapped start to finish narrative. This is a deck that can be shuffled in an infinite number of ways, and becomes more realistic in the process.

What is most surprising in the switch to a pre-watershed slot is the negligible loss of 'edge'. The body in the bath from *Woodentop* is a precursor to similar horrors in the early series, all of which were broadcast at 9pm. Along with the mixture of POVs between cop and criminal, they give this period an odd feel, tangibly different from the *Bill* we come to know in the 1990s. But the handling of violence is the best expression of the documentary style. It arrives suddenly and randomly, without any artistry to it. When Galloway discovers the body of a child molester who has slashed his wrists rather than face justice, he turns a corner and it is simply there, lying in a bloody heap: an unavoidable fact, not a series of fast-cut impressions. Likewise, when a gunman is assassinated, the combined force of the bullets punches him into a wall and to the floor in a single, merciless take. But, though the viscera is trimmed a little at 8pm, the world of Sun Hill remains a brutal one: a bus driver soaked in blood after a crash, burns to faces and hands after a car catches fire, even a stuntman flailing around in the midst of a genuine fireball.

At times the show exceeds not only its earlier incarnation but also its big screen cousins. The Season 1 episode *It's Not Such a Bad Job After All* deals with the suicide of a heroin-addicted teen, Amanda, drawn into making bubble bath porn movies. When the first *Lethal Weapon* film retells this story with remarkable synchronicity – same habit, same movies, same first name – it opens in a luxury penthouse where the girl is scoring. In a glossy softcore scene, all loose lingerie and billowing curtains, she obtains one last high before swan diving from another to her death. Compare and contrast with the scenes of drug addiction from *Bad Faith*, an early half-hour episode of *The Bill*. The police break into a flat and find a couple overdosed on crack: slumped in a chair, only half-alive, the woman stares glassy-eyed as a lump of vomit rolls down her pockmarked cheek. This is the view from the trenches, lacking in any style or beauty.

Another ingredient that flourishes in the old format and the new is the show's humour. *The Bill*'s gift for the absurd comes from its storytelling remit, to examine the whole of police business, which throws up all sorts – literally so, at the beginning of *Sun Hill Karma*, when PC Ken Melvin is forced to step into a cell that two dozing drunks have redecorated with puke. "Nah, it's only a mess when they shit all over the walls," says Cryer, with the nonchalance of a man who has seen this, and worse, plenty of times before. When the cleaners arrive they are furious at being delayed by the late arrival of a prison bus, but Cryer tells them they can start on the female cells: "I'm sure Glenda won't mind." "Oh, *Glenda's* in, is she?" one of them enthuses. "Hello pet, how are you?" she greets her favourite customer, settling down for an excited natter. When she emerges from the drunks' cell, she gives them both barrels – "If my cat made a mess like that I'd rub his nose in it!" – and is told to "piss off, you old bag." She goes for one with her broom and has to be warned off by Bob. "I should be a magistrate not a bleeding cleaner, I'd soon sort these buggers out!" "We could use her on the TSG," Roach tells Cryer as he saunters away.

This world has its own bizarre subculture that becomes completely normal to the people inside it. The arrival of a terrifying bag lady, who dents Nick Shaw's forehead by throwing a phone at it and has to be dragged into her cell, demonstrates that nothing can be taken at face value. Through the chaos, a quiet bespectacled man brought in for defrauding DIY stores sits in custody because there is no cell free for him. Finally he is bailed: "Another time, perhaps?" he asks hopefully. "You do see life, don't you sergeant?" Alone at last, Cryer steps into a cell, hops on the bed and tries a quick burst of the lotus position to soothe himself.

Crucially, the police are not just sober and collected figures watching the craziness unfold. Those dynamic renegades who dominate the show have the rise taken out of them along with everyone else. In *Home Beat*, Sun Hill's flame-haired terrier Galloway has to go about things more gingerly than normal when he picks up an ankle bite from his own kind. "I hear it died of rabies," notes a sad Cryer, who starts humming 'How Much is That Doggy in the Window' as Galloway limps off sullenly. Home beat PC Yorkie Smith is summoned to the DI's office and finds the big boss in his pants, climbing awkwardly into a new pair of trousers.

Galloway's fellow maverick Roach is similarly dressed down in a half-hour episode, *Personal Imports*. When his suit is ruined after he is shoved into a urinal, he glares his way through an interview of a suspect while wearing a T-shirt that proclaims, 'I've Done it in Corfu'. Cryer's musical ability rubs off on the rest of the relief. First, after a glorious defeat in a charity football match, substitute goalie Viv Martella is serenaded with the *Match of the Day* theme. Then Nick Shaw and Taff Edwards, both outsiders from the provinces, try to make a quick exit from the station on their community bicycles as they are forced to attend a tree-planting ceremony. Sneaking out behind them in the yard, their colleagues prove they are East End born and bred: "Daisy, Daisy, give me your answer do..." From here it's a short step to the command performance in *Good Will Visit*, another early half-hour, in which Alec Peters arrests an entire ship of ratings for trashing a bar and is forced to let them go after being berated by Chief Inspector Conway. "This has been one of the worst days of my life," he declares after seeing them off the premises – and is then piped back aboard Sun Hill by a line of PCs with thumbs in mouths.

It's notable that the show applies the same effort and choreography to its comic sequences as it does to action, recognising that timing is vital for both. Take the dance of Reg Hollis in *The Price You Pay*, after an old woman at the front desk hands in a gnome with a fishing rod. "Has it got a name?" "Grow up constable, of course it hasn't got a name!" Reg begins his pirouette through the station, a camera following him as he engages in a *pas de deux* with one colleague after another. "Fishing for compliments, Reg?" asks Inspector Frazer at the swing doors. Emerging from an office, Sgt. Peters ups the ante: "Ah, new gnome beat officer!" But the crowning move comes from the prima ballerina Mike Dashwood, as he and Roach pass by: "DI Galloway undercover?" Like many of the set-pieces in these early days, it isn't remotely integral to the plot: simply confirmation that this is the oddest of jobs. "Ah, the eagle has landed!" Penny declares at the end of *Trespasses*, when he steps into the collator's office to find a church lectern recovered in a burglary. Peters turns instantly to an annoyed Stamp: "Five quid. I bet him five quid that'd be the first thing you said." "Sorry for being so predictable," mutters Tom. In *A Little Knowledge*, Melvin brings in a balloon seller working a street corner without a licence. The crowd that has gathered for the crime of the century laughs as the balloons are crammed into the van. But the police have the last laugh when the suspect tries to do a runner in the yard and loses hold of his livelihood. "Don't worry, we'll get Northumberland to set up a roadblock," Taff reassures him as they watch it drift skywards. "The officer on the case thought that Air Traffic Control ought to be informed, in case they're a hazard," Viv radios from CAD. "No, straight up! Well, not quite straight up – more north-westerly really."

With increased output comes a growth in the writing pool, and the show's durability is proved in the ease with which it is picked up by different authors, old and new. This is a format that has room for the chaotic black comedy of Julian Jones, in which the police pursue domestic abusers and mental patients around the streets of London; for the probing questions of JC Wilsher, soon to examine the police's flaws in greater depth in *Between the Lines*; for the bizarre wordplay of Arthur McKenzie, an ex-DCI who delights in tying his dialogue in elaborate knots; and for the disturbing ghost stories of Peter J. Hammond, which take the police away from the comfort of canteen banter and into strange worlds occupied by strange people. *Guessing Game* is an exercise in horror in which nothing is seen, only implied: the story of a serial kidnapper who has died by chance of a heart attack, but may have left a final victim behind somewhere. The torturer's lair is found not in some dank basement but right at the top of a high-rise building, virtually touching the stars. It is a world by itself, totally unknown to the people below: desolation in the heart of a city. "All ready and waiting," Roach observes, after he kicks in the bedroom door and finds a single chair in a darkened room, with a single piece of rope on it. We see a glimpse of what might have happened, but also, in times past, what has happened – the nasty residue of a crime, even when the criminal has gone. The odd assortment of perverts, missing persons and "ding a lings" that populate Hammond's other episodes have the same enigma about them: a feeling that the truth is just out of reach of the police, who tomorrow will be confronted by a new set of people with fresh problems to not quite solve. Through its focus on atmosphere rather than elaborate plotting, Hammond's work follows *The Bill*'s guiding light: less is more.

What is most striking about *The Bill* in the 1980s is that, once it was established as a programme, disruption rained on it non-stop for the rest of the decade. For its second series producer Michael Chapman left temporarily, to be replaced by Peter Cregeen, who re-orientated the show by setting in stone the rule about seeing events solely from the view of the police. The following year, it was forced to move house due to strike action at its Wapping home, resulting in an eighteen-month break before Series 3 and a new Sun Hill based across town in Kensington. The year after that, the format was rejigged to become an ongoing half-hour show, with all the logistical headaches that came from two units shooting simultaneously. The year after *that*, it was change at the top again, as Chapman returned to take up the reins from Cregeen; and finally, at the turn of the 1990s, it underwent a second move across London, to its final home in Merton. But if anything, the quality gets better and better across these upheavals, suggesting that they were formative. Looking at the span of the entire programme, it could be argued that when *The Bill* got its own purpose-built station, it became too stable for too long; and that the resulting, increasingly outlandish efforts to shake it out of that stability helped to hasten its end.

What shines through in this early, tumultuous period is the unbreakable strength of the core idea: a blueprint that can be twisted and moulded every which way, that is bigger than any single character, and therefore detached from the need for 'stars'. In essence *The Bill* is the single play, holding the torch well into the next decade as it disappears elsewhere – and recognising the full potential in its subject. The police series is not just a murder mystery production line but the best possible tapestry for capturing life in all its awful glory.

© Edward Kellett

MAGGIE MAKES BRITISH TELEVISION HISTORY:
THE GENTLE TOUCH

On April 11th, 1980 - four months before British audiences were introduced to Inspector Jean Darblay in *Juliet Bravo,* and eleven years before they were introduced to DCI Jane Tennison (based on Flying Squad detective Jackie Malton) in *Prime Suspect* - Detective Inspector Maggie Forbes made history by becoming the first female police officer to feature as the lead character in a British television series.

Television has so often been far ahead of the reality of certain periods in history by featuring characters whose real-life counterparts are marginalised in a variety of ways and placing them in positions of authority and power, or simply showing them being treated equally to everyone else around them. Seeing such characters on screen brings hope to viewers who are finally able to see people either like themselves on screen, or aspirational role models, as well as generating necessary conversations questioning why society has not yet progressed to that point off-screen. In the case of Maggie Forbes and *The Gentle Touch* (1980-84)*,* British television was actually far *behind* the times in regard to screen depictions and the real-life achievements of British female police officers.

American audiences had long since already enjoyed their own groundbreaking moments featuring female police officers and private detectives on television. The very first occurred when the series *Decoy* (1957-1958) aired. *Decoy* was created for syndication and was the first American series to feature a female police officer as its lead character. Beverly Garland played Patricia 'Casey' Jones, a detective working undercover in New York City, who notably works alone while on her assignments, rather than with a partner.

Gwen Bagni and Paul Dubov's popular but short-lived series *Honey West* (1965-1966) had focused on female private detective Honey West (Anne Francis) and her partner Sam (John Ericson) a former Marine. The character of Honey was intended to be the American equivalent of the character of Emma Peel from the British series *The Avengers*. Honey was perfectly able to take care of herself.

Next came Robert L. Collins's hugely popular *Police Woman* (1974-1978), which turned Angie Dickinson into a household name for her portrayal of Sgt 'Pepper' Anderson, an undercover officer working in Los Angeles. Like Maggie Forbes, 'Pepper' was also shown to be liked and respected by her male colleagues and was in the job because she deserved to be there and was just as capable as the male officers.

The action-packed *Charlie's Angels* (1976-1981) saw the arrival of the 'kickass' team of female private detectives Sabrina Duncan (Kate Jackson), Kelly Garrett (Jaclyn Smith), Jill Munroe (Farrah Fawcett) and Kris Munroe (Cheryl Ladd). The women were hired to work for the mysterious and wealthy Charlie Townsend (John Forsythe) and were aided in their work by the adorable Bosley (David Doyle). [1]

In the decades before *The Gentle Touch* aired, British detective films and series had centred around male officers, with female officers featuring as minor characters. Popular detective series such as the realistic and hard-hitting *Z-Cars* (1962-1978) and the action-packed and violent *The Sweeney* (1975-1978) were all about hardened men, car chases and shootouts. *The Gentle Touch* changed all that.

In Maggie Forbes the series gave us a female police officer who was just as capable, memorable and interesting as the likes of Jack Regan in *The Sweeney*. *The Gentle Touch* also focused less on officers kicking in doors and running after villains, and more on time-consuming investigative police work, such as hours spent reading files and documents, running surveillance on suspects and speaking to witnesses, victims and suspects. The series was more interested in the human stories behind the names and case information in the reports and statements that come across the desks of Maggie and her colleagues. Most important of all, the series showed that the police force was no longer the sole domain of male officers.

Before exploring *The Gentle Touch* in some depth, it is worth offering a brief potted history of the evolving relationship between the real British police force and women officers. When the force was founded by Sir Robert Peel in 1829 it was a male-only profession. From 1883 the Metropolitan Police began to employ women under a special licence to visit female convicts while under police supervision. In 1889 fourteen women were formally employed as Police Matrons – supervising and searching women and child offenders in police stations and in the courts – to undertake duties which up until that point had been carried out by police officers' wives. In 1914, animal rights and women's rights campaigner Margaret Damer Dawson, and suffragette Nina Boyle, co-founded the Women Police Volunteers service which was renamed the Women Police Service the following year.

In 1915 Edith Smith became the first British woman to be granted full powers of arrest. Her appointment was brought about due to concerns in Lincolnshire regarding sex workers frequenting a local army base where fourteen thousand officers were billeted. Where possible Constable Smith tried to deter the women from going to the camp and issued cautions. She only arrested them if it was deemed absolutely necessary. In 1920 Florence Mildred White became the first female officer to attain the rank of Sergeant. She was 'attested' which meant that she had the same rights as male constables. White moved to Birmingham City Police a few years later and became the first female Inspector in 1930. In 1932 Lilian Wyles became the first female officer to attain the rank of Chief Inspector. Wyles's 1937 Annual Qualification Report lists her as being "very good" in regards to her power of command, influence over the men (the officers serving under her), tact in dealing with the public and her ability. Her experience as a police officer is listed as being "exceptional". Wyles retired in 1949 and published her memoirs, *A Woman at Scotland Yard: Reflections on the Struggles and Achievements of Thirty Years in The Metropolitan Police*, in 1952.

Shirley Becke joined the Metropolitan Police in 1941, was promoted to Sergeant in 1952, became an Inspector in 1957 and a Superintendent in 1960. Becke was behind new advertising campaigns during the 1960s aimed at recruiting female officers after the 1968 redesign of the female police uniforms by fashion designer and royal dressmaker Norman Hartnell. Becke also became the commander of the A4 Branch. In 1968 twenty-nine-year-old Sislin Fay Allen became Britain's first black female Police Constable. She had emigrated to Britain in the early 1960s as part of the Windrush generation. She had been working as a nurse before deciding to seek a career change and applied to join the Police. Sadly, Allen was subjected to racism by some colleagues and also received racist hate mail from members of the public. She remained in the force until 1972, after which she returned to Jamaica with her family and continued to work as a police officer there.

Dawson, Boyle, Smith, White, Wyles, Becke and Allen...just a few of the groundbreaking female police officers in the real world who predated Maggie Forbes in the fictional one of television drama. *The Gentle Touch* was made by London Weekend Television for ITV. Episodes aired on Friday evenings for the first four years of the series before moving to Saturday evenings for the fifth and final season. The memorable theme tune was written by British songwriter and jazz pianist Roger Webb, who is best known for fronting the Roger Webb Trio and Roger Webb Orchestra. He also wrote the themes for the series *Strange Report* (1969-1970), *Shadows of Fear* (1970-73) and *Hammer House Of Horror* (1980). The theme was haunting and slow during the first season and was then changed to be more upbeat for the remainder of the series.

The series was created by Terence Feely who had been the story editor of the British anthology television series *Armchair Theatre* and *Mystery and Imagination* during the 1960s. Feely was also the associate producer of the cult spy series *Callan* and had been instrumental in bringing it to the screen as a full series after the pilot episode *A Magnum for Schneider* aired as a 1967 episode of *Armchair Theatre*. Feely wrote for many British television series over the years including *The Prisoner, The Avengers, The Saint, UFO, Shoestring* and *The Persuaders!*

Jill Gascoine was cast in the lead role of Detective Inspector Maggie Forbes. She was born in Lambeth in 1937 and took up acting after leaving the boarding school that she hated. She performed at the Edinburgh Fringe in the late 1950s, went on to work with director Ken Loach at the Living Theatre in Leicester, and attended Dundee Repertory Theatre in Scotland, during the 1960s. Gascoine worked steadily in minor television and film roles throughout the 1970s – including a recurring role in the popular series *The Onedin Line* – but it was her casting in *The Gentle Touch* that saw her gain the major lead role of her career. She brought intelligence, strength, determination, playfulness and warmth to Maggie Forbes.

When Gascoine first read the initial treatment for the series, she immediately liked the character of Maggie. In a 1989 television interview with Gloria Hunniford, Gascoine recalled: "I liked the fact that she was a single mother. How assertive she was. That the programme itself depicted her professional life, as well as her private life, which I thought was very interesting. It was the first time it had happened on television and I like that." Gascoine also recalled the response of real police officers if they ever saw her when she was out in public: "I can remember once in Swallow Street in London there was a whole van load of policemen went past when I was walking down. They all jumped out of the back, and as I walked past, they all saluted me and said, "Good evening, ma'am." [2]

Maggie Forbes still feels like a groundbreaking character when you watch the series today; what is most striking is how normal the series makes it seem for Maggie to be in the job and to be in the rank that she holds within the force. She is not in the job merely to serve as a tick box exercise for management and become the token female officer assigned to a team. She is in the job because she deserves to be there. Maggie has the experience and expertise that the job requires. She has passed all the required tests; she can look after herself while out on the streets dealing with criminals and suspects; and she is just as capable of undertaking her duties as her male colleagues are. Maggie is tough and shrewd, with a no-nonsense attitude, and she always treats marginalised individuals respectfully and kindly – something which is frequently shown not to be the case where Maggie's colleague Bob Croft is concerned.

Unlike DCI Jane Tennison in *Prime Suspect*, Maggie Forbes is shown to be liked, accepted, respected and valued by most of her male colleagues from the very beginning of the series. Tennison, on the other hand, constantly finds herself disliked and disrespected by many male colleagues and senior officers who question her suitability to be a member of their male dominated profession. In this regard *The Gentle Touch* feels even more groundbreaking than *Prime Suspect*. An interesting point about Maggie is that she retains her femininity throughout the series. She never feels compelled to act overly tough or hide her emotions in order to be accepted by male colleagues. Nor does she feel that she must take steps to make herself appear physically less attractive or more masculine. Maggie is completely comfortable in her own skin. [3] The other thing that stands out about her is that – as Gascoine admired – she is a working single mother. For the duration of the series, we see Maggie attempting to juggle both her responsibilities at home and at work. British audiences would not see a female detective quite like this again until the arrival of DCI Janine Lewis (Caroline Quentin) in the series *Blue Murder* (2003-2009).

The Gentle Touch follows a Metropolitan Police C.I.D. team based at the fictional Seven Dials police station in London. In addition to Maggie Forbes, the team consists of DCI Bill Russell (William Marlowe), a veteran of the force who has seen so much over the years that it takes a lot to shock or horrify him these days; DI Bob Croft (Brian Gwaspari), a bigoted and irascible officer who often gives Maggie a tough time and is barely tolerated by most of his colleagues, much less liked by them; the ever dependable and steady DS Jake Barrett (Paul Moriarty); the baby of the team, DS Jimmy Fenton (Christopher Thompson); and DS Peter Phillips (Kevin O'Shea). Other recurring characters include Maggie's teenage son Stephen (Nigel Rathbone); her supportive father George (James Ottaway); and her boyfriend DI Mike Turnbull (Bernard Holley).

The relationships that Maggie has with Bill Russell and Jake Barrett are at the heart of the series. Jake and Maggie are great mates and confidants. There is a hint that Jake sometimes wishes they could perhaps become more to each other but that he will never act on that for fear of ruining their friendship. The more interesting relationship of the two is that between Bill and Maggie. The pair develop such a close bond and are so in tune with each other's moods and body language that they can read each other like a book. Bill always has Maggie's back and is convinced of her suitability for the job from the very beginning.

As the series progresses and Bill's relationship with his wife becomes strained and ends in divorce, there is a sense that Bill's feelings for Maggie are turning romantic, as he seems to find any excuse that he can to spend more time with her inside and outside of working hours. They would have made a good couple but, interestingly, the writers chose not to go down that route and instead left them as very close friends. The closest the writers ever got to developing this potential relationship further was in Tony Hoare's episode *The Conference*, where Maggie and Bill attend a police conference being held at a hotel. These days screen relationships which depict characters changing from colleagues to friends, and then from friends to lovers, have become a clichéd trope in detective series, but back then it would certainly have been meaningful and interesting if the writers had chosen to take Bill and Maggie's relationship in that direction.

From the very beginning of the series, the writers also highlighted how much of a toll being a police officer can take on both the officers themselves and their families. Maggie's husband Ray (a uniformed police officer) is shown to be worn out and at the end of his tether with the job in the opening scene of the first episode *Killers*, written by Brian Finch. Ray Forbes rages to Maggie about the violence the uniformed police are increasingly seeing and being subjected too, as well as the increasing lack of respect and appreciation they are beginning to receive from the public. When Ray Forbes is gunned down later in the opening episode, while trying to stop an armed robbery, the incident brings home to the audience the daily risks taken by the men and women who do this job. Ray Forbes's speech about the growing public anger, disrespect and hatred towards the police was both topical and would also prove to be prescient. [3]

When *The Gentle Touch* first came on air, women and girls across the country were terrified and furious over the police's handling of the 'Yorkshire Ripper' case. Between 1969 and 1980, lorry driver Peter Sutcliffe travelled around Yorkshire – and beyond – bludgeoning numerous women and girls with a hammer and murdering thirteen females with a mix of hammer blows and stabbings. The onus to stay safe from harm was placed solely upon women and girls. In 1977, they were instructed not to go out after dark by the police. This prompted outrage and led to the Reclaim the Night women's protest march in Leeds on the 12th of November, with several other marches taking place that night in other cities across the country.

Despite the hard work put in by many individual officers working on the case, the overall investigation conducted by West Yorkshire Police had been shambolically handled from the beginning. Sutcliffe was questioned nine times over the years; crucial evidence and key information in victim statements were dismissed; and precious time was wasted on the infamous 'Wearside Jack' hoax tape and letters. Arguably worse still were the sickening attitudes held by some of the male officers leading the investigation, directed towards the victims themselves – especially towards those who had been sex workers at the time of their death. Superintendent Jim Hobson infamously said the following during a press conference in 1979: "He has made it clear that he hates prostitutes. Many people do...But the 'Ripper' is now killing innocent girls." When the case came to trial in 1981, these attitudes were echoed by the Attorney General Sir Michael Havers, who had this to say about the victims: "Some were prostitutes, but perhaps the saddest part of the case is that some were not." Havers's speech led the English Collective of British Prostitutes to organise protests which were held outside the courts at the Old Bailey in London.

Inside the police force itself at the time of the Sutcliffe investigation, the experiences of female officers were mixed. Sexism was still rife but segregation between male and female officers ended in 1973. Before that year, female officers had belonged to a separate division to their male colleagues and were assigned different duties. Despite the decades of sexism and hostility found within the force, as I have highlighted we had seen some pioneering female officers make incredible strides towards equality, rising through the ranks decades before desegregation was even a consideration.

At the time Maggie Forbes arrived on our screens, the reality of life for women and girls in Britain painted a mixed picture. On the one hand, women were in a far better place in many regards than they had ever been before. Women had gained more independence and control over their own bodies – due to the arrival of the Pill in the 1960s and the legalisation of abortion in 1967- and had achieved equal pay (in theory) with male colleagues in the workplace thanks to the passage of The Equal Pay Act (1970) and the Sex Discrimination Act (1975). The country had elected its first female Prime Minister the previous year (a very different Maggie). The feminist movement had opened the eyes of women around the world to the fact that they could be mothers and wives yet also enjoy careers and lives outside of the restrictive gender roles they had been pigeonholed into for centuries.

On the other hand, women were still victims of rape, sexual assault and domestic violence; were still subjected to sexism and misogyny – all graphically highlighted by the 'Ripper' case. Marital rape would not be outlawed in England until 1992.

Given all the remarkable achievements of female officers over the decades, it is both disappointing and frustrating that we did not have more British films and television series like *The Gentle Touch* long before the 1980s. This in itself makes both *The Gentle Touch* as a series and Maggie Forbes as a character genuinely ground-breaking.

Several writers worked on *The Gentle Touch* during its five-year run. Recurring writers included Terence Feely himself; *Sapphire & Steel* creator P.J. Hammond; Roger Marshall, who wrote for many series including *The Avengers*, and was the creator of *Zodiac, Travelling Man* and the co-creator of *Public Eye*; and Neil Rudyard, the pseudonym of the actor William Marlowe. These four penned some of the series' most memorable and hard-hitting episodes.

The focus of the series was on Maggie, her colleagues and on the daily working lives of police officers; yet the writers also tackled topical societal issues such as homosexuality and homophobia, rape, euthanasia, sexism, racism, sex work, disability, abuse of the elderly and youth violence. The following episodes provide just a taste of some of the topical and hard-hitting storylines to be found in the series.

P.J. Hammond's episode *Solution* is the final episode of Season 3 and is arguably the bravest and most moving episode of the entire series. The episode features two separate yet interconnecting storylines. The first focuses on Clare (Sheila White) who is terminally ill with leukaemia and needs her partner Jean (Fiona Walker) to get her some medication so that she can take an overdose and pass away peacefully and quickly. This storyline is memorable not only because of its heartbreaking ending, but also for its focus on a lesbian relationship, and for depicting it as a normal and loving thing, at a time when homophobia was still rampant. The second storyline sees Bill, Maggie, Bill's wife Jean and Maggie's friend John, who is a doctor, attending a dinner party at Bill and Jean's house. Conversation turns to euthanasia as well as to the difficulties that come with caring for those who are severely ill or disabled. Maggie and Bill must both confront their own personal feelings on the issue. It is a topic which remains controversial and divisive today, and this episode feels even more groundbreaking because of the frank and sympathetic approach that Hammond takes to the subject matter.

Roger Marshall's episode *Blade* is the fifth episode of Season 1 and focuses on homophobia and gay relationships. When a young man is found murdered on a Tube train, Maggie and Bob Croft investigate and discover that the victim was gay. Croft's undisguised homophobia disgusts Maggie as the pair work the case. Maggie discovers the murder victim was having an affair with the older Doctor Thorne (Kenneth Gilbert). This episode looks at 'lavender marriage', which is a term used to describe a marriage between a man and a woman where one or both are gay and have entered into a perceivably heterosexual marriage for protection from homophobia. Thorne's wife doesn't know of her husband's sexuality, and he doesn't want her told because he doesn't want to hurt her. A cruel decision made by Croft regarding Thorne's situation leads Maggie to confront him publicly at work and magnificently deliver him a dose of his own unpleasant medicine. At the time this episode aired, gay relationships between men over the age of twenty-one had been legal in Britain and Wales since 1967 – interestingly lesbianism had never been declared illegal – and would be legalised in Scotland in 1981, in Northern Ireland in 1982, and in the Republic of Ireland in 1993. Despite the legalisation, many men and women within what we now call the LGBTQ+ community were still too afraid of being their true selves publicly due to the levels of homophobia which pervaded society.

The final episode of *The Gentle Touch*, *Exit Laughing*, was written by William Marlowe as Neil Rudyard and aired on November 24th, 1984. The episode sees Maggie receiving terrifying threats, and a series of thefts are reported in the Seven Dials staff locker rooms. The final shot of the series sees Maggie, Bill and the rest of the team meeting down the pub to discuss their futures. The end of the series wasn't the end of Maggie Forbes, however. The following year, Terence Feely's series *C.A.T.S Eyes* aired. This series sees

Maggie (who has now left the police force) join an all-female detective agency led by Pru Standfast (Rosalyn Landor). While not in the same league as *The Gentle Touch*, the series ran until 1987 and has gained a devoted fanbase over the years.

We have both *The Gentle Touch* and Jill Gascoine to thank for the creation of *Widows* (1983-1985) and *Prime Suspect* (1991-2006). Author Lynda La Plante started out as an actress and while training at RADA began to write stage plays. While guest-starring in Tony Hoare's Season 2 episode of *The Gentle Touch, Something Blue*, La Plante and Gascoine got the giggles during filming due to some of the dialogue. La Plante said to Gascoine, "I'd love to have a go at writing..." to which Gascoine replied: "So why don't you? Give it a go." [4]

La Plante took her encouragement to heart and wrote four scripts for *The Gentle Touch* which she submitted to the script editor. All four were rejected and returned, but on one somebody had written, "This is brilliant." The storyline of that script would go on to form the basis for La Plante's acclaimed television series *Widows.* If she and Gascoine had never had their chat during filming, it is possible that the aspiring author might never have gone on to create *Widows*, or her two famous policewomen -- DCI Jane Tennison and DI Anna Travis.

The Gentle Touch remains both a landmark and a highpoint in British television history and Detective Inspector Maggie Forbes undoubtedly paved the way for future British female screen detectives such as Jane Tennison, Janine Lewis, Rachel Bailey and Janet Scott, Vera Stanhope and Stella Gibson. We all owe a debt of gratitude to Maggie because of that.

© Madeleine Langham

1. Editor: *The Gentle Touch*'s five series run from 1980-84 crosses timelines with CBS' groundbreaking *Cagney & Lacey* TV movie and subsequent series – 1981-88 – which

combined elements of a female buddy film with the police procedural.

2. *LWT at 21*, ITV, 1989.

3. In that LWT interview, Jill Gascoine makes the observation that there is no reason why female police officers should not be 'glamorous' and she states that the real-life officer she partly based Maggie Forbes on was "even more" so.

4. Ray Forbes's speech about the growing public anger, disrespect and hatred towards the police preceded landmark events revolving around public hostility towards the force, especially amongst black Britons. The police and government response to the New Cross fire in 1981 – which saw thirteen young people killed and over fifty people injured when a fire was deliberately set at a house in London in which a sixteenth birthday party was being held – led to the Black People's Day of Action March in London on March 2nd, 1981. The Brixton riots, or Brixton uprising, of 1981, began on April 10th in response to rumours of police brutality against a black man. Following an arrest, the next day protestors began to fight with police and set fire to vehicles. The riots lasted for three days and left over 300 officers and civilians injured, as well as damage estimated at around £7.5 million. Riots would return to Brixton in 1985. These events were a stark reminder that it was not just women who felt marginalised by mainstream society and by Britain's police forces.

5. 'The Queen of Crime': Lynda La Plante. *Writing*, 15/06/2011.

BUREAU DES ÉTRANGERS: SUNSHINE & SHADY PEOPLE IN *BERGERAC*

"Bureau des Étrangers – Office of Strangers. How very Kafka!" (Hedley Cross, *Campaign for Silence*)

For a decade, *Bergerac* offered 1980s British crime drama viewers the opportunity to escape to the semi-exotic island location of Jersey. The series was an intriguing blend of action-adventure and police procedural, with an exploration of a wide range of topical subjects which was sometimes playfully light, yet often darker in tone. However, to get a full sense of the *Bergerac* formula, one must rewind to the pre-production history of another show, *Shoestring*, the series which, in effect, it replaced. As its co-creator, Robert Banks Stewart, explained in a BBC Four documentary:

"I was invited to go and join the BBC, to overhaul *Target*. About a week after I was there, the head of series, Graeme McDonald, came into my office and said, 'Why don't we scrap it, and do something new? Have you got anything you'd like to do?' Somehow, I found myself saying, 'Why is it that the BBC never make a really good private eye series, like Americans do - like *Rockford*? Why don't we really try and make a private eye series?' and Graeme McDonald said, 'You're on!'" [1]

As Banks Stewart would later acknowledge, offers like that are incredibly rare opportunities in television drama. The 'seed' for *Shoestring* came when Banks Stewart was listening to an advice programme on the radio and thought that it would be a fun, quirky idea to have a Private Eye/Ear character with his own radio show who then goes out of the studio to solve listeners' problems. Banks Stewart wanted to break away from what he felt was a "tired" formula: tyre-screeching, action-driven crime series starring well-known actors and shot in all-too-familiar, suburban London locations. Instead, he created a somewhat geeky main character who was sensitive and vulnerable, who had a past which had left him psychologically scarred, and whose private life was equally atypical or unconventional. Actor Trevor Eve – who had impressed Banks Stewart playing opposite Donald Pleasence and Laurence Olivier in an adaptation of *Dracula* – was initially reluctant to take a television series lead role, preferring theatre, film and one-off TV drama. However, Banks Stewart's unusual concept and Private Ear character drew him in:

"It seemed to be an opportunity to play someone eccentric. There had been the 70s tradition of straight-looking guys doing it 'right on the nose' and this was a character coming from left-field. He'd had a problem in his workplace and had wandered off. It was a chance to create someone from scratch." [2]

The methodical and innovative Eve brought his own creative ideas to the series, such as the crumpled-up suits and pyjama shirts that someone mildly eccentric and living part of the time on a leaky houseboat might wear. Having found a less well-known lead to play an unusual, offbeat character, Banks Stewart also wanted a more unfamiliar setting for the series. He rejected the BBC's suggestion of Slough and recommended Bristol as a city with an interesting variety of locations. Script editor Bob Baker has suggested that the city was a key "character" in the show. [3] Director Martin Campbell described the *Shoestring* locale in the following terms:

"The whole atmosphere around Bristol is very different. It was an interesting environment. Perhaps a lot of people hadn't seen it before so that added to the texture of the series." [4]

Add an eclectic main cast of support characters and a funky, harmonica-driven theme tune and, as broadcaster Hilary Oliver observes, the BBC had both a character and a series which "bucked the trend" of 70s crime series such as *Target* and *The Sweeney* which she describes as "testosterone-charged" dramas. [5] Oliver felt that *Shoestring* was a more modern show which helped drive the detective genre into the 80s. Trevor Eve's radio man/private eye Eddie Shoestring was a huge Sunday evening success, with ratings topping 20 million viewers. Those impressive figures are proof positive that you can attract a sizeable television audience with something a little alternative or – as Eve describes it – 'left-field', *if* the initial concept and lead character is backed up with intriguing scripts, quality guest actors and distinctive direction.

Forty-five years on, thanks to Trevor Eve's fun, flair and flawless portrayal, many viewers fondly remember the character of Eddie Shoestring: the cartoon caricatures which he swiftly sketches, his ability to slip into eccentric undercover roles, the running joke that he never has a private detective card on him for prospective clients, and the disarming and gentle charm of a character motivated by a moral code rather than money. After all, he is a rare private eye in that it is the radio station – rather than his clients – who pay him. The storylines frequently deal with hard-hitting subjects: a prostitute who takes her own life after a potential client turns out to be her own father (*Private Ear*); a woman left in emotional and financial disarray after her husband is killed by a drunk hit-and-run driver (*Knock for Knock*); a serial rapist who kills a female colleague because she has demonstrated that she can identify him (*Listen to Me*)...all within the first half a dozen episodes. At other times, *Shoestring* journeys down more unusual narrative roads for a 1979-80 series: the disadvantages men have in child custody cases (*Nine Tenths of the Law*), domestic abuse – both physical and emotional (*The Link-Up*; *The Farmer Had a Wife*) – and (in *The Dangerous Game*, a 1980 Christmas episode) the potentially fatal dangers of black-market toys.

Eddie Shoestring is not a miracle worker and sometimes the story endings are downbeat, particularly so in *The Farmer Had a Wife* where, as he offers a somewhat smug case summary on his radio show, it emerges that his client has taken his own life. In many of the stories, the police are seen as unwilling to pursue unsolved cases or reopen questionable ones. The writers were able to tackle these dark subjects while adding lighter touches, such as the ongoing relationship and rapport between Eddie and his landlady lawyer Erica (delightfully played by Doran Godwin) and a number of amusing, memorable physical encounters between Eddie and villains; the two which spring immediately to mind involve a messy fight with antique fraudster brothers in the estuary mud (*Knock for Knock*) and a scrap-chase with a blackmailer on the Romanesque stage of a seedy strip joint (*The Teddy Bears' Nightmare*). Many of Eddie's clients are morally grey characters, operating somewhere between victim and villain, illustrating the subtlety at play in the series. This even applies, albeit occasionally, to Eddie himself, illustrated by his insensitivity or blasé attitude when he visits a local women's refuge. Shoestring has some heroic qualities, but he is not a conventional action hero; he is even knocked out by a young schoolgirl in one episode (*Nine Tenths of the Law*). He is a likeable, (usually) empathetic human being and it is these 'everyman' traits – along with his quirky, maverick characteristics – which helped attract large audiences. Rewatching the series, you can see why Banks Stewart referenced Jim Rockford as being influential.

Given Trevor Eve's original reluctance to commit to a television series, it is unsurprising that he chose to step away from the role after two series. Despite the production team's frustrated sense that the show had untapped potential for further runs, the decision was made not to recast the lead. This was no doubt the correct one, given that a huge part of the quirky charm of *Shoestring* is Eve's own performance in a role he helped to create. As someone on Twitter/X commented to me: "Two and out, just right. We've done it. Let's do something else." What Robert Banks Stewart did, in effect, was to take many of the strands which had made *Shoestring* a critical and commercial success and weave them into a new show.

Eddie Shoestring was a character with an intriguing back story as a computer programmer who had a nervous breakdown and was trying to both rebuild his life and, in certain respects, reinvent himself. In creating policeman James Bergerac, Banks Stewart provided his new lead with an equally complicated past, one which is always present, haunting the detective and representing a key part of the overarching narrative: a history of alcoholism, career-threatening injuries, and a difficult relationship with both his ex-wife and father-in-law. In many respects, the 'divorced, recovering alcoholic policeman' is a cliché, yet Banks Stewart's interest in seeing the main characters and their relationships with each other evolve and develop takes us beyond cardboard cut-outs and the merely formulaic.

In casting John Nettles as Jim Bergerac, Banks Stewart was once again actively seeking out a relatively unknown actor (yet someone who he knew about) to play the lead role. While it would be ridiculous to describe *Bergerac* as a spin-off series, it is important to acknowledge the connective tissue it shares with *Shoestring* in terms of a winning formula. As the *TV Cream* website suggests, there is a sense that Banks Stewart took "the nuts and bolts" of the earlier series and used them to assemble *Bergerac*. [6] As if to emphasise the connections, seven of the writers and eight of the directors used in *Shoestring* would contribute to the new series.

Robert Banks Stewart already knew Jersey and, after revisiting the island, made the decision to use it as the new series' main setting and location for filming. Like Bristol in *Shoestring*, the unfamiliar locale would become part of the show's enduring charm. If, as Bob Baker suggested, Bristol was an important 'character' in *Shoestring* then this arguably applies far more so to the choice of Jersey.

Later in this book, I explore the importance and appeal of 'unknown' locations in Roger Marshall's Granada 1980s series: the canal network and its Industrial Revolution architectural landmarks in *Travelling Man*; the fishing port of Barfleur in *Floodtide*. *Bergerac*'s use of Jersey is another great example of a place which becomes far more than simply a picturesque backdrop. In Campbell's words, interesting settings add 'texture'. Jersey, as an island situated between England and France, where both languages are encountered, offers viewers a sense of something vaguely exotic or 'other'. George Fenton's BAFTA-winning main theme, with its accordion refrain, reinforces this. [7] There is the ironic concept of 'death in paradise'. [8] Jersey's very nature, as a small island, also provides us with a certain sense of (almost incestuous) claustrophobia in that most of the high-ranking figures – and shady characters – know each other or are connected in some way. James Bergerac's checkered past will be common knowledge to most of the influential people he comes across. Finally, as the description in the opening episode of the newly-created – fictitious – Bureau des Étrangers highlights, the island has an eclectic mix of visitors: "outsiders, offshore company people, tourists, foreign labour, conference visitors and immigrants in residence", a rich source for some of the 'nomadic' and/or mysterious guest characters who will pop up in the series.

If Robert Banks Stewart's *Bergerac* was initially seen by the BBC as a 'stop gap', it eventually ran for nine series: 87 episodes including six feature-length 'Christmas Specials'. [9] The consensus today is that BBC executives never felt entirely comfortable with the show, despite its popularity with the viewing public. The suggestion is that it was considered by the corporation's hierarchy as being too 'commercial', as in too 'ITV-ish'. I wonder whether part of this opinion was coloured by the fact that so many of the writers and directors involved were people who tended to work for the 'dark side of the dial': John Kershaw, Jeremy Burnham, Philip Broadley, Dennis Spooner, Terence Feely, Brian Clemens, Edmund Ward, Don Leaver, Gerry O'Hara, Robert Tronson...Back in the 1980s, there was still a sense of 'them and us', as my own father discovered on his rare forays from ITV to Auntie. With hindsight, there is an irony here in that *Bergerac* is, arguably, the linear ancestor of *Shetland* (2013-), a crime drama made by ITV Studios for the BBC. Times have changed, boundaries become blurred...

Robert Banks Stewart's introductory episode, *Picking It Up*, begins with the death of a colleague and friend of Bergerac's, DC Tom Draycott, 'killed in action' as he attempts to prevent a villain from taking off at the airport. His funeral takes place in a scenic cemetery overlooking the beach, an early visual nod to the 'death in paradise' concept. It is made clear to both Bergerac and the viewer that Draycott and our lead were secret sharer mavericks: "haphazard like you", often "working solo, without keeping in touch". As with Morse, there is an immediate sense that Bergerac is considered "a poor policeman and a very good detective".

Banks Stewart's initial script introduces us to many of the regular Series 1 characters: permanently suspicious Inspector Barney Crozier (Sean Arnold); frosty ex-wife Deborah (Deborah Grant); shady yet paradoxically naïve ex-father-in-law Charlie Hungerford (Terence Alexander); and police colleague Charlotte (Annette Badland), played here as a mildly flirtatious Bureau equivalent of Miss Moneypenny. Charlotte's character shares connective tissue with Radio West's receptionist Sonia (Liz Crowther). [10] Banks Stewart's plot also introduces Draycott's attractive French fiancé Francine (Cecile Paoli) as another of Bergerac's potential secret sharers, an outsider by nationality, just as Jim is by circumstance.

Picking It Up offers us a well-structured main plot – with Jim sidelined for medical reasons and acting almost as a private eye – while allowing the writer to drop in elements of Bergerac's back story and character, such as the ongoing question as to whether his significant injuries from a pre-series accident will end his police career, continuing doubts about his ability to stay away from drink, and his obsessional nature which makes forming both professional and personal relationships difficult. In a tale revolving around international arms dealers, Bergerac's ability to solve a case during "a spot of sick leave" sets us up for a series which will willingly tackle topical subjects while also centring on a 'tainted' man's ongoing attempts to prove himself as a detective, father, lover, recovering alcoholic...

Finally, the series opener introduces us to Bergerac's Triumph 1800 Roadster. Robert Banks Stewart had cut his writing teeth on 60s action-adventure series such as *Danger Man*, *The Saint* and *The Avengers* and there is surely a deferential nod to John Steed in the choice of another vintage motor car here. Many television series are almost as fondly remembered for their cars as they are for their lead characters. Restricting ourselves to the 1980s, we have Morse's Jaguar Mk11, Thomas Magnum's constantly borrowed Ferrari 308, Derek Trotter's Reliant Regal van, Arthur Daley's Jaguar XJ6...each choice tells us something about the character, and their vehicle becomes synonymous with them. Bergerac's Triumph 1800 Roadster has been gathering dust in Charlie Hungerford's garage and become the dumping receptacle for the few personal items left over from his failed marriage, such as his guitar. Despite Crozier's warning to exchange it as it is "against [police] regulations", we instinctively sense that Bergerac will keep hold of it. What does it tell us about him? That he is somewhat unorthodox, stubborn, a maverick, an independent minded character. With a hint, perhaps, that he may not always follow orders? [11]

The sense of the past impinging on the present is cleverly played out in the second episode, John Kershaw's *Nice People Die in Bed*, which tackles two more topical themes: global charities being misused for private profit; and the need for homosexuality to remain in the closet when the people involved are public figures. Beautifully directed by Martin Campbell, we see Bergerac at one point crashing down a fire escape in pursuit of a potential villain, some of the sequence artfully shot from beneath. This is cut through with flashbacks of the pre-series incident where – under the influence of alcohol – he attempted to leap on to a boat and inadvertently crushed his leg against a harbour wall. The flashback, and the x-rays the Bureau holds, remind us that, however successful Jim Bergerac is in recovering a sense of stability in both his personal and professional lives, his future will always be coloured or tainted by his past.

Bob Baker's *Unlucky Dip* continues the sense of an overarching narrative to *Bergerac*, with the detective still 'on probation' as he awaits a medical board. This third episode – exploring a cocaine trail from Algeria to Jersey – demonstrates the ambitiously wide canvas of the series in terms of location filming, with sequences filmed in St Malo, on a hydrofoil, go-carting on an expansive slice of sandy beach, St Helier's busy port, a clifftop cable car, and (most effective of all) a derelict coastal cement works, the perfect 'playground' for a stylishly shot, extended action sequence. While location managers and directors would be scratching their heads for fresh Jersey settings later in the decade, this episode highlights what the picturesque island brought to the show, cinematically speaking, including an almost Mediterranean splash of glamour.

Baker's script provides us with a clever early twist. Drug courier Raymond Dumoitier (John Rowe) is tailed from Paris by Bergerac, but when the police collar him at the St Helier ferry port he is empty-handed. We are as clueless as the police: did he pass the package on to another passenger, or has he dumped it? The eventual (ironic) reveal that he was pickpocketed on the hydrofoil crossing leaves everyone involved in the story frustrated: red-faced police chiefs; our already under-pressure detective, later accused of assault and taken off the case; Dumoitier's drug bosses, furious at the loss of £250,000 worth of coke; Dumoitier himself, under suspicion from police and villains alike, and given a brutal beating; and petty thief Simon Gibbins (Ian Bartholomew) soon discovering that he has – in Bergerac's words – "lifted something a little too hot". For everyone involved it has indeed been an 'unlucky dip'. Once again, as the plot evolves, we see how everyone connects in Jersey society, with Charlie Hungerford unwittingly friendly both with the drug boss – a fellow Yacht Club member – and the mother of the pickpocket. Baker's story satirises the veneer of respectability which high-level villains often lurk under: a luxury garage owner who services Rolls Royces for well-heeled clients like Hungerford, yet makes his serious money from drug smuggling and distribution; a well-spoken import-export businessman whose fancy house and life style – the Range Rover, children's private school fees etc – are paid for not by the perfume essence he takes to Paris for the Franciscan Brothers, but the Algerian cocaine he brings back on his return trips.

Unlucky Dip leaves us with some intriguing questions. Are middlemen such as Dumoitier any less culpable than the major players in the drug running business? Are alcoholics such as Gloria – subtly underplayed by Prunella Scales – drug addicts in much the same way as users of illegal substances? In a decade where Class A drugs, such as cocaine, were increasingly associated by the media with people in affluent society, such as City workers, company executives and their prospective clients, Bob Baker's script chooses to concentrate on the couriers, dealers and the 'barons' at the heart of the web. Baker was reflecting the fact that, in reality, these delivery men, like their users, could come from any social background or walk of life.

Alistair Bell's emotive *Campaign for Silence* weaves together a story which combines two themes: the long-term effects of PTSD and the debatable ethics of exposing war crimes. For Charlie Hungerford, retired Major Furneaux is simply a fellow Yacht Club member who is interesting company but never has the money to pay for a round of drinks. Behind closed doors, Furneaux, a former POW in Korea, lives his own private hell as he rewatches war footage. His decision to write his memoirs is stimulated both by the need for money and the desire to expose Kinthly, an officer who committed a chilling act of genocide during a scouting party. That man – who was later praised as a 'war hero' – went on to become a general and an MP. Both his former military regiment and the deceased Kinthly's psychopathic son are determined to keep the truth buried. Part of what makes this a stand-out story is the moral question of whether Furneaux is 'doing the right thing' by exposing a dead man's dark past. Equally compelling is the chilling realisation of just how far some people will go to maintain the silence. The main magical ingredient is Ian Hendry's truly outstanding guest performance as the alcoholic Furneaux.

In a world increasingly interested in keeping up appearances, it is disturbingly easy to maintain myths: that Kinthly was a war hero, that Furneaux is an unreliable drunk. Unlike medals, PTSD, as a mental illness, is invisible and, for some people, what can't be seen is simply dismissed. The casting is also spot on for lesser roles such as the charmingly cynical publisher Hedley Cross (his dialogue drily delivered by Simon Cadell) and the snobbish, patronising Colonel in his London military club (Neil Hallett) who presumes that an 'island cop' such as Bergerac will passively take commands just as his orderlies do. With Charlie Hungerford once again a friend of someone at the heart of the matter, there is almost a wink to the audience when he explains to Bergerac that there are "not many secrets on the island".

Gerry O'Hara's *See You in Moscow* is a fascinating story which takes us in to the Cold War spy thriller genre yet, ultimately, is both a tale about love and loyalty *and* a political satire. While we centre on Margaret Semple (Sara Kestelman), a leading civil servant who is in fact a Russian spy, O'Hara is equally as interested in satirising the cynical world of bureaucratic politics. On the surface, we have a simple plot in which it is a case of who will trap the fugitive Semple on Jersey, Russian agents or M16. However, Colonel Measures (Bernard Gallacher) is a two-dimensional figure of fun, resplendent in his MCC tie and continually condescending to the Jersey police in what he terms a "one horse town". Intriguingly, the presence of sleeper agents on the island – a seemingly normal couple who run a tomato farm – is tied into Jersey's WW2 occupation by Germany and the Nazis' use of people from countries such as Poland as wartime slave labour. The showdown between Semple and her Russian colleague/lover Gregori is played out in the iconic German Underground Hospital/Jersey War Tunnels, now a museum exploring the Occupation, a brilliant choice of location given the story's focus on both M16's own 'occupation' and the connections which O'Hara makes between WW2 and the Cold War. In true Le Carré mode, the writer here shows "no sense of transition from the one war to the other, because in the secret world there barely was one." [12] There are unanswered questions, such as why Semple became a spy and why the Russians want her back in Moscow, but the ensuing conflict between M16's cloak-and-dagger boss and Crozier's "island yokels" highlights the complex relationship – both fictional and real – between the self-governing island 'nation' and Whitehall.

Dennis Spooner's slow-burner *Portrait of Yesterday* tackles blackmail and bigamy in the build-up to a high society wedding. The back story of the bride's mother Sarah Mitchell (Sarah Lawson) – a stateless refugee in post-war Britain who paid a young soldier to marry her to gain a British passport – is intriguing. The twist that her elderly second husband (Derek Farr) takes the law into his own hands, trapping and accidentally killing the blackmailing first husband (Charles Kay) in a struggle, should have taken us into the morally grey areas of both vigilantes and crimes of passion. Unfortunately, the story's denouement lets the episode down. The couple's decision to dump the body on the beach, rather than call in the police, is clearly done to maintain their spotless reputation and allow their daughter's wedding to go ahead. Yet with both the dead man's car stored in their garage and the murder weapon left in their bedroom, the police are left with the simple task of piecing together what happened. Ultimately, it is hard to have much in the way of sympathy for the central character, who by her own admission chose to commit bigamy simply to marry into money. Even her wedding gift to her daughter – a portrait of herself – seems a bizarre, narcissistic one.

Philip Broadley's *Last Chance For a Loser* centres on a string of connected house break-ins at a time when, as Jim Bergerac observes, the "island's like a sardine tin": the height of the tourist season, a large-scale conference, and major yachting and golf events under way. This provides an interesting backdrop for a first-rate story which looks at the class divide on the island, one which is even reflected by the structure of the police force, as the Bureau's chief (Tony Melody) admits:

"It's our job to protect the wealthy and capture any villains who think they can come over here and prey on them. That is our speciality, so that the rest of the force can get on with the business of looking after ordinary mortals." [13]

This makes Jim Bergerac's position within the Bureau an uncomfortable one, given his confession that he hates "looking after the filthy rich". For Bergerac, both the game of golf itself and the people who belong to the island's exclusive clubs epitomise that idle rich society which he loathes.

Broadley's script creates two fascinating guest characters. Ex-professional golfer and ladies' man Eddie St Pierre – perfect casting for Patrick Mower – is all arrogant charm on the surface, yet with hidden depth. He acknowledges that, "You're talking to a marquee name reduced to the marquee", selling golf equipment in a tent at the tournament. Despite being involved in the robberies, he has certain ethics, including the insistence that there is no violence. Perhaps the fact that he is a rarity in the first series – a villain who 'gets away with it' – reflects the writer's grudging respect for his own character. [14] The shortsighted snitch Horace ('Horatio') Nelson is a wonderful character, played with aplomb by Kevin Stoney, and it is little wonder that he was used again several times in the second run. Being a script written by Philip Broadley, the tale is also seasoned with humour, including Bergerac's child-like jealousy that Francine has fallen for Eddie's roguish charm, and two of the burglars even talking in golf terminology about the robberies: "Five up and two to go". Interestingly, a frustrated Crozier (only half-jokingly) suggests that he would like to see rich homeowners becoming armed vigilantes. There is more than a hint that Jersey's millionaires have created a paradise for thieves, building mansions which are hidden away for secrecy and privacy. The robbers even use an arrogant resident's own boat as a get-a-way vehicle after burgling his property and we are almost encouraged to withhold sympathy for the victims!

If Dennis Spooner's first *Bergerac* script was something of a disappointment, he produced a super second tale in *Late For A Funeral*. It combines a WW2 backstory of Occupied Jersey with a modern-day treasure hunt, as a group of shady German businessmen and an even more dodgy local villain, Ronnie Bishop (Gary Watson), battle to find a pair of priceless Norman chalices stored in the wreckage of a Nazi plane on the ocean bed. Spooner draws on his *Avengers* background by introducing a third interested party, Henry Tuchel (James Tossins), who runs an eccentric private museum, has created a fantasy personal history as a squadron leader, and plays at being a fighter pilot in his simulator plane. The fact that his corpse ends up displayed in one of his WW2 flying machines adds a surreal, macabre touch to the proceedings.

Spooner ensures that humour peppers the plot. When police doctor Lejeune (Jonathan Adams) is given a forty-year-old skeleton to examine in the mortuary, he drily comments, "You're taking longer to get them here!" When we reach the (almost inevitable) underwater scuba diver battle at the end – nicely mirroring the opening scene – the confrontation is playfully foreshadowed by a piece of *Jaws*-like music. This episode could easily have veered into either deeply unpleasant choppy waters or foundered on the rocks of the downright silly. However, Spooner maintains a delightful balance between playfulness and dramatic suspense. *Late For A Funeral* is a perfect example of the variety on offer in the initial series, in terms of style, mood and theme.

Peter Miller's *Relative Values* takes us into Agatha Christie whodunnit territory when the suspicious death of an eccentric, but likeable, rich miser Henry Bernard (Geoffrey Bayldon) in his remote mansion seems to point the finger of suspicion at his housekeeper (Lynda La Plante), who will inherit his substantial assets. As viewers, we are the only ones who have been privileged to see the caring, close relationship they enjoyed, and her devotion to and affection for him. The conflict in the story is provided both by the arrival of his two grown-up, estranged children and the fact that, not for the first time in the series, it is only Bergerac who does not believe that it is an open-and-shut case. The twin twists that the housekeeper is in fact Bernard's illegitimate daughter and that the proud man was trusting her to "look after" his other two children add an irony to their decision to bump him off. The final reveal – that Charlie Hungerford has bought the dead man's estate as a future hotel investment project – simply adds to the overall sense of vultures swooping in a tale where only one person genuinely cared about the old man. The perfectly watchable, if unexceptional, episode adds an extra layer to the overall feel that in *Bergerac* we are in a moneyed world where most people know the (financial) price of everything but the (emotional) value of next to nothing, a Thatcherite theme in itself.

Terence Feely's budget-busting *The Hood and the Harlequin* brings the initial *Bergerac* run to a spectacular end. In terms of location shooting alone it is like a mini movie, with filming taking place in London, Paris, the Weymouth terminal, onboard a ferry, a ride on the iconic 'duck boat' – an amphibious ferry – scenic landmark Elizabeth Castle and its causeway. Admittedly, the plot itself is hard to swallow, particularly the idea that, with one of Europe's most wanted gangsters on the island, Jersey police seem to have no idea what Jacques Tabouis looks like. He is able to fool everyone, going undercover as a 'harmless' French-Canadian photographer, while a minor Parisian crook – himself undercover as a taxi driver – is mistaken for him. Perhaps you have to ignore the holes and just enjoy the ride. There are some impressive action sequences including Tabouis' motorbike ride across the causeway and Bergerac's leap onto the escaping boat. A young Greta Scacchi makes her on-screen debut as Annie Escale, Tabouis' double-crossing girlfriend, and Scacchi's magnetic presence here already demonstrates her star quality. Part of the charm of this final episode is watching Escale continually fooling the Sûreté tail in Paris and later achieving the same confusion with Bergerac and his colleagues. In many respects, Tabouis' darkly clinical dispatching of Annie's partner-in-crime is out of keeping in a story which is mostly played for its entertaining 007-'lite' action-adventure. With hindsight, even the episode title is playful, hinting that the plot will revolve around mistaken identity rather than a darker tale about gangsters. One topical question which the story does bring up is whether Jersey banks are regularly being used by international villains for money laundering.

There is a challenge facing any new television series. On the one hand, it can take time for a show to 'find its feet'; on the other, it is inevitably at its freshest in its initial run. *Bergerac* hits the proverbial ground running, partly explained by the fact that Robert Banks Stewart took a winning formula from *Shoestring* and reassembled its basic elements on Jersey. The island location was a masterstroke, ensuring that viewers experienced a weekly Sunday evening escape to somewhere that genuinely felt semi-exotic, despite the fact that it seemed to rain as often as the sun shone on the shoots. The presence of Banks Stewart as producer and John Kershaw as script editor ensured narrative continuity, while the fact that nine different script writers were employed in the ten-episode first series guaranteed great variety. That variety is mightily impressive in this initial run, both in terms of themes and style/ mood. In addition, there is a genuine consistency of quality. Even the couple of episodes which have weaker plots are still perfectly watchable more than forty years down the line. While *Bergerac* is 'of its time', it has not notably dated in terms of production values.

A further ingredient in the winning recipe was the cast, both the regulars and the guest actors. John Nettles was a fresh face for most viewers, and he plays every James Bergerac layer with subtlety: the determined, dogged, stubborn and sometimes prickly detective; the romantic lover with a suspicious streak of jealousy; the sense of melancholia which occasionally haunts him. Nettles could also handle himself in the action sequences. The support cast members were all reliable and Sean Arnold and Terence Alexander were the most significant contributors. [15] Among the guest actors there were some stand-out performances from the likes of Prunella Scales, Ian Hendry, Patrick Mower, Sara Kestelman and Greta Scacchi, if only for her cinematic screen presence.

However important the writing, acting, direction and locations are, a series such as *Bergerac* lives or dies by whether the lead character wins over the public. James Bergerac lacks the quirkiness and charm of Eddie Shoestring, but he shares his vulnerability. Part of Jim Bergerac's appeal is the sense that he is an 'everyman' on an island seemingly populated mostly by millionaires. Nor does he appear to have a chip on his shoulder about this. He seems happy enough to live in a basic, rustic apartment (ironically) on a vineyard and, in the final first series episode, when he reflects that Charlie's £65,000 yacht represents more than five years' salary for a Jersey policeman, it seems to be more an observation than anything else. Bergerac would never feel at home at exclusive golf clubs, yacht clubs... For all his faults, he has a hero's moral code and is living proof that Jersey "isn't only a sunny place for shady people". [16]

As a postscript to this chapter, it is worth observing how *Bergerac* illustrates how far the BBC had progressed in terms of production values in a relatively short period of time. Shaken out of any complacency by the success of Thames TV's Euston Films, the BBC had launched its first ever 'all-film' crime series, *Target*, in 1977. Until then, their standard approach had been to use videotape with filmed inserts. A 'glossy' BBC crime series such as *Bergerac* would have been unthinkable back in the mid-70s. As *Target* and *Shoestring*'s film editor Graham Walker has observed, this period was revolutionary for the BBC in terms of its production:

"In 1975 *The Sweeney* burst onto British TV screens. Probably the first truly modern drama series. Action-packed and shot entirely on location with lightweight 16mm film cameras, it looked and felt very different from everything that had gone before. It was a huge success. The BBC soon realised they had nothing in their schedules to counter this... I must give the BBC credit here. Instead of trying to develop their own methods of working – which they were prone to do – they listened to advice and followed the standard film industry (i.e. *not* television industry) practices which were well established for the production of multiple drama films; after all, the Americans had been doing it for years...It was fascinating to see during this period feature film industry terms such as Director's Cut, Picture Lock, Final Mix etc. creeping into the BBC's language..." [17]

© Rodney Marshall

1. *The Cult of Shoestring*, BBC 4 documentary, 2008.
2. *The Cult of Shoestring*.
3. *The Cult of Shoestring*.
4. *The Cult of Shoestring*.
5. *The Cult of Shoestring*.
6. *TV Cream*, 06/07/2009. The *Guardian* obituary of Robert Banks Stewart also connects the two series: "When Eve elected not to return for a third series, Stewart followed the same formula in creating its replacement – an eye-catching location, Fenton's music and the casting of the right actor for the part rather than a 'name'." *Guardian*, 15/01/2016.
7. George Fenton had also provided the equally distinctive, harmonica-driven earworm theme music for *Shoestring*. In terms of awards and nominations for scores, Fenton is unmatched in British TV history.
8. Comedian Peter Kay recently commented on the irony of cardboard cut-outs of John Nettles being used in 1980s travel agents to boost the Jersey tourist industry: "There's people being murdered every week [in *Bergerac*], even though it's only five miles wide. 'Come to Jersey!' That's rich!" (Steve Wright's *Peter Kay Christmas Special*, BBC Radio 2, 03/12/2023). In reality,

the TV series had a huge impact in terms of attracting tourists to Jersey.

9. It is impossible to do justice to the entire series in a single chapter and this essay solely explores the initial run of ten episodes. Amongst more conventional story lines involving robbery and murder, future plots would centre on, amongst others: the treatment of women in rape cases, protected birds, domestic abuse, escort girls/prostitution, drug addiction, paedophilia, racism, terrorism, the Mafia, black magic, war crimes, animal rights activists, Masonic Lodges, the use of steroids in sport, Apartheid...Like any long-running show, it would inevitably lose its freshness. I would suggest that Series 1-2 are the best, when Banks Stewart was at the helm of his creation. The charismatic presence of Celia Imrie in Series 2 as Bergerac's new lover adds an extra dimension. While Eve's departure from *Shoestring* left the production team and viewers with a sense of unrealised potential, *Bergerac* arguably outstayed its welcome. There is a growing sense that it had run out of creative 'steam' – and new locations – before James Bergerac became a French-based private investigator in its final run. The problem is that hindsight makes it far easier to detect or judge any series' 'peak'. At the time it would have been far harder, particularly for those inside the proverbial goldfish bowl.

10. Liz Crowther praised her casting as the Radio West receptionist, suggesting that she was "blazing a trail for plumper actresses...before that everyone seemed to be svelte..." *The Cult of Shoestring*. Annette Badland, as police receptionist Charlotte, continued this open-minded, left-field casting.

11. Just as Patrick Macnee had always found driving Steed's vintage cars 'challenging' in *The Avengers*, John Nettles discussed the dangers and pitfalls of driving the Triumph on country lanes in Jersey in BBC 4's 'Cult of *Bergerac*',

2008. "It was indeed a horror. In Jersey this thing was impossible to drive with any degree of safety because the roads are very narrow, the hedges are very high. You come to a crossroads, you've got to hang your bonnet out there in cannonball alley before you can see round the bloody corner."

12. John Le Carré, 'Fifty Years Later', David Cornwell's Afterword to *The Spy Who Came in from the Cold*, 2013 edition.

13. As Simon Cadell's character playfully hinted – "How very Kafka!" – there is something vaguely disconcerting about the Bureau's name and very nature, as if major crime on the island is only committed by outsiders, and that foreigners are automatically viewed with suspicion. In this respect, episodes such as the second series outing *Fall of a Birdman* help to redress the balance as a Portuguese worker/ornithologist is murdered by an islander (Richard Griffiths).

14. In many respects Eddie St Pierre is similar to Patrick Mower's Australian thief character in *The Sweeney*, Colin McGruder, someone certain to get under the skin of detectives but who viewers are happy to see escape the clutches of the law-enforcers.

15. Alexander's Charlie Hungerford – who would go on to appear in 85 out of the 87 episodes – captured the public's imagination. He is a character for Jim Bergerac to spark against and come into conflict with. Frequently the plots require him to be an unofficial snitch, a vital source of information. He is even, occasionally, brought into the action itself. In many respects the morally grey Hungerford is exactly the type of person Bergerac finds repellent. And yet he is capable of surprising us, of moving beyond type. As the series evolved, many regular characters would come and go, yet *Bergerac*'s various producers clearly sensed that he was a vital ingredient in the recipe. There is an element of the larger-than-life

Arthur Daley about Charlie Hungerford. It is hard, even in that initial run of ten episodes, to imagine Jim without him. It is fitting that the initial series ends with the detective rescuing Hungerford's yacht and Charlie bringing the convalescing Bergerac a bottle of non-alcoholic champagne. It feels like a thoughtful, significant act.

16. In the original quote, Somerset Maugham was talking about the French Riviera, in *Strictly Personal*, 1941.

17. *Shoestring*: An Interview with film editor Graham Walker, 23/09/2017, eustonfilms.blogspot.com (The Story of Euston Films: Celebrating the Thames TV Subsidiary – and more!)

MURDER AND MOZART:
THE UNCONVENTIONAL WORLD OF
INSPECTOR MORSE

The 1980s was a decade of great change, including fierce political battles over high unemployment and privatisation, public fears about nuclear weapons, and new health concerns ranging from AIDS to Mad Cow's Disease. Change was also happening within television, including a brand new fourth channel. 1987 saw the introduction of a completely new format for the British television series, in the form of the now widely loved and fondly remembered detective drama *Inspector Morse*.

Consisting overall of thirty-three, two-hour long episodes, the *Inspector Morse* series introduced a film-length format to the television series, one which broadcasters were initially wary of. With crime dramas never running longer than 60 minutes, the main concern was whether these slower paced, less action-packed stories would be able to hold the viewer's attention for as long as two hours. Ted Childs, the executive producer, was warned, 'You'd better get this right'. [1] With such a big budget and a two-hour time slot, *Inspector Morse* was a big risk for ITV's Central and their Zenith Productions subsidiary, but – with the benefit of hindsight – one worth taking. The first script, written by Anthony Minghella, was an adaptation of Colin Dexter's Inspector Morse novel *The Dead of Jericho*, and aired on January 6th 1987. *The Dead of Jericho* was an instant ratings success, and the series would later peak at 18 million viewers. [2] It was a rarity in garnering both large viewing numbers *and* many positive reviews from critics. This new two-hour episode format, sometimes coined the 'Morse format', has influenced other favourite detective series such as *A Touch Of Frost*, and *Midsomer Murders*, and has become a tradition for the Morse franchise, with its two spin-off series *Lewis* and *Endeavour* following suit. Ted Childs and the rest of the production team could therefore breathe a huge sigh of relief; they had definitely 'got it right'.

Part of the series' success is, of course, due to the flawless immortalisation of the character of Morse, brilliantly perfected by the late John Thaw. Having played various policemen throughout his acting career, notably the young and ambitious Sergeant Mann in the 1960s series *Redcap*, and the memorable, irascible, and ground-breaking Detective Inspector Jack Regan in the 1970s series *The Sweeney*, it could be said that Thaw was once again 'typecast' into yet another 'copper' role. Yet Thaw blows that thought out of the water with his portrayal of a gentle, vulnerable, educated and classical-music-loving DCI, a sharp contrast to his ambitious Sergeant Mann and the impatient and often violent DI Regan. In a 1987 interview with Adrian Furness for the *TV Times*, Thaw said, "I didn't say I would never play another policeman. I said I would never play another Regan. Morse is not like him in any way. He is much more laid back. He takes things coolly and calmly and uses his brain more than Regan." He then went on to say, "The only similarity between Regan and Morse is that I'm playing them, and obviously my personality has come into both. But, for Morse, I'm using a different side of my personality— the gentler, nicer side." [3]

The *Inspector Morse* series is not a single lead one, of course. Its chemistry would not be complete without Morse's faithful sidekick, Detective Sergeant Lewis. Portrayed wonderfully by Kevin Whately, Lewis acts as a foil to Morse, his working-class background and family-oriented lifestyle directly contrasting to that of the grumpy bachelor with his fixed set of assumptions and prejudices. The character of Lewis in the form of Kevin Whately is different to the Lewis originally written in Colin Dexter's novels. Whilst Dexter had written Lewis to be a 60-year-old Welshman and ex-boxer, the series transformed the character to the 35-year-old Geordie family man, acting as a better foil to the prematurely ageing and craggy Oxford detective. There were other noticeable differences from the novels, including a sanitisation of Morse himself – something I will come on to – and even a change of vehicle. Whilst Morse was meant to drive a Lancia in the books, the producers had trouble trying to source one. At Thaw's suggestion of Morse driving something "more British", the now iconic regency red MkII Jaguar was chosen.

When crime novels are adapted for television, a question is frequently asked, "Has the television series done justice to the books?" I for one would agree with the popular opinion that the television adaptations are an *improvement* on the novels. This is largely thanks to the reworking of Morse's character and John Thaw's brilliant portrayal of the Detective Chief Inspector. With the help of the series' developers, Thaw made the character of Morse memorable in his own way, changing him from the slightly sleazy bachelor with a penchant for pornography and seedy strip clubs as portrayed in the books, to the much more gentlemanly and vulnerable loner with a preference for crosswords and Chopin. [4] Whilst the *Inspector Morse* series may not be wholly faithful to the books, it can be seen as enriching them. Dexter himself thought very highly of Thaw's portrayal of Morse, and later changed Morse's car in the books to a Jaguar to fit with the TV series. [5]

Running from 1987 to 2000, *Inspector Morse* reached its peak with audience ratings reaching 18 million in the UK – as mentioned previously – during the mid-90s, and worldwide figures estimated at one billion spanning over 200 countries. It boasted impressive scripts from talented writers such as Anthony Minghella and Alma Cullen, and various episodes directed by Peter Hammond and Danny Boyle. The series was originally developed by both Minghella and Scottish producer Kenny McBain. After McBain's untimely death in 1989 at the age of just 42, the devastated production crew decided to keep his name in the end credits as a tribute to him, and to honour his contribution to a fondly remembered and ground-breaking series.

Whilst Morse as a character is arguably outdated and old fashioned, even its earliest 1980s context, the scripts were modern and often topical, focusing on then current issues. Examples include the Series Five episode *Promised Land* which references a prisoner dying from AIDS, and the Series Six episode *Cherubim and Seraphim* which deals with the rave culture of the 1990s. These explorations of contemporary issues serve to highlight the contrast between the ageing Morse and the modern world he operates in, down to his struggle with technology in *Driven to Distraction*, and his disgust at a man sporting a ponytail in *Death is Now My Neighbour*. (Rather ironically, it is the ponytail which inadvertently causes the man to be murdered). Morse resorts to classical music, crosswords and literature as a sort of 'comfort blanket', an intellectual 'opium' to help him deal with the horrors of his job, sometimes even helping him to solve a case. [6] It is these unconventional methods of case solving that make Morse unique (and sometimes irks Lewis, who objects to solving crime "like a crossword puzzle" in *Driven to Distraction*). That unconventionality can lead to him sometimes getting it wrong: arresting an innocent suspect, jumping to conclusions, and treading on the toes of his superiors, mainly Chief Superintendent Strange, played to perfection by James Grout. Indeed, it is Morse's flawed and vulnerable nature which cemented him into the hearts of millions of viewers for years to come.

No matter the role, John Thaw could make every single character he played lovable. With the *Morse* books, you were more in love with the convoluted plots and suspenseful mysteries than the main character. With the series, it was the opposite, a testament not only to the script writers but also to Thaw's innate ability to breathe life into every character thrown his way, from Sergeant John Mann (*Redcap*), through Jack Regan (*The Sweeney*), James Kavanagh, Monsignor Renard, Tom Oakley (*Goodnight Mister Tom*) and Endeavour Morse, amongst many others.

This *New Waves* book explores television drama of the 1980s. However, it is important to note that *Inspector Morse* ran for eight series during the 1980s and 1990s, with the final episode broadcast on 15 November 2000, titled *The Remorseful Day*. With far more television options in 2000, as opposed to 1987, almost 14 million viewers watched Morse finally decide to retire after a spell of bad health, but not before he solves one last case. After finally cracking it, Morse has a heart attack and collapses on the lawn of Exeter College, [7] later dying in hospital, his last words to Strange being, "Thank Lewis for me." It is an episode so brilliantly emotive that, if you are a hardcore John Thaw fan like me, it causes some internal conflict. I admire the superb script and acting, yet simply cannot rewatch it due to its heartbreaking ending.

Even though Morse passed away in 2000, and John Thaw sadly died two years later, their legacies live on. In a 2018 *Radio Times* 'Top 50 Crime Drama' poll, *Inspector Morse* was voted into first place, and in 2020 the grumpy detective came comfortably second behind Sherlock Holmes in the Radio Times' 'Britain's Favourite Detective' poll. As mentioned, *Inspector Morse* is also survived by two spin-off series, *Lewis* and more recently *Endeavour*, which saw John Thaw's daughter Abigail Thaw in the role of an investigative journalist called Dorothy Frazil (which is a clever pun on the 'Thaw' name, as 'frazil' means to de-ice). To me, that is sufficient evidence to show that, after all these years, the unconventional and cantankerous Morse is still widely and dearly remembered.

© Cailin Thomas

1. Cited by Kevin Whately in the *Radio Times* online, 03/07/2018. The running time was 100 minutes, excluding advertising breaks.
2. Editor: I vividly remember seeing *The Dead of Jericho* on that opening night in 1987. For me, it set the standard immediately. The extended running time allows Minghella the luxury of focusing so much more on the guest characters: the strange behaviour and disturbing tantrums of student Ned Murdoch (Spencer Leigh), the seedy,

suspicious stalker neighbour George Jackson (Patrick Troughton), and the sad sense – even early on – that Morse's relationship with Anne Staveley (Gemma Jones) is doomed. We already learn all we need to about the private Morse in this first story, including his child-like vulnerability and naivety when it comes to romance. For the guest actors, being cast in *Morse* must have been a dream, with no sense of having to rush towards a completed story in 50 minutes. The same applies to the writers and directors who were, in effect, shooting 'television movies'. Ironically, the quiet, narrow backstreet of terraced houses in Jericho – Combe Road in reality, 'Canal Reach' in the story – is just as memorable a location as the riverside pubs and college quadrangles will be; it adds a sense of stricture and claustrophobia; the sort of place where neighbours might easily spy on you!

3. Editor: we might add that Regan and Morse do share some characteristics: a level of cynicism, a tendency to upset the hierarchy, loners in terms of their personal lives and, while they are both great detectives, they are seen to get things wrong in cases. Arguably they both fit the label Morse is given by a former colleague: "a poor policeman and a very good detective". They also share a mistrust of the corridors of power in the police force, hence the barbed references to golf clubs (Regan) and Masonic Lodges (Morse).

4. Editor: I think that this is a perfect example of how 'sanitising' the lead character works well for a television adaptation. If TV Morse had been interested in pornography and striptease clubs, it would have been to the detriment of the character. Similarly, TV Lovejoy is no longer a man happy to physically assault women or steal from his friends. These adapted TV characters retain imperfections but become warmer and more sympathetic than the figures in the original novels.

5. Editor: the fact that the creator of Morse was happy to feed off the television adaptations in his own novels is, surely, the ultimate stamp of approval.
6. Editor: I guess that Morse's penchant for real ale is his more conventional 'opium'.
7. John Thaw had to repeatedly throw himself down onto the grass to get the shot due to the camera acting up. Editor: Cailin's reference does remind me that one of my (very few) complaints about *Morse* is the over-use of the Oxford colleges for plots. I fully understand the temptation to bring in the scenic 'dreaming spires' as often as possible, but it does arguably become a cliché.

LOCATION, LOCATION: ROGER MARSHALL'S GRANADA YEARS

By the mid-1980s my father, scriptwriter Roger Marshall, had built a reputation as someone who could create memorable scripts for a wide range of series – from the Edgar Wallace Mysteries to the increasingly outré *The Avengers* and landmark cop show *The Sweeney*. He had also demonstrated his ability to co-create new series, including *Public Eye* (with Anthony Marriott), *Zodiac* (with Jacqueline Davis) and *Mitch* (with Donald Zec). Most recently, he had made a rare venture over to the BBC to write a six-part serial called *Missing from Home* (1984), which knocked *Coronation Street* off the top of the weekly ratings, twice. The mid to late-80s would prove to be his most creative and happiest professional years. However, the seed for these was sown back in the mid-70s. It was while researching at the canal museum at Stoke Bruerne – for *Parasites* (1976), an episode of Terry Nation's *Survivors* – that Roger became interested in narrowboats and began "trying to set up a man-on-a-barge idea". [1]

"It took a long time to sell *Travelling Man*. It came here [Granada] twice, before Executive Producer Dick Everitt said 'Yes' and I think everybody at the BBC turned it down, even with John Thaw attached to it at that time, because John wanted to play the lead. But persistence won out in the end." [2]

With hindsight, Granada was the perfect ITV station to pick up Roger's treatment, as he later acknowledged. [3] The Northwest region had a vast canal network and notable industrial landmarks, all within an hour of the studios, including the Cheshire Ring and the Llangollen Canal, with plenty of spectacular locations which could be used. As had been the case with his memorable *Avengers* episode *The Hour that Never Was*, it would be a case of location visits frequently inspiring a story, rather than vice versa.

The overarching plot for *Travelling Man* (1984-85) was a relatively simple one: Alan Lomax, an ex-Drugs Squad officer, has been framed and, having served a two-year spell in prison, is released and sets out on his narrowboat (Harmony) – one of the few material things he has left – with a twinned mission: to find his grown-up son and to clear his name by unearthing the villains who set him up. There was an element of *The Fugitive* to the series, as Roger acknowledged, with the nomadic Lomax stopping to help various guest characters before, almost inevitably, being advised to 'move on'. The canal settings, with the narrowboat Harmony representing both home and transport, would dictate a slower pace to the series. This was never going to be a fast-and-furious, tyre-screeching drama full of car chases. The (clichéd) expression, 'location, location' would be key:

"The shows that I did at Granada, where I wrote all of them [*Travelling Man* and *Floodtide*]…because they were such a long stint of work, four years or something, I got to know all the Production Managers, and got to a sort of wonderful thing that you can't really achieve in television very often when I would be able to say to them, "Look, give me a location and then take me to it and show it to me, and then I'll write the script about what you've shown me," and they said, "That's fabulous", because it suddenly brings them into the forefront of the production, and it worked terribly well on both of those series. Not easy to do – I mean it was easy for John Ford to go up to Monument Valley and the rest of Hollywood will wait. Television doesn't work that way. Not often, but it did on these two occasions. The two series were both heavily full of location, but the locations came before the story, which was a lovely, luxurious way to work in that you were writing a scene for a place that you know exists and you can visualize it…a great privilege." [4]

Travelling Man was made entirely on location, an Outside Broadcast using single-camera video recording. This was a decision made by the production team, for aesthetic rather than financial reasons. Admittedly, this led to poor picture quality in some of the night-time shoots and was one of the reasons why the series lead, Leigh Lawson, chose not to stay on after the initial two mini-season thirteen episodes:

"The TV company had decided to experiment for the first time with shooting drama on video – this was 1984 don't forget…I had not been told of their intention before the start of filming. When filming started, I was very unhappy with some of the results". [5]

As Granny Buttons' blog observes, it is the technical quality, both video and sound, which is arguably the main weak point of the series, even if some critics (paradoxically) saw this method of filming as a plus. [6] On a more positive note, *Travelling Man* has several outstanding features.

First, the casting of Leigh Lawson – with Thaw no longer available – was a masterstroke from director Sebastian Graham-Jones. The two men had worked together at the National Theatre. As Lawson would acknowledge many years later, it was Graham-Jones' address book which would see so many fine actors from both The National and the RSC guest star in *Travelling Man*. The guest cast included: Terry Taplin, Colin Jeavons, Tony Doyle, Lindsay Duncan, John Bird, Tom Wilkinson, Freddie Jones, Judy Loe, Susan Fleetwood and Julian Glover. In addition, a number of up-and-coming young actors also featured: Kate Hardie, Dee Sadler, Peter Capaldi, and Alan Cumming among others.

Unlike Thaw, Lawson was not an actor well known to television viewers. His background was mostly in stage and film, including playing a memorably villainous Alec d'Urberville in Roman Polanski's *Tess* (1979). It made perfect sense to cast the thirty-eight-year-old Lawson as outsider Lomax, a man who has charm, sex-appeal, and a brooding presence, yet also character defects which make it hard to label him as a hero, an aspect I will return to later.

The canal setting – 'backdrop' would underplay its importance – was an inspired move on the part of Roger Marshall. The memorable landscapes and landmarks – such as the Anderton boat lift – which Lomax and his barge pass through are not simply attractive scenery; they often drive the narrative, as Roger observed. In much the same way that Lawson was an unknown for most viewers, the British canal system would have been something new, unexplored or 'other' for many people and Lomax's meandering journey on Harmony allows the series to gently progress, with the emphasis on characterisation rather than action, even though there is plenty of the latter too. Harmony and the network of waterways provide Lomax – and the plots – with freedom to wander. As he tells student Billie Young:

"Like being a snail, going everywhere with your home on your back …I don't like being cooped up, shut in…I like not having a telephone number. I like not having to pay rates…I like not having a postal code. I like not having a front door for people to knock on."

Yet this mobile lifestyle also makes him vulnerable to attacks from intruders on numerous occasions. In *The Collector*, arsonist Terry Naylor sets fire to the boat; in *Grasser*, professional hitman Barry Thomas tortures Lomax on his boat; in a dramatic Hitchcock-inspired sequence in *Moving On*, Lomax is attacked by a crop-duster helicopter while crossing Chirk aqueduct; and in the penultimate episode *Blow Up* the chief villain at the heart of the spider's web, Len Martin (Tony Doyle), places explosives on board with fatal consequences. In addition, several policemen invade Lomax's privacy, clambering on to Harmony to inspect the boat, while a teenage-tearaway plants drugs in the barge. [7]

A third vital ingredient is that *Travelling Man* is both a series and a serial. There is an overarching twinned plot and yet most episodes offer a self-contained story, until we reach the final two. Lawson would later reveal that he was disappointed the decision was made to bring the search for Lomax's estranged son to a premature end:

"I thought Roger Marshall's idea of Lomax searching for his son was a brilliant sub-plot and should have continued...I felt it needed that thread." [8]

Roger would later admit that this was an error of judgement on his part:

"One of the things I miscalculated badly, and should have known better, in *Travelling Man*, was the bond between Lomax and his son. A lot of people, when the series had finished, would say to me, 'Cor, I like that man looking for his son!' They never mentioned about the man on the barge, or the fact that it was lovely Cheshire scenery, or the helicopter was fabulous bombing him crossing the bridge. It was a man looking for his son. Which is a great theme. I think in retrospect, if we started again, I would build that in stronger." [9]

The final key ingredient which was central to the series' commercial success – with viewing figures of up to 13.2 million – was the powerful drugs theme, which would run on into *Floodtide*. It was a subject that he had wanted to tackle for many years:

"When I started writing television, I remember going to see a producer and saying, 'What about a story on drugs?' He said, 'Well there isn't such a thing. What are you talking about? There's no problem. This isn't America!' One couldn't entertain a drugs situation. Unfortunately, twenty years later, it's now commonplace." [10]

By the mid-1980s, the illegal drugs trade in the UK was being explored in the popular press and figures suggested that in 1984 there were at least 50,000 regular heroin users. It was clear that neither heroin addiction nor the recreational use of cocaine was a class-specific activity. Lomax is, of course, something of an expert, having been an Inspector in the Drugs Squad. In the course of the series, he encounters several middle-class characters whose desperate craving and addiction is dominating and controlling their day-to-day lives. These include former nurse Sally Page (Morag Hood), whose dependence on stolen pain-relief pills – following a ski accident – has led on to heroin. The scenes where we see her injecting into her foot pull no punches, from the frantic assembling of the kit, through the injection itself, to the zombified post-fix expression on her face. Highly intelligent student Billie Young (Dee Sadler) is caught up in a series of con tricks in order to raise the funds for her next fix. While Lomax is able to help Sally, Billie ends up taking her own life, plunging off the roof of a university tower-block, a reminder that at times *Travelling Man* delivers a hard-hitting, bleak message. As Lomax tells Sally in the opening episode:

"Once you've picked up a few dead, dirty, ruined bodies, shop doorways, derris, nice middle-class bedrooms, it gets so that you just hate the whole drugs business...your man in the little grey van, he'll suck you dry, and still come back for more."

To provide variety, and avoid a didactic approach, there are plenty of episodes which have nothing to do with drugs, such as the search for a missing child, stories which explore terrorism and snitches, Yuppie gangs, organised crime, sheep rustlers...Nevertheless, the impact which drugs can have on people's lives is never far away and many of the locations which we find ourselves in reflect the downbeat nature of the series: from post-industrial abandoned warehouses, seedy bedsits, squats, to laundrettes and back street bookmakers.

Lomax is an enigmatic, multi-layered protagonist. A drifter, a "gypsy of the inland waterways" as one character calls him. He does step in to help strangers – albeit often reluctantly – but he also demonstrates a lack of sensitivity, particularly when it comes to his sexual encounters with the likes of Chrissie (Lynne Miller), Andrea (Lindsay Duncan) and Maureen (Bobby Brown). It is made clear that he was an unfaithful husband, a 'roving Romeo'. He has the ability to charm women, but also a tendency to leave them mentally scarred. He seems oblivious to the emotional destruction which he leaves in his wake; he is shocked, for example, when Andrea explains how traumatised she has been by the arsonist 'collector'. As Maureen tells him: "You're a very attractive man. I've always fancied you rotten. And you've always used me." We could justifiably describe Lomax as a fascinating, but deeply flawed lead character.

One personal memory I have of *Travelling Man* is that my parents had just 'invested' in a VCR and Granada would send down a copy of each episode after editing, but before the music was added. Once I had watched the episodes when they were transmitted, it hit home to me what Duncan Browne's melancholic, panpipe-driven main theme added, in addition to memorable incidental scores. In a clever touch, many of the guest characters had their own personal riff or score, including Lomax's son.

Leigh Lawson chose to leave *Travelling Man* for several reasons, including his desire to return to The National to take one of the lead roles in Peter Shaffer's *Yonadab* with Alan Bates. This led Roger to rethink his initial idea of *Floodtide* as a sequel:

"That was a possibility, yes, but became an impossibility when Leigh …wanted to go back to the stage, and then it became – everybody thought – a much better idea to start with a completely new character." [11]

Canals were at the heart of *Travelling Man*, and the concept of the location-driven series would be equally pivotal in *Floodtide* (1987-88). Before a word of the first script had been written, Roger set off for Normandy with producer Steve Hawes:

"You're walking around Barfleur on the French coast, and you see the fishermen with their nets and you think, 'Oh God, this is all there, isn't it? I don't have to do anything!' It just required me to move the pieces around in the front, which was great fun." [12]

Barfleur was an inspired choice of location. Less busy and touristic than its far larger, more illustrious neighbour, Honfleur, it offers a compact, scenic beauty which can be captured by the camera in a single 360-degree sweep. All the ingredients needed for this part of protagonist Dr Ramsey's story – his 'playground' – can be found within a stone's throw: his cottage, the cobbled harbour walk, boules court, Serge's Bar de la Marée, the quayside boat moorings from where the mute Marcel takes the doctor fishing, the beach which Tessa and Dany will use for horse riding...As Roger commented, the location allowed the writer the luxury of simply 'moving the pieces around'.

There is plenty of connective tissue between the two series: the same creator, who also penned each script; the same production company and method of recording; an overriding sense that the enigmatic protagonist remains haunted by the past and has now turned his back on the world he previously inhabited; the presence of an 'insider/outsider' [13] who intriguingly becomes something of a 'secret sharer'; a similar use of attractive waterside locations, in the case of *Floodtide* the aforementioned picture-postcard fishing harbour; and the overriding theme of ruthless drug barons and the trail of destruction they bring with them. With the decision already made not to recast Lomax, the next challenge – as already stated – was to create a new lead character:

"I think it was Steve Hawes who said, 'Wouldn't it be nice if the guy wasn't a karate, ex-SAS expert, but a layman, with no special skills?' We finally settled on a doctor...at the back of my mind was the fact that he would have some medical knowledge about drugs, and that would be useful in the body of the series." [14]

Making Ramsey a 'layman' was an intriguing decision. For one thing, it means that, unlike ex-copper Lomax, he will be completely out of his comfort zone in the harsh, violent world of drug pushers and syndicates. This, arguably, has both a positive and negative impact on *Floodtide* as a piece of realistic drama. In some respects, it makes Ramsey an everyman, someone we can identify with. We share his fear whenever his safety or that of those dear to him comes under threat. As he tells DI Brook in *The Catch*: "Can I remind you, I have been beaten up, tailed, snooped on, shot at, customs gave my friend a working over. What happened to good old law and order?" His lack of 'action man' expertise can also be used for light humour, as in a rueful exchange he has with Tessa after he has been left black-and-blue following a hotel bedroom assault:

Ramsey: You should have seen the other guy.
Tessa: Really?
Ramsey: Wish I had.

As DI Brook amusingly reminds Ramsey: "In case you haven't heard, John Buchan's dead. The talented amateur, the gent in his Harris Tweeds and heavy brogues, he's out." Brook goes as far as to suggest that Ramsey has enjoyed playing the sleuth. Well, there is an element of truth in this, until the stakes are raised to the deadly serious. On the other hand, there are times when his ability to avoid the snapping jaws of death, such as in a series of car chases with hitmen in both the Peak District and Normandy countryside, or his night-time escape from a fishing trawler in Fleetwood, requires a willing suspension of disbelief on the part of the viewer. It becomes increasingly problematic, arguably, as the second mini-series progresses.

Floodtide would raise the bar in terms of budget and location shooting. [15] While *Travelling Man* had brought viewers some memorable sequences such as the aforementioned crop-duster helicopter attack on an aqueduct, the new series would require a Granada unit travelling to France to record extensive material and, as the series evolved, this French filming would not solely be Barfleur-based but would also include sequences shot in Dieppe, a cross-country road-rail chase, in Rouen and Paris – at iconic locations such as the Pompidou Centre and Sacré-Coeur Basilica at the top of Montmartre – in addition to the open countryside. Particularly effective is the use of the city streets in Rouen as a gang of henchmen casts an ever-decreasing net to catch Ramsey and Tessa in. In addition, UK rural locations included the attractive Cotswold market town of Fairford, the roofless splendour of Tintern Abbey, the Peak District National Park and the atmospheric, almost primeval Forest of Dean.

In both of Roger's 1980s Granada series, the main setting – the canal network and the harbour front – offers an ironic contrast between the picturesque, tranquil, holiday-feel location and the metaphorical darkness of the storylines. If there is an element of 'otherness' about the canals, then the French coastal village takes this a step further. As a location, it fulfils the British dream of an idyllic Gallic setting, with its colourful boats, harbour front cafés and restaurants, and pretty, shuttered stone houses with views of the sea. However, while the bilingual Dr Ramsey (Philip Sayer) is settled in France, for his visitors such as Tessa Waite (Gaby Dellal) and DI Brook (John Benfield) it is a place where linguistically and culturally they are out of their comfort zone. In Tessa's case this will be used for dramatic purposes, in Brook's for welcome moments of light relief. [16] Ramsey's reluctant return to the UK sees him equally like a 'fish out of water': he no longer recognises this mid-80s Britain of inflated property prices, wine bars, a broken-down NHS and a free enterprise culture where Class 'A' drugs are served – alongside the champagne – to prospective clients by company execs touting for business.

From the opening scenes in the first episode, *The Call*, it is clear that the canvas in *Floodtide* will be a broader one. When you have a senior Cabinet Minister and potential future PM dying while snorting cocaine in the teaser, we can already anticipate that any cover-ups – described by Exton Waite's lover Isabel (Connie Booth) as "a conspiracy of silence" – are going to be on a far grander scale than the one which framed Lomax and led to his personal mission to clear his name. In *Floodtide* we wait to see how all the seemingly disparate characters connect, from a small-time street dealer called Charlie – found glassy-eye dead by Ramsey in a bath in a squalid flat in *Observations* – to two seemingly respectable professionals, Doctor Wyn-Bennet (James Greene) and osteopath Simon Wood, both operating out of plush offices off Harley Street. The fact that we constantly flit between England and France will soon provide us as viewers with a sense of a narrative which crosses frontiers, just as the sophisticated international drug organisation will not respect borders. While the nomadic Lomax drifts from one misadventure to another, often simply by turning up in the wrong place at the wrong time, by contrast in *Floodtide* we have, in effect, a single narrative. Ramsey's decision to investigate the death of a former friend will see him increasingly caught up in a connective web of politics, policing and drug organisations, none of which he understands nor will any of the strands let him go. In one sense, the moment he agrees to support and help former lover Tessa, he becomes a ticking time-bomb.

Roger's description of Ramsey as a 'layman' is a half-truth. He may lack the streetwise skills of a Drugs Squad police officer – evidenced by his movie-inspired semi-comic unsuccessful attempts to break into a drug-dealer's flat by using his credit card – but, as the writer observed, his medical knowledge allows him to be immediately suspicious once Tessa has described the manner of her father's death. Ramsey has forensic skills which Lomax lacks, and both his proficiency as a doctor and the professional standing which that brings with it provide him with a certain gravitas which can 'open doors'. His medical connections and contacts help in his investigations, such as getting a sample of cocaine swiftly analysed and allowing him to meet twenty-two-year-old 'victim' Kate Ross (Michele Winstanley) in an NHS hospital after she has overdosed.

Ross offers us echoes of student Billie Young in *Travelling Man*, intelligent, middle-class girls from loving families who, nevertheless, have become trapped in a downward spiral of drug dependency. Kate is another lost soul, articulate, attractive, yet deeply damaged and seemingly beyond help. She is unwilling to heed Ramsey's warning about the limited time accorded to a coke addict: "From first puff to last pop – twelve years." "Bull shit!" Like Lomax with Billie, Kate's subsequent death leaves Ramsey with a deep sense of a missed opportunity, of regret, if not guilt.

Ominously, the level of violence escalates in *Floodtide*. While a tied-up Lomax's torture by a professional hitman on Harmony was suitably gritty – ratcheted up by his promise to return to finish the job off – that is mild in comparison to the scenes in the holiday cottage of drug-dealing middleman Simon Wood (Tom Chadbon). Even re-watching *The Trial* episode today, there is something genuinely shocking about the content, as Wood's male lover, Aubrey (Michael Lumsden), is both sexually mutilated and murdered – albeit off-camera – and Wood is forced to drink a poisonous, acidic cocktail. While Wood is no innocent victim – part of the lethal drug chain itself – the barbaric events which play out in the cottage are a sobering reminder, both to us and Ramsey, of the lengths to which the invisible bosses behind the 'industry' will go, both to keep their network operational and to silence anyone who attempts to step away from their position within the organisation. Or anyone who threatens to disrupt their business, as Ramsey does. Georges Trillat revels in his role as the all-seeing Lambert, offering genuine menace and a sense of mocking malevolence in these scenes. Lambert clearly enjoys his work as "a trouble-shooter". As the first mini-series comes to an end, Ramsey himself has killed a man, as self-defence turns into an out-of-control, frenzied assault with a bottle, and the body count in the series has already risen to eight. In some respects, the Ramsey we re-discover in the second run is already a broken man, suffering from recurring nightmares and hallucinations. [17]

As mentioned, both Lomax and Ramsey find themselves facing the twinned enemies of drug barons and state surveillance. Lomax is mistrusted by the police, while British Intelligence want Ramsey removed. However, a key difference between Roger's two protagonists is the way in which their personal narratives unfold throughout the course of the thirteen episodes. In *Travelling Man*, Lomax – on release from prison – has already hit rock-bottom. His wife has emigrated, his family disowned him, the marital home sold and just a meagre sum of money remains after legal fees. Lomax basically has nothing to lose as he sets off on his twinned mission. In contrast, Ramsey, a widower, has rebuilt his life: he has a profession, an attractive home, a social life in a vibrant community where he is well-respected, and a beautiful French lover and soulmate, Dany Faisan (Sybil Maas). Unlike Lomax, he has *everything* to lose. One of the things which makes *Floodtide* a 'tough watch' is to see a decent man gradually ground down: increasingly terrified as he is followed by the shadowy, feral Lambert and numerous other henchmen; barely escaping death after a night-time manhunt in Fleetwood; his ex-lover Tessa kidnapped and injected with heroin; the living nightmare culminating in the arranged overseas murder of his romantic partner, after which he is a shell of a man. While Lomax's twinned missions are, essentially, self-centred ones, Ramsey's crusade is 'for the greater good', a one-man operation to fight back against the illegal drug traffickers. This carries with it a tragic sense of doomed inevitability, for both Ramsey and those closest to him. As one police officer comments, he is like a modern-day Don Quixote tilting at windmills.

With Granada happy to give the green light to a further series, Roger took the decision to kill off the lead character in the ultimate of downbeat endings. Actor Philip Sayer was, by this point, terminally ill and my father felt it would be disrespectful to recast Ramsey. In hindsight, it is hard to see how a further series of *Floodtide* would have worked; I'm not convinced that, after everything he had gone through, Dr Ramsey had anything left to give. After all, he is not a professional private detective or law-enforcer. His death, in the final scene, seems fitting in more than one sense.

Floodtide was not meant to represent the end of the Granada adventure for Roger. The series had offered viewers a varied canvas of locations which the hard-hitting storylines play out against, from honey-coloured Cotswolds villages to the iconic Parisian cityscape. [18] However, a genuinely international third new series had already been rubber-stamped, even before *Floodtide*'s second run had been broadcast. Called *Grapevine*, it would initially be a six-part mini-series centring on an American ex-CIA agent now working for a European detective agency. Andy Robinson of *Dirty Harry* fame was cast in the lead role, having been attracted by both the character and the initial scripts he received. Speaking to Matthew Morgenstern in 1987, as the second mini-series of *Floodtide* was in production, Roger set out the location-wide scope of this forthcoming show:

"First episode is set in Italy, second episode is set in Holland and Germany, third episode is set in the UK, fourth episode is set in Paris. And so on." [19]

Indeed, director Don Leaver was already in Amsterdam, with location-hunting and casting also taking place in Rome for *Grapevine*, when the news came through that Granada had decided, at the last moment, not to make the series. It has been suggested that senior management was worried that the forthcoming Simon Dutton *Saint* reboot would be covering similar visual and thematic territory. [20] The news was devastating for both Roger and for Andy Robinson who wrote a wonderful letter to my father, explaining how much he had been looking forward to the project and how inspiring the scripts had been. In addition, my dad had a 'pipe dream' of a spin-off series for DI Brook/John Benfield:

"I think he's got the qualities, the combination, for a very successful series, an interesting character and a good actor." [21]

Sadly, neither *Grapevine* nor *Brook* saw the light of day. *Grapevine* would have completed a remarkable drugs-themed Marshall trilogy, as those Granada location-driven dramas expanded from the canals of Northwest England, through a rare Franco-English production, to a genuinely European series. This final, ambitious instalment would have (potentially) represented Roger's jewel in the crown. [22] Was this cancellation an indication that the region-based, high-budget television drama landscape was changing, shifting, shrinking even? [23]

Both *Travelling Man* and *Floodtide* are very much products of their time. Between them they reference a wide range of mid-80s social and political issues, from the new Yuppie subculture of wine bars and 'recreational' drugs, the HIV/AIDS epidemic, a failing NHS system, through to famine in Ethiopia, Médecins du Monde, and international drug smuggling. Roger recalled how much fuss there had been in the *TV Times* decades earlier about a character in *Public Eye* having a couple of 'reefers' in her drawer. "It just shows how the times have changed." [24] At the same time, those mid-80s Granada shows were created in an era before mobile phones and the internet, where a man on a barge is cut off – for better or worse – from the outside world and where, if an ex-copper or doctor wants to investigate crime or malpractice, there are no online short-cuts; he has no alternative than to use shoe leather. It would be an exaggeration to suggest that modern technology has killed drama, but it has certainly changed it.

Roger Marshall created two memorable lead characters in Lomax and Ramsey. Both Leigh Lawson and Philip Sayer were well cast in the roles. Both series benefit greatly from the guest actors attracted [25] and there is a satisfyingly organic feel to the plots, no doubt helped by having a single creator/writer throughout and the same executive producer in Richard Everitt. *Floodtide* also benefits from having just two directors, in Tom Cotter and Ric Mellis. The downbeat endings to both series are a sober reminder, as Matthew Morgenstern observes, that "the good guys can't always win". [26]

Nevertheless, for many viewers it is the locations themselves that live long in the memory. The production managers on both shows were central to the series' success, taking Roger to a succession of fabulous settings, tailor-made for dramatic storylines, from the Thomas Telford-designed Chirk aqueduct – lying parallel to an equally spectacular railway viaduct – to an abandoned naval fort on a remote Normandy rock. It was these locations which often inspired and drove the narratives, and which greatly explain the visual pleasure of returning to these mid-80s thrillers decades on.

© Rodney Marshall

1. *The Marshall Chronicles*, an interview with Matthew Morgenstern, *Primetime* Magazine, 1987.
2. *The Marshall Chronicles*.
3. "I figured because of the canals, Granada was the best bet and years later my agent sent it to a drama producer there. The script unit had already rejected it. Luck played a part and the right man, Dick Everitt, saw it..." (*Action TV*, Spring 2005, pp. 33-34).
4. *Spaces of Television*, an online interview with Dr Billy Smart, 13/09/2012. In this respect we can compare Roger's approach with that taken by Robert Banks Stewart for *Bergerac*, where he re-visited the island of Jersey and immediately realised that it was a location which was far more than simply an attractive setting; that it was a place which could drive the plots and overall narrative, adding 'texture'.

5. Cited by Granny Buttons, from Leigh Lawson's e-mail response, in his online blog, 04/06/2010.

6. Matthew Morgenstern, reflecting on the series in 2020, commented: "I think that the video images actually add something to the work, setting it firmly in the real world. It's Britain at a turning point between its industrial past and its service-industry future." Intriguingly, Matthew also suggests that, beyond the obvious themes of Lomax searching for his son and clearing his name, that this is a story about middle age: "the crime stories are really a packaging for the main drive of the series - an exploration of the themes of fall, disappointment, isolation, betrayal, self-destruction and, perhaps, redemption. On his travels, Lomax encounters numerous people in their 40s and 50s for whom life has not turned out as expected, and the series is at its best when it's addressing these themes." (*Facebook*, 17/10/2020) Matthew's theory is backed up by what Roger had to say about his one-off play starring John Thaw, *Whatever Became of Me?*: "The sort of phrase you start to think of in your forties."

7. There are practical issues, naturally, with setting much of the drama onboard a narrowboat. Looking back on what he considered to be "a special time in my life", Lawson recalled the difficult conditions for shooting on the narrowboat: "Most of my memories of filming on board Harmony are of being extremely cold and cramped. We shot a lot in winter and the windows had to be removed to obtain shots through them, as well as a camera crew inside." Cited by Granny Buttons.

8. Cited by Granny Buttons.

9. *The Marshall Chronicles*.

10. *The Marshall Chronicles*.

11. *The Marshall Chronicles*.

12. *Spaces of Television*.

13. In the case of *Travelling Man*, it is Fleet Street journalist Robinson (Terry Taplin); in *Floodtide* it is Detective

Inspector Brook (John Benfield). Both the characters themselves, and the fine performances from Taplin and Benfield, play a substantial role in the success of the two series. For one thing, given what Lomax and Ramsey are put through, each needs a secret sharer, both for sanity's sake and plot purposes. Second, Taplin and Benfield both bring a dry sense of humour and a certain degree of light relief. The growing rapport or 'cautious friendship' between Lomax/ Robinson and Ramsey/Brook helps establish a sense of natural plot and character evolution. Theirs are relationships where mutual trust must be gradually built up.

14. *The Marshall Chronicles*. 'Useful' would be underplaying the importance of Ramsey's profession, particularly in the first mini-series.

15. Despite employing the same method of shooting as *Travelling Man* – Outside Broadcast single-camera video recording – *Floodtide* does not suffer in the same way in terms of quality of sound and vision. Clearly the crew had learned, technically-speaking, from the earlier series.

16. Most of Tessa's experiences in France revolve around drama, including being kidnapped and drugged; weaned off heroin on a remote island rock; held hostage in a hotel bedroom. In contrast, Brook's French experiences often provide moments of light relief: his inability to order a beer in French or understand the currency; his romantic relationship with a female Parisian pickpocket who has taken his wallet on a bus but later shares love poetry with him.

17. The hallucinations involving a grinning Lambert are effectively nightmarish. It is a nice touch that, by the final episodes, Lambert the hunter has also become the hunted, with the cartel having decided to terminate him. *Floodtide*, arguably, could have been brought to a natural end when Ramsey discovers that his lover has been murdered in Singapore. At this point it is brutally clear that he can never

defeat the cartel. The following episodes feel somewhat drawn out, with the single goal of building towards an almost Western-style confrontation between Ramsey and Lambert, his nemesis. Once Ramsey has killed the Frenchman, he has lost his sole purpose for carrying on.

18. Despite filming in a number of attractive UK rural locations, *Floodtide* tends to offer an effective visual contrast between England and France in its use of locations. Barfleur's colourful and sunny picturesque waterfront is a world away from the greyness of the quay at Fleetwood. Ramsey's picturesque harbour cottage is in stark contrast to Brook's home on a soulless suburban estate, one which even the DI dislikes. The Paris we see in dappled sunshine seems far more attractive than the night-time images we are offered of London. As Dany says to Ramsey – somewhat teasingly – in their opening scene together, "Who in their right mind goes to England?" Ramsey himself describes England as somewhere which has "become a selfish place". Indeed, both the television series and its novelisations seem to be offering us a damning portrait of England in the mid-80s, a country where if you scratched beneath the moneyed veneer of those people who were profiting from Thatcher's entrepreneurial Britain, a very different, bleaker picture emerged. As a sidenote, one of the major challenges when casting *Floodtide* was finding bilingual actors who were equally comfortable delivering dialogue in both English and French. The lack of subtitles left some UK viewers dissatisfied, hence the tendency to mostly use English in the France-based scenes in mini-series 2.

19. *The Marshall Chronicles*. "Dick Everitt found a story in a French magazine and used it as the basis for an outline which he showed to his boss and it was commissioned." Roger Marshall, cited in *Action TV*, Spring 2005.

20. In Marshall's words, "Granada got cold feet and the project was cancelled". The article 'Private Thoughts, Public Eye' goes on to suggest: "Rumour has it that Granada heard that

LWT had their feature-length series of *The Saint* with Simon Dutton in the lead already in production and thinking that it was aimed at the same audience as *Grapevine* decided that they did not want to compete and threw the towel in." *Action TV*, Spring 2005.

21. *The Marshall Chronicles*. John Benfield would go on to star as DCS Michael Kernan opposite Helen Mirren in Granada's *Prime Suspect* (1991-95).

22. Granada had commissioned the highly ambitious *Jewel in the Crown*, first broadcast in 1984, with lavish location filming in India captured on 16mm. The Manchester-based company was making some exciting overseas drama at this point.

23. Certainly, the signs were ominous, as soon afterwards Granada "sacked every drama producer over fifty." Cited in *Action TV* magazine, Spring 2005.

24. *The Marshall Chronicles*.

25. As had been the case in *Travelling Man*, the guest cast list in *Floodtide* was impressive. In addition to the French actors employed, the list included the aforementioned John Benfield, Connie Booth, and Tom Chadbon; also: Linda Marlowe, John Fraser, Gina McKee, and Alfred Lynch who is pitch perfect as the seedy hotel porter, PF.

26. Matthew Morgenstern, private *Twitter* message received on 24/12/2023.

WITH THESE GLOVES YOU CAN PASS THROUGH MIRRORS: *STRANGERS*, *BULMAN* AND *THE PARADISE CLUB*

Once you get past Dennis Potter and Andrew Davies, whose seminal drama TV scripts during the 1970s and 1980s demonstrated what the genre was capable of as art, over and above what it could do as simple mass entertainment, you reach a tranche of scriptwriters whose work ranged across numerous popular drama series and who were rarely, if ever, named in newspaper TV reviews but who were always identifiable by the quality and individualism of their writing. Names in this tranche – recognisable to any serious student of television – include, in no particular order, Brian Clemens, N.J. Crisp, Roger Marshall, Troy Kennedy Martin, Chris Boucher, James Mitchell, Jack Gerson, Terry Nation, Jimmy McGovern and Wilfred Greatorex. However, in the same way that performer Matt Munro was described as "the singer's singer", a few lesser-recognised screenwriters have a justifiable claim on the title of 'the TV writer's writer'. One of these is Murray Smith. Never achieving the visibility or fanbase of those others, his quirky scripts ranged between gritty realism and equally gritty *sur*realism, elevating the simple UK 'cop show' into something approaching poetry in a similar way to that which Stephen Bochco accomplished in the USA.

Born in 1940, Murray Smith joined the British Army and was a Paratrooper and a Special Forces officer, before leaving Army life and using his professional knowledge to write scripts for television. At least, this is what can be gleaned from the meagre details that have emerged about the life of this apparently very secretive man. He proved himself quickly, writing for *Confession* (Granada TV, 1970), *The Sweeney* (Euston Films, 1975) and *The Mackinnons* (BBC Scotland, 1977). His work on *The Sweeney* and for Granada TV led to him being recruited to write for Granada's new crime series *The*

XYY Man (1976-77). Starring Stephen Yardley as cat-burglar 'Spider' Scott and Don Henderson as his nemesis, Detective Sergeant George Bulman, the first short series of three episodes, produced by Richard Everitt, adapted author Kenneth Royce's novel of the same name, while the second series of ten episodes (of which Smith contributed three) were original stories running in parallel with but ignoring four more Royce novels.

Bizarrely and unexpectedly, the character of DS Bulman was considered popular enough that he was transferred, along with his sidekick DC Willis (Dennis Blanch), into a bespoke Granada vehicle: *Strangers* (also with Richard Everitt as Producer). The title referred to their role as London coppers transferred to the North of England where their faces were not known. As Bulman explains to a colleague: "I was sent here to be a stranger in town, a face they didn't recognise." It's hard to think of any other popular series of the time where a lesser character took on an enhanced new life like that (although a few other examples will be mentioned later). *Strangers* ran for five increasingly weird seasons between 1978 and 1982 with Murray Smith writing twenty of the thirty-two episodes. He characterised Bulman as not exactly an anti-hero but as a collection of quirks (prone to violence and breaking the rules, regularly quoting Shakespeare, classic poets and philosophers, always pulling on woollen gloves when on business, obsessively using a nasal inhaler but only in his right nostril, studying for an Open University degree and carrying his possessions around in a Key Market plastic bag) and then allowed Henderson to link these quirks together into an irascible but bizarrely lovable whole.

Following *Strangers*, George Bulman was allowed to retire from the police force and set himself up as a clock mender and private detective in the Granada series *Bulman:* two seasons between 1985 and 1987, also and perhaps inevitably Executive Produced by Richard Everitt. Murray Smith wrote sixteen of the thirty-three episodes. In parallel, Kenneth Royce wrote several more *XYY Man* novels in which the character of 'Spider' Scott increasingly ceded prominence to George Bulman and the descriptions and background details gradually approached those of the TV series without ever actually colliding with them.

At first glance, the BBC drama *The Paradise Club* (twenty episodes running for two seasons between 1989 and 1991) might seem to be quite distinct from the intertwined series *The XYY Man*, *Strangers* and *Bulman*, with only primary writer Murray Smith (writing sixteen of the twenty episodes but also now Executive Producer) and lead actor Don Henderson (this time playing priest and former French Foreign Legionnaire Frank Kane – yes, I said Murray Smith was creatively 'odd') linking them. They do, however, take place in the same universe, as we will see later.

Given that we are looking in this book at the way the cultural and social background of the 1980s influenced series drama, this chapter will restrict itself to only those seasons actually in production during that decade – seasons 4 and 5 of *Strangers*, both seasons of *Bulman* and both seasons of *The Paradise Club*.

Shared Universe

The first cultural thing to leap out from these Murray Smith-heavy series has already been briefly mentioned – the shared universe aspect. Previously this was a rare occurrence in television in the UK, although the Granada series *The Odd Man* (1960 to 1963) spawned *It's Cold Outside* (1964 to 1965), which then itself spawned *Mr Rose* (1967 to 1978) while BBC crime drama *Z-Cars* (1962 to 1978) gave rise to *Softly, Softly* (1965 to 1969) which itself spawned *Softly, Softly Task Force* (1970 to 1976) and then *Barlow at Large/Barlow* (1971 to 1975). Similarly, ITC's *Department S* (1969 to 1970) gave rise to *Jason King* (1971 to 1972). Notably, however, each of these subsequent shows shared very little with their predecessors except the main character(s), who were always moving on and never looking back. In the USA, however, and in the UK a year or so later, the 1980s saw the birth of *Star Trek: The Next Generation*, which took place very distinctly in the same universe as the original 1960s *Star Trek* and used much of its established 'history', as well as several of its characters, and then led on to an entire interdependent universe of TV series and movies which shows no signs of stopping. Similarly, the hugely popular 1970s US dramatic soap opera *Dallas* gave rise to *Knots Landing,* which premiered in the USA on December 27th 1979 but in the UK firmly in 1980. As with the *Star Trek* universe, many characters crossed over between the two series over time. This would be a paradigm for the future of TV in the UK as well, starting in the 1980s and largely in *Strangers, Bulman* and *The Paradise Club*. The 1980s was the time when TV executives discovered that the viewing public had a voracious appetite for seeing the same characters move on from place to place and from situation to situation.

While the characters of Bulman and Willis moved from *The XYY Man* to *Strangers* with no callbacks, when George Bulman resurfaced in *Bulman* he was visited not only by old sidekick Derek Willis (two episodes) but also former boss Jack Lambie (three episodes, played by Mark McManus at the same time as he was playing the nearly identical lead character in *Taggart*, from 1985 until his death in 1994), MI5 maven Bill Dugdale (six episodes, played by the loveable and yet terrifying Thorley Walters), Bulman's saxophone teacher Sonny Boy Saltz (three episodes, played by real-life saxophonist Lol Coxhill) and Bulman's Russian equivalent, Inspector Pushkin (one episode, played by George Pravda). *Bulman* also contained numerous conversational references back to events and minor characters in *Strangers*.

When Murray Smith and Don Henderson crossed from Granada to the BBC for *The Paradise Club* they took with them Dugdale's shifty assistant Willie Bruce (recast from William Gaminara to Martin Clunes) and references to a near-legendary but never seen *Strangers* criminal event known as 'the Ice Cream Wars'. Had *The Paradise Club* continued to a third season or more, it is tempting to wonder what other crossovers could have occurred. George Bulman turning up, perhaps, still played by Don Henderson?

Politics and Sociology

It is easy now, looking back, to see that the 1980s was a key pivot point in TV, leading to the various future TV and movie universes of *Star Trek*, *Star Wars*, Marvel, DC, *The Game of Thrones* and *The Lord of the Rings*. But, more importantly, in the wider world broader movements were changing the country and reframing society.

Margaret Thatcher was elected Prime Minister of the United Kingdom in 1979 and remained in power until 1990. Thatcherism – an ill-defined set of beliefs and principles including an increased freeing of 'the marketplace' (however one defines that), reduction in Government spending and the rise of radical nationalism – came to symbolise, if not define, the politics of the 1980s. The later seasons of *Strangers* reflected the uncertain feeling of the times, not only with their use of decaying industrial landscapes, empty warehouses and urban wastelands as their many outside locations but also in an increasing focus on wealthy entrepreneurial criminals rather than the cosy cat-burglars and bent cops we formerly saw. As a police character says in the Glasgow-set *Strangers* episode *A Dear Green Place*, "The City is evolving into sophistication. We never had any organised crime up here, not really. It was all 'OK Corral' stuff. Not anymore, though. Now the hard men go round with teams of accountants and lawyers." The point applies to any major UK city, and later, in *Bulman*, the lawyers and accountants and, importantly, the businessmen who they work for often turn out to be the real villains.

Let us not forget, of course, that the public perception of the police itself was in the process of changing. The trustworthy and fundamentally decent PC Dixon, in the BBC's *Dixon of Dock Green* (1955 to 1976) had already been supplanted by the rough diamonds of ITV's *The Sweeney* (1975 to 1978), and George Bulman and his team continued the process. Fundamentally as decent as Dixon, but with a wealth of philosophical underpinning for that decency that Dixon never had, Bulman was known as a bully who could cheerfully break the temporal laws of the land in order to uphold a more spiritual law. "You coppers was always more vicious than us," one of his criminal informers complains as Bulman shoves him against a wall.

Bulman, despite being quirkier than *Strangers*, also continued probing at the rotting underbelly of British society. The season one episode *One of Our Pigeons is Missing* (an espionage story in which the humorous title only becomes clear as the punchline of a dark joke in the last few seconds) is set in and around the cracked concrete wharves and abandoned warehouses of the Manchester Docks and tells a gritty but strangely sad story about the lives of homeless people as seen through the eyes of an undercover Bulman. The characters and their sad stories are well drawn by Smith. Time moves on, of course, and that location is now MediaCity UK, home to the BBC and ITV. The irony can almost be tasted.

It may be an oversimplification, but an argument can be made that this kind of story could not have been told in the 1960s (Simon Templar living with vagrants!) and wouldn't have been told in the 1970s (Brett Sinclair or Jack Regan consorting with dossers!), but the 1980s was the decade which saw a move towards recognising that people on the edge of society are real people rather than borderline-caricatures and have stories: stories which need to be told. [1]

The economic path of the UK over the decade of the 1980s can be traced through the way that *Strangers*, *Bulman* and *The Paradise Club* use the iconic setting of the London docklands. In *Strangers* it is an urban wasteland that symbolises the decline and fall of the Port of London, at one time the world's busiest. After the docks closed the area become, by the early 1980s, derelict and poverty-ridden. In *Bulman* the area is beginning to be bought up and redeveloped, and in season 2 Bulman and Lucy McGinty move into the upper floor of a converted warehouse, as so many people and businesses did during that decade. In *The Paradise Club* lead character Danny Kane (the wealthy criminal brother of Don

Henderson's Frank Kane) is living with his wife and family in a new-build home in the area, part of the ongoing gentrification of the London Docklands, but close to where he and Frank used to play as kids. His neighbours have moved there from affluent Kensington. "Of course, you are, one suspects, an *old* Rotherhithe family," one of them says, rather cattily. "We, on the other hand, have migrated here – from South Ken." "Don't worry sweetheart," Danny's wife responds, "Nobody would guess."

Bulman in particular, sitting as it did in the middle of the 1980s, also reflected the general public's increasing distrust of both the upper classes and the organs of state (between which there was, and still is, of course, a notable overlap). The season 1 episode *Born Into the Purple* portrays the scions of high society as being a bunch of overtly superior party-going idiots out of touch with the 'real' world, while the season two episode *Chicken of the Baskervilles* (yes, seriously) draws attention to the fact that a large number of upper-class families have been hollowed out by death duties to the point where they cannot afford to heat or clean their country houses and so resort to selling off their paintings and antiques, but haven't got the skills to earn a proper living. This is in contrast to Granada's own elegant *Brideshead Revisited* (Granada, 1981), of course, but picks up from points made in the BBC's comedy *To the Manor Born* (1979 to 1981). As to the organs of state, the character of Bill Dugdale – a senior MI5 officer – is introduced in *Strangers* as being affable and bumbling, but in *Bulman* is increasingly revealed to be devious and treacherous. He obviously likes and respects Bulman but is quite happy to have him sent to prison in order to investigate a string of robberies being organised and manned by convicts (*A Man of Conviction*) and then have his sentence extended as he is proving useful 'inside'. Later, in season two, he knows that a Mossad hit squad intend murdering Bulman and Lucy but lets the plot run on as it furthers his own plans. It is only when Bulman calls him out on it that he decides to intervene. "People who don't exist have no need of warrants," he tells Bulman when the latter discovers that Dugdale has bugged his flat. In other words, as far as the State is concerned, the ends always justify the means.

On the wider international stage, the defining political and cultural landmarks of the decade were arguably the linked Russian movements of *perestroika* ('restructuring') and *glasnost* ('transparency'), in which the monolithic and repressive political/economic regime of the Soviet Union was opened up to Western eyes and influence in a process running between 1985 and 1991. *Strangers* anticipated this in the first episode of season 4 (*The Moscow Subway Murders*) in which Bulman's Russian equivalent travels to the UK in order to solve a baffling series of murders in which people are stabbed through the neck while on the Underground. Russians in British television before that had tended to be stereotypical spies, secret agents or diplomats, but Ivan Ivanovitch Pushkin (played by the wonderful George Pravda) is quirky, genial and a perfect foil for Bulman. While Bulman peppers his speech with quotes from Shakespeare, classic poetry and notable philosophers, Pushkin has learned his English from the novels of P.G. Wodehouse. It makes for some very quirky dialogue between the two. When they first meet, the suspicious Bulman gives his name as Ronald Reagan (who had just been elected President of the USA), but soon they are drinking together in a London pub ("Tracy – a large vodka, a gold watch and a pint of Nigerian lager please!") and Pushkin assists Bulman in the arrest of the murderer on a London Tube train while disguised as a woman – more on this later. Pushkin later turns up in season one of *Bulman*, in the episode *Sins of Omission*, now working for the KGB. In the season two episode *Thin Ice* we discover that Pushkin is dead, bludgeoned with an iron bar by a Moscow rioter, but his son (Jack Shepherd), a GRU officer, contacts Bulman hoping to defect from the Soviet Union to England but wary of a potential double-agent in Dugdale's organisation.

That episode, by the way, contains one of a number of moments in all three series – *Strangers, Bulman* and *The Paradise Club* – that sit firmly on the border between quirky and surreal. Pushkin's son is a saxophone player (for no very good reason), and a key moment in the episode has three saxophonists – him, side by side on stage in a pub with Bulman and Sonny Boy Saltz – all playing free jazz as part of a ploy to evade Dugdale's assistant (and possible traitor) Willy Bruce. Again, more on this later.

Minority Representation

A major shift in society and the shared consciousness of the UK during the 1980s is in the way black and Asian people were treated and portrayed on television. At the beginning of the 1980s TV comedies with black Indian/African/Caribbean characters such as *Love Thy Neighbour* (ITV, 1972 to 1976), *Rising* Damp (1974 to 1978), Mind *Your* Language (ITV 1977-1979) and *It 'Ain't Half Hot Mum* (BBC, 1974 to 1981) were fresh in the public's mind. Discussion still rages about whether these series portrayed their black characters in a stereotypical and racist way for humorous purposes or whether it was the white English characters' reactions to them that were racist, but undoubtedly those characters existed in the shows *because* they were black. That was their sole purpose.

In wider society, 1981 saw race riots in London, Liverpool, Birmingham and Leeds, while 1985 saw them happen again in London and Birmingham, but by the end of the decade attitudes in society had shifted somewhat, and representation on TV reflected that. From the mid-1980s onwards it became increasingly common for black actors to appear in roles in which their colour was irrelevant. *Strangers* walked a tricky line in its last two seasons. A major character in the second episode of season 5 (Edwin Luthor "Loco" Parmini, played by Trevor Thomas) was black and a definite villain, and yet the character was written and played as being complex, with motivation and a moral compass – although another character referred to him insensitively as "a sooty" (a racist epithet of the time). Other unfortunate racial slurs in season 4 of *Strangers* include "wogs" and "Pakis", although it could be argued that this merely reflected realistically the kinds of things that particular working-class characters would say rather than reflecting the attitudes of the programme-makers themselves.

There is a notable trend in the later seasons of *Strangers* of having minor characters ('walk-ons' in the parlance) be of Indian, African or Caribbean origin, reflecting society as a whole. One in a number of examples is in episode 2 of season 4, *The Loneliness of the Long Distance Copper*, in which Jack Lambie is stalked by the aforementioned escaped convict "Loco" Parmini who wants to kill him. At the climax of the episode, when Lambie seems set to be murdered, Parmini is clobbered from behind with a sack of rice wielded by an Indian shopkeeper. It could have been a white newsagent or grocer, and in other drama series it probably would have been, but the point is that here it wasn't.

Later, in season 5, Bulman's team expanded to include the West Indian DC Charlie Baker (Troy Foster), and during the brief remainder of the season he and WDC Vanessa Bennett (Fiona Millison) have a nicely underplayed interracial love affair, tragically curtailed when he is gunned down in the episode *Charlie's Brother's Birthday*. Or is this a subtler form of racism, similar to the 'bury your gays' trope identified in Hollywood movies? Would it have had more, or less, impact if it had been Vanessa Bennett who had been killed?

Bulman continued the trend of casting black actors in background parts, including a notable pair of West Indian hitmen in the season two opener *Chinese Whispers*. Later, *The Paradise Club* introduced, as one of its main cast, the black actor Leon Herbert as the oddly-named Polish Joe (more on Murray Smith's strange names later). Despite this up-front casting, the series has come in for some criticism – both at the time and more recently – for its supposed stereotypical portrayal of ethnic minorities. Times change, but they do not change overnight, and it was arguably the 1980s which acted as the crucible for this change.

Nudity on TV

The 1980s saw a sea change in the way women were treated in society, and thus also in the way they were portrayed on television. Feminism became an increasing force on university campuses, and the UK had its first female Prime Minister. In the decade before that, television dramas transmitted after the 9pm 'watershed' were liberally sprinkled with shots of topless women, usually for no plot-related reason. As Mark Lawson noted in *The Guardian* in 2013, "...from the 70s, post-9pm dramas on BBC1 and ITV specialised in the quick-flash tactic, in which a woman might show her breasts while rolling on top of a lover, or swinging out of bed, or offer a rear nude view while walking into the shower. The police series *The Sweeney* (ITV, 1975-78) was a specialist in this trick, so that, as John Thaw or Dennis Waterman answered the door, an undressed girlfriend might wander past on the way to bedroom or bathroom."

The first female full-frontal nudity on British television occurred in 1973, in Granada's drama series *Shabby Tiger*, but it took another ten years for equality to make its mark and for the first full-frontal male nudity to occur (the BBC's *Z For Zachariah*). There it was someone young and attractive (Anthony Andrews), but two years after that, in the *Bulman* episode *White Lies* Bulman carries on a conversation in a steam bath with a man in a three-piece suit while being himself fully-frontally naked. Don Henderson was many things, but he was no male model.

Anchoring in Reality

One of the defining characteristics of adventure series such as *The Avengers*, *The Champions*, *The Saint*, *The Persuaders!*, *Strange Report* and others of that ilk is that they take place in a kind of ethereal time and space, rarely referencing the politics and events that existed when they were being made. Arguably this made them more marketable overseas (especially the lucrative US market) and also meant that – while the cars, fashions and technology featured in them have aged – they maintain a certain (illusion of) timelessness. *Strangers*, like many other crime and thriller series of the 1970s and early 1980s, continued this ambiguous placing in time and space, whereas *Bulman* was deliberately much more anchored in the time in which it was made and set. Murray Smith, in particular, slipped in numerous references to events and personalities that the audience of the time would recognise but which might puzzle viewers ten or twenty (or, in the case of this chapter, forty) years later. In various episodes we get mentions of the Yorkshire Ripper (Peter Sutcliffe, convicted of murdering 13 women and attempting to murder seven others between 1975 and 1980), the Special Patrol Group (a controversial and secretive Metropolitan Police unit that was disbanded in 1987), the Brink's-Mat robbery (when £26m worth of gold and diamonds were stolen from a warehouse at Heathrow in 1983) and Umaru Dikko, a Nigerian politician discovered drugged in a crate marked as diplomatic baggage at Stansted airport in 1984, the apparent victim of a Nigerian government-sanctioned kidnap attempt. At a more minor level, references to celebrities such as Sylvester Stallone and John Belushi (died 1982) and movies including *Rocky* (1976), *Rambo* (1982) and *E.T.* (also 1982) serve to place the series very distinctly in time.

Smith, more so than any other writer on the shows, also anchored his characters and stories very firmly in London through a line in colourful vernacular and what purports to be Cockney Rhyming Slang. "A cock and hen" is a prison stretch of ten years and "the shovel and pick" is the Nick, or local police station. A "gold watch" is a glass of whisky while Bulman also refers to a pint of Guinness as "Nigerian lager" in what is an arguably off-handedly racist reference just because it is black and alcoholic (it is also referred to in one episode of *Bulman* as "Mother O'Grady's Morning Tea", which may itself be offhandedly racist). As for, "I'm goin' down the steps for a cockle!", well, who knows? "Going down the steps" means being convicted at the Old Bailey and being sent to the cells, but "a cockle"? That might just have been invented.

The use of popular music can also set a series in a particular historical and cultural context. *Strangers* and, to a much greater extent, *Bulman*, used music to punctuate and accentuate the drama in what was, for the time, a radical way. These days, of course, the use of a popular song even in a series like *Doctor Who* (BBC, 1963 to present) or in dramatic moments of US shows such as *Person of Interest* (2011 to 2016) and *The Blacklist* (2013 to 2023) is unremarkable, but in *Strangers* and *Bulman* we unexpectedly get at, various times, snatches of Steve Harley and Cockney Rebel performing *Come Up and See Me (Make Me Smile)*, the Flying Pickets with an *a capella* version of Talking Heads' *Psycho Killer*, Adam and the Ants with *Stand and Deliver* (mirroring the clothes and make-up worn by an eccentric hit-man in the episode), Orchestral Manoeuvres in the Dark performing *Locomotion*, Thin Lizzy with *Get Out of Here*, Wham's *(I Don't Want Your) Freedom* and Joe Jackson singing, *You Can't Get What You Want (Till You Know What You Want)*. Often the track used has some kind of relation to what is happening in the episode – none more so than the inclusion of *Psycho Killer* in the *Bulman* season one episode *Sins of Omission* to foreshadow Bulman's protégé Lucy McGinty (Siobhan Redmond) being tortured and nearly murdered by a psychopathic Soviet KGB officer. The bleakness of this episode, counterpointed by the whimsy of episodes like *The Chicken of the Baskervilles* is one of the hallmarks of this eccentric and yet brilliant series. [2]

The inclusion of the Joe Jackson track gives rise to a particularly quirky bit of dialogue that has no connection to the episode but points up how different the series is from anything else on TV at the time. In the season 1 *Bulman* episode *Pandora's Many Boxes*, Bulman is up a ladder painting over the old sign on his new antiques shop while listening to the radio. It is playing Joe Cocker singing a cover version of the lesser-known Beatles song *She Came In Through the Bathroom Window*. "I didn't know you were a fan of the Beatles, George," his protégé, Lucy McGinty says, emerging from the shop with a mug of tea. "It's Joe Cocker," Bulman corrects her. Pointless, but it enhances the episode in a strange, characteristic and almost indefinable way. A grace note.

Bulman's own musical preferences tend towards free jazz, as exemplified by his choice of instrument and teacher. He can frequently be seen (and heard) playing his saxophone in various episodes. On one occasion he and a drunken friend regale a pub with their own version of Don McLean's *American Pie*. On another, he tries to interrupt the rehearsals of a Russian jazz-rock group in order to find his friend Pushkin, but is ignored. Spotting an upright piano he gets their attention, and grudging respect, by joining in with his own jazz riff. The series also frequently breaks the action so that Siobhan Redmond can, for some plot-related reason, perform an old jazz number in a fine singing voice.

The oddest musical moment in the three TV series has to be in the final double-episode of *Strangers* (*Charlie's Brother's Birthday* and *With These Gloves I Can Pass Through Mirrors*), where Bulman is shot by a hit man and, while lying on the ground, is serenaded with the theme tune of *The Sweeney* by his saxophone teacher Sonny Boy Saltz (free-jazz exponent Lol Coxhill). It is a touching and surreal meta moment that almost, but not quite, breaks the fourth wall.

Following in the wake of *Bulman*, the eponymous location of *The Paradise Club* is a music venue inherited by reform*ing* gangster Frank Kane (Leslie Grantham) and his brother, priest Danny Kane (Don Henderson). With that backdrop it would be strange if music *wasn't* a key component of the show, and indeed many of the episodes featured contemporary, up-and-coming bands playing their songs live on stage. Bruce Dickinson of Iron Maiden also notably makes an appearance in the episode *Rock and Roll Roulette*. The use of live original music would come back to haunt the BBC, however. The series has only once been repeated (on UK Gold) and has never been released on video or DVD, largely because of the problems in tracking down the rights for some of the songs.

Quirkiness and Surrealism

Buried in the previous paragraphs are several bits of evidence pointing to Murray Smith's idiosyncratic writing style. He writes in extremes, moving from humorous escapades to gritty, brutal violence, from pastoral English landscapes to broken industrial cityscapes and from straight-down-the-line crime drama to surrealism (via quirkiness on the way).

Smith's choice of character names is one example of his left-field attitude towards dramatic conventions. Bulman, Willis, Lambie, Dugdale: yes, all well and good. But then we come across small-time crook Henry Vincent Van Gogh Hodges in *Strangers* – a name that is bestowed for no other reason than the sheer fun of it. The previously mentioned Inspector Pushkin (*Strangers* and *Bulman*) bears the same surname as the Russian writer Alexander Pushkin, a point noted by the characters in the episode. We also, amongst many others, have Police Commander Macheath (almost certainly a reference to Bertold Brecht and Kurth Weill's *The Threepenny Opera*) and hitman Sartine (presumably referencing 18th Century French statesman Antoine de Sartine). The names serve no purpose other than they make a change from Smith or Jones and add a bit of colour to proceedings.

The backgrounds (or sometimes foregrounds) of the shots in *Strangers* and *Bulman* are worth watching, just for the odd things that turn up. This is, of course, much more likely to be down to the various directors and the producer Richard Everett, but it links in with Murray Smith's quirky approach. In one episode of *Bulman* a blind man is reading a braille book in a pub while Bulman is talking to a contact. In another pub in a different episode, Bulman talks about making a phone call to a police informant's line using the code phrase "Fly's Eye", and two ladies sitting near him think he's got a horse racing tip and immediately rush to place their own bets. In yet another episode, a barber's shop where Bulman is meeting Bill Dugdale has a parrot on a perch by the door, while in yet another episode an old country house has an owl on a similar perch.

In street scenes we might see a group of Hare Krishna devotees in orange robes chanting as they go by, a man passes by carrying a euphonium, and the main character in the shot walks past a string quartet seated and playing classical music. None of this really means anything, but in television terms it takes longer to set up and costs more, and thus would be cut if it was not considered important. Its importance is in establishing a style, a look, a feel that is different from anything else at the time.

Eccentricity, or perhaps actual surrealism, became a 'thing' on television in the 1990s with, for instance, *Twin Peaks* (1990 to 1991) and *Northern Exposure* (1990 to 1995) in the USA, but also shown in the UK. The 1960s had its fair share of unreality on TV of course, what with *The Corridor People* (Granada again, 1966) and several episodes of *The Avengers* (ITV, 1961 to 1969), but those shows reflected the fashion and art of the time. The TV surrealism in the 1990s was a different thing entirely, a reaction against the hard-nosed reality of the TV of the 1980s. *Strangers, Bulman* and, to a lesser extent, *The Paradise Club* can be seen as precursors of this trend. The sight of the portly, middle-aged Ivan Ivanovitch Pushkin in drag on a Tube train in the *Strangers* episode *The Moscow Subway* Murders – for no reason that is ever properly explained – is one of many examples of how Smith could imbue an otherwise standard cop-show scene with a tinge of the eccentric and the bizarre. Elsewhere, in the episode *A Dear, Green Place* a key conversation takes place fittingly on the edge of the 'Bridge to Nowhere', an unfinished flyover that was meant to be part of the M8 motorway but was left, literally, hanging.

Other notable examples in later episodes of *Strangers* include Bulman smuggling himself into a siege situation in a block of flats in a coffin in the season 4 episode *A Dear Green Place* – something mirrored in the season 5 episode *Charlie's Brother's Birthday* when Bulman and Co. investigate a smuggling ring involving stolen coffins. The next episode – the final one of *Strangers* – is titled *With These Gloves You Can Pass Through Mirrors*: a three-way coded reference not only to Bulman's sartorial choices but also to this being the final episode and to the 1950 Jean Cocteau movie *Orphée*. That episode, by the way, contains what has to be one of the greatest lines of British TV, when an IRA hitman turns up over-armed for confrontation, only for Jack Lambie to laconically mutter: "Oh you naughty bastard...Chummy's got a rocket launcher!" That sort of thing never happened in *Juliet Bravo*.

In *Bulman*, and later in *The Paradise Club*, the bizarre aspects become almost comedic. The *Bulman* episode *The Name of the Game* has Bulman confronting a small-time conman while, behind him, an armed robbery is taking place without him realising. [3] In *Another Part of the Jungle* a cashmere-coated hitman with a sawn-off shotgun stalks through a Yorkshire village as if in a darkly surreal episode of *Last of the Summer Wine*. The second episode of *The Paradise Club - Family Favours -* has Danny Kane orchestrating a robbery in which one of his men literally swoops down, suspended from a crane and dressed in a superhero outfit, and snatches thousands of pounds from the hands of a security guard; a feat later referred to as "The Great Crane Robbery". That is the big set-piece in the episode, but a more minor and yet equally eccentric moment occurs when we see two cleaning ladies with dusters tied to their feet polishing the floor of The Paradise Club while dancing to the music of the band playing on stage. Perhaps *more* eccentric, as it serves no purpose other than to entertain. A few episodes later, in *Crack in the Mirror*, Polish Joe helps Danny Kane escape a tricky situation by deploying boots with explosive charges in the heels. "I hear your boots exploded", Frank says to him later. "Yeah, they do that sometimes", Polish Joe replies laconically.

So, there we have it – Murray Smith's trilogy of linked crime dramas, spread across two channels and thirteen years. Very much of its time in some respects, and ahead of its time in others. There is so much still to say about these series, and yet I will carry forever three snatches of dialogue that, for me, summarise them. One is Jack Lambie's "Chummy's got a rocket launcher" line, as already mentioned. Another is when Bulman accidentally wanders into the wrong Open University viva, expecting it to be Medieval Literature.

After bluffing for a few minutes with flowery French poetry, he is interrupted by one of the examiners saying, "You have a strangely personal view of geomorphology, Mr Bulman." The third is a very simple one. In the first episode of season two of *Bulman,* he and Lucy McGinty have returned from an extended sojourn in China, where they have been avoiding the murderous intentions of a crime boss. Lucy comes back early, and when Bulman returns six months later, he finds she has opened a dance class in Chinatown. "What the hell are you doing teaching Chinese to tango?" he asks. Lucy stares at him with the kind of innocent but slightly aggrieved face that only Siobhan Redmond can manage. "Well," she says, "someone's got to do it."

© Andrew Lane

1. Editor: in this respect US crime drama was far more advanced in tackling topical social subjects such as homelessness. *Goodbye, My Lady Love* (1959), for example, pulls no punches when tackling the community of derelicts in NYC's Bowery district, in *Naked City*. While *The Guardians* (1971) and *1990* (1977-78) both explore homelessness, these two dramas were dystopias set in the near future.
2. Editor: in the US, *Miami Vice* (1984-90) set a benchmark with its use of contemporary pop music.
3. Editor: a playful, deferential wink, perhaps, to the monkey scene outside a Parisian bank in *The Return of the Pink Panther* (1975)?

AND THEN THERE WAS *LOVEJOY*

Take a country in the middle of a time of excess, where short-term greed has overtaken long-term thought, add a series of novels about a rather unpleasant antique dealer, a pinch of genius in the shape of a decent adaptor and top off with an actor who hasn't perhaps quite fulfilled his early promise, but is still in gainful employment in the US and the UK. Simmer gently, then bring to the boil, and what have you got? *Lovejoy*.

Lovejoy wasn't the first antique dealer to feature as the lead in a TV series, nor was he the last. ITC's *The Baron* (1967) starred Steve Forrest as an occasional undercover agent whose day job was owning a top-end antique shop. The antiques never got in the way of the action much, and although it is profiling, it is hard to imagine the beefy Texan Forrest having much interest in antiques and fine art. Coming more up to date, *The Madame Blanc Mysteries* (Channel 5, 2021 – ongoing) centres around a female British antique dealer who lives in France. We shall return to Madame Blanc briefly later.

Lovejoy was the brainchild of a doctor, John Grant, writing under the pen name Jonathan Gash. The novels were a series of short, fast-paced adventures of a roguish and, at times, disagreeable antique dealer and his cronies, crossing the hinterlands of East Anglia, involving themselves in a series of scrapes and brushes with the law. The novels are barely readable now: Lovejoy is amoral, he treats friends poorly (and hits women) and often the books descend into sub-Hammond Innes territory with outlandish and unlikely climaxes. What made the books good, however, was the love of antiques, and the authenticity of the setting. When the stories came to TV, the last two aspects were what made the series stand out from the herd. [1]

Ian McShane was an actor who had had a promising start in the 1960s but had wandered ever since. By 1986, when *Lovejoy* began, he had been doing well enough, with supporting parts in international films and TV series, but stardom had proved elusive. That was all about to change, when someone suggested that if he was interested in a series, he could do worse than have a look at Jonathan Gash's *Lovejoy* books. McShane agreed, and enter Ian La Frenais, half of a top script-writing duo (the other half was Dick Clement) who were responsible for many great TV series (*The Likely Lads*, *Porridge*, *Auf Wiedersehen, Pet*) and were now doing very nicely, thank you, as screenwriters and script doctors in Hollywood. La Frenais was awarded a 'created by' credit and wrote the series 'bible'. In a very real sense, *Lovejoy* was his baby. (Dick Clement turned up as a writer occasionally as the series progressed).

The regular cast was filled out by Dudley Sutton, who played Lovejoy's associate, Tinker, a scruffy and occasionally disgusting figure in the books, sanitised for television at Sutton's request. Sutton, not conventionally handsome, had nonetheless enjoyed a good and eclectic career, and was a favourite of maverick director Ken Russell. Tinker was a lynchpin of the books, but the other three regular characters were not. Work experience Eric (Chris Jury) was basically added so that Lovejoy or Tinker could explain antique things to him, and thus the audience. Lady Jane Felsham (Phyllis Logan) was a will-they-or-won't-they love interest, with Lord Felsham (Pavel Douglas) lurking in the background and, occasionally the foreground. Finally, Malcolm Tierney, a respected stage actor, played Charlie Gimbert. Gimbert was Lovejoy's landlord and owned a successful auction house. He was also Lovejoy's arch-enemy, which sat uneasily with the milieu, and ultimately became unsustainable.

The series was shot on location in Essex and Suffolk, in and around picture-postcard market towns and villages with timber-framed chocolate box thatched cottages, [2] where the books were set, with occasional forays into the wider world, particularly when the series was revived in the 1990s. It was always summer. A lot of care went into the series, with lovely locations, classy guest artistes and supporting actors, top of the range writers and directors and, most importantly, a genuine love of the antiques which formed the centrepiece of all the plots. Compare and contrast with *The Baron*: "I've sold that bust" was more or less your lot. Care was also taken to introduce a handful of semi-regulars to give the series some grounding in a reality – fellow antique dealers, a café owner, a garage owner whose life's work seems to be bringing Lovejoy's car back from the brink of destruction.

Since adventure series like *The Baron* had ruled the airwaves nearly twenty years before, life had got tougher and faster, and by the mid-80s, it seemed to get harsher, as well. "Greed is good", remember? *Lovejoy* was an oasis of calm in a hectic 1986 world. Riding on McShane's charm (which was considerable) and exploiting the aforementioned assets, *Lovejoy* seemed to be a rock-solid antidote to the darker times falling upon us, a precursor to other 'cosy' series, like *Heartbeat* and *Where the Heart Is*. So why did it stall after one series, and not return for another five years? With all that it had going for it? What could possibly go wrong?

The series starts off with some introductions. Lovejoy and Tinker already exist, and so does Charlie Gimbert, but during the course of the first episode, *The Firefly Cage*, we meet first Eric Catchpole. Eric's dad has done a deal with Lovejoy. In return for cold, hard cash, Lovejoy takes on Eric as a kind of work experience boy. Catchpole Senior has despaired of Eric ever finding a job for himself, so he is prepared to set him on a path which will open his eyes to the world of antiques, acquiring a useful trade. Lovejoy, of course, ignores Eric initially, but soon finds himself in need of his motor bike and sidecar to pursue a buyer of an antique he (Lovejoy) was interested in. And could the woman that Lovejoy and Eric splash with muddy water as they drive through a village by any chance be Lady Jane Felsham? It could. 'Meeting cute', up to a point. The motorbike-and-sidecar is, of course, a comedy staple (Arthur and Olive in *On the Buses*, *George and Mildred*, the Battys in *Last of the Summer Wine*), without ever being particularly amusing. Fortunately, its use in

Lovejoy is limited. We are treated to a succession of 'character cars' over the course of the series, but that seems to be a staple to this day. Even poor old Alan Bates, about as distinguished an actor to grace the small screen in a comedy-drama as you could get, had to drive a character car in *Oliver's Travels* (1995). Perhaps showrunners think such things are amusing, but to the viewer they can be a tiresome gimmick. One yearns for the quirky detective-by-chance to turn up in a Mondeo, just once. Anyway, as early as the first episode we are introduced to two staples of the series. One, a bit of serious knowledge about antiques, accompanied by curiosity to find out more. This never bores. It is achieved so naturally by writers who have done their research that it becomes an organic part of the story. You come away having learnt something, even if you did not intend to. In this case, it is miniature sculptures made out of coal. Who ever knew there even was such a thing? The other staple is loyalty. When Lovejoy's friend Drummer is murdered, Lovejoy isn't happy, not happy at all, and this drives the second part of the story. Drummer is played by Ronnie Fraser, like McShane someone whose career waxed in the 1960s. Never a handsome leading man, Fraser was nonetheless in demand for decades. Also featuring are Sarah Lawson and Kim Thompson as this week's femme fatale. Because we are just getting to know the leads, the guest stars don't perhaps get as much of a look-in as usual: we're also introduced to Gimbert's assistant (Denys Graham) and niece (Cassie Stewart), and local mechanic Brian (Anthony Jackson, from *Bless this House* and *Rentaghost*), all of whom we will see again. Throw in Lady Jane and Lord Felsham and that is quite a cast of characters to meet in an hour, but it is all done professionally. The introduction of some endearing and interesting characters, an efficient plot and some excellent locations and photography, and *Lovejoy* hit the ground running. Tune in next week? Oh, yes.

The second episode, alas, was a bit weaker. *The Axeman Cometh* is...er...all about a bloke who comes after Lovejoy with an axe. Whether the title came first or the idea, I don't know, but they are not much of a hook. Of far more interest are the relationships.

Lovejoy pulls a fast one and acquires a dresser that Gimbert had his eye on. Cue much teeth-clenching and shouting of "Lovejoy!" by Gimbert, already getting a bit tiresome and we are only on episode two. We meet an acquaintance of Lovejoy called Frobel, played here by stage actor and writer Oliver Cotton. (The character would reappear, much later on, played by one-time matinee idol James Booth), and another two semi-regulars, Dandy Jack, an antiques dealer and friend (Geoffrey Bateman) and café owner Woody (Mark Monero). Woody never develops into much of a part, but he and Dandy Jack add to the community building up around Lovejoy, making 'Lovejoy World' all that more believable.

Another face eases her way into the series in episode three. Antiques dealer Helen, played by Jo Ross. She has her own shop, and like Dandy Jack is markedly more successful than Lovejoy. Lovejoy, despite his expertise (and apparent innate talent to divine a genuine antique – a 'divvy') is always broke, often with the tax man on his back. (That is the other part of the joke in the previous episode – Lovejoy doesn't just have an axeman after him, he has the taxman after him as well. And the taxman isn't a man either, she's a woman.) Tall Paul Antrim makes his first appearance as a not-too-unfriendly copper. Episode three is called *The Sting*, and it does what is said on the tin. Unfortunately, the victim of the sting is Gimbert, so what happens? Yep, teeth-clenching and shouting "Lovejoy!" But although the second and third episodes are treading water a bit, the series is getting into its stride – the milieu is settling down, the rapport between Lovejoy, Lady Jane and Tinker is established, and we're getting to know something about antiques, as Lovejoy and Tinker explain to Eric what's what.

Episode four brings us another story based on one of the original novels – the first episode was based on *Firefly Gadroon – Gold by Gemini*. Re-titled *Friends, Romans and Enemies* (supposedly more accessible) it is also the first episode since the opening one to end in violence. And just as in that first one, it sits uneasily in Lovejoy World. What was part and parcel of the books does not comfortably translate into the cosy world of comfort TV. We also get a trip to the

Isle of Man, in the company of two unexciting villains, and, despite our growing fondness for Lovejoy's usual haunts, the brief change of locale is welcome. Perhaps it put more of a strain on the budget than usual, because the guest cast is a bit lacking in star power, although cult favourite Sheila Keith puts in an appearance.

We stick with the books for episode five, and turn to the first novel, *The Judas Pair*. The antique argy-bargy is all about a pair of flintlocks (called throughout, for reasons that escape me, 'flinters') and is intriguing, although the episode title is a massive spoiler. Mark Kingston, a venerable stage actor (the first person to play the professor in the original production of *Educating Rita*) adds value, but the real joy to be had from the episode is the presence of Anthony Valentine. Although his 1970s heyday (*Callan*, *Colditz*, *Raffles* etc) is a bit in the rear-view mirror, he still dominates every scene he is in, slipping so expertly between easy charm and menace. He raises the episode, and not a second too soon, as the series needed something of a jolt. [3]

We are halfway-through, and it is worth reflecting on the quality of the series. Sure, it has not always been perfect (and remember, we are hauling over the coals forty years after the event, when it is very easy to pick fault and cavil at things of which the casual weekly viewer would not even have been aware) but it has held up, largely due to the focus on relationships, the quality of work done by the writers in getting up to speed on antiques, and the conviction of the actors in putting it across. When McShane and Sutton start bantering about 17th century treasures or whatever, they are talented enough to get it across that this is actually stuff they know – suddenly it is not a script anymore, it is two experts wandering the highways of history together. Earlier, mention was made of the current series, *The Madame Blanc Mysteries*. Everything that the producers, writers and cast got so perfectly right in *Lovejoy*, is completely ruined in *Madame Blanc*. Sally Lindsay, who created and wrote the series, must take a lot of the blame. Playing Madame Blanc, she gets the rest. Madame Blanc is, supposedly an English antique dealer who now lives in France and is called in by the local law whenever someone is murdered, which appears to be roughly once a week. Putting aside the unlikeliness of the basic premise, and the 'child of five could solve it' nature of the murders, the worst thing about the show is when Madame Blanc solves a crime because of her intimate knowledge of antiques. Her character's eyes glaze over, and she then recites it in a drone so flat, you keep expecting her to say, "Your call is important to us". How far we have fallen since *Lovejoy*. What do producers and script editors actually do now? Sally Lindsay, by the way, is also credited as an 'Executive Producer'.

Anyway, to return to the matter at hand, to a series made with love, care and attention to detail, and episode six of *Lovejoy*, *To Sleep No More*. The main plot is not what is important in this episode, although it cracks along, with a Russian doll quality to it. Lovejoy is in the pub with the aforementioned Dandy Jack and Helen, when he gets into an argument with unsavoury dealer Arnold (played by TV's go-to bully John Forgeham). The police arrive, and Lovejoy shifts the blame onto Gimbert, with Helen, Dandy Jack et al supporting him. This is important because it strengthens Lovejoy World – it is filling up with real people, who may not have much to do with the plot but expand the size of the bubble Lovejoy and co are bouncing about in. Malcolm Tierney, of course, gets full mileage out of that term 'teeth-clenching acting' here directed at Rose Bruford.

So, the series is picking up nicely, despite a few rocky moments. Episode seven takes us away from our comfort zone again, but this time only as far as Norwich, where smoothie Tony Palmer (Ray Lonnen) is setting up in business with Lady Jane. He is, of course, 'No Better Than He Should Be'. Lovejoy produces a dodgy spiral staircase (obviously they'd got fed up with antiques you could fit in your pocket by this point) and everybody gets terribly upset. More upsetting, however, is a couple of con artists (played by Jenny Runacre and *It Ain't Half Hot, Mum*'s lovable old Donald Hewlett) who make the cardinal error of pulling a fast one on a shopkeeper friend of Lovejoy. Again with the loyalty – Lovejoy and his team go to considerable efforts to avenge the shopkeeper, who is really no more than a nodding acquaintance. If there is one message to be had from *Lovejoy*, it is 'you stand by your friends'. When the series returns after its long hiatus, this rule is (very) occasionally broken, and no good ever comes of it. [4]

Episode eight is a little more reflective, and none the worse for it. Lovejoy gets hold of some Napoleonic letters, and traces the rightful owner, but they are not original. Those are in an army barracks. This gives rise to an interesting plot and counterplot, but the real interest is how Lovejoy gets caught up in the romance behind the letters – the value to him is not pounds, shillings and pence, but the story attached. Incidentally, far from 'looking after his mates' Lovejoy stitches Eric up over his road tax, but this, we presume, is not a serious business, merely having a laugh.

And now we come to the big one. It is a two-parter, and it is set in foreign climes (spoiler in title). It is *Death and Venice*. Dudley Sutton and Chris Jury probably saw the title and started looking for their passports. Unlucky. Of the regulars, only McShane makes the trip, but he is joined by Haydn Gwynne (from the time when she was better known on stage than TV), Alexander Knox and the wonderful Fulton Mackay. The plot involves a dying millionaire (Knox) who decides to save the artworks of Venice from the ravages of nature by replacing them with forgeries. Does it sound like the sort of thing a dying millionaire would come up with as he sputters his last? Still, nobody ever tuned into *Lovejoy* because they fancied a dose of gritty realism.

For some reason (probably not unrelated to the weather) the Venice on display here does not show up as well as East Anglia does in less ambitious episodes, which is a shame. The plot is over-stretched, but understandably so. If you are going to fly a crew out to Venice, you are going to want two episodes out of it. We should be grateful they settled at two. Mackay shines of course, but to return to a theme, when Lovejoy gets home, he goes to the pub, and all his friends are there – Tinker, Eric, Lady Jane, Dandy Jack, Helen and...Charlie Gimbert. Yes, they are all sitting together like old mates, all the slights, deceits, cons, threats, imprecations and teeth-clenching are forgotten. In Lovejoy World, nobody bears a grudge for very long.

And that was it. Over. No second series. Why? The first series was good, and popular (our *post facto* nit-picking is all very well, but at the time, the series was a refreshing change from what had come before). What went wrong? Well, apparently it was money. The BBC simply did not offer WitzEnd Productions enough to make it worth their while. [5] Obviously over the next few years things were resolved, but by the time the series returned changes were made. Lovejoy, Eric, Tinker and Lady Jane remained, but the rest of the supporting cast were never mentioned again. Even Gimbert did not make the cut, but this was probably just as well. All that shouting "Lovejoy!" through clenched teeth had got very tired, and Gimbert was set up as a cardboard character: his only role in life was to be Lovejoy's nemesis. He had no back-story, and none was even suggested until much later in the series' fourth run after he had come back and gone again. Malcolm Tierney deserved, one felt, a bit better.

But by the end of the first series, we sensed that we had got to know the characters well and liked them. Lovejoy, we felt, was a (reasonably) honest man in a dishonest world, although not averse to making a fast buck if he felt like it. He knew antiques and could spot a fake a mile off. He loved the freewheeling life and he loved his friends. Tinker was loyal to the bone, and he and Eric often provided comic relief. One might query the need for comic relief in a show that was, essentially, frivolous, but let us not forget that the original books had a darker tone, and the television series needed to ensure the light shone out of it. Eric was a bit of a fool, but he meant well, and sometimes he learnt well. Lovejoy, Tinker and the world of antiques gave him something to live for, and he stopped being the idle waster he once was. Lady Jane was a beacon of sanity. Calm, intelligent and forgiving (sometimes very forgiving) she provided a necessary link to the real world, if being married to a lord and living in a country manor house is the real world. If Lovejoy mooned after her, she ignored it, which was just as well, because few things bring a show to a grinding halt quite so quickly as unrequited love requited. We will never know what happened to all the other characters in Lovejoy World, which is a shame, because their characters were starting to be fleshed out when the series ended. Gimbert, we know, comes back, but he brings back the same problems, so his renaissance did not last.

As for the cast, during the series' hiatus Ian McShane carried on much as before, with international films, guest appearances in *Minder*, *Miami Vice*, *Perry Mason*, *Columbo*, and a run in *Dallas*, as well as a spell in the musical version of John Updike's *The Witches of Eastwick*. Post-*Lovejoy* he consolidated his stardom with the US series *Deadwood* amongst others, and the film *Sexy Beast*. His latest work includes the popular *John Wick* series of films. Phyllis Logan pursued a long and successful career, including every episode of *Downton Abbey*, as the housekeeper. Chris Jury wanted to become a director – it was why he eventually left the series – so he did. Dudley Sutton continued being Dudley Sutton – a one-off, often seen walking the streets of Fulham and Chelsea, occasionally in a beret. He died in 2018 at the age of 85 and was still to be seen in episodic TV up until that time. Malcolm Tierney died in 2014 at the age of 75, and was, fittingly, buried in Highgate Cemetery, close to the grave of Karl Marx. As a lifelong socialist, he would have appreciated that.

All of them conspired with top writers, producers, directors, guest actors and crew to transport us to Lovejoy World, where it was always summer, where the pub was always open, and where there was always an antique bargain to be had, as long as you got there first. We learned of snuffboxes and flintlocks, of divvies (Lovejoy) and barkers (Tinker), of love and loyalty, and, most of all, that if you live in a community and look after your friends, and they look after you, nobody stays angry much past opening time.

© Ian Payn

1. Editor: having re-read a couple of the novels recently, I agree that it is the detailed, passionate descriptions of the antiques and their remarkable craftsmanship histories which mark out the books as interesting and this aspect is used brilliantly in the television series. The flat but attractive and unspoilt East Anglia countryside also offers us a visual feast.
2. Editor: Bury St Edmunds and Lavenham feature heavily.
3. Editor: Anthony Valentine raising the standard as a guest star in 1980s TV is something of a common theme. He is wonderful across a range of series during the decade, including *Hammer House of Horror*, *Bergerac* and *Minder*.
4. Editor: Ian's observation here is another reminder of how *Lovejoy* the series provided us with a far warmer lead character than the original novels.
5. 'Contractual problems' – which is a euphemism for money – has often been cited as the reason, and *Lovejoy* would have been a rarity in those days as a BBC show made by an independent production company. According to Chris Jury: "We were hopeful of a second series in '87 – which would have been filmed in '86 – but the BBC made Executive Producer Alan McKeown an offer he couldn't accept and all power to him he walked away. The deal's the thing you see... In Spring 1989 Michael Grade left the BBC to go to Channel 4 and within three weeks WitzEnd, Alan's company, contacted my agent and we were back on...I always felt many of the metropolitan TV industry types [BBC executives] were slightly embarrassed by *Lovejoy*. It wasn't cynical, urban, edgy or cool enough for them. Like *Heartbeat* and *Last of the Summer Wine*, it was innocent, rural, funny and nostalgic – and of course immensely popular with the public!" 12/09/2011, *Adventures in Primetime*.

AND SOON THE DARKNESS...
HAMMER HOUSE OF HORROR

In the 1980s, the wind of change was to sweep across British independent television in many ways, not least with the latest round of franchise reviews for licensees, which brought forth a handful of new and reshuffled companies. Amongst those affected was Lew Grade's Associated Television (ATV). Despite having run a successful renewal bid in a restructured form, Grade was ultimately obliged to step away from the company after a boardroom coup in 1982. [1] Even prior to this, the television landscape had begun to change...

ITC – Grade's production arm under the auspices of ATV's holding company ACC – had become globally known across the 1960s and early-70s for producing polished, if light, action-adventure series such as *Danger Man*, *The Saint*, and *The Persuaders!* However, by the mid-1970s new, more dynamic and realistic formats (such as Euston Films' *The Sweeney*) had emerged and viewing tastes were changing. ITC's clean-cut action hero formula had one last hurrah with *Return of the Saint* in 1977, [2] but the company's prolific output – and export – of fantastical entertainment was, it seemed, reaching the end of the road. Then, out of nowhere came a very different format, offered by a company that had already experienced the death throes that were to come for ATV, but which had clawed its way out of the grave. [3] In 1979, Michael Carreras had finally lost control of his family business, Hammer Film Productions. Two former Hammer production executives then structured a buy-out deal with the company's creditors to trade under the Hammer banner in administration. These two long-time industry stalwarts (Roy Skeggs and Brian Lawrence) knew exactly to whose door they should run in the hopes of making a deal: Lew Grade's. A deal was thrashed out over lunch with ITC's top table (Grade, Jack Gill and Charles Denton) and an option was picked up for two cinema features, which would be upgrades of popular sitcoms (*Rising Damp* and *George & Mildred*). The TV spin-off market had been a lucrative sector for the original incarnation of Hammer and ITC no doubt took their risk in light of having a ready-made audience. However, the biggest part of the pitch had come in the proposal of a television anthology series in the traditional Hammer mould.

Hammer was renowned worldwide for their revolutionising of the horror genre in the 1950s, picking up the old black-and-white Universal monsters and adding a vivid splash of colour – mostly gore. Again, ITC was presented with what would most likely be a ready-made audience, based on the 'cult' following around the Hammer product, which was already well established with a track record of almost (then) a quarter of a century. Grade's company delivered a quoted figure of £2 million; it is not clear whether that figure was just for the anthology series, or the whole film and TV package. Television was not unused to the anthology thriller/horror/suspense series. Hammer itself had co-produced *Journey to the Unknown* (1968-69), and Anglia Television's *Tales of the Unexpected* (1979-88) was enjoying what would be a very long and successful run. ABC/Thames TV had covered several of the Hammer staples (such as Dracula and Frankenstein's monster) in their *Mystery and Imagination* (1966-70) series, and the BBC had produced their renowned annual adaptations *A Ghost Story for Christmas* (1971-78), as well as their own anthology collection *Supernatural* (1977). [4]

The ground was already well trodden, so much so that Michael Carreras' own attempts to lift his failing company by offering a similar product in both 1973 and 1976 had been unsuccessful. Like the original Hammer did with their cinematic monsters, Skeggs and Lawrence would emerge with a product that would break the televisual mode of horror entertainment, in a surprisingly strong small screen series. The emphasis would be heavily placed upon the fact that this was a Hammer production, set up to meet the expectations of an audience that the producers fully understood. It would be a significant divergence from the output for which ITC had been known up to that time. Running ahead of the establishment changes that would be imposed by the subsequent and notorious Video Recordings Act of 1984, *Hammer House of Horror* (as the series would be titled) was designed to make the darkest corners of its viewers' living rooms seem even darker.

Traditional tales of witches, lycanthropes and satanic cults were all to be given an update for the new decade, alongside several more psychological, murderous or just pure evil encounters. *Hammer House of Horror* acknowledged how the television audience had matured since witnessing the aforementioned supernatural offerings and looked to make it grow up even more. Whilst the Hammer stamp would be both strong and vital on the new series, the 'hands on' television producer was David Reid. Reid was a writer, director and executive producer for ATV, producing and executive producing series such as *The Power Game* (1965-69), *The Strauss Family* (1972) and *Clayhanger* (1976); he would be ATV/ITC's hand on the tiller. He had previously directed several episodes of the second series of *Catweazle* (1970-71) for London Weekend Television, and he went on to be the executive producer of ATV's *Sapphire & Steel* (1979-82). Similarly, there would be crossovers between ITC and Hammer in terms of production crews, with familiar names such as ITC make-up man Eddie Knight (*The Prisoner*) cropping up alongside creatives such as Hammer's renowned composer James Bernard. The 'New' Hammer brought a lot of experience together from both big and small screen to ensure that their 35mm scary tales would be as polished as they could be.

In fact, it is surprising how polished the finished films were, particularly given their rapid turnaround time. Cinema Arts/ Hammer took a lease upon Hampden House in Buckinghamshire (an allegedly haunted former school), as Roy Skeggs wanted to recreate the small studio atmosphere from Hammer's original era at Bray Studios, which by all accounts he succeeded in doing. At a time when unions were still quite strong, everybody seems to have chipped in behind the scenes, in true Hammer 'in house' style. This was very different to ITC's usual way of working, wherein staff at their Cumberland House H.Q. would have been responsible for arranging and booking studio time, often at third party studios such as ABPC Borehamwood. Skeggs deployed two units, working in tandem, "...which allowed us to shoot all 13 episodes in 14 weeks", he was to say in a subsequent publicity interview for the series. That does sound tight. Clearly the relaxed days of ITC production at Elstree or Pinewood were gone, but when you consider that the thirteen shows were almost all literally 'in house' at Hampden, the logistics would have been that much easier.

Shooting started on 9th June 1980 with *The Thirteenth Reunion* breaking ground for the phoenix-like company. Given Skeggs' assertion that the entire series was shot in 14 weeks, this would approximate shooting to end around the 12th September, just 24 hours before the series would go to air for the first time. Although *Thirteenth Reunion* was first before the cameras, the tale that opened the series' run was *Witching Time*, a story of a possessive witch, resurrected in modern times on the site at which she had been burned at the stake. In the early 70s, when Hammer Film Productions had to some extent begun to feel threatened as a new wave of horror emerged in cinemas, of which *The Exorcist* (1973) was the vanguard, the company reviewed its production approach. The outcome was that it took a decision to travel in a 'permissive' direction and began to include much more nudity in their films. This position was similarly reflected in the new television series.

Hammer House of Horror would go out in a primetime adult timeslot, 9:15pm on Saturday night, at the traditional September height of the new television autumn season. This post-watershed billing would allow for the tales to include similarly bared flesh, as was seen from Patricia Quinn as the titular witch, Lucinda Jessop. Whilst not wholly unprecedented – London Weekend's 1976 adaptation of *A Bouquet of Barbed Wire* was seen to be similarly 'racy' in its Friday night primetime 9pm slot – it is notable for the fact that Lew Grade's usual stance was for 'family entertainment'. When he entered the world of film production, he was ever reluctant to risk an X certificate for any of his films. Whilst *Hammer House of Horror* has many fantastical elements, it is not, unlike ITC's action hero output, truly suitable for family viewing, although I suspect that it being Saturday night, the watershed often went by the wayside, particularly given how many fans of my generation can recall the impact that the original screenings had! In his book *A History of Horrors*, author Denis Meikle says that during shooting the company was instructed to tone down the nudity, but uplift the gore, in line with concerns and requirements from the US networks. (ITC were, as ever, keen to secure international sales). As the series progresses you can see a fairly quick phasing out of the more overtly sexual elements.

Hammer stalwart Peter Cushing likened the film company's output to a ride on a scary rollercoaster, in that there would be thrills enough, but at the end of the ride your boyfriend would always be there with a comforting arm around you; good would always prevail. For this new series, however, in contemporary interviews Skeggs said that the fun thing about *Hammer House of Horror* was that, "It was like making the old Hammer Horror movies, except we had the joy of letting the baddies win!" They did win too, most of the time!

The next transmitted tale was *The Thirteenth Reunion*, which introduced those of us who probably should not have been watching to the deliciously gruesome topic of cannibalism. This tale is laced with some very darkly comic elements, such as the Burke & Hare style undertakers and lines like, "I'll bring some garlic. Dracula might try to turn us into the undead!" There is a lot of implied horror in the narrative, and psychological play, with a cold and ironic ending for the story's star, Julia Foster.

The next episode to be transmitted starts, like the others, with a 'teaser' sequence, although for *Rude Awakening* (starring the great Denholm Elliott and Lucy Gutteridge) the teaser is more of a *Space: 1999* 'This Episode' opener which gives away a considerable amount of the plot. Were they short on running time, or had no faith in the story, I wonder? The plot is driven by the psycho-sexual fantasies of Elliott's character, with some provocative imagery being exploited as he tries to bed his secretary (Gutteridge). The script leans heavily on the recurring nightmare style of Ealing Film's *Dead of Night* as it builds to a murderous and psychologically devastating impact. Then there is the twist ending, which creates uncertainty about the whole tale and the viewer is arguably trapped in recursion...

The following episode, *Growing Pains*, tackles the subject of genetics and food production, as well as the impact of absentee parents. For me it has very little to recommend it, and it is arguably the weakest story of the whole series, plagued by poor acting, unsympathetic characters and weak special effects. Then we come to one of the classics of the series, *The House that Bled to Death*. Anyone who saw the original transmission will recall with a joyful gleam in their eye, that notorious scene within the birthday party. It really did become burned into the memory of an entire generation. In line with the U.S. requirements, this tale ramps up the gore factor 100%, even if it is clearly poster paint running through the veins of the titular house. Looking back at it through grown up eyes, yes, perhaps the plot is a bit contrived or hokey, but the basic premise still comes out as chillingly cold and cruel.

Charlie Boy brings to the small screen another new and disconcerting element: fetishism. Stars Leigh Lawson and Angela Bruce fall foul of a weird, ugly, African tribal effigy in a tale that is laced with both tension and sexual imagery and – the most galling aspect – the fact that as Roy Skeggs said, the baddies do tend to win! Another classic follows when Hammer superstar Peter Cushing returns to the small screen as ex-Nazi turned pet shop owner

Martin Blueck in *The Silent Scream*. This fondly remembered tale is one of (again) cold cruelty and psychological terror as Cushing's victim (Brian Cox) is isolated and reduced to a near animalistic level. The story also has a wonderful, and very bleak, double twist ending.

It is back to familiar Hammer territory for the next tale with *Children of the Full Moon* and adventures in lycanthropy. The story is totally dominated by the central performance of Diana Dors as the welcoming yet weird Mrs. Ardoy, who has borne a large and unusual family in her remote house. A gory opening and laced with some wonderfully dark yet sparkling dialogue, "Come on in...I won't eat you..." perfectly delivered by Dors. A notable aspect is that the script offers up an implied rape of the central character. The tale builds perfectly on some familiar horror traits: old dark house; middle of nowhere; spooky dark woods...to deliver a memorable slice of Hammer horror, despite having been landed with a couple of bland principal protagonists. Dors' presence more than makes up for any shortcomings.

The next episode, *Carpathian Eagle*, very much broke new ground for television in presenting a narcissistic and utterly amoral killer, roaming the streets to find random, unconnected victims. Nothing new there then? After all, ATV's mid-70s series *Thriller* was jam-packed with similar types. In the case of *Carpathian Eagle*, though, there was a massive sea change: this killer was a woman. No shrewish, wronged woman either; leading the cast was attractive dancer-turned-actress Suzanne Danielle, whom the media had nicknamed 'The Body'. It would take television drama some years to catch up with the concept of a female serial killer, so Hammer was very much as innovative here as it had been on the big screen in the 1950s. Similarly unusual concepts within the tale are the initial considerations of one murder having a homosexual element, and the focus upon a drag artiste in the initial investigation. It was quite something to see the tables turned upon the *Thriller* type convention of the beautiful young woman always being the victim; this combined with the fact that another major convention was overturned in that good did not win out, as the viewer was left to consider what the killer's next move was going to be. [5]

We return once again to Hammer roots with the next story, *Guardian of the Abyss*, a tale founded on good old-fashioned Home Counties Satanism. The plot (very much in heroine-in-peril mode at first) revolves around the pursuit of an ancient scrying glass, wanted by a satanic cult to enable the summoning of a demon. It took several rewrites to knock the tale into shape but Don Sharp, its director, remembered it as being a good small screen facsimile of a classic Hammer tale. Again, there is a somewhat shocking opening for the timeslot, where a cult acolyte is seen starkly beating her head to try to get the evil out of her. As with a few of the series' tales, there comes a twist ending as the plot becomes resonant of another well remembered fantasy outing, *The Wicker Man* (1973). This story benefits from some great special effects – the mask of the demon being particularly notable and effective in that it brings a big screen feel to the box in the corner.

Visitor from the Grave, the next in the series, had been an early script penned by none other than Anthony Hinds, Hammer Film Productions' original driving force both as a producer and, over time, a writer. Despite the promising pedigree, I feel that the episode falls a bit flat. It starts strongly enough, with the shocking (off camera) rape of the lead character and the effectively gory shooting of her attacker, but then dwindles into a fairly basic plot of gaslighting, as her nefarious husband and 'friends' conspire to send her mad and thus get her money. Despite another strong touch involving suicide, the story goes for a somewhat hokey twist ending straight out of a 1950s American comic book. Not to mention a dreadful ethnic portrayal when they should have known better. [6]

The show bounces back strongly with another of the best remembered tales, *The Two Faces of Evil*. Ask anyone who saw the series' original run (or repeats for that matter!) and this tale will pop up alongside *The House that Bled to Death* and *Silent Scream* in the top rankers. In a brilliant piece of 'less is more', the realisation of the script manages to imbue a sense of sheer evil across the story, achieved with just some basic physical manifestations – such as a distinctive fingernail – which slightly change the familiar to create a living nightmare. The whole piece is built on a wonderful juxtaposition of good versus evil as the plot progresses. Following on from the film *The Omen*, this episode also brings to the small screen an encounter with a disconcertingly menacing child, as it builds to another shocking denouement. [7]

The series closes with what might be argued as being the most horrific tale of the series. *The Mark of Satan* is the darkest of stories, delving deep into the mind of a man who is having a nervous breakdown. Once again laced with gore – the central character works in a hospital mortuary – the story has a strong degree of realism; the character appears to be suffering from paranoid schizophrenia. A series of dark incidents – including a particularly disturbing threat to a new-born baby and a coldly effective but understated murder – snowball into a strangely off kilter ending. This really was 'strong' material for peak time Saturday evening; there is, perhaps, too much realism in this tale for it to be enjoyed as escapist entertainment.

In a suitably adult time slot, the original run of the series was quite successful, with Skeggs claiming in a subsequent interview that it hit the Top Ten in most weeks. In reality, from the only figures I have found, this is more likely the Top Twenty, with audiences averaging around 13 million. It was, undoubtedly, quite a divergence from all that had gone before under the ITC banner, being truly episodic without any connective tissue (in terms of characters) running throughout the series. The fact that it used some actors who had appeared in other ITC series was, as they say in the movies, purely coincidental; actors must keep working to pay the rent. Whilst scripts were produced by writers with (for the most part) established television records some with ITC/ATV backgrounds – the bulk of the directing work was done by Hammer cinematic alumni, and the house style was (as it needed to be) essentially Hammer.

As was often the case with ITC productions, Lew Grade was testing the water. A season of just 13 episodes would lend itself to a sale as a US network 'filler' slot in some form or another, without an overstretching commitment. In an interview with the *Evening Mail* less than two weeks before the series premiered on network ITV, Roy Skeggs said, "We're doing this 13, and another series next year. Hammer is definitely back". [8] Whether there was an ongoing commitment by ITC to a further run is not on record. As always, any decision by the company would be reliant upon the feedback that Grade received from the American networks, and early responses from them had not been altogether positive. Unfortunately, the hard facts of the bottom line meant that another ITC funded venture into the darkness was never to be, as the company had suffered $51 million losses in the summer of 1980 on the films *You Can't Stop the Music* and *Raise the Titanic*, losses that effectively ended ITC's production run.

In 1981 the new Hammer agreed a deal with Fox television in the US. A proposed second series emerged as the much watered down, *Hammer House of Mystery & Suspense*, a series of 90-minute TV movies with much weaker supernatural/horror elements. One critique of these tales noted that they were not distinguishable from any other 'Mystery Movie of the Week'. For all its faults and detractors – there were some! – *Hammer House of Horror* set a memorable standard at the crossroads of the decades, one which (in terms of both style and impact) it would take television at least another decade to catch up with... [9]

© Al Samujh

1. A notable, ambitious ITC project at this time was the acclaimed *Jesus of Nazareth* (1977).

2. The 1980 franchise decision stipulated that ACC needed to sell most of its shares in ATV and turn ATV Midlands into a new business, one which began broadcasting as Central in January 1982. The IBA felt that the company had been ignoring its Midlands broadcast area, while concentrating on making glossy productions (for export) in London.

3. Editor: As Al Samujh suggests here, *Hammer House of Horror* is the end of the road for ITC drama in many respects. As Robert Sellers remarks, "the final hurrah...for ITC itself, being the last significant television series commissioned by the company." *Cult TV: The Golden Age of ITC* (Plexus, 2006), p. 272.

4. Editor: we could throw in the success of Brian Clemens' *Thriller* (1973-76) which ITC had distributed to foreign markets such as the US. Unlike *Thriller, Hammer House of Horror* would rely (almost) throughout on British actors in lead roles.

5. Editor: in this respect the story was genuinely ground-breaking as it daringly moved away from the cliché of the lone, young female trapped.

6. Editor: the only thing we can say in defence here is that Gareth Thomas is playing an actor who dresses up first as a policeman then as an Indian Swami. The ethnic disguise is to fool Penny, not us.

7. Editor: visually, for me this is the most striking episode, from the horror and disorientation of the initial car crash to the blinding whiteness of the cottage hospital. It becomes a waking nightmare for the female lead which we are forced to share.

8. Evening Mail, 04/09/1980.

9. Editor: as a final note, it is worth emphasising how strong most of the casts are in the mini-series: Jon Finch, Julia Foster, Warren Clarke, Denholm Elliott, Leigh Lawson, Marius Goring, Peter Cushing, Brian Cox, Diana Dors, Suzanne Danielle, Anthony Valentine, Sian Phillips, and John Carson all give impressive performances...A few of these

were ITC veterans, but many of the guests were undoubtedly attracted by the 'one-off drama' nature of the series, captured on cinematic 35mm film.

BOUCHER'S HIGH FRONTIER:
STAR COPS

When Chris Boucher died in December 2022, there was a collective sense that we had lost a unique talent, a voice of wit and creativity that very few have matched in television. [1] He was a writer who, to many, had created some of the best *Doctor Who* stories in its 60-year history, and had guided *Blake's 7* to greatness not only with his inventive editing of its scripts, but also by writing some of the most highly regarded stories that the series had to offer. Nor was he just a science fiction writer, as his roles on various high-profile crime and police dramas such as *Shoestring*, *Juliet Bravo* and *Bergerac* proved. With hindsight, there seemed to be an inexorable pull to combining these two genres that he had become associated with, and a desire to create something of his own, both original and unique. Very much like the man himself.

Star Cops had a huge and lasting impression on me, so much so that I wrote a book – *Above The Law* – on the making of the drama. In my introduction I explained why it made such a personal impact; a serendipitous case of the right time and the right place as it was my first introduction to 'hard' science-fiction and, to some extent, high concepts. For me it was a new experience and, as is so often the case, these can burn themselves into your thoughts and memories in so many ways.

The idea of a dystopian future had leached into 1980s British drama from the 1970s, from *Doomwatch* (1970-72) and *Survivors* (1975-77) to *The Day of the Triffids* (1981), *The Nightmare Man* (1981) and, more viscerally, *Threads* (1984). Reality and factuality would often be heightened to act as warnings or metaphors for man's callous disregard for the planet in the pursuit of money, and both the death and trauma it would ultimately bring. These productions were entertainment, but they had also been created to make you think. And nothing makes you think more than death, loss and loneliness. An initial sense of isolation, bereavement and longing gradually shifting, under the need to adapt and evolve, is a feature that all the main characters go through in *Star Cops*, and something that grounds us all in reality much more than time vortexes and walking plants. However, threaded throughout the series is a sense of determination and humanity and the collective idea of overcoming any hurdles and fighting for survival and a future.

Set in 2027, *Star Cops* explores the theme of where there is life there is crime and the need for policemen. As mankind extends its reach to permanent bases on the Moon, then opportunities arise to test the boundaries of law and order away from Earth. As space exploration begins to branch out from the Moon and its various bases and facilities, then industrial, medical, trade and political exploration begin to open themselves up to misuse and criminal activity; all in conjunction with the natural avarice of man. As someone comments in the opening episode: "space exploitation". It is a new world of developers and seekers and colonists, much like the conquering of the Americas by the Europeans, and there is a need for this "hostile environment" to be protected by a sheriff. There is no coincidence that a suggested title for the series was *The High Frontier*.

Star Cops was always promoted as a crime series first and foremost. Once past the melancholic theme tune and title sequence – the first indication that this was not going to be your conventional sci-fi series – the viewer becomes a witness to two brutal and mirrored murders on Earth and in space. The publicity material took great pains to reiterate that this was cops and robbers, not aliens and monsters – "Spacemen are ten-a-penny, what we need out there is a good copper". The science-fiction aspects of the series were all carefully chosen to either juxtapose and heighten reality – spacecraft hijackings, computer viruses, clone experimentation – or accentuate the dangers and isolation – explosive decompressions and lonely outposts. It explores logic and the illogical, machine and humanity, and that grey area where both use each other:

"...the show's creator Chris Boucher was anxious to 'get away from the gee-whiz elements of space opera, and back to nuts and bolts with an intelligent detective series set in an alien environment. I certainly didn't want to boldly leap where lots of people have leapt before'." [2]

Realism was always the foundation of both Boucher's and the production team's vision. 2027 wasn't filled with flying cars, hover-boards and silver suits, but a recognisable world of restaurants, muggings and prejudice, in smart suits. Space travel was now as familiar as getting the bus to the shops, and here lies the skill of Boucher and his world building in that we believe the extraordinary to be mundane.

At its very heart, it is a character driven drama that benefits (and succeeds) by having a superb group of actors that effortlessly co-create some of the most believable and enjoyable central characters. Even one creation that wasn't human seemed to be Boucher unconsciously continuing his exploration of machine intelligence replicating human characteristics, following on from the mad computers and Voc robots in *Doctor Who*, and Orac, Zen and Slave in *Blake's 7*, with Box an "intelligent listening device" supporting the lead in his journey through policing on Earth and in space, as well as trying to cope with all that life throws at him.

The realisation of *Star Cops* took a long and tortuous path. Originally devised for radio but rejected due to the drama allocation already having been met, the scripts were adapted for television. Initially Boucher had proposed and written a two-part opener, but this was vetoed by then Head of Drama Jonathan Powell, with a request to cut the two scripts down to one. From the very start, there was a rocky relationship between Boucher and his producer, Evgeny Gridneff, with the latter demanding rewrites to all the scripts. Boucher would later disclose that things had started out badly and simply got worse: "Some producers you get on with and some you don't, and unfortunately Evgeny Gridneff and I just didn't." [3]

With the rewrites that had been imposed on Boucher, time was now running out to fill the ten-episode run and so two further writers were brought in by Gridneff to write half the episodes. The template and aesthetic for the series had already been set, the guidelines were solid within Boucher's scripts, and so both John Collee and Philip Martin had a strong foundation on which to build and create, while adding their own unique take on the drama. Part of that template was that the dialogue was sharp and as witty as the characters, and the world building effortlessly extended beyond the studio sets.

Philip Martin had, at this point, two *Doctor Who* stories to his name after years of writing gritty crime drama in the form of *Gangsters* (1976-78). To those who had seen that series, this was no ordinary, formulaic venture into the criminal underworld of cops and robbers, but a side-step into the depravity of organised crime, drug dealing and racism in a multi-cultural city. John Collee had trained as a doctor but only had a single television script to his name. *Star Cops* would provide him with a launch pad for a burgeoning writing career which soon included four scripts for *Bergerac* as well as the film *Paper Mask* (1990), adapted from his own 1987 novel that drew on his hospital experiences, a thriller that impressed reviewers with its technical expertise.

Nevertheless, the challenges to the production would continue from beginning to end. The truncating of scripts was nothing to losing a complete story through BBC electricians' industrial action, and the series recording was delayed for weeks. Then one of the primary actors became seriously ill and had to be written out of the final episode. The production team knew that they had something special on their hands, but the general atmosphere of apathy to all things science fiction from the higher echelons of the BBC was palpable. Whilst the early 1980s saw a continued dedication to creating new or original output, a managerial change at the top of the corporation saw a huge shift in emphasis that would be detrimental to the genre.

During the series' initial development, *Doctor Who* had been axed, reinstated, then reduced in screen time. The final part of *The Tripods* trilogy (1984-85) was scrapped as it was considered an expensive ratings failure, leaving home-grown science fiction a little thin on the ground. Amongst this, *Star Cops* was championed by BBC Controller Michael Grade as something adult and unique:

"BBC TV's head of drama, Jonathan Powell, has commissioned two scripts for a brand-new sci-fi work called *Star Cops* which could start next year. Now it is thought that this project is dear to Mr Grade's heart and he considers *Dr Who*, which started in 1963, to be dated and whimsical. But the BBC said: "In no way is it seen as a replacement for *Dr Who*. We categorically deny that. In fact, they are so different. *Dr Who* is a fantasy with monsters and the new project, if it went ahead, is straight science-fiction. They could cheerfully be run in the same week, just as *Dr Who* was with *Blake's 7*." [4]

On ITV, John Thaw cruised his way to murder scenes in his vintage Jaguar as Colin Dexter's *Inspector Morse* was adapted for television. On BBC2, David Calder vomited his way through astronaut training as Nathan Spring, the soon to be appointed Commander of the International Space Police Force. Whilst *Inspector Morse* undoubtedly reinvigorated the crime drama with its high production standards, orchestral score and Oxford college scenery, it was *Star Cops* that blasted the genre literally in to orbit by combining a police procedural with science fiction. It was bold, fresh and brave whilst also being adult in tone, combative in nature and not afraid to explore the cramped, sweating environments of Moonbase and people's minds.

Whilst Boucher and series producer Evgeny Gridneff may not have got on, they did share the central ethos of subverting the viewers' expectations right from the beginning. The slow, melancholic and beautiful title sequence, consisting of close-ups of a spacesuit, paired with Justin Hayward's soulful theme tune 'It Won't Be Easy', is as far removed from initial expectations of a *Starsky and Hutch* in space as you can get. [5] The mature tone continues in the opening of the first episode, as a man being drowned in a deep lake on Earth is juxtaposed with that of an astronaut being 'drowned' in space. Throughout, the viewer is embroiled in this world of hijacking, kidnapping, familial resentment, germ warfare, the Mafia and revenge.

This sense of loss, loneliness and hurt underlies and permeates the series to its very core, with Nathan Spring acting as a gravitational pull. His girlfriend, Lee, sees the chance of them having a child diminish as he is put forward to become Commander of the ISPF; an immediate future of months without him and only sadness as company. The roles are then reversed – in the second episode *Conversations With the Dead* – as all hope of a future of marital bliss and children is brutally extinguished as Lee is murdered in an horrific plot to politically manipulate Spring in his new role as Commander.

The series' lead actor, David Calder, is first-rate. He is regarded by many as one of this country's finest actors, and his portrayal of Spring is believable, nuanced and rounded. The sense of grief at the loss of his partner is palpable and barely controlled, and echoes down the series as he lies in his cramped quarters on Moonbase and painfully vocalises how much he misses her. His anger at her death is channelled into his job as this authoritative but quietly spoken man uses every means possible to get the criminals, including physically assaulting a suspect in a sauna and killing two men in self-defence. Despite Boucher's initial concept of a much younger lead, the series was boosted by, and fortunate to have, Calder's involvement:

"I just liked the stories. Very simple, nothing complicated at all. It's thrilling for an actor to be offered what is essentially the lead in a television series, with a view that it might not just be one series but maybe two or three sets. Until the shelf life runs out. So there's that sense, or there are the peripheral things that come with it like your status in the business, the fact you are in front of the public in a consistent way means people really get to know who you are as an actor. I don't care about the money. I really do not give a toss about that, but I like to know that they can put that face to that kind of acting which is another matter. And you get paid! Not to be over romantic about it, but it's a privilege. And that's a lot of pluses. And you only have to read one script for an actor to know, 'Yeah, I'll be comfortable in that skin'." [6]

At times it was, and is, uncomfortable viewing. Colin Devis, superbly played by Trevor Cooper, is a bigot, sexist and racist. With a libido higher than his IQ, he is frequently admonished and so begins the very gradual process of seeing his institutional behaviour as unacceptable. As the series progresses, this coarse, ex-London copper has the rougher edges of his nature filed, but never loses his power to stun his colleagues with his outdated views. Likewise, Australian engineer Pal Kenzy, a fantastic portrayal from Linda Newton, is introduced as a gambler and out to protect her back, until she is sacked from the ISPF by Spring. After publicly foiling a hijacking, and becoming the media face of the Star Cops, she is back in uniform a little more vulnerable but just as argumentative and anti-authoritarian as before. Kenzy is smart, hot-headed and a rare example of an equal female character on television at the time. And here is one of the reasons that the series succeeds so well: the development the lead characters undertake over the nine episodes.

Each character grows in complexity and believability, and it is Boucher's initial dialogue that superbly builds them up from potential stereotypes. The series got lucky with its casting, as the actors were skilful in analysing their scripts to create a set of leads that were believable, with a naturalistic camaraderie offset by an almost familial annoyance and frustration with each other.

If Spring was the father of the team, then American David Theroux, played to perfection by Erick Ray Evans, is the relaxed uncle who is fun to be with but doesn't mess around. Along with us, he is Spring's introduction to space and the International Space Police Force – smart, witty, warm, but again with an edge and a secret that mentally paralyses him. [7] It was always the production team's intention to up the 'international' in ISPF as Boucher replaces the disgraced French Moonbase Co-ordinator with a bold move of having the Russian Alexander Krivenko (Jonathan Adams) take his place. On broadcast, the Berlin wall was still up, and despite some considerable thawing thanks to Thatcher, Reagan and Gorbachev, the Cold War was still ongoing. The only character that Boucher did not create, and wished to disown, was that of Japanese doctor Anna Shoun (Sayo Inaba) who would endure sexist and racist remarks from Devis but would – ironically due to Boucher's handling – become a harder and just as important member of the team.

Admittedly, and perhaps by necessity due to having to create a character shorthand in only fifty minutes, the series did often resort to stereotyping. On paper, the Brits were stiff-upper lipped; the Japanese cold-hearted; Americans jingoistic; Russians sneaky; Arabs couldn't wait to cut your hands off; Italians were knee-deep in Mafia corruption; whilst journalists wafted around in long macs reeking of alcohol. But the directors either played to this or played against this with great success, as the guest cast is exemplary and brings in the huge talents of people like Daniel Benzali (pre-*Murder One*), Geoffrey Bayldon (playing against type) and Brian Gwaspari in a dual role.

However, it is not all grim and gritty. As with any Boucher script the humour is very much present. Boucher had a style unique to himself, not so much with stories (which were always original and beautifully crafted) but with his dialogue. His writing is clever and imbued with dry, quotable wit that permeates everything he has crafted. His lines were never there just to get the plot across, but a masterclass in how to write, with every exchange continually building and creating, whether it be the plot, a character or a world.

His dialogue always hit the ground running, with the much cited 'Boucher sarcasm' liberally applied with often dark and well observed put-downs. But these fast-paced, clever exchanges could also shift in to deep and often profound sadness in *Star Cops,* a trait that would be picked-up on by the other two writers. The series was also incredibly witty, a reflection of the fact that Boucher started out as a gag writer on *Braden's Week*, *Dave Allen at Large* and *That's Life* during the late 1960s and early 1970s, as he explained in an online interview:

"All characters have to come from inside yourself and anyone who says differently is even less sane than the rest of us. I'm glad (people) find the lines witty - I've been accused of being glib, but then I think glib is fine. I began by writing three-line quickies (basically a comedy sketch told in three lines of dialogue). Funny is quick but quick takes time to work out. And witty is what you wish you'd said at the time but didn't think of till much later. Like the man said - brevity is the soul of wit. All of which waffle means I have no idea...I don't think I actually have a method. I have a plot idea - a variation on a news story I've heard or an idea I've found interesting, something like that, and then given a series framework or production limits I set out to write it. It sounds a bit haphazard, but I just sort of follow my nose and hope it all works out in the end. I'm not above going back and correcting something that doesn't quite fit but as far as I remember that didn't seem to happen all that often. I do work carefully, scene by scene though, and try to make each one complete and right (and hopefully entertaining) before I move on to the next one - maybe that gives my brain time to work out how to get where I want to go." [8]

This was Chris Boucher's series, his "baby" as Gridneff would later call it. As its creator, Boucher had intended to be its sole nurturer by writing all the scripts himself. You can see all that had gone before distilled into his five scripts that defy the test of time. It would also be fair to say that while both Martin and Collee may have stood on the shoulders of a giant, they were clearly inspired by what Boucher had created. It is evident that Collee loved playing with these characters and thrived in his bid to equal the dialogue in his strong scripts. Collee recalled:

"The pilot script was really good and the concept seemed strong. I think the series was a little ahead of its time... I was quite new to TV writing so it was a learning process which may account for a certain uneven-ness in style between my episodes. Science background helped a lot. I knew nothing about crime writing! In those days writers tended to do a lot of work independently." [9]

Production standards are high throughout, with the concept of a NASA-based modular design ethos permeating each episode and working better when the lighting is low and sympathetic. [10] Even with two designers (Dick Coles and Malcolm Thornton) there is a continuity that is metatextual throughout the series, as specially created companies, brands and logos are prominent, lending the drama a sense of believability that is so often overlooked in other series. Designer Malcolm Thornton felt that the aesthetics would dictate the 'suspension of disbelief' by emphasising the environment:

"We felt the interiors should be much more atmospheric and technical, as living and work spaces. Space is a dangerous environment, and the interiors should reflect the technical demands of men and woman working and living in space."

To make the weightless effects (using Kirby wires) as realistic as possible, the interior of a huge American space station was even built on its side so as trick the eye away from any wires or pulling of harnesses.

"The American Commander's office was very complicated to design; we storyboarded every shot and then designed the set to suit the action and the technical demands of the actors on wires. The set, as I remember, was basically on its side with the desk attached to the end wall, with the chair fixed to the wall with the actor 'lying' in the chair. There was a slot in the 'roof' of the set to allow for the actors' wires." [11]

By having only two directors, Christopher Baker and Graeme Harper, this sense of style continued to encompass the series, and it was distinctive. At times it was as near cinematic as a 1980s, BBC videotaped, studio-bound drama ever got. It sometimes battled the cliché of being over-lit and static, often during the times that required complex sequences that were in danger of creating an over-run of studio time, but at others the series exuded a stillness and dynamism with its cramped, airtight chambers, low-level shots and blue lighting. It constantly aimed higher and tried to buck the trend, and when it succeeded it just shouted of the possibilities of more time, more episodes and being made on film. Videotaped drama was gradually being replaced by single-camera filmed series, and *Star Cops* missed out, but it was clear that the production team not only saw the strength and quality in the scripts, but the sheer potential of making something unique, as Harper recalled:

"Evgeny, when he saw my episodes of *Doctor Who*, was now becoming a producer and he was developing *Star Cops* and he thought that it would be a fantastic relationship. So, he asked me if I was interested and I was terribly flattered because this was new, this was us creating the whole environment that we were about to shoot, and my involvement in that case was much more than it had been before. *Doctor Who* was already set up, here was a chance to really develop and create a series with another director, so I was really flattered when I got asked. We were all serious, trying to make something that nobody had done really, not in television anyway. We hadn't done this kind of living on the moon and being out in space. I mean, there had been series in the 60s, hadn't there, but this was a serious attempt to show how it really is going to be in 30, 40 years from now because you're using the technology that was being designed for that." [12]

But film *was* used, and to sublime effect. The award-winning visual effects by Mike Kelt still impress today, with a power and beauty that seems to be timeless. This is, arguably, as close as British television has ever got to the majesty of Kubrick's *2001: A Space Odyssey* and in a pre-CGI world. Again the importance of creating a world that viewers could believe in was foremost on the designer's mind, as Kelt explained:

"The directors and producers were open to suggestions. They were completely flexible about the look of the spaceships. So it was a perfect opportunity to take a lead. I was very keen that the various vehicles looked practical, and believable. The show was not set that far in the future so the first research concerned NASA and McDonnell Douglas, both of whom were extremely helpful. I was frankly tired of streamlined spaceships – after all, why would it be streamlined in space! [Unless, like the shuttles and Hermes they were entering the atmosphere]. It was also important to establish some continuity, such as air locks, and container pod designs on the basis that development would have gone down a logical cost effective route. So if anything the design process was more complicated – you were effectively trying to design something that was, or at least looked, practical." [13]

Even the uniforms were inspired by contemporary NASA clothing, with the set being visited by former NASA Commander Pete Conrad, the third man to walk on the moon during the Apollo 12 mission, to provide advice. It was this level of enthusiasm and design skill that elevated the series and still impresses today, but in 1987 it was something that very few dramas had even attempted by creating its own micro-world for its characters to exist in.

Once beyond the Kirby wires and CSO blur, the stories have an inexorable pull. In 1987 it was a case of 'could this happen?' and now it seems to be a case of 'when will this happen?' They are clever and unique and always played well when one of the lead characters was at the heart of the story, either investigating or becoming the victim. The series' final episode *Little Green Men And Other Martians* subverts everything that had gone before by daring to shift the series into what it had been advertised as *not* being about. In an almost Nigel Kneale sense of bravery, the story warps and twists the finding of an 'alien' artefact on Mars, which leads to one of the most daring and breathtaking final moments of the series and left many open-mouthed with Boucher's audacity.

For a drama set in the future, it played with contemporary concerns, but eschewed the obvious by incorporating another element as the threat. The IRA were still active, and the prospect of a channel tunnel between Britain and France rang alarm bells as a natural object of attack. Bombs would be too obvious for Boucher, and so a poem-activated computer virus infiltrates the safety programs and causes mass destruction. The superpowers were still circling each other with the threat of mutually assured destruction, and the fear of self-imposed mistakes being made combined with internationally vetoed germ warfare, leads to unnecessary suspicions. Crack cocaine usage was on the rise in the inner cities and the series showed there were no borders to addiction or even the ethics of drug experimentation. And, most disturbingly, whilst London and Birmingham still reeled from race riots, the series saw technology being used to create weapons that could target skin pigmentation: "So the bastards have created a racist weapon!" And this summed up *Star Cops*. It was new, unique, exciting and by trying to do things that had never been done before it did 'boldly go'.

When asked whether Boucher drew on his two genre strengths of crime and science-fiction in creating *Star Cops*, he replied: "Yes. And it went against what I knew which is that hybrids are almost never successful. Let me rephrase that: hybrids are *never* successful." [14] I disagree, and history does too. The series gained a cult following and several awards. The years that followed brought reappraisal and the solid belief that it was ahead of its time with it having more in common with such groundbreaking dramas such as *Edge Of Darkness* (1985) and *A Very British Coup* (1988). Novelist Terry Pratchett believed it to be, "...the genuine, pure quill of science-fiction...It was clever and well thought out." [15]

In 2006 BBC4 and BBC Scotland created a season of programmes looking at 'cult' dramas, ranging from *Doomwatch*, *Survivors* and *Adam Adamant Lives*. [16] Naturally *Star Cops* was included, and people began to prick-up their ears upon award winning writer, critic and journalist Kim Newman's summary:

"If it had come back for another couple of seasons, I think it may well have been the BBC's best science-fiction show. I think the strength of *Star Cops* is the writing..." [17]

It could and should have been a success, but anything being put out in the middle of summer, at 8.30 in the evening and on BBC2 was going to struggle. [18] Yet it was a series that lingered in the mind of those who saw it. It was a show that, despite being cancelled after nine episodes, never died and spent nearly thirty years being championed by those that loved and admired it and could see its numerous merits. At the time, the whole production team believed that they had created something special, unique and powerful, so were bitterly disappointed when there was no second series. David Calder also strongly believed that to schedule a relatively expensive new drama against a popular, low-cost situation comedy was an act of "sabotage and absurdity". [19] He had also pushed for the series to be repeated, as he was confident in picking up a fresh audience and, on the back of this, a second series:

187

"The BBC, as far as I'm concerned, fouled-up miserably the series, and threw away such a, potentially, good idea. With good scripts, good writing and good acting. And something which was really quite fresh and new at the time. And I think they didn't understand what they had. Not only them, but unfortunately part of, well some of, the production side too didn't know what they had and didn't understand it. And when the BBC chose to put it out was just so crazy. The middle of summer, in a heatwave! The final days of the test match with their top show on the other side - we were on BBC2! It was extraordinary. Well to me, I just thought 'they've well and truly sunk this!' and so move on, bye-bye." [20]

Fortunately, it wasn't bye-bye. The series remained hovering in the periphery with its successful release on VHS and DVD. Chris Boucher reworked his scripts into a novel and the pages of genre magazines would often see the series feature in articles. It was a slumbering beast.

On Thursday 9th November 2017, Big Finish announced a relaunch of *Star Cops* as an audio drama. The series had come full circle from Boucher's original idea. Starring David Calder, Linda Newton and Trevor Cooper, people began to experience what many had seen back in 1987. There have now been a further twenty episodes and two audio novels, far outweighing the initial output. But the concept of the series is still there. It still takes risks. It still violently smashes past, present and future realities and problems together. It is still smart and funny and as cynical as it ever was. It was if it had never been away and all thanks to the vision of Chris Boucher.

Now, 2027 is within our grasp and it's not just space that could do with a man like Nathan Spring to sort everything out. *Star Cops* was set forty years in the future; maybe it was forty years ahead of its time?

© Paul Watts

1. Editor: Toby Hadoke's Guardian obituary praised Boucher's writing in one of his *Dr Who* stories, *The Robots of Death*, for four aspects: sardonic exchanges, well-drawn characters, world-building through dialogue and hard sci-fi concepts. All of these aspects are there in *Star Cops*.

2. *Radio Times*, 04-10/07/1987, *Star Cops* preview. Editor: in that opening episode, *An Instinct for Murder*, the first scene with Spring makes it clear that he is very much a policeman who prefers to use human instinct and 'shoe leather' rather than lazily relying on technology, despite his use of 'Box'.

3. Kaldor city – online review with Chris Boucher by Alan Stevens. Editor: I particularly like Boucher's original idea of filming the Earth-based sequences on location and on film, with the space-based scenes on videotape in the studio. It would indeed have given *Star Cops* a 'unique' look.

4. Paul Donovan, 'War over *Dr Who* as Grade plans new sci-fiction series', *The Mail*, 01/03/1985.

5. Editor: while Boucher clearly did not like the theme song, I agree with the producer and Paul Watts that it works well as both an emotive score and as a warning that this will not be your average sci-fi series.

6. David Calder, interviewed by Paul Watts, 2017.

7. Editor: Spring and Theroux's mutual love of classic movies is a nice touch. It helps them to bond and is used throughout the series, adding connective tissue and a sense of a story arc.

8. The *Star Cops* site, online interview with Chris Boucher.

9. John Collee, interviewed by Paul Watts, 2017.

10. Editor: there is a contrast between the approach the two directors took to lighting, with Baker preferring brightly lit, ordered interiors and Harper going for dimly lit, dingy ones. Like Paul, I prefer the low lighting, however, personally, I don't feel that the contrast has a detrimental effect in terms of continuity.

11. Malcolm Thornton, interviewed by Paul Watts, 2017.

12. Graeme Harper, interviewed by Paul Watts, 2017.

13. Mike Kelt, interviewed by Paul Watts, 2017.
14. *Blake's 7*, The Merchandise Guide – Mark B Oliver. Interview with Chris Boucher, 2012. Editor: Boucher stated on *'The Cult of'* BBC4 programme that he should have asked to produce *Star Cops* himself and thereby maintain creative control. It is hard to disagree with that. Mind you, hindsight is a wonderful thing, and he admits that at the time he did not want the responsibility!
15. SFX magazine. 'Top 50 SF TV Shows of All Time'. Terry Pratchett (1991).
16. Editor: this was followed up by a 2008 run of BBC 4 'Cult Of' documentaries re-examining Sunday night dramas such as *Shoestring* and *Bergerac*. There is a well-balanced online review of the series at vulpeslibris.wordpress.com
17. *The Cult of Star Cops*, BBC Scotland/BBC 4(2006).
18. Even that 8.30 pm slot was not a constant.
19. *The Cult of Star Cops*, BBC 4, 2006.
20. David Calder, interviewed by Paul Watts, 2017.

A BOX OF DELIGHTS: BBC CHILDREN'S DRAMA IN THE 1980s

Viewed at a distance and through the prism of a 21st century audience, the confidence, aplomb and sheer range of drama commissioned and made by the BBC Children's department throughout the 1980s now seems nothing less than staggering. Although these days the BBC has two dedicated children's channels, the content is heavy on animation and repeats. The punishing costs of drama mitigate against there being much of it across the schedules and, even when they are able to greenlight a project, contemporary commissioners tend to play safe. Series which can be made in high numbers (to bring down costs) predominate. However understandable this is in our crowded, competitive and noisy multi-media world, the past is a different country.

At the start of the 1980s, the BBC Children's department was reaping the fruits of one woman's extraordinary mission to expand and revitalise its content. Monica Sims had been made head in 1967, taking on a department which, just a few years before, had been heavily cutback and curtailed, its output restricted to a mix of young children's programmes – chiefly *Play School* (1964-88) and *Jackanory* (1965-96) – sundry 'magazine' shows – the most notable and successful being *Blue Peter* (1958-) and *Vision On* (1964-76) – and a ragbag of imported material and bought in animations. Drama and light entertainment had been hived off to the Corporation's mainstream Drama and LE departments. LE offered the likes of *Crackerjack* (1955-84), *The Basil Brush Show* (1968-80) and, later, the egregious (and now sinister) *Jim'll Fix It* (1975-94). Drama delivered *Doctor Who* and the Sunday classic serial, with the occasional thriller thrown in to play during the afternoon block of children's programmes. Such was the typical inter-BBC rivalry and suspicion, there was next to no communication between the departments. *Doctor Who* was wildly popular with children but Sims often felt it crossed lines in terms of its scary themes and casual violence. Meanwhile, as the catch-all name implies, the Sunday classics strand focused on dramatisations of famous novels – some more suitable for children than others. But across these offerings there was almost nothing reflecting the contemporary lives of children or the issues and themes to which they might particularly relate. Sims was determined to change all this and to reclaim the real estate, rekindling drama within her department and enshrining its autonomy to commission it.

In order to do so, she enlisted the help of her departmental manager, George Ageros. Ageros was adept at the art of 'robbing Peter to pay Paul' and by 1971 had squirreled away the money for a few tentative adaptations, among them *Joe and the Gladiator* (based on a novel by Catherine Cookson and set against the background of an impoverished North East) and a six-episode contemporary science fiction thriller *Mandog* (1972), written by the distinguished author Peter Dickinson. The prime mover behind these initial efforts was producer/director Anna Home. Home would quickly become the key player in the resurgence of BBC children's drama, and would later succeed Sims as its Head. She was born in 1938 and, as a child, had been a voracious reader of everything from John Masefield and E. Nesbit to Biggles and Enid Blyton. In 1960 she joined the BBC straight from Oxford as a radio studio manager, one of the few avenues (other than secretarial or administrative) then open to women keen to explore a more creative and challenging career. Home's television break came as a junior member of the production team of *Play School*, an imaginative daily programme for young children, which started with the arrival of the brand new BBC2 in April 1964. Home was soon able to get closely involved in the aspect of the series which most appealed to her: the storytelling. This led to her joining *Jackanory* – a simple concept in which a narrator (usually a well-established actor or comedian) read an illustrated adaptation of a book over the course of a week's worth of 15-minute episodes. As time went on, *Jackanory* experimented with dramatized inserts and it was shooting these which gave Home her first experience of drama. "I cocked up from time to time quite badly", Home admits, "but Monica was very patient and she wanted as much as I did to get the drama back into what she perceived as being its proper place. Nobody ever *taught* my generation anything. No-one trained me. Classic BBC. What I learnt, I learnt in the studio from the Vision Mixers and, on location, from the camera people. Dorothea (Brooking – a seasoned and highly experienced director/producer) was a great influence in terms of overall production. A fantastic woman and someone we looked up to. But in the very early stages of the resurgence of children's drama, she wasn't around very much." [1]

For many years at the BBC, it was an unwritten principle that in order to get official funding for certain projects, there first had to be proof that there was an audience for it. It was a kind of internal guerilla warfare in which programme makers sought by smoke and mirrors (and the patronage of a head of department willing to bend the rules) to get the material they wanted to make on screen. A prime example was the annual *Ghost Story for Christmas* – the first, in 1971, was made on a shoestring. Only once it had proved a success were subsequent efforts properly allocated and budgeted for. It was the same story with the children's department's gradual return to the genre. "It was always a struggle", comments Anna Home. "They didn't want to spend money on kids' drama." What was important was that these early efforts quickly found a keen audience, and this encouraged the view prevalent within the department that it was essential to commission drama made specially for children and, in particular, contemporary drama rather than the ubiquitous bonnets and wigs of the Sunday classics. "We had a completely different pitch on it," explains Anna Home. "We did do some of the traditional stuff, but we wanted to do something different, of now, not of then. We were very much wanting to reflect the world in which our kids lived. A good story, well told, is what you were looking for all the time."

By the close of the 1970s, children's drama had been fully revitalised. Anna Home became the Executive Producer in charge of the slate and two other key players had emerged, directors (and occasional producers) Paul Stone and Colin Cant. Stone was a former child actor who had cut his directing teeth on *Blue Peter* while Colin Cant had been a designer at BBC Glasgow. He worked as assistant to Ridley Scott, who inspired him to become a director. Cant had been directing at Granada on *Coronation Street* and the autobiographical John Finch saga *Sam* when the call came via his agent that BBC Children's department was looking for a director for their football series *Striker* (1975-76). Over the next two decades, Cant proved to be both the most consistent and gifted of the directors at work in the children's department. "I was terrified most of the time," laughs Cant, looking back. "The last day's shoot was always what I was aiming for – but I loved the editing, sitting in that dark room with the editor, sewing it all together." [2]

On average, each year's budget allowed the department to make a trio of (typically) six-episode serials and a longer run of *Grange Hill*, which quickly became the drama flagship for the department. From its very first (shorter) series in 1978, *Grange Hill* established itself as a powerhouse. The ratings alone were extraordinary. Throughout the 1980s, it would dominate the children's TV landscape with its characters and content driving a huge and often controversial debate. The tidal wave of appreciative feedback from children was counterbalanced by the many complaints, chiefly from adults – parents, teachers and even MPs – horrified at what they saw as a glorification of the bad behaviour and poor standards in many urban comprehensive schools.

"Anna originated the concept of *Grange Hill*," said Paul Stone, in an interview he gave me in 1988. "Phil Redmond created the specifics."

"The 'schools things' that had been done by the BBC in the past had all been in the sort of *Billy Bunter* tradition," observes Anna Home herself. "I wanted to do something that was contemporary and reflected the world of the comprehensive school. When Phil first came to me, it was with a comedy. I wanted something tougher. To begin with, Phil was a bit dubious about it."

Redmond had already touted the idea around several ITV companies, all of whom had turned it down. "We all sat down as a group and discussed the idea," Stone explained. "There was much criticism on the basis that children wouldn't want to come back home from school to have it reflected back at them. We had been battling before *Grange Hill* for a greater naturalism and a greater chance to reflect social issues back to children."

The series certainly provided a consistent platform to satisfy both these concerns. Phil Redmond remained closely involved, though it was quickly apparent that with the scale of *Grange Hill* he would not be able to write every episode. This led to the forming of a team of writers – notably Alan Janes, Margaret Simpson, Barry Purchese, Jane Hollowood, David Angus and John Godber – with a script editor to guide and hone the narrative. For several series in the 80s, this post was held by the brilliant Anthony Minghella.

During this time, there was only one significant misstep. Broadly speaking, the principal characters were all popular with the audience. Todd Carty's effervescent portrayal of the cheeky chancer Tucker Jenkins set him apart, however; he was phenomenally successful in the role. In the 1982 series, as Tucker was fading out, there was a new arrival, Jonah Jones, played by the high-spirited Lee Sparke. Jonah was just as cheeky as Tucker, and Sparke undoubtedly had as much star quality as his predecessor. The mountain of fan mail reflected the immediate impact he made. Alas, behind the scenes, Sparke's sometimes riotous behaviour, though essentially good-natured, began to cause concern. For the smooth running of the show, producer Kenny McBain determined to make an example of Sparke and he and Minghella decided to kill off the character. Although nothing new in soap terms, this was a brave move for a children's drama. A previous, lesser *Grange Hill* character had been killed off, but the treatment of this story was so cautious and tentative, especially in its aftermath, that there had been no emotional resonance for the audience. This time, McBain and Minghella realised that the death of such a well-loved character would be bound to cause a seismic reaction, off screen and on. But they had reckoned without their juvenile star and his family. The Sparkes declined to take part in such a storyline and so Jonah disappeared abruptly between series. Minghella hastily rewrote the storyline to involve the somewhat implausible Jeremy (Jonah's unlikeable cousin) instead but, in consequence, the storyline was inevitably diluted. When Edward Barnes (who had taken over from Sims as Head of Children's in 1978) learnt of the decision, he was incandescent and threatened to sack McBain for dispensing with such a stand-out star, but, in the event, calmed down and kept him in post. When McBain eventually moved on, it was to produce the high-profile *Inspector Morse*.

The BBC had done somewhat better with their management of Sparke's predecessor Todd Carty, giving him his own spin-off series, *Tucker's Luck* in 1983. This was part of a brief but glorious expansion of the department into shows aimed at teenagers and screened in a special early evening slot on BBC2. *Tucker's Luck* neatly tapped into the depressing 'dole culture' experienced by so many young people during the early to mid-80s, though it did so with a light touch. The other major entry in this slot was *Maggie* (1981-82), based on a series of books by Joan Lingard, where the focus was on a feisty Scots girl determined to break free from the confines of her working-class Glasgow roots. The setting was important in itself, as Anna Home explains: "It was about reflecting the *whole* audience not just the South East and London. We wanted to break the barriers."

These teenage dramas were a chance to explore deeper emotional relationships too, which generally bored a younger audience. In *Grange Hill*, for instance, a boyfriend/girlfriend storyline usually played out to the open derision of at least a couple of the other characters.

When you look at the 1980s run of *Grange Hill*, some of the storylines seem staggeringly raw and uncomfortable – the bullying and racism in particular. Language is used which would no longer be permitted in most adult drama, never mind in a series aimed at children. As the wearisome disclaimer goes, it reflects the attitudes of the time and so has become a useful time capsule of once standard behaviours. There is, for example, a casual acceptance of occasional physical violence towards children, both from teachers and parents. Shoplifting and smoking both feature in prominent storylines. "That was the great thing about Phil," says Colin Cant, who directed and produced many episodes. "He really zeroed in on what was real."

At its best, *Grange Hill* is brought to life not just by the writing and direction, but through the performances of many of the cast. Children from Anna Scher's pioneering theatre school, based in Islington, provided some of the stand outs. Scher worked with real inner-city kids and her methods were the antithesis of the more traditional 'eyes and teeth' stage schools. "You could guarantee a good performance from one of her students," remarks Colin Cant.

It was halfway through the decade that *Grange Hill* delivered its defining storyline: Zammo Maguire's slow disintegration into drug dependency. Nothing afterwards could match the reach and influence of this saga; to raise funds for charity, there was even a successful (if artistically lamentable) cast single, *Just Say No* and a one-off documentary special to discuss the issues raised by Zammo's decline. That BBC Children's Drama were willing to commit to such a challenging story is a sign of the assurance which then existed in the department. There would be complaints for sure, but these met with a robust defence, rather than the cringing apologies more familiar from TV companies today.

Complaints were not confined to *Grange Hill*. There was always an adverse reaction from some when the BBC embarked on anything to do with the supernatural. 1988's wonderfully imaginative and spooky fantasy *Moondial* triggered a robust debate about what was acceptable in the regular teatime drama slot (Wednesdays at ten past five). Plans to dramatise the (literally) haunting *Ghost of Thomas Kempe* (the work of the distinguished Penelope Lively) came to nothing in the wake of fears about the likely response.

Another proposed production, of John Christopher's dystopian *The Guardians*, was nixed when it became apparent that the adult drama department was embarking on the same author's epic *Tripods* series. These kinds of casualties were unusual, however. As a self-governing fiefdom within one of the 'ghetto' departments of the BBC, drama was able to run its own show with a remarkable lack of back seat driving from the 'grown ups' in mainstream television management. Strong audiences provided a kind of insulation and so children's drama was largely left to its own devices and discretion. This creative freedom, unheard of now or in the last 30 years in TV, encouraged a flourishing confidence and freedom to experiment.

The department benefited enormously from its connections with many of the pre-eminent children's writers of the time. The period from the 1960s to the 1980s was a boom time for children's publishing and a kind of 'golden age' of high-quality writing emerged from key names – among them, Leon Garfield, Nina Bawden, Penelope Lively, Helen Cresswell, KM Peyton, Bernard Ashley and Robert Westall. The best of their work had helped to fuel *Jackanory* and allowed relationships to develop between them and Anna Home, in particular. "We nurtured these relationships," she says. "Helen Cresswell, for example, was one of my best friends by the time we'd all worked together for so long. It was a wonderful period for that generation of writers."

The work of this cabal of fine authors inspired most of the adaptations which defined BBC children's drama throughout this heyday. There was a strong degree of trust: writers knew that their work would be respected, taken seriously and shared with an audience of many millions. If they were so inclined, there was an opportunity to adapt their own work and certainly to have a degree of involvement with the actual production itself. This was in marked contrast to the experience of many authors in the shark-infested waters of adult drama. There was space, too, for the fledgling writer, for new voices to be commissioned and nurtured. One such was Richard Cooper, who contributed the (then) topical tech spy thriller *Codename Icarus* in 1981. Cooper went on to write the epic and unjustly overlooked *Knights of God* for ITV (filmed in 1985 but only screened somewhat belatedly in 1987). In the decade to come it was Russell T Davies who was given his first major commissions from the department.

Knights of God was among a string of ambitious and interesting productions commissioned by Anna Home during her time at the ITV company TVS (1981-1986). At the BBC, she had been succeeded by Paul Stone as the Executive in charge of drama and when she returned to the department as its Head in 1986, he remained in place for the rest of the decade. "I'm often asked whether I proportion out the drama between established writers and newly commissioned work," he commented. "There is never a format except that instinctively I've tried for quality. The greatest and best writers for children in the world are based in this country."

By now, there was a regular 'rep' of directors specialising in children's drama, some staff and some freelance; along with the enduring Colin Cant, other stand-out names include Marilyn Fox, Christine Secombe, Roger Singleton-Turner and Renny Rye. It was a collegiate environment. "The teams were very caring, but they also enjoyed it very much," says Home, "and I think that was one of the great things about the BBC of that time, that it was hard work but it was great fun. They could speak up for things that they wanted to do. It wasn't all coming down from me; it was being generated from below as well."

Colin Cant pays tribute to the freedom Anna allowed her creatives: "Once you got the script and the budget, you didn't see her again until the edit. And even then, there was very little interference. That was the good thing about children's drama – they left you to it."

Funding, however, remained a challenge. "It was always tight," Home continues, "and I have to say that there wasn't a great deal of interest in what we had to say at Offers meetings. [Offers were part of the BBC's internal system, in which heads of department pitched ideas to the channel controllers and sought backing for their annual slate]. On the other hand, there is something to be said for not being considered madly important so that you just get on with it quietly and hope people don't quite realise what you are doing..."

The 1980s were rich with productions unflinching in their attempts to engage children with a rich and diverse variety of emotionally intelligent drama. Bernard Ashley was a prominent source for these, starting with his *Break in the Sun* in 1981. This followed a girl called Patsy, who decides to run away from a toxic and abusive home life. In 1986, there was *Running Scared*, a tough thriller set on the crime-ridden streets of London and 1989's *Country Boy* carried a prescient theme of the dangers of environmental pollution. "Bernard had been a teacher and headmaster," comments Anna Home, "rooted very much in the East End and he knew the detail of that world very, very well. They were real kids in his stories."

Vivien Alcock's unsettling *The Cuckoo Sister* (1986) told the story of a child, stolen from her pram, who is subsequently reunited with her birth family, and her sister. As well as the terrifying central conceit of the story, the serial is a depiction of class conflict too – the 'returned' sister is seen as 'common' by her sibling. In Berlie Doherty's *White Peak Farm* (1988), the aftermath of bereavement provides the focal point of the drama. There was room for comedy/drama too. Helen Cresswell created the delightful *The Bagthorpe Saga* (1981) which focused on an eccentric family living in a country village and there were two series of the likeable *Seaview* (1983-85), about two siblings growing up in a Blackpool guest house. *Jossy's Giants* (1986-87) showcased the adventures of a children's football team and was written by darts commentator and TV personality Sid Waddell. "I think what we were trying to do was to provide children with the kind of range of drama that was available to adults," suggests Anna Home.

Not everything worked, of course. There were some notable clunkers. In 1982, there was a trio of duff efforts, a leaden adaptation of E Nesbitt's *The Treasure Seekers* and two serials transmitted back-to-back: *Jockey School* (the title says it all) and *Break Point* (about the competitive world of junior tennis). "There are a lot of kids who like horses and sport," points out Colin Cant, who directed *Jockey School*, "but one of the major problems is that it's very hard to cast young actors who can ride (or play tennis) well enough. And the kids who can, tend not to be very natural actors."

The following year, *The Baker Street Boys*, a much-vaunted spin-off from the world of Sherlock Holmes, did not quite come off either. It was made as a mixture of film for exteriors and studio for interiors and this did not help the necessary atmosphere or suspension of belief. Although the film/studio mix was then the traditional and widespread approach in much TV drama, it was not so predominant in Children's TV. Many of their most successful series were shot entirely on location. "It was about the reality of it all," observes Anna Home. "It was much easier for the child actors to be out on location in places they felt familiar with rather than being in studios and leaping over cables and all that sort of stuff." Perhaps the other issue with *The Baker Street Boys* is that it aspires to be nothing more than a slice of light-hearted fantasy escapism. Nothing inherently wrong with that, but out of kilter with the usual approach within BBC Children's to period drama. Many of these were remarkably gritty and unflinching. 1980s *Our John Willie* (from a book by Catherine Cookson), shot entirely on location, was set in a poor mining town and focused on two brothers' struggle to survive a hostile world, exacerbated by the fact that one of them, the John Willie of the title, is deaf and dumb. Portraying a central character with a disability was ground-breaking and yet there was absolutely nothing 'tokenistic' about it. Another fine example was 1983's *The Machine Gunners*, based on Robert Westall's novel about a group of poor but sprightly Geordie kids during the Second World War who get more than they bargain for while souvenir hunting for shrapnel and exploring a crashed enemy plane. Critics of the book had focused on its uncompromising portrayal of working-class kids from the North East who did not speak 'properly', and that the story itself was too dark and alarming for children. The BBC version is a triumph – with a brilliantly natural young cast – authentic to the book, utterly real in its treatment and thus its effectiveness.

In 1986 Leon Garfield contributed the marvellously atmospheric *December Rose* (which, in a reversal of the normal process, he also novelised) which centred on the misadventures of a hapless chimney sweep. There was nothing 'cosy' or counterfeit about this depiction of the harshness of Victorian society's treatment of many of its unfortunate and unwanted children. "It was this thing of constantly going back to reality, rather than fantasy," says Anna Home. "We did fantasy as well, but the core of the stuff was real and relevant, even if it was set in another time." "Whenever I did fantasy," adds Colin Cant, "I would have pages of questions for the writer as I knew I might have to explain the plot to one of the actors. But I didn't always get the answers I was looking for!"

It must be said that none of these productions, notable though they undoubtedly are, achieved the lasting reputation or prestige of either of the 'giants' of the era: first *The Box of Delights* (shown in 1984) which undoubtedly paved the way for the second, CS Lewis's *The Chronicles of Narnia* (three series from 1988 to 1990, starting with the most famous of the books, *The Lion, The Witch and the Wardrobe*). *The Box of Delights*, in particular, has become something of a cult with devotees rewatching the episodes in the run up to Christmas each year; the final instalment takes place on Christmas Eve. Effects which were then state-of-the-art have inevitably dated, but one can only admire the *chutzpah* of the production teams who wrestled with the myriad problems of how to conjure up such magical fantasies in an analogue world. The *Narnia* series is slightly undermined by a horrible piece of miscasting with one of the leading children but, overall, the success of the series finally led the Children's Department back to reclaiming the prestige Sunday classics slot which it continued to occupy with distinction for the next decade, before the funding and support finally evaporated. "That slot was important," explains Anna Home, "because it was where an audience who wouldn't normally catch it, saw it. You weren't entirely dependent on the child audience – it was back to the family."

For me, the jewel in the crown of the BBC's 1980s period dramas for children is the much lesser known but perfectly exquisite *The Children of Green Knowe* (1986). Based on one of a series of idiosyncratic books by Lucy M Boston, *Green Knowe* is a ghost story sophisticated in its suggestion of a family's past interwoven with its present, in the solitary form of the lonely and slightly 'other' small boy, Tolly, played with great sensitivity by Alec Christie; the 'present' being sometime in the 1950s. Everything about this production delivers: the casting is perfect, the shooting (all on video, on location) is sublime (special kudos for the magnificent lighting) and the story, albeit slight and slow moving, is perfectly paced between the whimsical and the creepy. It fully captures what it is like to be an intelligent, small child seeking to understand an enigmatic world and to make sense of the passage of time and its strange tricks.

The final period piece of the decade was also set in the 1950s, and was another fantasy, an adaptation of one of the most magical and satisfying children's books of the 20th century, Philippa Pearce's *Tom's Midnight Garden*. This was actually the third time the BBC had adapted the novel but the earlier versions (which used the same script) – in 1968 and 1974 respectively – were unsatisfactory, both in terms of the need to truncate the narrative and because of the limitations of the production and cast. The six-episode 1989 version, by contrast, is a masterpiece which manages to distil the dreamy aura of the original book into a beautifully paced screenplay. The child leads – Jeremy Rampling as Tom and Caroline Waldron as Hetty – are exemplary and there is the added bonus of Paul Reade's wonderful score.

If you have gained the impression that series were where it was at, you would be right; there was rarely the money for more than the occasional one-off. There were, however, some noteworthy efforts, including an attempt to establish a tradition of Christmas specials. In 1980, this was *The Bells of Astercote*, based on a novel by

Penelope Lively, an effective ghost story blurring the divide between a village now and in the time of the plague. The following year came *John Diamond*, a splendid mini-adventure from the assured pen of Leon Garfield and, like much of his work, Dickensian in tone and language. Finally, in 1982, another ghost story, the Brummie based *Ghost in the Water*, with a strong theme of less tolerant times for young lovers. This was a fairly dark story for Christmas time, but beautifully shot all on film. Other one-offs worthy of mention include 1982's *Billy Boy*, a poignant depiction of how the Troubles in Northern Ireland affect the main protagonist, 1983's *The Winner*, about Cheryl, a talented athlete under increasing pressure because of her sporting ability and 1986's *Sticks and Stones*, about a troubled Glaswegian boy caught up in the racial tensions of inner-city London.

At the very end of the decade, a vibrant new drama arrived on Children's BBC. Set in a Newcastle youth centre, *Byker Grove* had a large cast of engaging Geordie kids and was an instant success with the audience. Like *Grange Hill* before it, this first series of six episodes was something of a trial run. When it returned the following year, it was promoted to a full 20-episode season, and it was in this form that it continued to run, alongside the now perennial *Grange Hill*, until the early years of this century. Today *Byker Grove* is principally remembered for bringing the world the enduring talents of Ant and Dec, but its significance in terms of BBC children's drama is that it was a fully indie production rather than being made in-house. In this way, it was a signal of the changing times in the television industry which, slowly and inexorably, eroded the creative community which had been built up and sustained so successfully and for so long within the BBC. Today, nothing remains of the range, complexity and diversity enjoyed by BBC Children's throughout the 1980s. "The context of now is so completely and utterly different that I don't think you can talk about it in the same breath, really," comments Anna Home, who remains the Chair of the pressure group the Children's Media Foundation. "It's a completely different set up now. The audience has split and fragmented. It's a problem. *YouTube* is now the channel of choice and we would like it to be regulated to include public service content. The big question is whether children's content is going to continue, other than in animation? All you can do is hope that at some stage, someone will be able to trigger another rebirth." [3]

© Richard Marson

1. Private interview/meeting with Anna Home, 11/01/2024. All subsequent Anna Home quotes refer to this.
2. Private interview/meeting with Colin Cant, December 2023. All subsequent Colin Cant quotes refer to this.
3. My thanks to Anna Home and Colin Cant. Many of the productions mentioned can still be found on DVD and in some cases purchased on streaming services: available titles include *Grange Hill*, *Jossy's Giants*, *Ghost in the Water*, *The Box of Delights*, *The Children of Green Knowe*, *The Chronicles of Narnia*, and *Tom's Midnight Garden*.

HOME THOUGHTS FROM ABROAD: *AUF WIEDERSEHEN, PET* AND CONDITION-OF-ENGLAND COMEDY UNDER THATCHER

[This essay is dedicated to Arthur Knowles, my dad, as a working-class man, working in a factory rather than on a building site, but someone who lived through this period and stayed afloat.]

The comedy drama series *Auf Wiedersehen, Pet* (1983-1986; 2002-2004) was voted ITV's favourite programme of all time in a 2015 poll to celebrate the broadcaster's 60th anniversary. Alongside this measure of substantial popularity, it has also received critical recognition: its first series placed 46th in the British Film Institute's top 100 British television programmes in 2000. In spite of these measures of esteem, though, it has received little critical attention in comparison with its peers in 1980s television drama or comedy, something this essay aims to redress. *Auf Wiedersehen, Pet*'s identity in the marketplace of early to mid-1980s British television shows its hybridity and ability to capitalise on developments in television genres, in broadcaster profiles and branding, and in the relationship between viewers, TV shows and the cultural politics of the time.

In this essay I confine my discussion to the first two series of the show, as those were products of the 1980s, being produced by Central (then holder of the Midlands ITV franchise) and screened on ITV in 1983-84 (series one) and in 1986 (series two). It is a testament to the show's enduring popularity and its position in viewers' and producers' cultural memories that it was revived over fifteen years later by the BBC, with a third series being screened on BBC1 in 2002 and a fourth, plus a concluding two-part Christmas special, in 2004. As well as the fact that this essay collection focuses on 1980s television, I am arguing that the later BBC revivals of the show, while the work of the same writers, Dick Clement and Ian La Frenais, are effectively the show's homage to itself and to the mythology of the 'Seven' set up in the original ITV series. The original format was brought to a forced end with the death of Gary Holton, who played Wayne, in 1986 towards the end of the filming of series two. As a result, the later series are compelled to envision a different future for the characters which shows how age and changing times have treated them, but which functions consciously as an echoing of the earlier group without being able to recreate that group or the specific cultural, social and economic circumstances that brought them together. My concern here, then, will be with *Auf Wiedersehen, Pet*'s representation of the early to mid-1980s cultural landscape with which its protagonists are grappling, and its use of hybrid generic forms to convey the shifting aspects of its central theme, men 'out of place' in terms of their personal lives, social identities and sense of masculinity as an increasingly embattled arena of life.

As a show comprising 13 one-hour episodes in its first two series, *Auf Wiedersehen, Pet* fits unproblematically into the drama format. However, it was written by two celebrated comedy screenwriters, Dick Clement and Ian La Frenais, held in high esteem for a range of sitcoms including *Porridge* and *Whatever Happened to the Likely Lads?* As such, it occupies a hybrid position, as, I would argue, an early example of 'comedy drama' which attempts not to blend the two seamlessly, but to incorporate both in order to balance out the bleaker aspects of 1980s social situations with a lighter perspective. [1] Clement and La Frenais are documented as having 'felt liberated by the freedom of writing a series of one-hour dramas' [2] and Clement in particular stated:

"There is a feeling in comedy that each page must have a laugh on it, so it was nice to get away from it and write something 'real'. Not that we wanted to be preachy or write a searing indictment of

Thatcher's Britain. But the politics were there and the context was a good one in which to write." [3]

Many fans of Clement and La Frenais' previous work might well contend with the idea that this was somehow less than 'real'; their situation comedy output has frequently been praised for its naturalistic representation of characters and scenarios, and the awareness in those representations of the impact of social change in Britain. I would argue that *Auf Wiedersehen, Pet* can be seen as very much a successor to their enduring portrait of the transitions of the early 1970s in *Whatever Happened to the Likely Lads?* (which itself can be viewed as a recreation and darker reflection on their 1960s *Likely Lads*). In short, they are drawn to refresh themes of their existing work in new series, considering as they do how the present-day context is now shaping their protagonists. In addition to this, having moved to Los Angeles as a result of their success, the opportunity to write specifically about the North-East again was also an opportunity to demonstrate their continuing connection with their roots in both a regional and a political sense, as they note in their memoir:

"The (mostly) Geordie brickies working the German building sites in Thatcher's Britain reminded viewers that we had not disappeared into the Hollywood Hills and were still firmly on the side of the have-nots." [4]

Auf Wiedersehen, Pet therefore demonstrates the writers' personal desire to be, and be seen as, socially engaged with the condition of their homeland. It also indicates the climate of TV production as one which encouraged and valued explorations of the everyday as political. Roddam and Waddell note that one obvious point of comparison with *Auf Wiedersehen, Pet* was Alan Bleasdale's *Boys From The Blackstuff*, originally a one-off play and then screened as a five-part BBC2 drama in 1982, and acknowledge that *Auf Wiedersehen, Pet* was not "overtly political" or "angry" in the manner of Bleasdale's work. Dick Clement, while initially discouraging comparisons of the two, then goes on to do just that, stating:

"There was room for both [...] Alan's characters were in despair, drowning. Ours had taken action and got out, so they were swimming, albeit with some difficulty. I'm not saying it was better, just different." [5]

The strong presence of both anger and despair as characterising *Boys From The Blackstuff* is undeniable, and *Auf Wiedersehen, Pet* certainly handled its comparable theme with a lighter touch. I would argue, however, with regard to Clement's view of his own characters as having "taken action" that their decision to go to Germany is a rare example of them doing so. It is a persistent lack of agency that dominates the lives of the seven protagonists, which itself can be connected to the social climate in which they are rooted and, specifically, the challenges to traditional masculinity which their situation presents. They take opportunities that turn up but do little to actively seek out ways of improving their situation; likewise, they are relatively passive in managing their relationships, often seeming to pay them scant attention until a crisis arises, as with Dennis' and Oz's marriages, and Hazel's second thoughts over marriage to Barry. Nevertheless, Clement's portrayal of his protagonists as "swimming, albeit with some difficulty" is fitting: they experience difficulties, even crises, but, ultimately, stay afloat. This precarious condition, while well aligned with the pressures being exerted at the time on working-class men and traditionally masculine fields of employment, was also a prefiguring of the more developed and recognised 'crisis in masculinity' that would only be fully anatomised later in the 1980s and beyond, of which both *Auf Wiedersehen, Pet* and *Blackstuff* are fictional examples.

Lez Cooke notes that while *Boys From The Blackstuff* was billed, and indeed received, as "serious arts television" it nevertheless also had impressive viewing figures for a BBC2 broadcast, with 4 million viewers rising to 8 million for its final episode. [6] It is important to remember that *Auf Wiedersehen, Pet* was broadcast in a quite different television context, as a mainstream ITV series, in a period when ITV was by some way the most watched of the four terrestrial channels. As such, it offers a representation of Britain's social and cultural position that is less overly political, but in which, in Clement's words, "the politics were there" for a popular audience. Philip Schlesinger, writing in the year that *Auf Wiedersehen, Pet* was first screened, assesses the commercial and audience-led context in which it was appearing:

"Commercial pressures operate with particular force on the popular series and serials that are central to the rating battle between the two main networks, BBC & ITV. To attract a mass audience they need to work with images and ideological themes which are already accepted by the widest range of potential viewers." [7]

Schlesinger argues that popular series are often assumed to be uncritically conveying "official" perspectives, but that they can work with alternative perspectives that the viewing public have accepted, e.g. that Thatcherism can be debated, if not defeated. In this respect, *Auf Wiedersehen, Pet* plays a role that I contend is analogous to that which Ian Green (also writing in 1983) argues is found in the Ealing comedies of the post-war period. Green argues that the Ealing comedies negotiate informal and formal censorship which allows for the conscious criticism of contemporary situations, particularly of institutions: government and the state, by using comedy as a way of raising these issues but then "drowning" them in laughter and thus dismissing active, overtly political discussion of the concerns. [8] *Auf Wiedersehen, Pet* is able in this way to frame the effects of Thatcherism as significant in the lives of its protagonists, and by implication, Britain at large, yet to distance itself from a "searing indictment" (Clement's words again) of those issues by the deployment of comic moments in the narrative.

An emblematic example of how this operates can be found in one of the most memorable and also political monologues from Oz.

210

Over the course of both series one and two, Oz is the character who articulates some of the most stinging anti-Thatcher comments, but his self-centred and prejudiced remarks provide regular comedy and he is very clearly a partisan and unreliable narrator of events. In *The Return of the Seven: Part One*, the opening episode of series two, Oz is seen delivering an angry speech to an initially unseen audience on his return to the UK from the Falklands:

"You know the reason I left this country in the first place, divvn't you, eh? I'll tell you. In a word, Margaret bloody Thatcher, that's why. Because I'd had it, I was up to there with what she'd created. Bloody wasteland. Desolate. Nae joy, nae hope, nae nowt. Where kids get to 21 and have never done a day's work in their life. Honest men have to gan oot thieving to feed their families. Young bairns can buy heroin in the bike sheds at school. Oh dear. But I thought, "Nah, nah, nah. It's got to be getting better. It cannae be as bad as what it was, can it?" I was willing to give you lot the benefit of the doubt on this one, you know. But no, no, no. What happens? What happens is I've been back on my native soil for fourteen minutes, and I'm subjected to this act of fascist intimidation! 'Cos that's what it is, you know! That's what it is, and I'll be writing to my MP about this!"

As Oz concludes, we see that he is naked and about to be strip-searched by a customs officer. This exemplifies the show's capacity to vocalise genuine dismay and discontent about contemporary Britain, but then to undercut it by showing that Oz is motivated here by purely individual resentment at being singled out for suspicious treatment. Green's concept of "drowning in laughter" is enacted here: the scenario is raised as a social concern, but no further consideration of change or resistance is developed because the comedy framing takes effect, revealing Oz's words in the context of the strip-search he is about to undergo. The "searing indictment" of Thatcher's policies gives way to Oz as comic subject about to find himself in trouble yet again.

This pattern is one repeated across series one and two: criticisms of Thatcherite Britain and wider aspects of the current social order are present but without any sense that a solution to these problems can be found. As with their personal and employment problems, the forces imposing this new way of life on them are simply too powerful: the lads have no answer other than to drift on and wait for developments. However, while they are generally resigned to a lack of agency, along the way small victories are possible by unified action. Working together offers day-to-day comradeship and support, and also the potential to act together to right a wrong – these are the localised, yet collective, routes to greater life satisfaction that *Auf Wiedersehen, Pet* represents as being within the reach of its protagonists.

The success of *Auf Wiedersehen, Pet* can be seen in both viewing figures and in viewer and reviewer comments on its appeal. It had been scheduled in a Friday evening 9pm slot, something which worried both Jimmy Nail, playing Oz, and the director Roger Bamford, on the basis that "this is about brickies, about lads, and they all go to the pub on a Friday night". [9] The Friday night scheduling slot is also aligned with comedy or entertainment programming rather than serious drama. Nevertheless, it was received well by newspaper TV critics, with positive reviews in the *Daily Mirror, Sunday People* and the *Guardian;* perhaps predictably, the *Daily Mail'*s review criticised its "coarse language" [10] but still enjoyed aspects of the show. The first episode attracted 10 million viewers, with this figure dropping in the second week, settling at around 9.5 million in the early weeks but then rising to over 11 million by the second half of its run in January 1984 and achieving 13 million viewers for the series finale. [11] Reviews of the finale were particularly positive: Anthea Hall in the *Sunday Telegraph* referred to "this exceptional series, in the very best traditions of British comedy" [12], and, like other TV critics, expressed hopes for a second series. When series two aired in the spring of 1986, it was able to capitalise on this success, with between 13 and 16 million viewers during the run. [13] Its commercial prospects for renewal would have been extremely good, but for the sudden death of Gary Holton towards the end of filming for series two, which proved devastating in permanently ending the possibility of the seven established protagonists appearing together again. It is indicative of the viewing public's enduring affection for the show and of its capacity for popular success that, over fifteen years later, the BBC picked up the show to develop its second life in the form of series three and four plus Christmas specials. Those series attained success of their own, but are part of a different era, and given the remit of this collection to focus on 1980s television, will not be discussed here.

The original show's appeal is further illuminated through contemporary academic studies of television audiences. David Morley's 1986 book *Family Television: cultural power and domestic leisure* was based on research with families on their viewing habits, conducted in spring 1985, and it is notable that *Auf Wiedersehen, Pet* is mentioned a number of times, with series one having concluded its run a year earlier in 1984. The 18 families interviewed by Morley all came from one area of South London, demonstrating that while the Geordie accents may have given unfamiliar viewers trouble, there was no north-south divide in terms of southern viewers relating to the show, its humour and its characters. They also all owned video recorders, which, coupled with the significant presence of unemployed men in Morley's research participants as heavy television viewers, indicates that the series may have had a reach greater even than that shown by official viewing figures in being watched as time-shifted viewing by these audiences. One such individual, an unemployed avid TV viewer and film fan, names *Auf Wiedersehen, Pet* as a favourite series: "That's a terrific programme". [14] Another man interviewed says of the show, "It was really terrific. After a while the characters were fantastic. That's something that I wouldn't miss." [15] A third man expands on this with:

"*Auf Wiedersehen Pet*—it's fantastic. I work in the building industry and it's typical of what goes on on a building site. I'd really like to see another series. It's a terrific bunch of characters." [16]

This interviewee's praise for the show as "true to life" echoes the feelings other male viewers stated. Even if not matching their personal experience in all ways, they clearly identified with the representations of contemporary masculine experience on offer. Morley himself comments that shows like *Auf Wiedersehen, Pet, Boys From The Blackstuff* and other named favourites such as *Hill Street Blues* were "providing precisely that sense of a connection between personal experience and the broader societal dynamics which construct that experience". [17]. Even given regional differences, the sense of a shared form of experience was clear from these male viewers' responses.

Interestingly, the potential regional divide, and a different view, arises in another Morley interview with one woman discussing her husband's preferences:

"He likes to watch *Auf Wiedersehen Pet*—I fall asleep in that. I can't even understand what they're talking about. I can't understand it. He's laughing and I couldn't honestly tell you about what. I find it such a strain I just fall asleep. They may as well be talking Dutch—because I don't understand it." [18]

This seems to be, at least in part, an issue with understanding accents as well as one of gendered viewing preferences. However, other female interviewees depart from this view, on the grounds of 'masculine' taste and also of age. One Morley interviewee has a preference for 'realistic' drama of a kind which is displayed by the men in the other families interviewed. "I like regional things [...] *Auf Wiedersehen, Pet*, and the *Likely Lads*, those sort of things...and the *Boys from the Blackstuff*." [19] In another empirically-based study, Ann Gray's *Video Replay* which interviewed women viewers (based on a thesis submitted in 1989 so with interviews being conducted in

214

the several years before) notes that Sandra, who at 21 is the youngest woman in the study, says: "I like to watch *Auf Wiedersehen, Pet* and *The Young Ones*. My mum and dad can't stand them, they don't see how it can be funny". [20] Gray and other feminist television scholars have noted the gendered differences in viewing preferences and also the extent to which, in the 1980s, men still held considerable sway in determining the family's real-time viewing. However, we can see from this that *Auf Wiedersehen, Pet* was able to appeal beyond its assumed core audience of male viewers on the basis of its regional representation, and also to younger viewers on the basis of its comedy status. Consequently, the characteristics that made it less explicitly political than shows like *Boys From The Blackstuff* were also those that allowed it to attract a significant, mainstream audience, and in this capacity represent 'the context' of its protagonists' struggles, through a comedy frame to those who may well have never switched on something they saw as 'political'.

Men out of place: masculinity in changing times

The enthusiastic responses of the men interviewed in David Morley's research show that *Auf Wiedersehen, Pet* was felt to excel in representing current masculine experience as well as the challenges of working-class life in 1980s Britain. It is significant that this originates from the 'fish-out-of-water' scenario of having to leave their home country and become Brits abroad, examining and comparing their own country, its industry and the resulting sets of values held with those they encounter in Germany. However, across series one and two, the protagonists continue to experience the feeling of being not at home, either abroad or even, later, in their own country. This is represented as a common, unifying masculine experience, which crosses regional divides, rivalries and other differences, but which reinforces the underlying class identity they share. Being away from home prompts this awareness of themselves as 'strangers in a strange land', and the inherent nostalgia and sense of dislocation that persists in Germany and after their return. This happens in spite of the protagonists being more widely travelled than ever given their class position; despite them roaming the globe in search of work (and play) they remain essentially provincial in outlook. Consequently, they aim to recreate this sense of their own locality, often in the form of a comfortable drinking location, their literal 'local' – and lost sense of Britishness wherever they go. This engenders, for instance, Oz's hopes for and then disillusionment with the Falkland Islands as a defiantly British territory and scene of military victory, but still lacking in the social amenities he craves after a day of manual labour, prompting his return to the mode of continual complaining about all things German he deployed in Dusseldorf.

The seven protagonists are not outliers in deciding to join the black economy in Europe in response to a lack of work locally. In *Who Won The War Anyway* Dennis says "there's 30,000 of us over here". Moreover, it is not just British workers who are seeking a better situation. When items start going missing in the hut, and the seven look for the culprit, Oz's suspicions fall on 'the Abduls', as he refers to the Turkish workers on site who live in separate huts. On voicing his thoughts, Neville asks "What's wrong with the Abduls?" (it is notable that the derogatory terms used by Oz are also used by more wholesome members of the group). Oz isn't short of a reply:

"They account for half the crime in German cities. The dirty parts are where they live."

Dennis, however, is able to contextualise these points, responding with:

"They're over here as sweated labour. They get the worst housing and the lowest wages".

This seems to be tacitly accepted by the others, who are far less hostile to other nationalities than Oz, though they – even Neville – still seem to regard them as an alien group, one they are somehow different from as Englishmen, although they would prefer to live peaceably but at a slight distance from them. The view seems to be that the Turks do indeed suffer from racism, but that there is nothing the English workers can, or should, do about that. The resigned acceptance of inequality can be traced back to the disadvantages they themselves have experienced; life is simply not fair to the ordinary working man, who may rail against this – as Oz certainly does – but is powerless to change it.

Any attempts to challenge workplace unfairness in the first series of *Auf Wiedersehen, Pet* are made on an individual, case by case, basis. Dennis thus tries his best to get Neville, as a young and naïve man, restored to his job after the deception where they initially pretend that he is a carpenter, to get him the only other available vacancy on the Dusseldorf site. When Oz is sacked for causing trouble, though, Dennis declines to get involved, and the general feeling in the hut is that Oz deserves it for his constant boundary-pushing with their German bosses. This can all be viewed in opposition to one of Thatcher's most infamous assertions, that there is 'no such thing as society'. In contrast, in series two, the seven are seen, during a period when trade unions were under specific attack from the government, to take collective action and to succeed in doing so. They act in unity to help Barry renovate his house to make it a marital home; to take revenge on Wayne's behalf for their treatment at the hands of the local landlord, the snobbish Arthur Pringle, while working on the nearby Thornley Manor; and, most significantly, refuse to work until Ally Fraser, the underworld Newcastle businessman to whom Dennis is in debt, agrees to cancel the punitive level of Dennis's debt from then on. The informal nature of this arrangement – agreed on out of personal loyalty to Dennis – does not undermine the fact that when working men assume a united front, they prevail against the rich businessman, managerial classes and bitter pub landlords that aim to exploit them.

Series 2 was broadcast during 1986, with the ignominious end to the miners' strike in March 1985 still very much a fresh memory. This may well have seemed like unrealistic nostalgia for a time when such collective action had a far greater chance of success. However, *Auf Wiedersehen, Pet* had been from the start a series which foregrounded the plight of working-class men like the protagonists, in a society which seemed intent on modernising in a way which displaced and devalued them. Having already lost so much, it is perhaps not surprising that the protagonists are allowed their own small victory. As seen on many other occasions in the series, the struggles of working-class men can be ameliorated by the friendship and support they can provide for each other, from a perspective of knowing and understanding the struggles faced by other members of the group. While *Auf Wiedersehen, Pet* frequently draws on the noted reluctance of men like this to open up and disclose their feelings, using this for comic purposes, it also includes a number of scenes where they divulge their fears, hurt and insecurity.

The seven's work skills are, above all, portable. That is what enables them to work informally in Germany in the first place, what allows them to move freely through the UK and Europe when work is available, and ultimately what they see as their recourse in the final episode of the second series, where they seem to be headed for Morocco on Ally Fraser's boat as it flees the pursuing Spanish authorities. Powerless to influence their course of travel, they continue to drink, and Bomber says, "Well, there must be some work in North Africa", to which Moxey replies, "There's bound to be. I mean, they built the pyramids, didn't they?" The series ends on a note that affirms the paradoxical constants in the Seven's lives: they are on the move again, to a destination dictated by someone else, again, but with the expectation that they will pick up their trowels and get working on arrival, as what else is there to do?

Gender and social change

Left behind by the social changes affecting traditional masculine roles, the *Auf Wiedersehen, Pet* protagonists find that working unofficially in Germany is their only option because there is "nae graft up our way" as Oz puts it. As this shows, in one sense Thatcher's impact was felt and resisted on a regional and class-driven basis, particularly so in the north and midlands where the decline of traditional heavy industry and high unemployment, particularly for manual workers, was creating a significant economic downturn with a major effect on local communities. Jackson and Saunders note that this was treated as a necessary by-product of Thatcher's vision for the UK:

"[Thatcher] was adamant that there was no alternative to the pain of economic restructuring, despite the social pain it caused [...] the collapse of the old industries was inevitable, heralding a new prosperous beginning." [21]

The bitterness felt by unemployed north-east brickies like Dennis, Oz and Neville was familiar then to many other working-class men from a similar regional background, where a dislike of the Thatcher government deepened and for many has endured to the present day. Again, Jackson and Saunders indicate that this exacerbated an existing sense of north-south and other regional divisions between parts of the UK, fuelling in turn "the growing perception of a distinctive 'territorial' dimension in British politics. The 'national' dimension was part of the mix of British regional anti-Conservatism, but the prime driver was socio-economic". [22] As such, *Auf Wiedersehen, Pet*'s cast of protagonists from across England demonstrated the dire straits in which many working-class men found themselves – even Wayne, the Londoner, has had to go to Dusseldorf to find work as a carpenter. Early worries about the show being 'too' regional faded with its ratings success, but arguably at least part of the affection felt by viewers was tied to its representation of different regional identities – English ones, at least – something those regional audiences could all appreciate.

While in series one more attention is paid to German-British differences, the English-set episodes of series two feature more references to the class divisions within British society itself, in a way which dovetails with regional divisions when the protagonists are based in a rural Derbyshire village to work on the conversion of Thornley Manor for Dennis' criminal boss, Ally Fraser. As they arrive at the manor, Moxey states, "I lived in a place like this once... a borstal near Prestatyn". Oz is, unsurprisingly, the character who voices the most pointed comments, as when he adopts a faux-upper-class voice to appear at the door of the manor and says:

"There's a notice there what clearly states that members of the working class will be exterminated."

Or when he remarks when an Alsatian barks at them on their walk through the village:

"That's an attack dog, that is, it's trained to go for the working class".

Even Neville becomes uncharacteristically sharp when responding to the well-spoken local campaigner who urges him to keep "the glorious heritage of England intact" with:

"I was brought up on a council estate in the north-east of England, pet, I mean Mrs Bellamy. I've seen precious little of the glorious heritage of England."

On returning from that conversation, Neville adds that he feels "more a foreigner here than I did in Germany". This stark difference between regions of England is underlined by the exchange between the two police offers pursuing Ally Fraser when they travel to Newcastle, with one asking the other if he considers himself working class, and on being told that he does, "Wait till you spend the night in Newcastle. You'll realise you're middle class." Phil Wickham notes in his book on *The Likely Lads* that in spite of its characters' universalism for many, the north east was seen as "different", [23] and this returns as a distinct presence in both series one and two of *Auf Wiedersehen, Pet*, where the Newcastle location of Dennis, Oz and Neville becomes dominant in establishing the detail of 'left behind' communities under Thatcherism, while remaining relatable as one location in a web of many similarly affected others.

Barry is the keenest member of the seven to be seen as socially aspirant. Early in series two he outlines his progress:

"I'm a very different person from the one you knew in Dusseldorf. Saved me money, bought this place, started me own business, learnt elementary Spanish and joined the SDP. And I've travelled, and I don't just mean the Falklands. Last year Hazel and I took a villa in Gozo."

Moxey obliging notes, "You're obviously very upwardly mobile these days, Barry" in response, but this list brings together Barry's intellectual aspirations, which were evident in series one, with markers of not only personal success such as buying property and owning a business – key aspects of aspiration which the Thatcher government strongly encouraged – but also mid-1980s modernity and progressive thinking, such as Barry's membership of the SDP. While Thatcherism and its cultural framework had permeated day-to-day life, this co-existed with at best a deep ambivalence and at worst a passionate hatred of its ideology from many ordinary people. Barry may be the protagonist of whose achievements Thatcher would be most proud, but he made his position clear in series one in his comment about the lack of work available in the north-east, saying, "I blame Thatcherism. It's a misguided policy, misguided and misconstrued". Aspiration may be desirable but the policy context that has made it so central is still a troubled subject.

Nevertheless, Barry is the most forward-looking of the group and the one most keen to speak the language of the future, though this, like Oz's regressive comments, is mocked (more gently) by the others. When he says, "I'll give my business a couple of months, and if it still don't take off, I'll try one of those sunrise industries", Bomber replies, "Can't see you as a milkman, Barry". It is no surprise that Barry is able to say to the young women he and Wayne are attempting to charm at the start of series two, "I should think Prince is more your mark, eh?" whereas Oz resolutely sticks to his more traditional preference for country music, and indeed its more old-school masculinity. Oz is predictably dismayed when he discovers his son Rod's preference for American football, which Channel 4 had started showing soon after their launch in 1982, over Newcastle United, as another marker of cultural change which is leaving him behind. However, neither Oz nor Barry is represented as being suited to the combination of ruthless self-centredness and ambitious self-starter energy that truly Thatcherite success required. The protagonists are able to adjust, with some reluctance, to cultural change but are trailing forlornly in its wake, weighted down by their regional and class-based roots.

Most importantly, the new insecurity of previously secure jobs in traditional industries was above all a problem for men. This was the central aspect of the 'crisis in masculinity' being experienced by men in the early 1980s, as was already being documented by Ian Miles in 1989:

"Fewer jobs involve heavy manual labour, more jobs involve working with keyboards and dealing with other people, for example. The everyday equation between types of work and gender, then, is harder to sustain than heretofore [...]. Mass unemployment has also weakened the correlation between masculinity-femininity and breadwinner-dependent, even if this ideology still maintains considerable force (and is able to inflict untold psychological stress on unemployed men and their families)." [24]

Series one shows this primarily from the men's perspective, as their undocumented work in Germany allows them to regain their breadwinner roles in their families by either sending money home (though not in Oz's case) or to accumulate money that will give them access to their own family life, as with Barry's saving for a mortgage and wedding to Hazel. There are also occasional moments where we see the protagonists as able to adapt their skills to circumstances: where Bomber is sewing Wayne's jacket to repair it, and when asked by Wayne where he learned this, he replies that he has picked up all sorts of things in his time. However, for the most part they live resolutely undomestic lives in Dusseldorf, and even with the exception of Barry's plan to paint the hut to brighten it up, Bomber undermines his egalitarian demonstration of domestic skills by objecting to first pink, then yellow, as "not a man's colour". The protagonists' lives are stripped down to working and socialising, which means the family lives they have left behind are glimpsed rarely from occasional scenes back home and Neville's phone calls to Brenda: even this, though, conveys clearly the "psychological stress on unemployed men and their families" that Miles refers to.

Series two, partly set back in England, gives a fuller view of how marital and gender roles are shifting, with Brenda the breadwinner in her job as a nurse, and Neville, unemployed once more, grappling with housework, childcare and cooking. Brenda, shown as clingy and dependent in series one, is now taking this in her stride, saying "Things are changing for women, you know, Neville. Even on Tyneside", whereas Neville is adjusting to his wife's earning status more easily than to her socialising with her male doctor colleagues at suspiciously upwardly mobile venues and activities like a badminton club. Series two also represents a broader shift of the gender dynamics for the protagonists and their relationships, in that rather than being in the background, back at home while the lads in Germany are able to seek out other female company if they wish, now the women are in the position of picking and choosing. Having been able to choose between his new relationship with

Dagmar or returning to his wife Vera at the end of series one, in series two Dennis' marriage has again collapsed and he is the rejected party, living with his sister. Marjorie finally breaks ties with Oz and is planning to move to Italy with her new partner, creating a storyline where Oz moves from being an absent and neglectful father to his son, Rod (whose age he can't remember in series one and is castigated by the others as a result), to one who experiences belated remorse and realisation that his son is effectively lost to him, largely through his own actions. Wayne's marriage to Christa, the German girl he has successfully wooed at the end of series one, has also broken down; Hazel, Barry's fiancée, is shown early in series two having cold feet about marriage while Barry ploughs on, unaware, with renovating their future marital home. The overall picture shows considerable ambivalence on the wives' part about whether marriage and the traditional nuclear family set up continues to offer them much, and either withdrawing from it altogether or remaking their role in it as Brenda has done. Even when Barry and Hazel eventually marry in the final episode of series two, this happens because Barry is finally able to offer the socially ambitious Hazel a wedding she deems more glamorous and enviable, on the exiled criminal Kenny Ames's ill-gotten yacht. The dynamics now show the lads at a relative disadvantage in their relationships.

Alongside this runs the storyline of Vicki, the gangster Ally Fraser's girlfriend, who at the start of series two is introduced as a stereotypical airheaded trophy partner whose role is to look decorative and go shopping. As the series progresses, though, even Vicki becomes dissatisfied with her lot, complaining that there is nothing for her to do in the Spanish villa and worrying about Ally's long-term plan to stay in Spain: "I'd die if I thought I was never going to see Newcastle again". Ally is also portrayed as an increasingly dark character as the series progresses, culminating in his violence against Vicki when she dares to challenge him: this proves to be the seal on his progression from local hard man made good to out-and-out villain. In comparison, the brief concern for the

Turkish brothel owner's partner as a victim of male violence in series one fades away as seemingly something that is out of the lads' ability to influence, long term. Vicki's position is seen as more akin to Dennis' indebtedness to Ally: in both situations, the lads feel the need to step in and make a moral and practical stand in their respective defences. While Dennis' role as the 'gaffer' has consistently earned the lads' loyalty, their support for Vicki – led by Oz, who is written towards the end of the series as a more suitable partner for her – shows that even the lads are now acknowledging in a broader sense that "things are changing for women…even on Tyneside" and regarding them as people with real aspirations, needs and desires of their own.

Though this 'provider and family man' role is the norm, it is not homogenous. Wayne is earning money for a single man's life of socialising and enjoyment, saying in series two: "Give me any income you like, and I'll live beyond it", though admitting that his constant pursuit of women and accessories like his sports car do not help. Working away from home does not particularly hamper this lifestyle, only the imposition of having to share a hut, and then his uncharacteristic feelings for Christa, interrupt it, but Wayne then continues through series two as an unreformed rake who thus escapes the patriarchal responsibilities of family life. The popular theme song for the show, "That's Livin' Alright" sums up Wayne's experiences most closely, even though he is something of an outlier.

In contrast, Moxey seems to be there because he is bereft not only of employment opportunities, but also of any relationships where he has to care for anyone else, or to be cared for himself. While Moxey is a marginal figure in the group – in ways that contrast with Wayne's more hedonistic outlier status – his criminal past is the basis for exploring the consequences of the rootless man's life at different points in the show. In series one, he comes under suspicion as a known criminal when money and valuables go missing in the hut; in series two, he is forced to seek out and live under a new identity, having absconded from his open prison, and eventually ends up travelling to Spain on his new false passport. Noticeably, Moxey does not share the wistfulness of Neville for his home country, having no-one and nothing to return to: he announces, as part of a discussion of future plans: "England's finished. Someone should stick a bloody great notice on it – 'out of order'. I've got no desire to go back and watch it going through its death throes".

While Bomber observes that this seems connected to the fact that "if you go back, they'll stick you in clink", there is an undeniable aspect of truth to Moxey's statement, which connects with Dennis' retort to Oz in series one that blokes like him spend a week away from the UK and "become ridiculously nationalistic for the country that can't even bloody employ them in the first place!" It is Moxey who points out the illogicality of Neville's wish to be in "some manky pub in Gateshead" instead of the sunny coast of Spain, and notes that "wherever you are, you've always wanted to be somewhere else… if he [Neville] was there, he'd wish he was here". Moxey exemplifies the extreme version of masculine rootlessness as represented in the show, but as such is also able to comment on the irony of other protagonists' attachment to a country that has arguably given them little to be attached to. Neville is the character who voices fully the nostalgia that permeates the show, and its dual meanings. Nostalgia was originally coined as a term denoting homesickness but has mutated into indicating a longing for another *time* instead of, or as well as, another *place*. [25] Both apply to the nostalgia experienced by Neville and others, which they experience as a longing for both a time when their expected social roles were more readily achievable, and for a place that felt familiar, secure and like home.

However, one different sense in which the lads are 'out of place' is one in which there is also some small gain for them, alongside the alienation felt by being away from their homes and home country. Bomber, another of the 'family men' among the group, gives voice to a different form of disquiet about what they have missed out on in the expected process of settling down to family life:

"I don't know, you goes to work every week, hands it over to the wife, pays for the house, new clothes for the kids. It don't leave much for yourself, like."

None of the group are newlyweds: even Neville as the youngest and most uxorious has been married for some years before they depart for Dusseldorf. All the others have been seen in previous episodes to be at least tempted to be unfaithful, usually having gone out drinking, seeming at times less than fully committed to their families back home. Bomber's wistful speech here is a reminder that these men married young and have been husbands, fathers and providers since then, but without having first had the space to act out, sow wild oats and indulge themselves in self-centred pursuits. Their time working away, while in many respects a hardship to be endured, also offers them a kind of delayed adolescence where day to day they are responsible only for themselves, and once money has been sent home, family obligations have been met, leaving them free to drink, relax and socialise as they please. The series' creator, Franc Roddam, recounts this:

"For those not inclined to be homesick, the life was a good one; sitting around drinking beer with your mates, watching the girls go by. Many of the men had married painfully young, often to the first girl they slept with. Suddenly, barely in their twenties, they had wives and kids and adult responsibilities. Then these same men found themselves in Germany ten years later with a wage packet and few responsibilities other than sending a few quid home. Having fun became an integral part of the experience; it was a chance to act like single men with no ties." [26]

The various dislocations the protagonists endure foster a kind of restrained hedonism, or perhaps a passively acquired version of the time-limited relief often found in comedy narratives where characters let go and break out of the expected social order, as theorised by Bakhtin in his work on carnival. Nancy Glazener says of Bakhtin's conception of carnival laughter: "It is ambivalent in that it affirms and denies at once, diminishing the individual but ennobling him or her through the medium of the collectivity". [27] I noted earlier that the protagonists' victories come from uniting in collective action as a group; they also find more low-level, day-to-day satisfaction in uniting to enjoy their leisure time as men who have done their required work and are off the clock until the next day. Having been squeezed by social and political circumstances into a position where they are displaced from their expected roles and responsibilities, and resigned themselves to a lack of meaningful control in the long term, short-term moderately carnivalesque enjoyment is what is left to embrace, given that, as the lyrics of "That's Livin' Alright" say: "Tomorrow you'll be back on the site".

The popular success of *Auf Wiedersehen, Pet*'s blend of comedy and drama elements can be seen as marking the advent of various developments in television. One was the introduction of overtly 'hybrid' genres and labels like comedy-drama or dramedy, both of which gained in currency in the late-1980s. Another was increasing recognition of the ability of regional identities to be present on TV in roles that extended beyond the confines of stereotypes, comic relief or sentimental tales of unalleviated class-based suffering. Finally, something which struck a chord with many viewers was the show's highly relatable depiction of working-class men struggling to deal with changes in their domestic and working lives.

It continues to be the object of enduring fandom forty years on from its first broadcast, with active fan forums still discussing the show, and a sell-out 40th anniversary live event in Newcastle featuring members of the original cast. Baker and Hoey argue that *Minder*, another ITV comedy drama of the period that offers a London-based epitome of Thatcher-era contradictions, does not endorse British pretensions to greatness, but instead, "its depiction of likeable low-life characters, trapped in an ossified class structure safeguarded for the ossification of the self-regarding rich, is more an indictment of the seemingly perpetual hankering after past glories that continues to skew public and political life in the UK". [28] Much of this is present in *Auf Wiedersehen, Pet,* yet it offers different satisfactions comprised of a nostalgic yearning for a more secure past version of masculinity, alongside the temporary but finally available pleasures of collective social action and leisure. Importantly, it uses its comedy framing to set up what we can see as a condition-of-England comedy, enabling the examination of contemporary social life and politics but also fulfilling the requirements of a mainstream show and entertaining large and varied audiences.

© Joanne Knowles

1. This was long before the term 'comedy-drama' entered the mainstream. Thirty years later, in 2013, TV critic Mark Lawson can be found referring to it as an 'increasingly fashionable tag', Lawson, M (2013) 'The Americans, Love and Marriage and the rise of hybrid TV genres'. *The Guardian*, 04/06/ 2013. Editor: Comedy-drama equally fits another La Frenais 1980s creation/adaptation, *Lovejoy*.
2. Roddam, F and Waddell, D, *The Auf Wiedersehen, Pet Story: That's Living Alright*. BBC Books, 2003, p. 17).
3. Cited in Roddam and Waddell, p.17.
4. Clement and La Frenais, *More Than Likely: A Memoir* (Weidenfeld and Nicholson, 2019, p. 5.
5. Cited in Roddam and Waddell, p. 46.
6. Cooke, Lez, *British television drama: a history*. London: BFI. 2015 2nd edition, p. 141.
7. Schlesinger, P, et al. *Televising Terrorism: political violence in popular media* (Commedia Publishing, 1983, p.77).

8. Green, I, 'Ealing in the comedy frame'. In Curran, J. and Porter, V (eds) *British Cinema History*. (Weidenfield and Nicholson, 1983, p. 207).
9. Cited in Roddam and Waddell, p. 48.
10. Cited in Roddam and Waddell, p. 58.
11. Cited in Roddam and Waddell, pp. 59-62.
12. Cited in Roddam and Waddell, p .62.
13. Cited in Roddam and Waddell, pp. 95-105.
14. Morley, D, *Family television: cultural power and domestic leisure* (Commedia, 1986, p. 61).
15. Morley, p. 121.
16. Morley, p. 136.
17. Morley, p. 82.
18. Morley, pp. 86-87.
19. Morley, p. 93.
20. Gray, A, *Video playtime: the gendering of a leisure technology* (Routledge, 1992, p. 123).
21. Jackson, B and Saunders, R, eds. *Making Thatcher's Britain* (Cambridge University Press, 2012, p.172.
22. Jackson and Saunders, p. 174.
23. Wickham P, *The Likely Lads* (Palgrave Macmillan for BFI Books, 2008, p. 23).
24. Ian Miles, *Demystifying Social Statistics* (Pluto, 1989, p. 51).
25. Stern, B, 'Historical and personal nostalgia in advertising text: the fin de siècle effect'. *Journal of Advertising,* 21:4, 1992, pp. 11-22. Tolley, Gail, 'The hidden history of homesickness' (Wellcome Collection: The Heart of Homesickness, 2020, part 2.)
26. Roddam and Waddell, p. 13.
27. Glazener, Nancy (1989) 'Dialogsubversion: Bakhtin, the novel and Gertrude Stein'. In: Hirschkop, K and Shepherd, D (eds.) *Bakhtin and Cultural Theory*. (Manchester University Press, pp. 109-129).
28. Baker, S and Hoey, P, 'The picaro and the prole, the spiv and the honest Tommy in Leon Griffith's *Minder*', *Journal of British Cinema and Television*, 15:4, p. 529).

ARMED AND ARMOURED WITH LAUGHTER: *DESMOND'S*

"Channel 4 was set up on the ethos of actually having multi-racial production companies...and trying to champion various new voices." [1]

Trix Worrell is arguably best known as the creator of Channel 4's longest-running sitcom, *Desmond's* (1989-94). It represented the writer's first foray into situation comedy, and in many respects the show helped to revolutionise and re-energise the genre, yet we can find his acute social commentary about 1980s Black Britain fermenting in earlier 'straight' dramas, including a one-off play which Worrell originally wrote as a piece of theatre. Ironically, it was a play script that won a Channel 4 award but then nearly didn't get made into a televised drama. [2]

In the forty-minute play *Just Like Mohicans* (1985), the Saint Lucian-born Worrell had already displayed both his ability and desire to explore Black Britain in intriguing contexts. Initially, we are plunged into a dimly lit night-time underworld of bored teenagers roaming the streets. We follow a black seventeen-year-old, Barrington (Gary Beadle), as he breaks into a house with two white mates, looking to burgle the property, only to discover that the owner is a seemingly vulnerable, elderly black widow, Shirley (Mona Hammond).

Once the other two thieves have left, the initial menace of violence and flick-knives subtly evolves into a two-handed drama in which the characters gradually share their contrasting backgrounds. Barrington is not as 'cocksure' as he first seemed, nor is Shirley the meek-and-mild victim we may have assumed. It becomes a story about immigration and roots, the problems of forging an identity and a sense of belonging as a black person in Britain. Worrell is keen to break through cultural stereotypes: Shirley, for example, does not look back on her old life in Jamaica with rose-tinted glasses. For Barrington, who has served time in a youth detention centre, there is a sense of not belonging anywhere. He barely understands his older family members when they use Caribbean patois; he has never visited his parents' home island, Saint Lucia. Equally, he felt uninspired, alienated and was bullied as a black kid at school in London, and senses that his current white friends are just as likely to mock him or drop him when it suits them.

Despite the sense that Barrington and Shirley become – albeit briefly – secret sharers, Worrell never allows the play to become too cosy. Having grasped the opportunity to bear his soul, Barrington still steals her late husband's silver cigarette case from her at the end. Yet there is a genuine warmth at the heart of a drama played out in the context of a mid-1980s society built around marginalisation, unemployment and consumerism. We are left with the feeling that Barrington – who reveals himself to be intelligent, articulate and sensitive – has a potential which only Shirley has seen and fired up. Rather than offer us a didactic message, the playwright leaves us to decide whether Barrington has self-destructed or has been let down by the system: school, detention centre, probation officers, family, the wider community etc. Either way, we are left with a powerful and overwhelming sense of disconnection.

Having won Channel 4's *Debut* writing competition, Worrell was invited to come up with a new concept for a black sitcom. What followed was a genuine moment of serendipity. Sitting on the top deck of a Number 36 bus, riding from Peckham into central London, at a red traffic light he took in the scene at a West Indian barber shop:

"It was called Fair Deal, and there were these barbers, their noses pressed against the front window, chirpsing the girls walking past. And I could see the customers in their chairs, half-lathered and half-shaved, waiting to get their hair cut, but thinking nothing of it." [3]

It was a 'lightbulb' moment for the writer, who had been unsure what to present to producer Humphrey Barclay. While there had been Black British sitcoms before *Desmond's*, including *The Fosters* (1976-77) and *No Problem!* (1983-85), Worrell's concept would be very different from the domestic sitcom approach, centring instead on a sense of community:

"The black barber is...a drop-in...a space where black people can just be black." [4]

Persuading Barclay, though, about the setting for the sitcom proved to be a challenge. In Humphrey Barclay's words:

"My heart sank at his pitch. There had already been several series set in salons, which tended to feature ladies with blue hair. So I wasn't excited at all. But he shook his head and said, 'Have you ever been in a West Indian barber shop?' Then he started to tell me more. The more he told me, the more I liked it." [5]

Trix Worrell's recollections of his sales pitch to the producer include the following observation he made in his 'interview':

"This is not a barber's shop – this is a community centre. You don't go there to get your hair cut! You go there to eat, watch sport and talk bollocks. You might get your hair cut – but only if you give yourself three to four hours!" [6]

Given Worrell's previous 1980s scripts, including the effectively, unremittingly bleak portrait of Thatcherite Britain in *For Queen and Country* (1988), [7] *Desmond's* was always destined to be more than just a sitcom:

"We knew we were doing something different. I have to take my hat off to Michael Grade [Channel 4 chief executive] who supported us when it was a real risk. But it reflected the growing violence on the streets." [8]

233

Despite never having written comedy before, Worrell felt that there was a close connection between immigration, racial minorities and humour. In one recent interview, he refers to laughter as being part of the "armour as a migrant", [9] while in an earlier one he observed:

"If you're a minority in a predominantly white society, you have to laugh. Comedy is what keeps you going." [10]

While the initial idea for *Desmond's* came from that chance sighting (from the upper deck of a London bus) of a barber shop he used to frequent, a more deep-lying inspiration was the writer's anger at how he felt black people were being portrayed in the mainstream media, an issue tackled even in the opening episode:

"I didn't write *Desmond's* for black people. I wrote it for white people so they could see how black people really are. At that time, the negative press about muggings and shootings was all we seemed to get. I was fed up with it." [11]

We might describe Worrell's approach as using the safety net of situation comedy as a medium to voice something dissident and subversive, even countercultural. Humour as a means of questioning and breaking down stereotypes and prejudices. [12] In addition, by setting a sitcom in a *black* barber shop, it was inviting *white* viewers to step into a space they would never enter in real life. For them, there would be a sense of 'otherness'. This, in itself, arguably makes *Desmond's* a landmark series. As actor Ram John Holder would later remark:

"It's an important part of the cultural history of this country. An artistic achievement." [13]

Desmond's, like any television drama, was not created in a cultural vacuum; it was a product of its time and place. Nevertheless, it proved to be surprisingly popular in the US. It gradually built-up

234

British audiences of 5 million, but also had a lasting impact on the local community, evidenced by Theatre Peckham's 2019 sell-out event to celebrate the show's thirtieth anniversary. [14]

The casting of Norman Beaton and Carmen Monroe in the lead roles was all-important, and part of the joy of watching the series is the magical chemistry between them. The scenes they share offer us a master class in both comic timing and – when called upon – dramatic acting. In addition, it offered a deferential nod to *The Fosters* which they had both starred in during the 1970s.

The casting in general was spot on and the main characters who populate the barber shop all connect to Worrell's interest in people's (contrasting) dreams, fantasies, aspirations and challenges, as previously explored in *Just Like Mohicans*. While Desmond Ambrose (Beaton) has an idyllic dream of returning to his roots in his native Guyana, his more forward-thinking wife Shirley (Monroe) is happy to remain in her adoptive London and witness their children hopefully fulfilling their own ambitions. Older son Michael (Geff Francis) sees himself as a go-ahead (Thatcherite?) banker and entrepreneur, while daughter Gloria (Kimberly Walker) wants to establish herself as a career-minded, independent female. Younger son Sean (Justin Pickett), a talented musician and rapper, is a computer wizard and academically gifted, albeit prone to peer pressure. Perpetual student Matthew (Frederick Christopher Gyearbuor Asante) has fed his family back home in The Gambia a fantasy about being a successful businessman, while Porkpie (Ram John Holder) is a charming layabout who shares Desmond's nostalgia for Guyana and was a fellow member of the aptly named band Georgetown Dreamers.

In that sense, the characters offer us a fascinating melting pot of personalities and traits, ones which anyone can identify with, regardless of background. Holder observes that, in some respects, "It didn't matter if you were black or brown or white. It was the story of every family." [15] As *Guardian* columnist Ross Davies puts it, "its warmth transcends racial fault lines." [16] As if to emphasise this, as the series develops, several white characters are introduced and fully integrated into the barber shop world of chat, gossip, dominoes and – if the customer is lucky – an occasional haircut. Some of the comedy revolves around the fact that Desmond is a terrible barber, and woefully outdated in the haircuts he provides younger customers. The introduction of young, trendy Tony (Dominic Keating) early in the first run (of six episodes) is a masterstroke. First, he is a white guy who appreciates 'black music' from the Desmond/Porkpie era, illustrating how music can connect people from different ethnic and age backgrounds. In addition, the Desmond/Tony exchanges about their profession are a source of cracking comedy:

Desmond: You gonna cut my wife's hair?!
Tony: Look, Desmond, we've been through this thing before: you cut hair and I style it. You chop and I caress.
Desmond: You caress my wife and I'll chop *you*!

Barber shop banter is part of *Desmond's* enduring charm. Much of the humour centres on the bickering between the Ambrose family members, a reminder that despite the barber shop setting there is still more than an element of the domestic sitcom. In addition, while in many respects *Desmond's* is an atypical sitcom, it still draws on running gags, and quirky 'side' characters, many of whom offer what soon become familiar interjections, such as the snobbish intellectual Matthew boring everybody with his "old African sayings".

Given that the remit of *New Waves* is to exclusively explore 1980s tv, only the initial series of *Desmond's* fits into the timeframe, a reminder that television shows do not respect all-too-neat decade divides. Indeed, in this latter half of my chapter, I am going to focus my attention exclusively on the opening episode. It is worth observing, though, that over the course of its six series and 71 episodes, the writers were able to explore a variety of subjects not usually found within a 'traditional' sitcom: 'random' police checks on black men; teenage knife culture; single mothers; poverty; menopausal depression; muggings; adoption; unemployment; the questionable nature of YTS schemes; cultural differences and conflicting senses of identity between migrants and their British-born children. The barber shop is even held up by a pair of confused teenagers in a two-parter. Each of these topics is tackled through comedy, but the viewer is left to find a more serious undercurrent, if s/he chooses to read between the lines. As Worrell had envisaged from the start, he wanted to reflect the times, specifically – though not exclusively – from a black perspective.

There is no sense of the first episode representing a pilot or introductory story. It instantly offers us a distinct flavour of what *Desmond's* would be bringing to the world of the 'British' sitcom…

French Lessons seamlessly and effortlessly introduces us to almost all the main characters, in addition to the charmingly haphazard, dysfunctional, yet welcoming world of a barber shop which regular visitors like Porkpie and Matthew treat as a free café/social club. Shirley is immediately established as someone with a dry sense of humour. Having surprised her daughter by instantly identifying which Bronte sister wrote *Jane Eyre*, she comments:

"I used to have a brain once, you know. It's just that I put it away when I married your father."

Underneath the humour, there is the frustration of an intelligent, well-read woman pigeonholed by her family as wife-mother-cook. Shades of *Butterflies*, apart from the culinary skills! Desmond is swiftly introduced as a somewhat vain, loveable grump, stuck in his musical past back in Guyana and out of touch with the younger generation. As he stares into the barber mirror, his opening line in the series is the briefest of soliloquys:

"Desmond Ambrose! 57, boy, and still handsome!"

Despite the delightfully witty, quickfire dialogue, Worrell often spikes it with more serious undercurrents, such as Desmond reminding Matthew that *The Sun* is unwelcome in his barber shop because of its racism and sexism. Rather than making it a didactic comment, it comes coated in a layer of humour, as does Desmond's attempt to lay down a 10.30 pm curfew for his daughter and her friend:

Gloria: That's too early. We're only going down the road.
Desmond: I know what I'm worried about: muggers, rapists and perverts -
Gloria: Dad, it's alright. We know who they are – we go to school with them.

The 'generation gap' provides much of *Desmond's* humour, whether it is the youngsters lacking interest in their West Indian roots, Desmond baffled by his younger son's rap poetry and computer skills, or wide-boy wheeler-dealer Lee (Robbie Gee) showing off his £100 new suit, leading to a typical exchange:

Lee: What do you think, eh? Miami Vice?
Porkpie: For a suit like that you need legal advice.

As much as anything else, the opening episode swiftly establishes that Worrell's characters are realistic, and fully rounded, rather than cardboard caricatures. For example, teenage Gloria and her white girl friend Louise (Lisa Geoghan) are academic and independent-minded, but that doesn't prevent them from sitting around discussing men's faces (and imagining their bums) from a 'male order' dating agency catalogue. Worrell is offering us a subtle soufflé of humour, satire and social commentary whisked into a sitcom that is more than just 'comedy':

"I don't write comedy. I can't retain a joke. However, if it is a character with comic flaws or comedy within them, I can put that person in a situation and make you laugh." [17]

In a quite brilliant scene towards the end of *French Lessons*, where Desmond and Shirley argue over both her late night out with a male French teacher and his ongoing dreams of building a house back in Guyana, we have a perfect example of the show's desire to push beyond comedy:

Shirley: Stop dreaming, Desmond. This is England 1989 and we're no nearer building a house back in Guyana now than we were in 1969.
Desmond: You think I aint going to make it? You think I aint going to get there? Well, I'm going to build that house if it's the last thing I do, even if I don't live there. It would be for the children, so they can know their country of origin, their culture, its roots. So if one day Thatcher decides to throw us out, we have somewhere to go to. [18]

It is a moment and comment where the "raucous" live audience (which the series was recorded in front of) quietly applauds, yet you sense that there is a hesitant poignancy to their muted reaction. It is a reminder that *Desmond's* is full of characters with roots, dreams, fantasies and fears, many of which were shared by some of the viewers.

In this first episode, Trix Worrell introduces us to the warmth, camaraderie, banter and humour of the barber shop. A space which – as I cited earlier – he described as somewhere "black people can just be black." This is, arguably, a half-truth, illustrated by the references to *The Sun* and Margaret Thatcher. The cruel outside world can encroach at times. Nevertheless, there are also positive cultural references in the episode. Characters talk about aspirational black role models: Lloyd Honeyghan, John Barnes, Linford Christie and Daley Thompson. There is adversity outside that shop, but there are tangible hopes and ambitions too. That central paradox also plays out in the unmistakeable, catchy theme tune which Norman Beaton sings, *Don't Scratch My Soca*:

"From the long warm nights with an ocean breeze
To the damp and to the rain of London city.
We come from the sun to live in the cold,
I miss me rum, I want my coconut tree."

Yes, the lyrics remind us that there are exotic, precious things left behind in Guyana and other islands by the Windrush generation and now sorely missed in grey 1980s Britain. Yet Beaton/Desmond goes on to celebrate the positives:

"Don't scratch my soca
Til the party's over;
Let's keep the music sweet,
Whine up your waist and feel the beat." [19]

It is the rhythms and the beat of daily life that make *Desmond's* barber shop such a vibrant world to enter. Trix Worrell arms his cast and characters with humour and warmth. He described the show's live audience as being "off the Richter scale" [20] and the fun was shared by millions of television viewers. Little wonder that Danny Boyle shared a clip of the show in his 'best-of-British-TV' section at the Olympics' opening ceremony in 2012. [21]

Just Like Mohicans has retained much of its dramatic power, almost forty years on from its initial broadcast, thanks in no small part to the spellbinding central performances from Beadle and Hammond. [22] Its Windrush theme has lost none of its relevance, sadly. The latter is also referenced in *Desmond's* main titles sequence. There is plenty of connective tissue between Worrell's one-off drama and his long-running sitcom. However, *Desmond's* demonstrates that if a television writer wishes to tackle social issues which have been either ignored or misrepresented in the media, then using the genre of a sitcom can work brilliantly: both arming and armouring yourself with laughter.

© Rodney Marshall

1. Trix Worrell speaking at a BFI Q&A event, 08/02/2019. Worrell went on to explain that he felt that Channel 4 had lost its way in terms of that original ethos and he also stated that he would like to see the *Debut* writing award brought back: "I still think that having a broadcaster run a writers' competition for new voices is really significant because it is so difficult to get in."

2. At the BFI event, Trix Worrell explained: "What was difficult about that award was that I got paid for it, but there was no guarantee that they were going to screen it. So I just kicked up enough fuss and I said, 'So what's the point in having this sodding competition if I, as a writer for theatre, win this award and you're not even going to show it?' And the reason they didn't want to show it was because single drama costs so much money. So, in the end we really took them to task about it. So, begrudgingly, they made it." In his BFI interview, Worrell explains that the theatre play ending differed from the televised version, and that it was a member of the cast at the Albany Theatre who entered the play for the Channel 4 competition. In fact, when Channel 4 rang him to congratulate Worrell on the award, he thought it was someone playing a joke and so he put the phone down on them. (BFI, 08/02/2019).

3. *Desmond's at 30, Guardian*, 04/01/2019.

4. *Desmond's at 30, Guardian*, 04/01/2019.

5. *Desmond's at 30, Guardian*, 04/01/2019.

6. *'You didn't go there to get your haircut!' – how we made Desmond's, Guardian*, 31/01/2022.

7. Trix Worrell also co-wrote the film script for the Denzel Washington movie *For Queen and Country* (1988) which was not a commercial success but was praised by, amongst others, Caryn James in the *New York Times*: "With a cruel, keen edge, this taut social drama slices deeply into Thatcher's England to expose a grim underbelly of racism, cynicism and despair." 19/05/1989.

8. *Desmond's at 30, Guardian*, 04/01/2019.

9. *Great British Life*, 01/10/2022.
10. *Desmond's at 30, Guardian*, 04/01/2019.
11. *Desmond's at 30, Guardian*, 04/01/2019.
12. In this respect, one might compare Worrell's use of the sitcom genre with Rod Serling's use of sci-fi/fantasy. Serling instinctively knew that it would be easier to make powerful social observations under the safety net of a show like *The Twilight Zone*, and this may equally apply to comedy, so often a great vehicle for dissident voices.
13. *Desmond's at 30, Guardian*, 04/01/2019.
14. The sell-out event brought some of the original cast back together with Trix Worrell for a Q&A after professional actors had read the first ever script while youth theatre members acted it out. Afterwards, Worrell commented: "The evening has moved me beyond words. The inclusive remit and the strong sense of community at Theatre Peckham was there for all to see...I saw young people, none of whom were born when it first aired, capture the spirit of the show and make it their own." (*Southwark News*, 16/01/2019). In a *Guardian* interview, Trix Worrell observed that "Black Entertainment Television, a TV network in America, started showing *Desmond's*, which gave us a great platform." He referenced Whitney Houston and Ice Cube as being amongst the show's celebrity fans. In the same article, Ram John Holder claimed that Nelson Mandela was also a fan of the show. *'You didn't go there to get your haircut!' – how we made Desmond's, Guardian*, 31/01/2022.
15. *Desmond's at 30, Guardian*, 04/01/2019.
16. *Desmond's at 30, Guardian*, 04/01/2019.
17. *Great British Life*, 01/10/2022.
18. In a cruel example of life imitating art, *Desmond's* came to an end due to Norman Beaton's ill health and the actor returned to Georgetown, which had also been Desmond Ambrose's dream. Beaton passed away a few hours after arriving at the airport. Desmond's death – in honour of the

actor – is referenced in the first episode of the spin-off series *Porkpie* (1995-96).

19. 'Whine' is Caribbean patois for the way you move your waist in circles while keeping the rest of your body still. Norman Beaton was a talented calypso singer, with a Number 1 hit to his name before emigrating to England. In Liverpool he played guitar with what became the Liverpool Poets. He went on to write musicals.

20. *Desmond's at 30*, Guardian, 04/01/2019.

21. Despite going on to further success, working with major companies in LA, and winning several awards, Trix Worrell reflected on the 30th anniversary of the series: "When I started out, they made braver choices in television. While there might be all these workshops today to increase the presence of minorities on screen, it's just about boxes being ticked." (*Desmond's at 30, Guardian*). At the BFI event he backed this up by saying: "It just feels like they're ticking boxes and what writers really want is experience. They want their voices to be heard." (BFI, 08/02/2019). Worrell's comments open an interesting debate about both commissioning and casting. They also serve as a reminder of how *Desmond's* offered viewers a sitcom which seemed to fit naturally into its late-1980s (and early-90s) landscape.

22. Mona Hammond and Carmen Monroe were two of the founders of Talawa Theatre Company in 1986, today the primary black theatre company in the UK. Hammond was later cast as Monroe's flirtatious sister Susu in the first series of *Desmond's*. Although Susu is a character introduced for chaotic comic effect, she also offers Desmond a warning that he is remembering Guyana with rose-tinted glasses.

THE COMIC STRIP PRESENTS... PASTICHE, TRUTHS AND EVERYTHING IN BETWEEN. OR, FIVE GO MAD ON 1980s CULTURE, SOCIETY AND POLITICS

2nd November 1982 marked the start of a new television age. A fourth channel began broadcasting for the first time in Britain. Channel 4 launched its programming late afternoon, with its key programmes being *Countdown* at 4.45 (still running at the same time today!), *Brookside* at 8pm (a soap drama, considered ground-breaking for its time), the first ever *Film on Four* production *Walter*, at 9pm, and its late night offering *The Comic Strip Presents* at 10.15 pm. The original Channel 4 press pack called *The Comic Strip Presents* a "taster...of highly individual films" suggesting that the new series would be different compared to other anthologies and comedy shows. [1] This description is in tune with the Independent Broadcasting Authority (IBA) remit for The Fourth Channel, namely that it will "have its own distinctive character...take advantage of freedom, enterprise and experiment...addressing sections of the audience who want something particular...or different". [2] Indeed, those references to "distinctive", "experiment", and "different" could be describing 'alternative comedy' itself, a new wave which had arrived on the scene not long before the new channel...

Margaret Thatcher became Britain's first female Prime Minister in May 1979, the same month in which the Comedy Store opened in Soho. It is a venue which many see as representing the beginning of 'alternative comedy'. Both the performers at the Comedy Store itself (in Dean Street) and Peter Richardson's 'breakaway' Comic Strip cabaret (in Walker's Court), also situated in Soho, were seen –

244

like Channel 4 – as pioneers, offering new types of material, and breaking away from the traditional fare of stand-up comedy, much of which by now seemed outdated and offensive with its Working Men's Club repertoire of mother-in-law jokes and racial and sexual stereotyping. The Comic Strip pioneers were Alexei Sayle, Rik Mayall, Adrian Edmundson, Nigel Planer, Dawn French, Jennifer Saunders and Richardson himself. While the twinned timing of Thatcher becoming PM and the Comedy Store opening in May 1979 is purely coincidental, we might argue that Thatcherism created the perfect conditions for this new wave of comedy to thrive. As Peter Richardson would later comment: "[Thatcher] gave us something to write about". [3] Historian Gavin Schaffer backs this up with the observation that "Thatcherism created an atmosphere where alternative comedy could thrive". [4] Nevertheless, it would be misleading to label all of these performers as rebellious, radical and motivated by a political agenda. Some of them, such as Sayle, no doubt saw comedy as an agent for social change, while others saw it as something principally to be played for laughs. 'Alternative comedy' certainly gave more of a voice to female and minority comedians, but how revolutionary was it? Many of the individuals emerging in the alternative comedy scene were still university educated, albeit via polytechnic and red bricks (unlike their Oxbridge 1960s satire boom predecessors). [5] Schaffer observes that the backgrounds of many of these new performers was hardly 'alternative':

"Despite their claims of breaking down social elitism, the alternative comedians emerged almost exclusively from university-educated, middle-class communities, the same breeding ground as their comic predecessors in the satire boom—and many punk bands". [6]

The televised *The Comic Strip Presents* – the subject of this essay – had its roots in the Comic Strip cabaret which had run at the Raymond Revuebar (1980-81) and subsequently gone on successful tours of the UK and Australia. The format for the Channel 4 series of self-contained mini-films was that the cast would consist of (mostly) the same actors each week but with a completely different plot, not too dissimilar in that respect from classic British comedy *Carry On* films, perhaps a stylistic link between classic and 'alternative' comedy. Its debut on the opening night of Channel 4 reflected the fact that alternative comedy was at the forefront of Channel 4 programming.

The very first episode of *The Comic Strip Presents*, *Five Go Mad in Dorset*, was a 1980s pastiche of Enid Blyton's *The Famous Five* novels. The latter were still popular books, despite their outdated attitudes to class and gender. *Five Go Mad in Dorset* demonstrates – and exaggerates – to the audience the full extent of just how outmoded the original books now were, while also reflecting on 1980s prejudice. One of the first scenes shows the children arriving at a railway station, with a porter sorting out their luggage, who happens to be black, with the children laughing. "I say Julian, that man looks foreign!" "I expect his name's Gollywog!" "Yes, or Tarzan!" "I think we'd better call the police just as soon as we get back to Kirrin cottage". The porter ends up walking the entire way with a push wagon of suitcases, and as soon as he gets to the cottage, the police drive by and arrest him. There are layers to the comedy here: satirising the outdated attitudes of the original books; a rebellion against racist jokes from 70s comedy; and commenting on modern police attitudes. This minority character is not the butt of the joke to the audience, only to the fictional children.

By 1982 there was still a lack of 'minority comedians'; even the main line up of *The Comic Strip* troupe were all white. It was Channel 4 where many minority comedians, writers, actors and other creatives first got their chance on primetime television. [7] One of the key ideals in alternative comedy was that it was there to "reject ... the easy techniques of racist jokes", contrasting to traditional stand-up where there was plenty of stereotypical profiling and jokes about ethnic minorities. [8] One of Channel 4's ideals was to be liberal in what it broadcast. "Channel 4 can represent minority groups and minority interests", again referring back to its targets as set by the IBA. [9]

Another scene in *Five Go Mad in Dorset* sees the children, having arrived at the cottage, eating dinner. "Thanks Anne, you really are a proper little housewife, not like George, she still thinks she's a boy!" "I think it's stupid being a girl, I wish I was a boy!" "Really George, it's about time you gave up thinking you're as good as a boy!" George is the outlier; a girl who does not want to conform to sexist stereotypes. The pigeonholing of the 'proper little housewife' offered a comedic contrast for 80s female viewers in a postindustrial society where an increasing number of women were embracing their freedom to take up a career, be financially independent, and spend less time in the kitchen, partly thanks to the emergence of 'convenience foods', such as the legendary Marks and Spencer's oven ready Chicken Kiev, launched like Thatcher and the Comedy Store in 1979!

Upon discovering a criminal, the children are unimpressed: "Urgh, what a horrible common voice he's got!" "Oh well, I suppose I better go down the police station and get nicked then". This attitude that the working classes must obey the middle and upper classes – famously satirised in the 1966 Frost Report class sketch – was, arguably, less prevalent by the 80s. After all, Thatcherism – in theory – allowed people to work their way up in society: starting their own businesses, buying their own council houses. There were, seemingly, fewer social barriers in place. Nevertheless, it would be naïve to assume that elitism and class snobbery had been eradicated.

The final scenes in *Five Go Mad in Dorset* show the children ratting out their own uncle for being homosexual. "Who would have thought that of Uncle Quentin?" "I'm glad he's been safely locked up, I never liked him one bit anyway". Is there a reflection, here, of the very mixed public attitudes towards male homosexuality in the

1980s? More liberal approaches had been adversely affected post-1981 by HIV/AIDS, with some people fully believing that they could die if they came in close proximity to gay men. In response to this media-fuelled panic, there were also increased gay rights protests. Of course, in the original context of *The Famous Five*, being different in any way would have been frowned upon.

Music, fashion, society, as well as comedy, continually evolve. One of the most noticeable changes during the 70s was the rise of both heavy metal and punk: movements which had their own subculture of music, fashion and ideals. The fourth *Comic Strip Presents* film, *Bad News Tour* (1983), follows the fictional titular band in this mockumentary style film. *Bad News* has four members, each a varying degree of anarchist. *Bad News*, being 'alternative music', share some similarities to alternative comedy. Most of the band members are actually middle class. Rik's character enjoys a comfortable lifestyle at home but lies about it and exaggerates his anarchic acts. He is only a part of the band because he brings the PA system and pays for things, tying in with the sense that left-field music, like comedy, was still predominantly made by the middle class. "We're just not simply heavy metal...we're trying to break a few barriers." "Are we?" The early 80 music scene was a paradoxical one. There was a barrier or divide in the music world, between anti-establishment anarchist music and the songs that became popular hits, which tended to be far less explicit about ideals. Yet, at the time *Bad News* aired, there was still a wide variety of musical genres represented in the charts, in an era before the Stock, Aitken and Waterman's Hit Factory.

The 1980s saw a revolution in media consumption: the VHS (and the higher quality, but shorter lived, Betamax) had become widely available, and more affordable, to the average household. This meant that, for the first time, viewers could buy or rent a film they wanted to see as and when they chose, without having to wait for a television repeat. The emergence of the VCR also meant that you could record live TV to watch at leisure, with no more rushing home from work to desperately try to catch something or missing an episode and hoping for a repeat. This was, after all, an era when even soaps did not have a weekend omnibus until 1991, with the first to do so being Channel 4's *Brookside*. [10]

However, VHS tapes could be illegally copied, leaving a new black market open for pirated videos. Unregulated tapes of so-called Video Nasties became popular, films that were unfit for cinema exhibition, often bizarre horror films or blatant pornography. These Video Nasties could be brought straight into a family home. This meant that children could watch wildly inappropriate material, especially in those financially better off households where a child might have their own TV and VHS player, and share dodgy tapes acquired from school friends. It was not until the introduction of the Video Recording Act 1984 (VRA) that age ratings became mandatory on home released media. [11] *Dirty Movie* aired in January 1984, at the very height of moral panic surrounding Video Nasties, and it was not until the September that the VRA was introduced.

Bean (played by Adrian Edmondson), the postman, gets excited by news of a 9am screening of 'The Sound of Muzak', a film that happens to be his favourite and which is being shown at a good time for his shifts. Little does he know that he is about to deliver a film to the cinema manager's home address, one which Terry Toadstool (cinema owner Rik Mayall) is eagerly awaiting. The film delivered is a 'dirty movie', which is disguised with a sticker reading 'Sound of Muzak'. Naturally, Toadstool was not expecting anyone to turn up to watch a film showing at the unheard-of weekday morning slot; he was planning on watching the 'dirty movie' by himself. In reality, explicit erotica was banned from cinema exhibition by the BBFC and Toadstool is already breaking the law by attempting to screen such a film. Morning weekday viewings were rare back in 1984, with cinemas opening for afternoon matinees and evening films. One was more likely to find a midnight screening than early morning. Bean points out that such early showings would be beneficial to shift workers such as himself: "A 9 o'clock showing? How enterprising". Many working-class people would have been shift workers, and did not have 9-5 jobs, so would often struggle to see evening films, especially on weekdays.

Toadstool eventually gets the film rolling. It is revealed to the audience that Bean's traffic warden wife moonlights in 'adult films' and turns out to be the star of this particular film. *Dirty Movie* shows Bean and his wife as a happy couple; Bean has no idea about his wife's double life. If he had got into the screening, he would have been doubly disappointed: that it was not the film he wanted to see, *and* the revelation that his wife was working for the porn industry. The rise of the 'permissive society' since the 1960s was something Thatcher was seen to attempt to reverse, with a return to so-called Victorian values and modesty. Throughout the 1970s 'soft' erotica had been easily available and not barred under the Obscene Publications Act, tabloids had 'Page 3 models', and magazines such as *Penthouse* were readily available in newsagents, not limited to special licensed adult shops. Ironically, the new VCR culture – and satellite television – would contribute towards thwarting Thatcher's plans.

Another major theme in *Dirty Movie* is police brutality, corruption and incompetence, all of which were being heavily scrutinised in the 80s. 1981 saw riots take place in Toxteth, and the infamous Brixton Riots, where the Metropolitan Police came under fire – literally and metaphorically speaking – for being racist. So much so that Lord Scarman was enlisted to complete a report about the force. There was a lot of public distrust in the police. There was a popular image of the force as being full of ignorant males wanting to affirm their masculinity and flaunt weapons, rather than concerning themselves with public safety. [12] In *Dirty Movie* there are two policemen on a stakeout looking out for what their inspector terms "photography, hard photography", corrected by the uniformed officers to "pornography", furthering the idea that even commanding officers were incompetent. The slapstick comedy revolves around a series of bungles: a stakeout of what turns out to be their own inspector's house, rather than Toadstool's; an attempted raid on the film screening, where they drive into a parked car...There are topical jokes (and physical gags) about police brutality. The references to violence and corruption make *Dirty Movie* very much a product of its time, mirroring public distrust and stereotypes of British policing during the (often volatile) 1980s.

It would be hard to address the 1980s without talking about Margret Thatcher's policies, especially with regards to the whole notion of the enterprising individual and self-made man. Thatcherism was based on ideals of self-help, using one's own initiative and starting a business, even as a way of escaping unemployment, tied to the notion that anyone, from any walk of life, could start their own successful business. This was a key feature of 1980s popular television entertainment. Del Boy (*Only Fools and Horses*), Arthur Daley (*Minder*) and Loadsamoney (Harry Enfield, *Saturday Live*) were all products of 1980s free enterprise and Thatcherism. [13] However, none of these aforementioned characters delved into the music industry (although they may have dabbled slightly!).

Private Enterprise (1986) satirises the 1980s music industry. It is the second *Comic Strip* film to centre on it, but this film is based heavily on the music production side, with little emphasis on the performers. This instalment shows greedy music producers not caring for their artistes or the standard of music, simply concerned about rivalries with other producers, no matter what devious scheme they concoct to make the most money. *Bad News Tour* showed youthful optimism of the 70s; *Private Enterprise* shows purely money-making opportunists trying their luck in the music industry, without any passion for the product. Derek, the record producer (Nigel Planer), is shown to be purposely looking for a terrible band. "I must admit we're looking for a tax loss. I chose your band, and they are the worst of everything", cementing the notion that the industry values the quantity of money, not the quality of the music. Keith (Peter Richardson) steals a tape by the band Toy Department, after gate crashing a recording session whilst delivering toilet roll; there is no doubt a joke in there about the quality of music. "That's theft that is!" "I like to call it 'private enterprise'!" ... "Oh, what you nicked it?" "Borrowed it".

Much of the plot of *Private Enterprise* is dependent on one little compact cassette tape. Although in contrast to the rise of VHS tapes, compact cassette tapes have been around since the 1960s, it was the invention (in 1979) and rising popularity of the Sony Walkman that revolutionised the way we listened to music and increased the importance of cassettes. One could not easily listen to a 12" record on the go, and although many cars had some form of cassette player (often an eight-track), music was never fully portable. The Sony Walkman was a cassette tape player, and personal headphones, lightweight and, most importantly, pocket sized, meaning that it could be taken (almost) anywhere.

The late 70s and 80s saw significant changes in music, not only in terms of the sounds. Each genre of music had its own fashion, from the aforementioned Punk with spiked Mohawks and safety pin adorned ripped jeans, to Ska rock with Doc Martens and checkered blazers, and New Romantics with dramatic make-up, pixie boots and frilly shirts. Kitson (Rik Mayall, lead singer of Toy Department) is arguing with fellow band members: "Just because I dress more fashionably than you, I'm too pretty to know anything about music, am I?", suggesting that his New Romantic look directly accompanies the music inseparably, despite being told that his fashion choices are too distracting against the "demo tape 85" Toy Department are making.

Keith literally crashes into a music producer's office building and decides to walk in and pitch the tape that he stole. The producer agrees to launch the single with a 'mystery band' as a press gimmick, and for Keith to hide the fact that he does not know how to reach the band. It turns out the single becomes a hit, and not the terrible tax loss Derek was hoping for. It also transpires that the band have split up, moved to Sweden and are untraceable. Derek persuades Keith to find the band so that he can produce a tour. Out of desperation, Keith arranges it so that the venues where the band are going to play are all mysteriously destroyed before the concerts can begin. Instead of admitting that he stole a tape, Keith finds it easier to commit arson and pretend to be a terrorist. He ends up escaping arrest for fraud and arson. *Private Enterprise* ends with Keith, and accomplice Brian, acquiring plane tickets to leave the country and we see them driving down the motorway. Not one character has enjoyed a successful enterprising moment: neither the music producers, nor Keith, nor the band itself.

1980s television comedy wasn't all about 'alternative' voices. A favourite sitcom of the decade was *Hi-de-Hi!*, first airing in 1980. It allowed viewers to escape into a nostalgic portrait of post-war British holiday camps. It is often left out of 1980s social/cultural history discourse, due to its cosy and family friendly ethos: "too gentle, too conservative, too nostalgic to be fashionable". [14] Nevertheless, the 1980s represented tough times for many people, so escapism and nostalgia played a key part in keeping morale up. Two particularly noteworthy Comic Strip offerings were *A Fistful of Travellers Cheques* (1984) and *The Bullshitters: Roll Out the Gunbarrel* (1984), which both offer us nostalgic views of bygone times, although neither is done without pastiche and a critique of vanished eras.

Post-war cinema saw a rise in heroic action films, with the domineering genres being war movies and Westerns, the latter often romanticising the American Wild West. For British audiences, Westerns were exotic: after all, the Frontier – with its pioneering spirit – is a socio-geographical location and concept completely alien to us. The genre includes 'Spaghetti Westerns' made by directors like Sergio Leone, (mostly) shot in Spain, doubling up for America. Films like Leone/Eastwood's *A Fistful of Dollars* (1964) became iconic. *The Comic Strip Presents* visited Spain to offer its own distinctive homage.

A Fistful of Travellers Cheques was the first of *The Comic Strip* films to run for more than half an hour. Also of note, it was the first not filmed in Britain. Much of the comedy presented in this film was not strictly alternative comedy. There was little in the way of 'new wave' political edge, but rather classic pastiche, which in itself could be considered nostalgic, as there had been many film parodies and spoofs before *The Comic Strip Presents*. There is also an element of "atmospheric comedy", where the *mise en scene* gives us more of the comedy than the script does. [15]

A Fistful of Travellers Cheques follows two West Country students on a holiday to Spain, wanting to do "the whole spaghetti Western thing", and pretending to act as hard men. The students, using fake names throughout, Carlos (Mayall) and Miguel (Richardson), are about twenty years of age. Being born in the early 60s, they would have grown up with Westerns during their formative years. Romanticised Western men, the ideal male? These characters certainly had some form of macho self-indulgence. Carlos and Miguel insist they are "mean, ugly, gun slinging bastards", although they struggle to keep up the tough persona: "How comes there's no soft toilet paper?" "You want soft toilet paper? You go to Hotel Gayboy". The fact that Carlos and Miguel are students suggests that they are more middle class than they appear; they can afford to take a holiday abroad whilst studying (a stark contrast to Rik's character in *The Young Ones*), and clearly have free time to enjoy watching classic Westerns, probably on videotape players. The 1980s saw a sharp rise in Britons taking holidays in Spain, cheap package deals and all-inclusive deals with warm sun was in stark contrast to the likes of Butlin's: cold, damp summer holidays in breezy coastal areas. There was also the availability of partying /clubbing holidays abroad. [16] Carlos and Miguel, being young students, would perhaps have been expected to go on a club 18-30 style holiday, when in fact they visit Spain for the sole purpose of pretending to be cowboys. We do not find out what Carlos' and Miguel's real names are, or indeed what they are actually studying.

The film ends with a fist fight in a café. Carlos and Miguel do not partake in the fight, instead indulging in a steak and rosé wine dinner (gourmet choices for students!) They leave the café, only to be confronted with armed police – with real guns, unlike the blanks they have been using. They look at each other and decide to shoot back. We do not see what the outcome is. It ends mid-action and we hear the sound of gunfire. We are left to assume that they have been injured or killed. Perhaps living, and dying, in a fantasy world was more preferable to British student life.

One of the best-known British television series which crossed over from the 1970s into the 80s was *The Professionals* (1977-83). Criminal Intelligence action heroes driving classic cars. Yes, it is now dated of course, but many fans look back on it fondly. Is this another example of the rose-tinted effect of nostalgia? *The Bullshitters* not only pastiches *The Professionals,* but also the actors' lives behind the camera. Bonehead (Keith Allen, playing Lewis Collins as Bodie) has started a training camp for TV tough guys; Foyle (Peter Richardson, parodying Doyle as played by Martin Shaw) is pushing his vegetarianism and performing in new wave artsy, 'socially aware' plays. By the later 1980s, the real-life Collins was heavily typecast and had a dwindling acting career. Although he did not open a "school for TV tough guys", he applied to join the Territorial SAS, but was rejected due to his celebrity status and all-too-recognisable face; maybe Collins missed a trick!

Like *A Fistful of Travellers Cheques*, *The Bullshitters* features an 'ideal male' from a previous era. Here we are presented with two slightly different offerings; the cunning anti-hero cowboy, maybe showing more brains than brawn, in comparison to *The Bullshitters'* caring, but tough male partner, the full-on all-hero action man. *The Professionals* has remained to this day a cult favourite, even if one now looks back on it as nostalgia TV, almost 50 years after it aired.

In contrast, *The Bullshitters* was from 1984, only one year after *The Professionals* ended. Was there already a nostalgia for the late 70s? Were people looking for escapist action-adventure fun?

The 1970s had also had its fair share of strikes, political disagreements and social issues, but did not have any equivalent of a decade-long era of Thatcherism, nor such a long-running mediatised conflict as the battle with the miners. *The Strike* aired in 1988 and follows a Hollywood production company making a film about the 1984 Miners Strike. Paul (Alexei Sayle) writes a screenplay about Welsh miners during the strike, based on his own experiences, and it grabs the attention of a production company, Golden Films, who "made their money from violent sex films". Paul had written a realistic Kitchen Sink plot, about Arthur Scargill and the everyday lives of miners in the South Welsh Valleys. However, Goldie (played by Robbie Coltrane, head of Golden Films) thinks the script is too boring and adds in action: "a mine collapse...a whole heap of miners trapped underground during a flash flood". This helps create a complete deviation from any form of social realism. The producer already has the idea that Arthur Scargill will be played with Hollywood action, "this Scarface – Scargill...this hunky hero". Al Pacino played the titular Scarface, who the company equates to Scargill, therefore decides that American audiences want to see the actor as Scargill. It is important to remember that the fake film *The Strike*, within *The Comic Strip* episode of the same name, is being made for an American Hollywood release. Eventually, the film within the film ends up as nothing short of "overblown commercial rubbish", with plots about Scargill saving his daughter from a mine collapse and threatening to blow up Sellafield. [17]

The Miners Strike of 1984 had created friction all round: between the workers themselves – those on strike and those refusing to strike; between miners and the police doing overtime to combat civil unrest; it also divided opinion within the general public and amongst politicians. The plot of *The Strike* becomes warped from any real event of the 1984 strike, sourcing its comedy (to British audiences) from its outrageousness. Ultimately, *The Strike* pastiches the film industry more than it does British socio-political history of the 1980s. This is partly because the strike had only finished three years earlier, so would have been considered too recent and raw to mock. Besides which, there was high unemployment and resentfulness amongst affected mining communities. [18]

The Comic Strip Presents followed a similar approach with its film *GLC: The Carnage Continues,* produced in 1989 but broadcast in 1990, with the format of a Hollywood blockbuster version of British historical events. There are certainly parallels between *The Strike* and *GLC*, with British actors playing Hollywood stars playing British political figures. Both films show overtly (fictionalised) Americanised views on British social issues and some of the comedy comes from the ridiculous idea of casting Al Pacino as Arthur Scargill, or Charles Bronson as Ken Livingstone. Both offer us a film-within-a-film and, whereas in reality a Kitchen Sink drama would have been more suited to tackle the two subjects, instead *The Comic Strip* sprinkles anarchic Hollywood glamour.

"You've never had it so good. Thanks to the Tories every household has a colour TV and the shops are all full of potatoes… vote for me for free enterprise."

Sir Horace Cutler (Leslie Phillips) is trying to maintain his place as leader of the Greater London Council. The real-life Cutler was an early advocate for privatisation of services, as well as council housing buying schemes, a sharer of Thatcherite ideas. In *GLC*, Cutler is shown to have a plan of flooding the docklands to make a resort marina. The London Docklands had been going through a major regeneration scheme under Thatcher. Perhaps it is not that far-fetched to imagine the real Cutler suggesting a luxury marina on the Thames.

There's a *Rocky* styled workout montage for Cutler's election campaign, Hollywood romanticised style, running parallel to

Livingstone cooking for the homeless. Upon the readout of the election results, Cutler has lost to Livingstone and is invited into the Prime Minister's office. "Mrs Thatcher will see you now". "You lost." "Yes, I'm sorry Mrs Thatcher, I really am." "Come here!" "I need a change." "You know what I'm going to do? I'm going to change your face". It turns out that Thatcher/Ice Maiden (Jennifer Saunders) is some sort of robotic killing machine, and physically mutilates Cutler's face. The comedy was feeding off the public mediatized image of the real-life Thatcher, the notion that she was The Iron Lady, which some opponents interpreted as characteristic of a cold, heartless robot.

Livingston immediately brings in a new cabinet, and notably chooses someone from a black minority background, with a stammering speech impediment, to be the new Lord Mayor: Sly, played by Gary Beadle, an entirely fictional character. "Halve the fares, old people travel for free." "Pardon sir?" "You heard me!" "Go to the bank, borrow money for CND, I want those cruise missiles out by Christmas!" "I want you to take care of the black minorities, set up theatres, sports centres, recreation grounds". "Start a new movement, call it gay pride, let's get those gays out of the closet." "Let's shake this city up". The real Livingstone did introduce cheaper bus fares as one of his first policies and did campaign for ethnic and sexual minority rights. Nevertheless, he was another divisive figure, looked up to as a hero by many, but also earning the nickname Red Ken, and a reputation of the GLC as the 'Loony Left' from critics in the right-wing popular press and government. [19]

We are introduced to a Lee Van Cleef styled Tony Benn (Peter Richardson). "If you're going to win, you need support of the party." "Screw the party, I'm doing this my way". The real-life Benn was a staunch leftist, if not Marxist, often appearing to be too left wing even for the Labour party. Benn was never a part of the real GLC, and in the film *GLC* Benn is clearly shown as someone independent of Livingstone's policies and ideas.

This fictional Thatcher is shown to be against whatever the public want. "She's banned the GLC, too popular." Livingstone visits the Prince of Wales (Adrian Edmondson) for help after realising Thatcher is out of control. Pottering in his garden, we have the satirical figure of the prince as an organic gardening enthusiast. "But you see, I have to remain impartial, it's very important for democracy!" The Beefeaters successfully drug him and hold him hostage. Livingstone hears and goes to break the prince out, in a full-on Hollywood action sequence. This is where *GLC* becomes a fully fictional Hollywood action film, bearing no resemblance to the actual decline of the GLC. Livingstone gets kidnapped and held hostage. Neil Kinnock (Derren Nesbitt) is portrayed as a bumbling politician unable to make a point, who is then shot by Benn out of frustration. There's a meta cameo where alternative comedians refuse to fight Thatcher, prioritising their careers, perhaps even an in-joke to the alternative comedians using comedy as a socio-political weapon, against those just simply wanting to make people laugh. The prince makes it to the balcony of City Hall: "The power of this country should rest with the people, and not with a woman whom one suspects is not of this Earth". The soldiers support the prince and Livingstone unconditionally, dropping their allegiance to Thatcher/Ice Maiden. Outraged, Thatcher then tries to kill Ken, but ends up being stabbed herself, bleeds yellow and howls. Definitely not human. It is suggested that this alien Ice Maiden was a being that had invaded Thatcher, controlling her, again a very Hollywood sci-fi ending. Underneath the far-fetched farce, we are left to decide if the Comic Strip was reinforcing the notions that Livingston was part of a 'loony left' and Thatcher inhuman/inhumane in her policies. [20]

The Comic Strip Presents was one of the first shows broadcast on Channel 4, on its landmark opening night. As the decade evolved, it played a role in 1980s popular culture, both reflecting and satirising the times. It was also a seminal show for alternative comedy, something which was becoming increasingly more mainstream. [21]

A new wave of anarchic comedy had arrived, and a new corporation – Channel 4 – provided a platform for it.

© Lucy Smith

1. Channel 4, Weekly Pack No 1, 02/11/1982.
2. *Television & Radio 1981*, ed. Eric Croston (Independent Television Publications Limited, 1980), p. 10.
3. Peter Richardson, *Laughing at the 80s*.
4. Gavin Schaffer, 'Fighting Thatcher with Comedy: What to Do When There Is No Alternative', *Journal of British Studies*, 55.1, (2016), pp. 374-397.
5. Editor: As if acutely aware of this, Rik Mayall, for example, who completed a degree in drama, later suggested that he did not turn up for the Finals' exams and had failed the course.
6. Schaffer, pp. 374-397.
7. Kamm Jürgen and Birgit Neumann, *British TV Comedies: Cultural Concepts, Contexts and Controversies* (Palgrave Macmillan, 2016).
8. Peter Rosengard, Roger Wilmut, *Didn't You Kill My Mother-In-Law?* (Methuen, 1989), p. xiii.
9. Dominic Strinati, *An Introduction to Studying Popular Culture* (Routledge, 2000), p. 167.
10. *TV Times* (Thames/LWT), 2-8 March 1991.
11. BBFC, *The Video Recordings Act*.
12. Lauren Piko, Evan Smith, 'Thatcher's Bloody Britain! Unemployment and Gender in Neoliberal Britain in The Young Ones and Men Behaving Badly', in *Gender and Austerity in Popular Culture: Femininity, Masculinity, and Recession in Film, TV and Literature*, ed. by Helen Davies, Claire O'Callaghan (CPI Group, 2017), pp. 87-110.
13. Editor: the creation of Arthur Daley predates the Thatcher government, but as the 80s evolved he does appear to satirically represent some of the Thatcherite policies.

14. Dominic Sandbrook, *Who Dares Wins: Britain, 1979-1982* (Penguin, 2019), p. 164.
15. Peter Rosengard, Roger Wilmut, p. 154.
16. Sina Fabian, 'Flight to the Sun: Package tours and the Europeanisation of British holiday culture in the 1970s and 1980s', *Contemporary British History*, 35:3, 2021, pp. 417-438.
17. Rosengard, Peter, Wilmut, Roger, p. 262.
18. Jonathan Winterton, 'The End of a Way of Life: Coal Communities Since the 1984-85 Miners' Strike.', *Work, Employment & Society*, 7.1, (1993), pp. 135-146.
19. Esther Webber, *The Rise and the Fall of the GLC* (2016) www.bbc.co.uk/news.
20. Editor: the film certainly satirises the right-wing press' vilification of Ken Livingstone, as in the tabloid headline, "Red Ken Ate My Baby!"
21. Editor: which, I guess, leaves us to debate whether comedy can be both 'mainstream' and 'alternative'.

CUFFY AND A DECADE

The 1980s. Like every decade since the 50s, it encompassed partial or full runs of countless television shows. However, 80s series seem to garner a disproportionate amount of attention from today's viewers compared to their predecessors from earlier decades. There are many possible reasons for this. 1980s series are more recent and therefore are still remembered by a larger portion of the population, who saw them during their initial run. 80s series also pick up new viewers due to their continued availability on retro television channels and streaming services. That availability can, in turn, be attributed to broadcasters believing these series will be better received by modern audiences than older shows, as they have more sophisticated production values and are not shot in black-and-white. Regardless of the reasons for the continued popularity of so many 80s series, it only seems fair that some of the pages of this book be used to give a series that has received relatively little attention over the years a turn in the spotlight. Hence the topic of this chapter: *Cuffy*, the 1983 sequel to the 1980-1981 ATV series *Shillingbury Tales*.

While *Cuffy* is unquestionably an 80s series, it is not a prototypical example of television from that decade. Indeed, from an aesthetic standpoint, only the fashions and hairstyles of some of the characters mark it out as taking place in the 80s. *Cuffy*'s quiet village setting is a timeless one, an anachronistic, bucolic locale free from the trappings and worries of contemporary life. This lack of modernity suits lead character Cuffy Follett to a tee, as he is an old-fashioned, anachronistic character, one who describes himself and his profession using the archaic term "tinker", and views modern technology either with suspicion (he is uncomfortable using the telephone) or as an entertaining novelty (advanced ovens and washing machines) or a means of turning a profit (buses full of tourists). The earthiness and simplicity embodied by the show's lead character and setting serve as a refreshing antidote to the predominant 80s culture, which became increasingly obsessed with money, power, and glamour as the years wore on. Indeed, the episode *Cuffy and a Fashion Show* directly acknowledges that the show is going against the cultural grain. It centres on fashion designer Tony Millington and his collaborator wife, Claudia, a prototypical 1980s power couple, who not only dress the part by donning the latest fashions, but also sell their designs to others in pursuit of the wealth and influence idealised by 80s culture. Seeking out a new marketing angle for their latest fashion line, the Millingtons decide to have a fashion shoot and show in Shillingbury precisely because its homespun aesthetic is the antithesis of what they and the other fashion lines embody, and will therefore stand out in the fashion world. *Cuffy*, similarly, stands out in the 80s television landscape by wilfully refusing to buy into the decade's trappings and trends.

That refusal does not make *Cuffy* the very best series that the decade has to offer. Its accent slants toward the comedic, with Cuffy getting into scrapes that devolve into cartoonish slapstick, making it ideal fodder for children. But, as the likes of *Catweazle* proved so brilliantly, it is arrogance, if not outright foolishness, to dismiss a series as having nothing of merit to say simply because it appeals to children. And *Cuffy*, despite being framed as tame family viewing, has much more to say than its slapstick set pieces suggest. Appropriately, given that the series is named after him, Cuffy is the means by which many of these messages are conveyed.

Cuffy and a Characterisation

First, however, it must be acknowledged that Cuffy, despite often being the vehicle for the show's messages, is far from a perfect character, neither deified nor depicted as preternaturally wise. In fact, in many instances, Cuffy is an irritant, and sometimes a liability, to those around him. Many of his attempts to assist others, particularly local farmer Jake, result in disaster and not insignificant amounts of property damage. For example, in *Cuffy and a Holiday*,

Cuffy knocks over a ladder while Jake is on it, sending Jake to the hospital. To make matters worse, Cuffy fails to call an ambulance due to his lack of proficiency with the telephone, and instead runs through the village telling everyone from local Mrs. Simpkins to the pub landlady to Reverend Norris to call for an ambulance or a doctor. As a result, a host of doctors and ambulances turn up at the farm, undoubtedly much to the displeasure of those in charge of the distribution of medical resources. Later, in a misguided attempt to be helpful and make amends, Cuffy visits Jake in hospital, only to eat all of the food he brings Jake, covet Jake's tea, and generally aggravate him. The *piece de resistance* occurs when Cuffy gets knocked off a ladder himself, winding up in the bed next to his unfortunate victim, leading a distressed Jake to contemplate a long, less-than-peaceful convalescence. In *Cuffy and a Fashion Show*, Cuffy is similarly disaster prone while participating in the titular fashion show, shooting an arrow that takes Mrs. Simpkins' hat off and pulling the set down while trying to unsnag a model's bridal veil from a prop. In *Cuffy and a Downpour*, Cuffy's pet sheep Calamity escapes and Cuffy and Mandy's pursuit of her causes them to leave a trail of destruction in their wake. Jake returns to his farm to find broken eggs, knocked over vats of milk, and a muddy Cuffy and Calamity in his bedroom, leading Jake to scream that Cuffy should be sent away to the North Pole where he cannot trouble people. If Cuffy and his catastrophic antics took place in real life, there is no question that Jake (and likely many others) would be in desperate need of insurance, and his premiums would be sky-high!

While many of Cuffy's disastrous attempts to render assistance stem from a genuine desire to help, or at least to be compensated for a job well done, the show does not depict him as wholly lacking in guile. Indeed, in some ways, Cuffy is a bit of a con artist. He has a habit of telling white lies, such as when he intentionally misdirects a model to a different town so he can take his place in a fashion show in *Cuffy and a Fashion Show*, and when he tells the Reverend's sister, who he is in love with, that he designs architectural monuments, paints, and conducts orchestras in order to impress her in *Cuffy and a Green Eye*. In *Cuffy and a Status Quo*, Cuffy uses subversive tactics to encourage the well-meaning parish council to sack him from the caretaker job they imposed on him, either performing his duties extremely lackadaisically – for example, when asked by the chairman to make tea for the parish council, Cuffy interrupts the proceedings to bring in the tray, tosses biscuits to each person at the table, makes noise and comments while the chairman is talking, throws sugar noisily into cups, reaches into a full teacup to remove excess sugar, and licks the spoon used to stir the tea – or adhering strictly to every rule regarding showing identification and paying for parking. He is similarly subversive in *Cuffy and a Carpet-bagger*, which sees him attempting to pay for a pint with a £10 note. The landlady tells him that she cannot make change for the large bill, and offers to let him pay for his pint later. Cuffy replies that he is happy to help her out by not giving her the money, and returns to his pint looking pleased with himself. A passing Jake sees what has happened and tells Cuffy that he is well-aware that he is working a con. Cuffy feigns being wounded by the accusation, protesting that he offered good money for the pint. Jake is not fooled, but does not make any effort to punish Cuffy for his behaviour. The fact that Jake comments on Cuffy's deception at all demonstrates that the occupants of the town are well-aware of Cuffy's manipulative tendencies, but generally let them go. This renders Cuffy's actions less dastardly – after all, the people who are being manipulated generally know they are being manipulated, and Cuffy knows that they know, so there is little or no real deception going on. The relatively mild nature of Cuffy's con artist tendencies becomes even more apparent when Cuffy gets himself mixed up with a genuine con artist later in the episode. Said con artist, Tom, pretends to befriend Cuffy, when, in fact, he is merely roping Cuffy in as an unwitting accomplice in his quest to relieve the residents of Shillingbury of their valuables. The fact that Cuffy is so easily drawn in by Tom demonstrates his naivety and the low stakes involved in his own conniving. In addition, Cuffy's shock and hurt when he discovers that Tom was only using him to rob his fellow villagers speaks to his inherent sense of honesty and unwillingness to perform any seriously devious acts. Telling Tom that he believed that they were friends, Cuffy expresses disappointment that all he received in return for the kindness he showed Tom was Tom eating the meat and potato pie that Mrs. Simpkins made for him and being arrested for unknowingly acting as a diversion while Tom committed his crimes. These comments speak to Cuffy's innocence, purity of heart, and character, and are so powerfully and sincerely professed that they make the glib Tom feel guilty for roping Cuffy into his scheme, to the point that he confesses to the police that he was the one behind the crimes, attests to Cuffy's innocence, apologises to Cuffy, ensures that Cuffy's £10 is returned to him by the police, and gives Cuffy another £5 as a goodwill gesture. Cuffy's interactions with Tom are therefore perhaps the best indicator of all that Cuffy, despite his white lies and small scams, is inherently good, capable of making even the most cynical and self-serving of people take a hard look at themselves in the mirror, a conclusion that is bolstered by Jake and the Reverend's willingness to act as character references when Cuffy is arrested along with Tom.

Along with his small-time scheming, another of Cuffy's less-than-flattering qualities is his penchant for emotional manipulation. He is not above using his plight as a man of few material resources to guilt people into providing him with whatever he needs or desires. For example, when caught out in the rain in *Cuffy and a Downpour*, Cuffy cuts the most woebegone, bedraggled figure possible in the hopes that Mandy, Jake's daughter, will take pity on him, override her father's wishes, and invite him to shelter in their warm, dry home until the rain has passed. However, it is revealed in the same episode that these bouts of emotional manipulation are not the products of a cunning individual who delights in preying on the goodwill of others in order to extract as much benefit for himself as possible. This becomes evident, ironically, shortly after Cuffy has wangled his way into Jake and Mandy's home to wait out the rain. While there, Cuffy tells his friends about his childhood, recounting how he lived with his mother and brother and another family in terrible council housing that was riddled with disease. Staring off

266

into the distance as he talks about how his brother got sick and died, it is clear that Cuffy is so caught up in his painful memories that he is not conscious of the effect his story is having on the people he is telling it to. Still distant, he explains to them that, after his brother's death, he and his mother went back to living outdoors because they believed being indoors was unhealthy. He also tells his friends that he has no memory of his father, and that his brother had a different father, but makes these statements frankly, without any indication that he feels ashamed of his parentage. Indeed, Cuffy speaks warmly about his mother, recounting how she was loving and played with and read to her children for hours on end. Cuffy then wistfully says that he wishes he knew how to read. What is notable is that Cuffy has clearly never told anyone in the village about his past before – both Jake and Mandy treat all of the information he imparts to them as new – meaning he has never thought to use it to emotionally manipulate his friends into doing him more kindnesses. Furthermore, Cuffy never mentions this painful chapter of his past again, to Jake, Mandy, or anyone else, even though it would be the perfect story to trot out whenever he wanted to guilt someone into giving him something. In addition, while he does mention on other occasions that he cannot read and write (*Cuffy and a Status Quo*), lost his one love interest to someone else (*Cuffy and a Green Eye*), and has never had a holiday (*Cuffy and a Holiday*), he does not frame these admissions in a way that would indicate that he is using them to wheedle something out of people. If Cuffy were truly a completely exploitive individual, out to get whatever he wanted using any means possible, he would happily milk his childhood tale of woe (and all of his other misfortunes) for all of it was worth. The fact that he does not, demonstrates that Cuffy is not as nakedly emotionally manipulative as he may sometimes appear.

Cuffy and an Economic Message

Because Cuffy is a flawed individual, but not egregiously so, he is the perfect vehicle to convey the series' many messages. His humble circumstances and imperfections demonstrate that one does not have to be irreproachably virtuous or wealthy to abide by the principles he models and adheres to. Many of these are demonstrated through Cuffy's way of life. While Cuffy's reasons for leading the lifestyle he does largely stem from the circumstances and events of his childhood, the show implies that there is also inherent wisdom in his decision to opt out of a conventional way of living in favour of something more unorthodox. Though it is highly unlikely that those behind the show believed that the average person should give up most of their worldly possessions, live in a dilapidated caravan, have only one set of clothes to their name, and rely on the kindness of strangers and whatever odd jobs they could scrounge to survive, there is a definite message woven throughout the series that urges the average 1980s person to reassess how they are living their lives and define 'success'. Perhaps the most explicit censure of the quintessential money-driven 80s way of life is contained in a story Cuffy tells Jake in *Cuffy and a Holiday*. In order to warn his friend about the perils of stress and drive home the need to rest, Cuffy tells Jake about the time he was in a pub with a man whose business had just received a large, lucrative order. Buoyed by this development and the influx of cash it promised, the man offered to buy drinks for everyone in the pub, then promptly dropped dead, the stress and excitement of his 'success' proving to be too much for him. Cuffy – as well as the show's creatives – clearly does not think much of the man or his life choices if he is telling the story as a cautionary tale.

Of course, one could argue that it is hypocritical for Cuffy to deride those who are caught up in their careers and their businesses when his own life is heavily dependant on the support of those in the community who have careers and businesses! In a decade in which people were encouraged to make their own way, therefore, why should Cuffy be allowed to opt out and expect the village to support his lifestyle choices? However, this perspective is very one-sided. While it is true that Cuffy is supported by the community, he offers plenty of value to the village in return, both with his labour and his mere presence. This is demonstrated on more than one occasion. In *Cuffy and a Holiday*, Cuffy takes a "vacation" from his work and regular routines. One would expect that the villagers would be relieved to have a break from having to support Cuffy. However, the villagers very quickly find that Cuffy's absence is not a welcome reprieve, but a source of inconvenience. Farmer Jake, typically annoyed when Cuffy shows his face, complains that Cuffy has left him short-handed at harvest time, while Mrs. Simpkins is irked when Cuffy refuses to mow her lawn.

A similar situation unfolds, to even more dramatic effect, in *Cuffy and a Status Quo*. Having determined that Ted Summer, the village hall caretaker, should retire, the parish council ponders who would be willing to take on the "rotten job" for the meagre salary that is paid for it. Three members of the council – Jake, Reverend Norris, and Mrs. Simpkins – then happen upon the "brilliant" idea that they should arrange for Cuffy to get the job by using their influence to persuade the chairman of the council that Cuffy is the ideal candidate. Their justification for giving Cuffy the job conforms with the mercenary 1980s attitude to economics – everyone must pay their own way. As Jake tells Cuffy, they cannot have one person "scrounging" off the rest of the people in the town, while Mrs. Simpkins states that Cuffy only does things for her because she gives him a meat and potato pie for his efforts. Similarly, the Reverend points out that Cuffy comes to the church and gets food there. However, the villagers ironically seem to have forgotten the other half of the economic principle to which they are adhering: people work for compensation. As an offended Cuffy states, he never scrounges because he offers labour in exchange for the things he receives, such as Mrs. Simpkins' pie. If she failed to provide him with anything in exchange for doing her yard work, that would amount to exploitation, but she acts as though he is "scrounging" because he receives something for his labours. Cuffy himself reminds Mrs. Simpkins of this fact in *Cuffy and a Holiday*, when she describes what Cuffy does as begging. Begging implies that someone is being given money for nothing, but an outraged Cuffy states that he provides services in exchange for what he receives. Unfortunately, this point does not seem to have been absorbed by Mrs. Simpkins or the rest of the parish council in *Cuffy and a Status Quo*, which leaves Mandy, seemingly the only person other than Cuffy with a grasp of basic economics, to list the tasks that Cuffy performs in exchange for the food and other benefits he "scrounges": spreading muck and digging ditches for Jake; clearing away dead leaves and other compost that the Reverend sweeps into the crypt; and mowing the lawn and gardening for Mrs. Simpkins. Cuffy also mentions performing tasks such as these for £1 an hour (or in exchange for goods and services) in other episodes, such as *Cuffy and a Carpet-bagger*, in which he reiterates that he does not beg and outlines his weekly schedule: Mondays are for Jake's "mucky" jobs; Tuesdays for helping the Reverend at the church… Cuffy therefore is not a mooch, but contributes to the town by performing tasks in exchange for a relatively modest income, while also providing 'social goods', like company, to the town's occupants.

However, Jake, the Reverend, and Mrs. Simpkins fail to heed Mandy's proof that Cuffy is not scrounging. Instead, they double down, so convinced are they that their perspective that Cuffy contributes nothing to the village is correct that they resort to outright bullying. Jake accuses Cuffy of wanting to carry on with a way of life that does not help the village, and – in response to Cuffy's agreement to accept the job on a temporary basis to "help [them] out" – of being ungrateful after they "bend over backwards" to get him a job. Mrs. Simpkins tells Cuffy that the job will help him to improve himself, thereby implying that Cuffy is deficient and needs improving if he is to have any value as a person. Mandy recognises this behaviour for the bullying it is and steps in, asking Cuffy if he really wants the job. Cuffy replies that he is determined to do the job, even though he does not want it, because he does not want anyone to be able to say that he is not part of the village. Even Mandy changes her tune slightly at this point, saying that helping others sometimes means doing something that one does not want to do, and crafting a speech for Cuffy to deliver during his interview that states that he wants to repay his debt to society and devote his energy to helping the community, and that the price of Cuffy's "individualism is a certain selfishness". This suggests that she, like the parish council, believes that Cuffy's actions and lifestyle are self-serving and that he could be more useful to the village. Cuffy, mercifully, never buys into the council's reasoning and takes the job to prove to the council that he is far more useful in his current role than they realise.

It does not take Cuffy long to be proven right – and the council to be proven very, very wrong. After Cuffy is awarded the caretaker position for a seven-day probationary period, the very members of the parish council who accused Cuffy of "scrounging" and not offering anything of value to the community begin to whistle a very different tune. Mrs. Simpkins brings Cuffy a meat and potato pie while he is working at his new job to show him that she has not forgotten about him even though he no longer comes to see her. This implied criticism demonstrates that Mrs. Simpkins valued Cuffy's visits both for the labour he provided and because she enjoyed socialising with him, and that she is angry that she no longer receives those visits. However, Cuffy points out that he cannot come to see her because he is working at the job that she forced him to take, an irony that she does not seem to grasp. Irony is then heaped upon irony when Cuffy begins to diligently perform his duties and demands that she pay for parking. Mrs. Simpkins points out that she just gave Cuffy a pie, but, unlike when Cuffy performed her yard work, the pie is no longer acceptable as payment. She is therefore forced to pay the fee with real money, a reality that she is clearly unhappy about, but which forces her to realise how much she valued being able to use non-monetary modes of payment where Cuffy was concerned. Cuffy replicates this pattern in the next two encounters with his unwanted benefactors. When Jake arrives, Cuffy asks Jake for identification, claiming it is required to gain admittance to the village hall. When Jake fails to produce any, Cuffy gives him a parking pass to act in lieu of it, but then charges Jake for it. This makes Jake's visit to the hall more difficult, but, again, Cuffy states that he is merely performing his job duties diligently, leaving the implication that Jake has created this inconvenience for himself unsaid. Jake then asks Cuffy to do a job for him on Sunday, which Cuffy refuses to do because it is his day of rest. This is inconvenient for Jake, as he is used to Cuffy being available to do jobs at short notice and at all hours, something that he clearly considered a valuable perk of employing Cuffy. Having forced Cuffy into an inflexible schedule, Jake finds he has done himself a disservice. Finally, the Reverend arrives and laments that he missed Cuffy that morning, implying that he valued his visits, but is again told that the job he imposed on Cuffy prevented the latter from making his usual rounds. Cuffy then provides the same overly correct service he gave the others, asking the Reverend for identification and the nature of his business, before stamping his dog collar in an example of administration taken to extremes.

Back at the farm, Mandy receives so many calls from people wanting Cuffy to perform odd jobs that she ruefully comments that one would think she was running an employment agency. On top of the requests from the community at large, Mrs. Simpkins admits that she wants Cuffy to work on her garden, Jake confesses that his farmhands refuse to dig ditches – work Cuffy previously performed – because they consider it to be "beneath their dignity", and the Reverend states that the women he has cleaning the church are not up to the task. While Jake mutters that it does not say much for the village that it grinds to a halt in the absence of one tinker, Mrs. Simpkins disagrees, implying that she has realised that the fact that Cuffy is embroidered into the fabric of their village in a mutually beneficial way is a sign that their town is a good and kind place to live. Mandy then tells the parish council to apologise to Cuffy and give him more money and appreciation in the future, conditions the council members all eagerly agree to, as they are keen to have Cuffy back in his old role. They have finally realised that he provides value to the town, not only of the type calculated in £s and pence, but in a form best described by another economic concept: "utility", the value, happiness, or satisfaction that a person garners from something. When Cuffy is not present in his normal capacity, the townspeople's utility decreases to the point that they agree that any monetary cost of helping Cuffy to survive is more than compensated for. This prioritisation of non-monetary value would be alien to many seeking wealth in the 1980s, which only serves to demonstrate just how shallow many people's understanding of the very economic principles they believed themselves to be in service of was (and continues to be).

Cuffy and a Lifestyle

Aside from negating the value that Cuffy brings to the town, the series demonstrates that there is another issue with the trio's plan to force Cuffy into gainful employment: they have failed to understand the inherent value that Cuffy places on his lifestyle. When the Reverend first puts the job offer to Cuffy – complete with communion wine to sweeten him up – he tells Cuffy that the job will change his life, provide for the future, open up new horizons, and lift him from his nomadic existence. He then talks up the benefits of the job, telling Cuffy that he will have regular hours, luncheon vouchers, and 2 weeks' paid holiday, and will never again have to worry about earning a little bit here and a little bit there. To the Reverend, it sounds like the ideal sales pitch, so he is stunned when Cuffy says he does not want the job. What the Reverend sees as a security, Cuffy sees as a lack of freedom. Getting a little bit here and a little bit there may be unreliable, but, at the same time, it gives Cuffy the flexibility to set his own hours – he can work as much or as little as he likes on any given day, and at whatever time of day he chooses. If he does not feel like working, he can simply not seek out a job that day. In addition, as Cuffy tells Jake, he prefers to live and work outside. A stable job would dictate his workspace, whereas his bit here and bit there allows him to choose work that can be done in his preferred surroundings. Cuffy's lack of a regular job also allows him to turn down any work he does not want to do. By imposing the job on Cuffy, therefore, the parish council's kindness is transformed into a virtual prison, depriving

Cuffy of the liberty to live his life in the way he chooses and that makes him happy. That freedom clearly holds such immense intrinsic value for Cuffy that it is worth much more to him than all the paid holidays, certainty, and luncheon vouchers in the world. [1]

Cleverly, the series reinforces this point about the value of being able to choose one's way of life by comparing Cuffy's plight to that of another character whose agency has been impinged upon, one who is easily forgotten by the audience, as he does not appear onscreen, and is also completely overlooked by the parish council: Ted, the original caretaker. Rather than consulting him about whether he has any plans for retirement, or even wishes to retire, the parish council simply dismisses Ted as old and due for retirement, assuming that, of course, at his age he must want to give up his job. Even Mandy, when asked by Cuffy why Ted wanted to retire, trots out the same line – that he is old – as a justification for giving him the heave ho. Cuffy replies by asking why Ted did not say something if he wanted to retire, and suggests that it is because Ted did not want to leave his job and will be bored stiff without it. Cuffy advocates for Ted's interests again after resigning as caretaker, pointing out once more that no one bothered to ask Ted if he wanted to retire, just as they did not ask Cuffy if he wanted the job. Cuffy describes this as people meaning well and causing trouble – the council has good intentions in allowing Ted to retire and giving Cuffy his job, but, in doing so, they deprived two people of their ability to make decisions about their own lives. Cuffy then advises the council to give Ted his job back at a higher rate of pay, thereby asking them to respect Ted's wishes rather than imposing their own on him.

The series returns to the theme of depriving people of the ability to manage their lives, this time with an emphasis on the condescension inherent in doing so, in *Cuffy and a Downpour*. While contending with his caravan's leaky roof, Cuffy receives a visit from the Reverend, who claims that "the Lord" has asked him how Cuffy is doing. Cuffy is unhappy to have a visitor while he is trying to cope with the storm and unimpressed by the suggestion that he should be flattered by the divine interest in his life, grumbling that God must know he has sent terrible weather down on Cuffy and therefore that he is not doing very well. Furthermore, Cuffy points out that if God wanted to know how he was, He could have asked Cuffy Himself. The Reverend replies that God would not talk to Cuffy directly, to which Cuffy curtly asks why He would not, since "He talks English like me, don't He?". The Reverend counters that God prefers to converse with those who talk to Him, like the Reverend himself, to which Cuffy exclaims, "Fat lot of good if He leaves it 'til March to find out how I am. There's been times this winter I thought I was going to meet Him face to face!", a rebuke that reinforces his earlier comment that "people think I hibernate in winter like a squirrel...out of sight, out of mind", and implies that, in addition to God, no one in the village worries about his welfare when the weather turns cold.

Cuffy's responses to the Reverend's words demonstrate that, while the Reverend means well, his visit and behaviour are condescending. By framing himself as the only one who has a direct link to God, and Cuffy as unworthy to converse with Him, the Reverend positions Cuffy as the "lowly" tinker who should be grateful that both God and His messenger have deigned to show an interest in the likes of him. Furthermore, the Reverend has chosen to fulfill his "divine" mission of looking in on Cuffy at a time that is convenient for the Reverend himself, rather than when the person whose welfare he is meant to be concerned about could most use the help. Had the Reverend really had Cuffy's best interests at heart, he would have excused himself when it became clear that his presence was nothing more than an imposition, and would instead have looked in on Cuffy earlier in the unforgiving winter and done something to alleviate his life-threatening circumstances. The Reverend therefore treats Cuffy as a godless charity case whom he can both feel spiritually superior to and congratulate himself for "helping" without inconveniencing himself in any way. The Reverend then adds insult to injury, deciding that he will help Cuffy now, whether he likes it or not, and decide the form that that help will take. If the Reverend had bothered to ask Cuffy how he could be of assistance, Cuffy would have told him that he needed warm, dry shelter in which he could wait out the bad weather, and provisions to keep him alive. Instead, the Reverend makes an executive decision to fix Cuffy's leaky roof. Ignoring Cuffy's desperate pleas to leave his roof alone, the Reverend goes up on the roof to inspect the damage. The frail caravan roof cannot support his weight, and the Reverend falls through, leaving a gaping hole through which the elements pour in and soak Cuffy's meagre belongings. Cuffy wails that, while his caravan may not look like much, it "happens to be my home…it's all I've got". The Reverend's condescending treatment of Cuffy – which led him to ignore Cuffy when helping him was inconvenient, believe that he knew what Cuffy needed better then Cuffy himself, and "help" Cuffy against his wishes – therefore results in Cuffy being left worse off than before. Failing to learn from and be humbled by his arrogant behaviour, the Reverend instead doubles down and climbs onto the roof of the caravan to repair the damage – again in spite of Cuffy's protests – then falls through a second time. All of this misery could have been avoided if the Reverend had not condescendingly believed that he knew better and could take liberties with Cuffy's life "for his own good" rather than asking Cuffy how he could make Cuffy's life easier. While this message would be worth relaying at any time in history, it packs a particular punch in an 80s context, when those of few means were particularly perceived as "lesser" and therefore in need of being condescendingly told how to properly run their lives.

Cuffy and a Vulnerability

The series illustrates other instances in which Cuffy is treated with condescension or simple thoughtlessness by the townspeople in order to demonstrate how wrong it is to subject those who are vulnerable and have few means to such treatment. In *Cuffy and a Carpet-bagger*, Cuffy's attempt to raise a legitimate concern about the arrival of Tom, who has parked next to Cuffy's caravan and, therefore, on Jake's land, is dismissed by Jake. This pattern of dismissing Cuffy is repeated as he moves through the village attempting to find someone who will listen to his concerns: the Reverend is worried about an infestation of a beetle in the church; Mrs. Simpkins is busy walking her dog; Mandy is in a rush and cannot stop to talk. It is clear that, because Cuffy is nothing more than the village tinker, anything he has to say is only acknowledged at the townspeople's convenience. In *Cuffy and a Holiday*, we learn that, because Cuffy is the tinker, the villagers consider him to be unintelligent. When Cuffy explains that he is taking a holiday because a doctor told him he was on the verge of a nervous breakdown and needed a rest from work, Mrs. Simpkins unkindly replies that stress is caused by overtaxing the brain, and therefore a tinker cannot have stress, implying that tinkers are unintelligent. Cuffy bristles at this, arguing that tinkers' stresses outstrip those of others, who only have to worry about not becoming tinkers, i.e., becoming poor. This exchange also reveals how little thought that the villagers give to the vulnerability of Cuffy's circumstances and how they shape both him and his behaviour. In *Cuffy and a Downpour*, he expresses fears about his clothes being damaged or lost in the washing machine, as they are the only ones he has, but Jake responds to his concerns with annoyance rather than sympathy, not realising that Cuffy's comments are evidence of his extreme vulnerability. In *Cuffy and a Carpet-bagger*, an angry Cuffy complains about Tom's presence in Shillingbury, stating that it is his village, as he has lived there nearly all his life. Of course, Cuffy has no right to lay claim to the village, but his concerns are clearly rooted in fear, as he tells Mandy that there is hardly enough in the way of job opportunities for one tinker "to scrape a living". This demonstrates the precariousness of Cuffy's existence: if someone competed with him for his jobs, he would be destitute. At times, the villagers not only do not think about the vulnerability of Cuffy's situation, but actively use it against him. In *Cuffy and a Green Eye*, Jake, not wanting Cuffy to compete with him for the Reverend's sister Delia's affections, threatens to not let Cuffy bring his caravan down to the farm for the winter unless he does it while Jake is spending time with Delia, and actually drags the caravan away from its usual location while both Delia and Cuffy are inside, destroying the infrastructure around the caravan in the process. This is a prime example of cruel vindictiveness, with Jake leveraging Cuffy's vulnerability to his own advantage, paying no thought at all to the fact that he is victimising someone who has no means to fight back and who could actually die if deprived of shelter. Such situations demonstrate that the townspeople rarely put themselves in Cuffy's shoes, and that Cuffy suffers due to their thoughtlessness in ways big and small, thereby encouraging viewers to reassess how they treat the most vulnerable.

Cuffy and Appearances

The series also uses the villagers' treatment of Cuffy to illustrate how people are often influenced and fooled by appearances, and treat people better or worse accordingly. For example, because Cuffy is scruffy-looking and has a rather pungent odour due to not being able to bathe regularly, the villagers make unkind quips about his bouquet and use it as a reason to dismiss him as someone with nothing meaningful to say (*Cuffy and a Green Eye*, *Cuffy and a Holiday*, *Cuffy and a Downpour*), while Mrs. Simpkins takes in Cuffy's appearance, scoffs at the idea that anyone would find him attractive, and clearly perceives Cuffy as being the lesser for it (*Cuffy and a Green Eye*). However, in *Cuffy and a Green Eye*, Delia, the Reverend's sister, looks past Cuffy's scruffy exterior and sees what the villagers have overlooked: an interesting person with a life and a past, one who deserves to be treated with respect and kindness, rather than dismissed solely because of his appearance. Not only does Delia see that Cuffy is more than his surface appearance, she demonstrates that recognition by asking to sketch Cuffy, and being willing to do so either at the tip or in his decrepit caravan. The fact that both of those environs are less than glamorous does not faze her in the least, indicating that she sets little store by the conventional trappings of wealth and success. Instead, she values people in their own right. The villagers, in contrast, are dazzled by glamour and wealth. This is particularly evident in *Cuffy and a Fashion Show*. Upon hearing that a fashion show and shoot are going to take place in the town, Jake initially dismisses both events, describing them as "girls prancing up and down showing off everything they've got...prostitution, no more and no less". However, as soon as Jake hears that there is money to be made from participating in the shoot, and that both events are being overseen by his celebrity crush Claudia Millington, he changes his tune. The Reverend is also interested in participating, and the group giddily begins to imagine how good everyone from Mrs. Simpkins to Mandy would look in front of the camera. To be fair, Cuffy is equally keen to participate, telling Claudia he is a male model in the hopes that it will persuade her to take him on. However, Cuffy's keenness to be involved in the shoot does not lead him to present himself differently. Instead, he shows up for the open call for the shoot covered in muck from Jake's farm, and argues that they might want him to be involved because he is the "genuine article", i.e., a real village tinker, rather than a poser. The rest of the villagers, in contrast, are so dazzled by the idea of being in a glamorous fashion shoot that they are willing to make changes to how they behave and present themselves. Jake makes every effort to get Cuffy out of his house before Claudia visits the farm, lest the sight of the scruffy tinker ruin Jake's chances of being involved in the shoot, and is willing to allow Claudia to make condescending comments about himself and others if it means she might grace him with a touch of her glamour. Elsewhere, Jake and the rest of the townspeople answer the call for participants in the photo shoot while dressed in their best outfits, the parish council tolerates Claudia condescendingly telling them that only "the people who matter" will be included in the photos, and the Reverend quotes Mickey Rooney in a desperate attempt to impress. Cuffy does not put on such airs, even when he insinuates himself into each photo taken during the shoot after Claudia rudely rejects him during the open call. This suggests that Cuffy's keenness to be involved in the photos is not due to him being dazzled by the glamour of the fashion world, but is motivated by a simple desire to not be left out of a new, exciting event in the town. This is further reinforced by the fact that, unlike his fellow villagers, he does not treat Claudia and her hangers-on with any reverence. Their diverging reactions to the photo shoot therefore illustrate a fundamental difference between Cuffy and the townspeople: Cuffy's friends buy into the idea that being invited into the fashion world improves their status, and are willing to sacrifice who they are in order to be a "better" version of themselves, while Cuffy stays true to himself and prioritises being part of the community, to the point of donating his fee for the fashion show to the local church.

Cuffy's willingness to continue to be himself no matter what also positions him as the polar opposite of Tom in *Cuffy and a Carpet-bagger*, who is also used by the series to illustrate the dangers of being fooled by appearances. However, this time it is Cuffy, not the villagers, who is dazzled. Tom uses his looks, genial personality, and slick patter to bamboozle, charm, and overwhelm people into letting him take liberties which, in turn, enables him to take their belongings. Tom's entitled and dishonest nature is foreshadowed in his first scene, when he wanders into Cuffy's caravan while Cuffy is away and snoops around. While Cuffy is initially suspicious of Tom, and the likes of Mandy are intrigued by the fact that he is, in her words, "tall, dark, and handsome", the villagers quickly take the measure of Tom after interacting with him. When Tom visits the church and rattles off his spiel to the Reverend, complimenting the church and flattering the Reverend by saying that he must have a large congregation – all the while sizing up the church's property to see what he might be able to steal – the Reverend is immediately sceptical, and murmurs to himself that Cuffy should be careful as he watches the pair depart. Similarly, Mrs. Simpkins immediately mistrusts Tom in spite of his charm offensive and offers to help her with everyday tasks, to the point that she is reluctant to give Tom the meat and potato pie she made for Cuffy, despite Tom's promise to pass it on to Cuffy. Tom makes a better impression on Mandy, as she clearly finds him attractive, but Jake expresses his reservations about Tom to Cuffy, pointing out that Tom has not helped Cuffy in any way and predicting that he will cause trouble for Cuffy. Cuffy, in contrast, is more taken in by Tom's spiel and showmanship the longer he knows the man. After initially railing against his presence, Cuffy finds himself at a loss when Tom invites himself into Cuffy's caravan (omitting to tell him that he has already been inside), and bombards him with his incessant patter on a number of topics while helping himself to Cuffy's coffee, bread, and cheese, all of which Cuffy can little afford to share. By turns, Tom flatters Cuffy by saying that his caravan is much better than Tom's own and asking Cuffy if he has had it assessed; pumps him for information about Mandy, on whom he clearly has designs; lies about just passing through the town; and dazzles him with his singing and spoon playing. When Cuffy tells Tom that his spoon playing reminds him of the circus where his mother helped with the balancing act and Cuffy cleaned the rings, Tom uses this information as a segway to make his move and ask Cuffy to collect the money earned from his musical performances. His promise to split the earnings is the clincher for Cuffy, who now sees Tom as a friend. While Cuffy is not dazzled by Tom's looks or lifestyle, as his friends were by the fashion people's, he does fall afoul of his quick tongue, proving that he is not immune to being deceived by people who put on a front. However, it should also be noted that, while the villagers are dazzled by the fronts put on by others because they want a piece of their money or glamour, Cuffy is sold on Tom's charm because he is naïve. When the scales fall from Cuffy's eyes after the pair are arrested due to Tom's pickpocketing, he is not upset that Tom has not brought him any glamour or glory, but that Tom sold him on the idea that they were friends, a relationship that Cuffy entered into in good faith by expressing a willingness to share jobs with him, introducing Tom to others in the village, and vouching for his good character. Cuffy therefore falls foul of an illusion, not because he is shallow like his friends, but because he takes those who express goodwill at face value.

Cuffy in a Nutshell

When Cuffy compares himself to Tom by saying that "some of us have got less obvious attractions", he is describing himself as well as the show. Both are easily underestimated but had plenty of wisdom to impart in the avaricious and status-conscious 1980s, and still do today. All we have to do to discover these valuable insights is check our preconceptions at the door and look beyond *Cuffy* the series' child-friendly amiability and Cuffy the person's well-worn raincoat.

© JZ Ferguson

1. Editor: One could argue that *Cuffy* connects to a wider interest of 1980s television drama in alternative lifestyles. We even have 80s 'straight drama' characters turning their backs on more conventional ways of living. Ex-policeman Lomax, in *Travelling Man*, enjoys a frugal, nomadic existence on his narrowboat, while in *Floodtide* Dr Ramsey prefers to live quietly and in harmony with the locals in a working-class fishing village in rural France, rather than operate out of a money-spinning Harley Street private practice. Part of the charm of characters as disparate as Cuffy, Lomax and Ramsey – or even Jim Bergerac in the rustic vineyard flat he lives in, in the initial series – is that they share an ability to cherish simpler lifestyles, unlike others who seem to know the price of everything but the value of nothing.

JAN ŠVANKMAJER'S WONDERLAND AND WHAT YOU WILL FIND THERE

In a well-known scene from Monty Python's *Life of Brian*, the question, 'What have the Romans ever given us?' is inevitably followed by a long list: the aqueduct, sanitation, roads, irrigation, medicine, education, wine, public baths, public order, freshwater system, public health...

In much the same way, if asked what Channel 4 has ever offered us, we could provide an equally long list...of movies which Channel Four Films invested in, partly for its *Film on Four* platform. Originally, the idea was to fund or part-fund films exclusively for television screenings, but this soon expanded. Within two years of its launch, Channel 4 Films was investing in a third of the feature films being made in the UK. [1] Working with independent film companies such as Goldcrest and Merchant Ivory, Channel 4 at least part-funded a number of landmark films in the 1980s and 90s, including: *The Draughtsman's Contract* (1982), *My Beautiful Laundrette* (1985), *A Room With A View* (1985), *A Month in the Country* (1987), *Waterland* (1992), *Peter's Friends* (1992), *Four Weddings and a Funeral* (1994), *Shallow Grave* (1994), *Trainspotting* (1996), *East is East* (1999) and the list goes on...One could write an entire book on the cultural impact of these projects, and their role in elevating now household names such as Daniel Day Lewis, Kenneth Branagh, Ewan McGregor and Hugh Grant to the international big-screen 'stage'.

Perhaps less well known is that in the 1980s Channel 4 was also investing in overseas films, through its FilmFour International arm which was set up in 1985. One example is *Alice*, (*Něco z Alenky; Something From Alice*), a live-action/stop-motion animated reimagining of Lewis Carroll's *Alice in Wonderland*, piloted by Czech artist/writer/director Jan Švankmajer and released in 1988. Švankmajer had drawn global attention through his distinctive style

283

of filmmaking throughout the 70s and early 80s, culminating in his short film *Dimensions of Dialogue* in 1983, one of his most acclaimed works, winning the short film prize at the Annecy International Film Festival that year, and cited by Monty Python's animator Terry Gilliam as one of his top ten animated films of all time:

"Jan Švankmajer's stop-motion work uses familiar, unremarkable objects in a way which is deeply disturbing…His films always leave me with mixed feelings, but they all have moments that really get to me; moments that evoke the nightmarish spectre of seeing commonplace things coming unexpectedly to life." [2]

Alice provided Švankmajer with his first venture into full-length feature filmmaking, but it was not the first time he had tackled Lewis Carroll: he referenced the *Jabberwocky* poem in a 1971 short film of the same name, which not-so-coincidentally was also adapted by Terry Gilliam six years later. Channel 4's decision to invest in a niche Czech animator who had never made a full-length feature film before was a risky one, especially at a time when Czechoslovakian authorities were strictly monitoring the arts and restricting what was allowed to be made and distributed. Alongside Swiss TV/film production company Condor Films, Channel 4 initially invested £70,000, despite knowing full well that the film might never see the light of day.

From the 1960s through to the 80s, British audiences would be mostly familiar with stop-motion in the form of small children's entertainment. Series like *The Herbs* (1968), *The Clangers* (1969-72, 1974), *The Wombles* (1973-75), *Paddington* (1976-80) and *Postman Pat* (1981-96) are etched into the memories of adults to this day, remembering them fondly as meaningful parts of their childhood. If anything, animation targeted at pre-school/young children has been Britain's great contribution to the global animation landscape, with Aardman serving as the most recognisable name, responsible for the TV Morph character in the 70s and the *Wallace and Gromit* franchise which began with *A Grand Day Out* (1989). More recently, *Peppa Pig* (2004-), not stop-motion, but British, has attracted mind-boggling international fame, being aired in almost every country on the planet and becoming so popular in China it has become part of the anti-establishment culture.

Animation as adult entertainment, however, would remain a mostly foreign concept. Disney's campaign to dominate the animation industry in the West, producing harmless, family-friendly viewing experiences, had firmly cemented the general view of animation as nothing other than that. That said, Disney's animation department itself was at a low point in the 80s, releasing *The Black Cauldron* in 1985, their biggest ever box-office flop. They would only save their reputation with the arrival of *The Little Mermaid* in 1989, setting off what is now coined as Disney's Renaissance era of animated features which includes many of their most beloved properties like *Beauty and the Beast* (1991) and *The Lion King* (1994) and their return to status as the industry's behemoth. *The Black Cauldron* is noteworthy for sharing a similar gloomy atmosphere to Švankmajer's works, a departure from what one would come to expect from the studio, yet still attempting to appeal to children. It suffers immensely, in my opinion, from being neither the typical fun and songful event, nor a grittier, more gruesome take on the Disney formula; it decides to commit to neither and ultimately comes across as directionless. The dystopian, cyberpunk action film *Akira* would arrive in UK cinemas in 1991, a couple of years after its domestic theatrical run in Japan and introduced a British audience to a world of truly daring animation that Japanese audiences had been long accustomed to. *Akira* and *Alice*, funnily enough, would compete against each other at the Annecy festival in 1989 for best animated feature, where *Alice* would take home the trophy. Considering *Akira*'s reputation as one of the most lauded films in animation history, this is especially noteworthy. [3]

Anyone tuning in to Channel 4 to watch a new animated adaptation of a children's classic and expecting to see a spritely fairytale in the vein of Disney's 1951 version would have been shocked at how dark *Alice* is. The full uncut film was shown at midnight on New Year's Day 1990, which would communicate that the film was not directed at children; however, the film was also commissioned as a children's six-part serial by German TV channel Hessischer Rundfunk, and a censored version was also aired on Channel 4 in 1989 over the Christmas holidays, weeks before the uncut version.

Švankmajer employs the same signature style that became synonymous with his previous short films. The most obvious is the very dim, de-saturated colour scheme. The dark and hidden areas – "chipped walls, the dirty staircases of blocks of flats, mysterious cellars, hidden courtyards" [4] – around Prague where Švankmajer spent his childhood manifest themselves here, such as the low-ceilinged rooms Alice finds herself in, the stairwells she journeys through, even the larder where she picks up a jam jar. In many interviews, Švankmajer brings up how important his childhood memories are in influencing the direction of his films, and his childhood fear of cellars and underground spaces is brought up in many of his films. It also invokes the sense of confinement Švankmajer experienced while trying to make films in the shadows of the strict supervision of then communist Czechoslovakian authorities, who did not approve of his work.

The distinctive sound design is another important element of Švankmajer's signature style. It is intimate and raw, amplified by the complete lack of music throughout the film. This makes it oftentimes sound goofy, bringing with it an element of humour, not unlike the foley you would hear in a Scooby-Doo-esque cartoon. A good comparison would be in the 'Breakfast' section of his short film *Food*, another production part-funded by Channel 4 which he made in 1992, a few years after *Alice*. The strange, slapstick nature of the film suits the sound design perfectly in my opinion, and a similar soundscape – creaking doors, furniture and machinery; lip-smacking and gulping etc – drives the comedic factor or element in *Alice*.

More of Švankmajer's signature which comes through in *Alice* is in the themes. I have already mentioned the idea of claustrophobic confinement and being trapped, but another glaring one is the theme of consumption. It organically makes its way over from the source material: Alice in the original story is just as obsessed with the idea of eating as Švankmajer is. So, whereas the dark, closeted setting of the film feels more like artistic liberty to bring the story of *Alice in Wonderland* in line with Švankmajer's vision, the ideas surrounding food feel like the perfect marriage between the source material and Švankmajer. Seeing the 'Drink Me' bottle, 'shrinking' cakes and the tea party rendered by Švankmajer feels particularly fitting.

Another aspect of the original which works to Švankmajer's strengths is the dreamlike storytelling. It allows him to completely ignore the rules of reality and create his own rules of how the world functions. Even if he chooses to divert from the plot set out by the book it does not matter nearly as much as there is no risk of defying logic or creating plot holes. This in turn could explain why Lewis Carroll's work resonates so much with Švankmajer. The surreal, dreamlike nature of Carroll's stories lends itself well to the magical imagery Švankmajer is interested in creating:

"So far, all adaptations of *Alice* present it as a fairy tale, but Carroll wrote it as a dream. And between a dream and a fairy tale there is a fundamental difference. While a fairy tale has got an educational aspect – it works with the moral of the lifted forefinger (good overcomes evil) – dream, as an expression of our unconscious, uncompromisingly pursues the realisation of our most secret wishes without considering rational and moral inhibitions, because it is driven by the principle of pleasure. My *Alice* is a realised dream." [5]

A striking difference between the style of stop-motion which a British audience would be familiar with and that which Švankmajer would introduce is in the texture. Švankmajer's lifelong experience working with puppets is evident, with models that look like real-world trinkets and toys that a child might play with, in a way that makes their integration with live-action elements not at all jarring. Clay models in the style of *Wallace and Gromit*, by contrast, would obviously look completely out of place. The biggest advantage of using a claymation world crafted from the ground up is the sheer amount of control at the animators' disposal. A mouth shape to convey every possible sound when talking can be created, every set piece can be meticulously crafted to allow for what the storyboards demand, and from every possible camera angle. Ultimately, what you are sacrificing is the sense of reality, that the world you are seeing really exists. Švankmajer's style of animation, especially in *Alice* where most set-pieces are of real-world scale (or roughly so), feels distinctly grounded and lived in. Švankmajer mirrors this sentiment in interviews, where he expresses a distaste for CGI animation and finds value in what he calls "tactile experimentation and explorations": using worn-down objects that have been touched by people and which have stories behind them: cutlery, keys, wardrobes, desks, rolling pins, socks, dentures...In his words: "I miss the tactile dimension that gets lost in digital animation. Computers work in 'non touched' reality, which I believe deprives animation of one important emotional level." [6] This feeling translates through the screen and adds to the film's overall appeal, in the same way that practical effects provide a distinctive quality over CGI – which is especially true in today's landscape where overworked CG studios are so relied upon that disinterest or emotional detachment in a film universe dominated by poor, hastily put-together CGI has become the norm.

Caryn James' 1988 review described *Alice* as a film which "does not violate" the original source material, an "extraordinary film which explores the story's dark undercurrents...Mr. Švankmajer never lets us forget we are watching a film in which an actress plays Alice telling a story...With its extreme close-ups, its constant motion and its smooth animation, the film is so visually active that it distracts us from a heavy-handed fact – this is a world of symbols come alive." [7] In the latter part of my essay, I will briefly explore a few of the elements which for me illustrate what makes the film an 'extraordinary' Wonderland and I will examine what you will find there, amidst 'dark undercurrents' and 'symbols'.

At the heart of Švankmajer's surreal Wonderland is a collection of inanimate objects which are brought to life. In the first room we visit, before Alice descends into Wonderland, we see a wide range of lifeless items which we will encounter later in more animated form (pun intended): sewing spools, animal skulls, jars, cakes, teacups, a doll – the latter being one version of Alice we will see shortly. Rather than the White Rabbit magically appearing as if from a conjuror's hat, here we first see it as a piece of taxidermy displayed in a glass cabinet. As it shatters its glass prison, the White Rabbit is then seen eating its own insides – sawdust – tying in with the themes of surrealism and consumption.

As Alice attempts to follow the White Rabbit across a barren wasteland and into Wonderland through the first in a series of (Russian Doll) desk drawers, she pricks a finger on a mathematical compass which draws blood. We are encouraged to read this sequence symbolically: the tyranny of education, and/or Wonderland's hostility to Alice, mirroring the attempts by the state to prevent Švankmajer from exploring his own Wonderland's anti-establishment vision. In this sense, Alice is almost a projection of the director himself. As she descends in a lift, she passes shelves of props: puppets, playing cards etc., again foreshadowing what is to come. As with the sawdust she tasted earlier, here she tries jam from a jar, only to find that it contains drawing pins – a disturbing detail which was cut from the children's serial version. Even the food in Wonderland is both hostile and unappetising: tins can contain maggots; slabs of meat drag themselves along like slugs. Alice swallows ink and chews on a slice of wood. She will eat or drink anything. Even when her life is on the line, during her interrogation by the Queen of Hearts, she casually helps herself to a cake which was being used as a piece of evidence. She refuses to follow conventional guidelines or rules, just as Švankmajer's filmmaking does.

Alice is our guide through Wonderland and, while we anticipate that the surreal world around her will be in a state of flux, we expect her to remain unchanged. Instead, she morphs between a child actor (Kristýna Kohoutová) and a doll. This subverts our expectations. The one hoped-for constant, our human companion in a world of inanimate objects – who should offer us stability and our point of human reference – is revealed to be unreliable. The first time she shrinks into a doll, we lose our bearings, and the world she inhabits suddenly becomes more precarious and dangerous. She almost drowns in her own tears and Wonderland creatures which were previously harmless become genuinely threatening. Indeed, it is now figures such as the White Rabbit who are empowered, who order her around, rather than fleeing when she attempts to speak to them. As Alice morphs back from doll to child actor, the White Rabbit takes a saw to her bare arm, a graphic example of those 'dark undercurrents', of the disturbingly adult nature of this version of Wonderland.

Arguably the most effective use of inanimate objects brought together to create a Wonderland creature is the collection of items which become the caterpillar. A sock appears and takes on a set of dentures and a pair of glass eyes, while a wooden spool fills the role of a mushroom which the creature sits on, later sewing over its eyes to go back to sleep. Part of the visual appeal here is seeing the caterpillar assemble itself, keeping the film grounded in the real world while, paradoxically, reminding us of its artificiality. The Mad Hatter is a wooden puppet whose strings would suggest that it cannot move independently, yet the character ignores these logical constraints, just as the Queen of Hearts – a cut-out from the playing card she represents – is seen to turn her head sideways which clearly defies the real-world physics. This mirrors the nonsensical, illogical nature of both dreams and Lewis Carroll's story.

The remit which the newborn Channel 4 was challenged to provide was to offer fresh content which was "distinctive...different...and experimental". While some of the British films it broadcast during the 1980s did this while critically examining the state of the nation, such as *My Beautiful Laundrette*, *Alice* equally fits the criteria, partly by undermining adult viewers' preconceived ideas that both Wonderland and animation itself are solely playgrounds for children. Švankmajer's art and life represent dissident voices. There is something almost magical about the way he filmed *Alice* in a cramped, tiny Prague studio. At a time when British television and film makers were relatively free to create anti-Establishment work, the production and post-production history of *Alice*, made and exported under the cloak of secrecy, is a sober reminder of the challenges faced by artists in far more hostile regimes.

© Tomas Marshall

1. "Channel 4's involvement in feature films was not planned from the outset. Although it began transmission with a regular slot entitled *Film on Four*, the original idea was that this would be filled by low-budget TV films, with commissioning editor David Rose generally able to offer £300,000 per project. During this period, Channel 4 embarked on negotiations with the Cinema Exhibitors Association with the aim of modifying the traditional 'holdback' arrangement, whereby there would be a gap of at least three years between a film's cinema and television premieres. This was designed to protect the interests of cinema operators, but it acted as a strong disincentive to television companies to invest in film projects, since they would have to wait too long before they saw any return on their investment. Though the CEA was reluctant to scrap the original agreement outright, a compromise was reached that allowed Channel 4 to screen films shortly after the end of their theatrical run, provided their production budget was no greater than £1.25 million. The immediate upshot of this deal was that the second season of *Film on Four* included substantial arthouse hits broadcast just months after their original release at a time when their critical acclaim was still fresh in the memory." Michael Brooke, *Channel 4 and Film*, BFI screenonline. As Brooke acknowledges in his article, arguably the 1980s was the decade when Channel 4 took its greatest "risks", including *Alice*.

2. Terry Gilliam, *The Ten Best Animated Films of All Time*, *Guardian*, 27/04/2001.
3. Editor: it is worth noting here that *Akira* had a ¥700 million production budget, in contrast to *Alice*'s modest six figure one, making the latter's Annecy film award even more remarkable.
4. *Electric Sheep* online interview, 2011.
5. *Electric Sheep* online interview, 2011.
6. *Cider Spoon Stories* online interview, 2016.
7. Caryn James, *An Alice for Adults*, New York Times, 03/08/1988.

NUCLEAR TV & *EDGE OF DARKNESS*

When someone mentions the 1980s what comes to mind? Perhaps it is Live Aid, fond memories of a new wave of synth-based bands or the surge of slick music videos on the fledgling MTV? Maybe it is the glossy fashion, striking make-up or extraordinary gel and peroxide hairstyles? Could it be the rise of yuppies with huge mobile phones, the surge of privatisation, the Falkands conflict or the miners' strike? It is probably not the threat of Armageddon caused by a global thermo-nuclear war or terrible nuclear accident. However, this was a very real fear which resonated throughout the 1980s and, unsurprisingly, became a core theme – a nuclear core if you like – of the culture of the decade.

This was not new of course. Ever since the creation of "Oppenheimer's deadly toy" [1] nuclear catastrophes have been a rich source of inspiration in popular culture. A raft of 1950s B Movies featured mutations created by nuclear tests including *Godzilla*, *Them* (featuring rampaging giant ants) and *The Incredible Shrinking Man* based on a Richard Matheson novel. In comics, Peter Parker becomes *Spider Man* having been bitten by a radioactive spider and Bruce Banner transforms into *The Incredible Hulk* following exposure to gamma rays during a nuclear test. The film *Seven Days to Noon* has an atomic scientist threatening to destroy London with a bomb unless the nuclear weapons programme is closed whilst *The Day the Earth Caught Fire* has the Earth's axis shifted by nuclear tests with a devastating impact on climate change and society. Auric Goldfinger plans to detonate a nuclear device in Fort Knox, flooding the US gold reserve with deadly radiation whilst *The Time Machine* and *Planet of the Apes*, based on novels by H G Wells and Pierre Boulle respectively, show future humans reduced to stone age societies after atomic devastation destroyed civilisation. Famously, Kubrick's *Dr Strangelove* was a blisteringly funny satire on Cold War tensions where a mad US general triggers a series of incidents that cause a nuclear war.

Although popular culture also portrayed foreseen benefits of harnessing nuclear energy such as powering supercities of the future, super-fast aircraft or sending spaceships to the stars, by the 1980s its focus was firmly pessimistic. This was fuelled by escalating East-West tension and the proliferation of a nuclear arms race between the USA and USSR – with the seeming increasing threat of a nuclear war – plus concerns about the safety of nuclear energy, the practices of organisations and governments in how it was being used and the potential dire consequences.

In the UK, the early 1980s saw a huge surge in the membership and profile for CND (Campaign for Nuclear Disarmament), whilst protesters set up peace camps near US airbases in the UK, most famously the women's camp at Greenham Common in Berkshire, protesting against the UK Government's decision to allow cruise missiles to be stored on the bases.

In the late 1970s and early 80s the Government created the "Protect and Survive" media campaign, including a booklet, series of information films, and audio recordings offering guidance on how the public could protect themselves during a nuclear attack. The films and audio recordings, voiced by actor Patrick Allen, were intended for broadcast if a nuclear attack seemed imminent. Although originally restricted, leaks to the media resulted in the booklet being posted to every house. Its guidance on surviving a nuclear strike, such as hiding under a table and whitewashing windows to shield the nuclear flash, was understandably greeted with ridicule and led to the book "Protest and Survive" by EP Thompson, a prominent voice in CND. Meanwhile Raymond Briggs's book and animated film *When the Wind Blows* told the touching story of elderly couple Jim and Hilda who follow the advice in "Protect and Survive" which proves useless against the inevitable appalling consequences of radioactive fallout.

Clips of Allen's commentary from the campaign films were included in Frankie Goes to Hollywood's anti-war single *Two Tribes* which reached number one in 1984. Its memorable video featured lookalikes of US President Ronald Reagan and Soviet Secretary Konstantin Chernenko in a wrestling match. Numerous other songs from the decade reflected the threat of nuclear war such as Ultravox's *Dancing with Tears in my Eyes*, Nina's *99 Red Balloons*, The Clash's *London Calling*, OMD's *Enola Gay*, Sting's *Russians*, and Kate Bush's *Breathing*.

In cinema, John Madden's techno-thriller *WarGames* (1983) concerns a young computer hacker who accidentally breaks into a US military supercomputer which controls nuclear missile launches and initiates a programmed simulation. This makes US Military leaders believe that an imminent USSR missile strike is likely and almost triggers World War III. Concern about nuclear energy and the motivations and behaviour of energy companies was the focus of Mike Nicholl's *Silkwood* (1983). It is a biographical drama about Karen Silkwood who works at a plutonium plant and blows the whistle on the unsafe practices of the plant owners which result in Silkwood and other workers being contaminated by radiation. The movie suggests that she was killed in a car crash by unknown forces to stop her revealing damaging information.

Inevitably such huge and current topics were also fertile ground for television. The harrowing 1984 television movie *Threads* was written by *Kes* writer Barry Hines. Despite its low budget, the film realistically portrays the horrific impact of nuclear war and its aftermath on ordinary people in Sheffield. Going about their daily lives, the residents ignore the imminent threat of a nuclear war reported in newspaper headlines and in TV and radio coverage. A Russian nuclear attack and the subsequent exchange of weapons decimates the United Kingdom, kills millions of people, and leads to long term devastation. We witness ordinary homes and shops vaporised, unflinching scenes of death and injury and the terrible consequences for survivors struggling to cope with the effect of radiation and a nuclear winter. Without power, food, clean water and facilities, society breaks down – there is mass starvation and death and a return to an almost barbaric existence. The film caused shock, revulsion and controversy but was critically praised, winning five BAFTAs in 1985.

The film is extremely similar both in tone and content to the 1983 US television film *The Day After* directed by Nicholas Meyer. The latter features more of the build up to a nuclear war, though, once again, this is largely ignored by people going about their daily lives until it is too late. The film then, once again, explores with horror the devasting impact of a nuclear strike and its aftermath on a collection of ordinary people living in Kansas and Missouri and the breakdown of society that follows. The film was greeted with critical acclaim and terrified audience appreciation alike. It remains the most watched television film in US history.

The fictional drama-documentary *The War Game* was finally televised on 31st July 1985, part of a week of programmes commemorating the fortieth anniversary of the Hiroshima atomic bomb. *Threads* was also repeated in the same week. Originally made in 1966 but withdrawn before screening following government pressure because "the effect of the film has been judged by the BBC to be too horrifying for the medium of broadcasting…" *The War Game* is another brutally realistic and shocking depiction of the devastation of a nuclear strike – but the effect is made even more realistic by the almost emotionless documentary style and narration. People are shown suffering the effect of horrific radiation burns, buildings and furniture ignite and people are left to suffer and die in agony, or struggle to survive with no food, water, and facilities. Inevitably, as with *Threads* and *The Day After*, civilised society soon breaks down.

Although such programmes are admirable in traumatically highlighting the terrifying risk of nuclear catastrophe and shocking realities of the consequences, it could be argued that they ultimately have less audience impact than a great popular drama or comedy which covers such themes but with more reach. One example was the 1982 US two-part mini-series *World War III*, also shown in the UK. Broadcast at the height of the decade's Cold War tensions, but set a few years ahead in 1987, the glossy and star-studded series portrays a rapidly escalating series of political and military events that lead to nuclear war.

Although *World War III* is very much a 'Hollywood' doomsday action saga, with some inevitable soap elements and stereotype characters, it is also a tense and stylish drama featuring a great cast and some excellent performances. Whilst the scenario is highly fictionalised, there are several realistic elements which make the escalation of events disturbingly plausible. The context of two political leaders facing immense domestic pressures and fading popularity, whilst trying to manage the conflicting views of hawks and doves within their own administrations, against the backdrop of an ongoing Cold War standoff, was all too realistic in the 1980s. Consequently, the series gives a persuasive insight into the terrifying risks of the proliferation of nuclear weapons and a mutual assured destruction military strategy where a single rogue act can tip the scales of delicate brinkmanship between the global superpowers, triggering Armageddon.

A similar story of unfolding events escalating out of control and leading to nuclear war was the subject of another programme broadcast in 1982, but this time it was played for laughs. London Weekend Television's six-part comedy series *Whoops Apocalypse*, written by Andrew Marshall and David Renwick, featured a host of established and up-and-coming television actors and comedy performers, instantly recognisable from other hugely successful comedy series, including: John Barron, Peter Jones, Geoffrey Palmer, Richard Davies, Bruce Montague, David Kelly. Richard Griffiths, Alexei Sayle and John Cleese. It also starred Barry Morse as President Johnny Cyclops and Ed Bishop as TV newsreader Jay Garrick, both of whom were more usually seen in dramatic roles. There are also wonderful cameos from Charles Kay, Nicky Henson, Michael Melia and Rik Mayall amongst others. The scripts poke fun at virtually every nation, culture, institution, and political dogma, essentially suggesting that the whole world is run by clowns and lunatics.

Each episode opens with a panning shot over a desolate wasteland comprising a fire-ravaged orange sky, destroyed buildings, and burnt vehicles, accompanied by a slow melancholy violin piece. The camera zooms in on a smart middle-aged woman rattling a tin and holding a tray of mushrooms labelled "wear your mushroom with pride". The music suddenly cuts to a jaunty tune over a split screen title sequence featuring many of the principal characters, brief clips, and images of capital cities before the words "Whoops Apocalypse" appear, followed by the episode title. There is another cut to a black screen with the week number printed in large white letters underscored by a brief dramatic theme. This is usually followed by a summary of news headlines read by Jay Garrick (brilliantly played by a deadpan Ed Bishop) which are hilarious but also neatly summarise key events and escalating tensions.

The series is, in many ways, a series of zany comedy sketches through which the story develops.   Morse is superb as the hapless and deeply unpopular US Republican President Johnny Cyclops, an ex-star of old Tarzan movies and clearly a parody of Ronald Regan. He is advised (or more frequently controlled) by his God-fearing right wing fundamentalist advisor, The Deacon, played wonderfully by John Barron. Reminiscent of Barron's character CJ in *The Fall and Rise of Reginald Perrin* who often used to remark "I didn't get where I am today..." The Deacon is prone to stating that "If the Good Lord had meant..." followed by a dubious reference such as, "....meant us to be optimists he would never have given us life assurance" and "...meant us to panic, he would never have given us clean trousers". Meanwhile, the Soviet Union is ruled by Premier Dubienkin (Richard Griffiths) who is, in reality, a collection of clones. As one version dies in the middle of meetings, it is replaced by another. The character closely resembles and parodies the frail Leonid Brezhnev, the then leader of the Soviet Union; there were frequent rumours that he had actually died and been replaced by a double.

298

In the best tradition of satire, *Whoops Apocalypse* successfully uses exaggerated humour to deal with the most serious of subject matter and highlight the alarming absurdities of the contemporary world. When first shown on late Sunday evenings, it proved enormously popular and, whilst over thirty years later some of the comedy does not quite stand up, much of it remains hilarious. The scenes involving President Cyclops and The Deacon, along with those involving the UK Prime Minister, Chancellor and Foreign Secretary (Peter Jones, Richard Davies and Geoffrey Palmer) are particularly joyous thanks, in part, to the deadpan brilliance of the performances. Ed Bishop's regular interjections as newsreader Jay Garrick are also side splittingly funny.

Some elements of the series are definitely 'of its time' and might be uncomfortable viewing for a 21st audience. Fantastic though Bruce Montague and David Kelly are, it is unlikely that having white actors wear dark make-up to play Iranian characters would be acceptable today, even in a deliberately absurd comedy. In addition, there are hardly any female characters in the whole series and those that do feature have minor roles, including a British newsreader who reads the news topless for some inexplicable reason. It feels unnecessary and misogynistic, especially when viewed today.

Some sketches remain glorious, however. Peter Jones's straight-faced and increasingly absurd assurances that he is Superman and the reactions from Richard Davies and Geoffrey Palmer are joyous. A scene where Barry Morse's President Cyclops lies in a hospital bed anxious to assure everyone that he is not crazy, whilst his psychiatrist pours water over him, wears a revolving tie and rides a real pink elephant, is brilliant. The constant crazy humour makes the last sombre moments of the show, when President Cyclops prepares to launch the US missiles and we realise that the enigmatic woman selling mushrooms in the title sequence is his wife, all the more impactful. It is similar to the effect of the memorable closing moments of *Blackadder Goes Forth* when Blackadder and his men go 'over the top' for the last time.

For me, the best piece of 'nuclear television' of the 80s (and any other decade for that matter) was the six-part thriller *Edge of Darkness*. Originally broadcast in November and December 1985 on BBC2, it was so immediately successful that it was repeated on BBC 1 within a few days to gain an even wider audience. It was written by Troy Kennedy Martin, whose CV includes co-creating the ground-breaking television series *Z-Cars*, adapting *Reilly, Ace of Spies* and writing episodes for popular TV programmes such as *The Sweeney* – created by his brother Ian Kennedy Martin – in addition to screenplays for films, including *The Italian Job* (1969), *Kelly's Heroes* (1970) and *Sweeney 2* (1978).

Troy Kennedy Martin had been frustrated about what he saw as a lack of political drama series on British television in the 1980s, particularly given the contemporary climate and events which he felt offered important subject matters, such as the policies of the Thatcher Government, the Falklands conflict, the Miners' strike, and Cold War tensions between two increasingly hard-line superpowers. He had originally planned a series based around the Miners' strike but felt it was not working and so abandoned the idea in favour of a story about the nuclear industry. He was inspired both by President Reagan's speech announcing the Strategic Defence Initiative (the so-called Star Wars program) and by James Lovelock's book on his Gaia hypothesis, conceived with biologist, Lynn Margulis.

The Gaia hypothesis, named after the Greek goddess of Earth, proposes that the biological and inorganic systems of the planet co-exist as a single self-regulating entity to ensure conditions for life are maintained. This was contrary to previous theory which assumed a planet's ecology was a response to its physical conditions. The hypothesis was informed by observations that life had persisted on Earth for over 3.8 billion years despite increasing solar luminosity and numerous major catastrophic events. Life finds a way.

As Kennedy Martin was preparing to write the script, Lovelock published a paper to illustrate the plausibility of the Gaia theory, using the Daisyworld computer simulation. Daisyworld is a hypothetical world orbiting a star with slowly increasing or decreasing radiant energy. The planet has just two life forms: black petaled daisies which absorb light and white petaled daisies which reflect light. The simulation tracks the two daisy populations and the surface temperature of Daisyworld. As the sun cools, the black daisies flourish and absorb the light, thus warming the planet. As the sun heats up, the white daisies become dominant, reflecting the sunlight and therefore cooling the planet. The two types of daisies provide a self-regulating control mechanism to counteract the variations in the solar output, ensuring the surface temperature remains almost constant. This would become an important reference for the series.

Edge of Darkness opens with Yorkshire CID detective Ronnie Craven (played by Bob Peck) discussing his investigations into a possible case of union vote fraud with leader James Godbolt (Jack Watson). Afterwards, he collects his student daughter Emma (Joanne Whalley), from her university campus. As they arrive home, an unknown man steps out of the bushes and shouts "Craven!" She steps forward and is brutally shot dead. Craven's commander, DCS Ross (John Woodvine), believes that the killer must be associated with one of Craven's old cases and identify a man called Lowe as their chief suspect. Craven is unconvinced and decides to investigate matters himself, guided by what seems to be the ghost of his dead daughter.

In one sense, *Edge of Darkness* is a superior political thriller highlighting the shady world of espionage, governments, and their murky relationship with a sinister privatised nuclear industry. It is also so much more, however. It is a murder mystery, a conspiracy drama, a fantasy which draws on the mythology of ancient Britain and Greece, an allusion to the powers of the mystical world and natural world in combating the folly of mankind, a ghost story, and a character study of grief. It is this blend which makes it such an accessible and entertaining series, as well as one which has some serious points to make.

The series also expertly weaves together reality with fiction, both to re-enforce a sense of realism but also as a commentary on the political climate of the day. The Labour politician Michael Meacher is shown speaking to students at Emma's university; Craven is interviewed by the broadcaster Sue Cook about the investigation into Emma's murder on BBC's *Crimewatch*; the newsreader Kenneth Kendall appears, reading bulletins which both reference the fictional inquiry into the proposed takeover of IIF by the Fusion corporation and genuine contemporary stories such as the Miners' strike which feature in clips. Craven also briefly watches Robin Day interviewing Margaret Thatcher about trident missiles. The original title of the series was Magnox, which is the name of a type of nuclear power and production reactor. Interestingly, it was also the name of a company set up in the 1990s to decommission a number of nuclear power stations.

At the heart of the series is a tour de force performance by Bob Peck in his first major television role, having spent much of his career in the theatre. Craven is a sort of everyman character. From his introduction when meeting with Godbolt, he comes across as morally principled and determined, but also world weary and dour. This feeling is emphasised by the constant heavy rain of the opening scenes. We later discover – through emotional flashback sequences following Emma's murder – that his wife died from cancer many years before and it seems as if he has never truly recovered from her loss.

Craven's mood lightens only when he collects Emma from university, immediately identifying her importance to him and the impact she has on his life. This theme – and the depth of the relationship between Emma and Craven – is continually reflected throughout the six episodes. Part of Craven dies when Emma is killed, and when he thinks her ghost has abandoned him he seems lost; an empty shell staring blankly and without feeling. He is

302

literally haunted, not just by Emma's ghost but also by grief, guilt and regret. Craven is driven solely by the need to discover the truth about the death of his daughter. Although he agrees to work with the CIA's Darius Jedburgh (Joe Don Baker), and on behalf of civil servants Harcourt and Pendleton (Ian McNeice and Charles Kay), ultimately, he does not care about them or their motivations, the various conspiracies, the nuclear threat, or the government enquiry. He only cares about finding out what happened to his daughter and why. Only intelligence agent Clemmy (Zoe Wanamaker) comes close to making him care about something else.

This focus gives Craven almost a death wish. He seems not to care about the risk of exposure to radiation when breaking into Northmoor. He deliberately invites terrorist McCroon (Sean Caffrey) to break into his house by asking Ross to remove the security detail. He knows this puts his life in danger and, even when McCroon puts a gun to his head and confirms he killed Emma, Craven continues to goad him. His aim is to get McCroon to reveal who arranged this and he is devastated when a police marksman kills the hitman before he can speak. After breaking into the MI5 computer facility, knowing that they have only a few minutes before they are traced, he risks his own capture and that of his associates in order to find the information he needs. In tracing Jedburgh to Scotland and discovering the location of the plutonium he seems to knowingly enable the CIA assassins to find them. This is a reflection of Craven's sense of duty to stop the plutonium being used as a bomb, but also a realisation that he and Jedburgh are dead men anyway. As a gun battle between Jedburgh and the assassins plays out, Craven sits impassively at the kitchen table waiting for his own death.

Only occasionally does the dam break and Craven's grief is released. Driving down to London after visiting Emma's body in the mortuary, he imagines talking to her as a child and cries for the first time. In the park, walking with the ghost of Emma, he seems to be momentarily overcome with what has happened and argues with her as she pleads with him not to give up. When McCroon is killed, a blood-splattered Craven collapses to the floor, pounding the table and howling in anguish. The belief that his one way of finding the truth has gone, combined with the fact that Emma's ghost has disappeared, provokes a temporary breakdown. In hospital, admitting to the psychiatrist that he sees Emma's ghost, Craven suddenly seems a beaten man. When Emma's ghost returns, this immediately rejuvenates him.

Craven's relationship with Emma – both before and after death – is an integral theme of the series. Kennedy Martin's original concept was to make Emma's appearances as a creation of Craven's imagination, triggered by his inability to deal with the grief of her loss. After her death, Emma was going to appear just as a voice – and indeed that is how we first become aware of her presence when we hear her speak to her numbed father as he 'matter-of-factly' puts blood-soaked clothes in the washing machine. The next idea was that Emma would appear on screen, but she and Craven would only be shown reacting to each other and not appear in frame together. This would demonstrate that she was a manifestation of Craven's mind.

However, in early shooting, director Martin Campbell filmed a scene with a young Emma in the back of a car reaching out to hug Craven from behind, so they appeared in shot together. In conversation with Kennedy Martin, they agreed that this meant Emma should really be a ghost. This changed the dynamic of their relationship and made a more interesting concept. Emma now becomes an essential character, driving Craven forward. As a ghost she becomes someone with whom Craven can have an honest conversation and seek answers. Emma drops hints and clues to guide Craven through the complex chain of events, and through this he and the audience gain a better understanding.

In the opening episode, when Craven collects his daughter, it is clear they have a close relationship. When Harcourt asks Craven whether he agreed with Emma's views on nuclear energy he responds that he doesn't, "...but I enjoyed the conversation". In a touching scene shortly after Emma is murdered, we share Craven's flashback memory of the time when his wife died; that evening his little girl tells him that she will look after him, "I think you should sleep with me tonight, Daddy". After her death, he lies on her bed clutching her teddy bear and goes to sleep. This appears to be the catalyst for Emma's appearance as a ghost and her subsequent help in him finding the truth. Even in death, Emma was looking after her father, just as she promised as a little girl.

Craven's relationship with Darius Jedburgh is also a key component of the series. Jedburgh is a fascinating character, brilliantly portrayed by Joe Don Baker in a complex larger-than-life role that could have been written for him. Jedburgh is a tough and intelligent CIA operative, energy attaché and veteran of Black Ops activities across the world. He is also at his happiest playing golf or settling down with a snack to watch *Come Dancing* on TV. It is a surprise to discover that Jedburgh established Gaia. Initially this seems slightly incongruous, but Jedburgh explains that this was a means of monitoring the practices of the nuclear industry in the UK during a time when President Jimmy Carter had wanted to reduce plutonium levels. All of this changed when Reagan announced the Strategic Defence Initiative. Nonetheless, Jedburgh's loathing of Grogan and the activities of the Fusion Corporation of Kansas and his speech at the NATO conference indicate that Gaia's views may also closely reflect his own.

Jedburgh and Craven are an unlikely but effective partnership, brought together through their own distinct but related agendas. For different reasons both seem to have become disillusioned lone wolves – weary of death, duplicity, and the double crossing of others. They first meet in a memorable scene, set late at night in a London restaurant where Jedburgh has enjoyed a meal and numerous drinks with some old CIA buddies. Jedburgh is a hard drinker who has whisky for breakfast, so is in full control whilst his friends pass around him. He and Craven end up singing to each other as they try to remember the lyrics of a song. Apparently, this was an improvised scene between Bob Peck and Joe Don Baker, but it cleverly establishes a curious mutual connection and unusual respect between the two from the outset. We see this throughout the series, including their final meeting when Craven tracks Jedburgh down and they drink, talk, and sing before the CIA assassins arrive.

Despite the bleak theme and dark atmosphere, the series is elevated by some wonderful humour. The brilliant characters of Harcourt and Pendleton are both shadowy figures but also immensely likeable. This is thanks to their typically dry English charm, caustic wit, and amusing interplay but also to the outstanding performances of Charles Kay and Ian McNeice who make both characters fully believable, appealing and, ultimately, vaguely heroic. They are sort of Ying and Yang characters, and we gain the impression that they are both fond and distrustful of each other (and everyone else) in equal measure. When Pendleton first introduces Harcourt to Craven, he describes him in fairly disparaging terms. He jokes with Harcourt that a CIA assassin might be hunting for him after his altercation with the Minister of Defence and also does not fully reveal to Harcourt all of Craven's telephone message when he calls to report that he has found Jedburgh.

Although both characters always seem to know more than they are letting on and are one step ahead of everyone, neither are in full control of events. Whilst investigating what they perceive to be 'wrong doings' of the nuclear companies and other government departments, they must also ingratiate themselves with all these players. They rely on others, including Gaia, Craven and Jedburgh to do their dirty work. Although they are keen to find proof of the activities at Northmoor to influence the Government enquiry into the proposed sale to the Fusion Corporation, ultimately they have no power over its outcome or proceedings. On presentation of his investigation report to the Minister of Defence, Harcourt is also genuinely shocked to discover the Ministry was aware that Northmoor was manufacturing and storing plutonium all along and actively encouraged this for national energy security.

In addition to a magnificent cast and wonderful script, *Edge of Darkness* also benefited from an outstanding director in Martin Campbell. Considered one of the rising stars of television direction at the time, Campbell went on to direct *Goldeneye*, *Casino Royale* and two Zorro movies amongst numerous other projects. Campbell brings an intense cinematic style to the series which feels edgy and realistic, thanks to the frequent use of handheld cameras, extensive interior and exterior location shooting, grainy film, and natural lighting. It created a style for many other filmed TV dramas that followed.

The brooding mood is set from the outset, as the camera approaches the building in which Craven and Godbolt are meeting from the perspective of the police on duty outside. It is dark and raining heavily, which gives it a claustrophobic atmosphere. We are made aware that the officers think there is a prowler in the grounds which immediately establishes a sense of threat.

Emma's murder is brutally violent and shocking: her bloody body flung backwards by two close range shots and her blood mingling with water from the pouring rain. The episode was actually filmed during a drought, so gallons of water had to be pumped from a nearby lake to recreate the rain. The scene afterwards is a panning shot which scans across the police in Craven's house, examining what is now a crime scene. It is accompanied by a soundtrack of mixed conversations which cleverly provide a brief background to Craven and his tragic family history.

There are numerous other examples of where Campbell's direction sets the tone. Each episode features a scene of a clanking goods train at night carrying what seems to be nuclear waste as if to emphasise a shadowy operation of the nuclear industry. When Jedburgh enters Terry Shields' house (to find his dead body in a bath) a handheld camera precedes him as he suspiciously climbs the stairs – emphasising his alertness to danger and a sense of inevitability about what he will find. The scenes in the caverns with Jedburgh and Craven are intense, but the mood is suddenly changed when they enjoy a lavish meal in an ornate room filled with paintings, grand furniture, and a spectacular wine cellar. It highlights the bizarre contrast of this luxurious facility installed in a nuclear fallout bunker in a cave! A similar point using a meal is made towards the end of the drama. Whilst Jedburgh and Craven talk about their imminent deaths over a whisky and food in a gloomy kitchen, Harcourt, Pendleton, Grogan, Bennett and others enjoy fine dining in a London hotel.

Another coup was the choice of Michael Kamen and Eric Clapton to provide the highly original theme and incidental music. Despite the low payment that the BBC could offer a world-famous rock star, Clapton was sufficiently intrigued by the project to come on board. He and Kamen created an extraordinary theme where the electric guitar sounds like a piercing scream, reflecting Craven's anguish under which the pulsing synthesiser strings create a dramatic ongoing pounding tension.

An intriguing element of *Edge of Darkness* is the sense that the audience cannot entirely trust any of the characters or their behaviour. Pendleton, Harcourt and Jedburgh operate in a world of shadows and double bluffs, and we are initially unsure of their true motivations, yet all prove to be acting honourably. Godbolt is an ex-miner who now works for the nuclear industry. At first it seems as if he might be in league with the industry, but we later discover that he helped Gaia break into the facility. Terry Shields appears to be a selfish idealist who cheats on Emma, but he is also an informant for British Security. Ross is a caring, by-the-book police officer who goes out on a limb to protect Craven, but his refusal to believe there may be more to Emma's murder raises suspicion of whether he is trying to cover something up. Craven himself is not entirely heroic, encouraging Jedburgh to accompany him to the dangerous Northmoor facility and later recklessly allowing the assassins to find him. Is he nobly pursuing the truth? Or has grief made him dangerously obsessed, or even mad? Even Emma's ghost seems to use her father; sometimes driving him to pursue the truth, but at other times misleading him or disappearing.

The metaphysical elements lift *Edge of Darkness* above a more conventional thriller. The concept of Gaia and Mother Earth is central. A spring appears on the spot where Emma dies, suggesting a form of reincarnation in nature or that Gaia is honouring one of her children. Emma refers to her father as being like a tree – with the inference that he is sturdy, rooted, but also part of nature. Just as Grogan is passionately advocating the benefits of the nuclear state to the NATO conference, claiming that by harnessing nuclear energy, "for the first time, man will be in charge", Emma is explaining the Gaia hypothesis to Craven and warning that, if necessary, the planet will fight humanity to defend itself. Grogan's inevitable death, followed by the appearance of the black flowers at the end of the final episode, infer that this is what is happening.

The title *Edge of Darkness* itself is open to interpretation. Is it a reference to Craven's state of mind, driven by grief and madness? Does it refer to a world of conspiracy and political shadowy figures where countries, corporations and individuals cannot be trusted? Is it a metaphor for the state of global politics and the threat of nuclear devastation? Does it refer to the origins of a dark universe and the light brought to it by the energy of plutonium? Or it a reference to the Gaia theory – where Earth will find a way to survive, even on the precipice of the world's end?

Personally, given the brilliance of the whole series I felt the closing scenes of the final episode to be a slightly disappointing ending. It feels a little rushed, with several loose ends. Apparently, Kennedy Martin wrote about fifteen different endings – including one where Craven turned into a tree! (This idea was firmly rejected by Bob Peck). Perhaps this suggests that he was not completely sure how to end the series himself. The final scene is largely described in a commentary from Harcourt to Clemmy, reassuring her that Gaia is safe, although it is not clear why he is doing this. Earlier, Grogan seemed to have suffered no ill effects from his radioactive exposure at the NATO conference, but now we are told he is dying. Craven is last seen on a mountain screaming, "Emma!" This might suggest that, driven by grief, he has succumbed to a final madness, or it could be a reference that he has gone wild and is becoming part of the natural world. It could be his agonising rage to the world at the death of his daughter, or perhaps infers that she has abandoned him in his final days. Perhaps the loose ends, uncertainties and mysteries of the final episode are the point. This is not a 'happy ever after'. Not everything is neatly resolved. The heroes and villains – and what happens to them – are not clear cut. The future of the planet is still in question – but we do know that, somehow, life will find a way.

Concerns with nuclear energy and the threat of potential nuclear war are as relevant today as they were in the 1980s, which begs the question why there are so few nuclear-themed television series today? Has the world moved on? Do we think it is safer than it was in the days before the fall of the Berlin Wall? Have we become more immune to these fears, so that stories on a nuclear theme do not carry the same interest? Are there other catastrophes and concerns that feel more relevant – for example the impact of infection and disease, climate change, economic meltdown, the rise of populist politics?

Later, both *Edge of Darkness* and *Whoops Apocalypse* were made into very different and very inferior films. At least we can celebrate the original series, and the other programmes mentioned in this chapter, which illustrate the importance and originality of 1980s 'Nuclear TV'.

© Trevor Knight
1. Lyric from *Russians* (1985) by Sting.

THE ROAD TO NOWHERE: THE STORY OF *DOCTOR WHO* IN THE 1980s

By 1980 *Doctor Who* had been a mainstay of Saturday night television and an integral part of British popular culture for over seventeen years. In 1989, however, the programme was cancelled – taken off air seemingly forever. During the 80s, *Doctor Who*'s popularity rose to new heights before its fortunes steadily declined, leading to the show's eventual demise. Nevertheless, in some ways its final years laid the foundations for its eventual triumphant return sixteen years later.

This is the story of the most dramatic decade in the history of the world's longest running science fiction television programme. It is a story of continuity and change; of national politics and BBC politics; of a transforming television landscape, of controversy, criticism, and conventions, of personality tensions, power struggles, protests, pantomimes, and pop records (well, one at least).

As the credits rolled on part four of *The Horns of Nimon* on 12th January 1980, season seventeen of *Doctor Who* drew to a close. Tom Baker had played The Doctor for six years – already the longest period that anyone had been in the role – and was hugely popular. With his big eyes, toothy smile, mop of curly hair, long multi-coloured scarf, and resonant voice he was instantly recognisable and for many had become synonymous with the character, not just in the UK but worldwide, including the United States where the programme had gained popularity. Given the length and success of his tenure, and the fact that he cared deeply about the programme, unsurprisingly Baker had become very proprietorial about the show. Some directors and writers complained that he could be difficult to work with – frequently moody, often adding or changing lines which he felt worked better.

Baker had also grown visibly older, seeming to age more than the actual years passed since he took on the role. An all-consuming production schedule and related promotional activities, combined with various behind the scenes challenges, may have taken its toll. These challenges included budgetary restrictions made worse by the impact of high inflation and recurring industrial action by BBC technicians which reduced available studio time. In late 1979 the latter led to the cancellation of *Shada,* the last scheduled story of the season. Baker also entered a tense, spikey romantic relationship with his co-star Lalla Ward, who played the Time-Lady, Romana. Being companions in the Tardis and in real-life caused friction on and off-set. To the amazement of many, the couple married in December 1980, though the marriage lasted only sixteen months.

Change was in the air, however. Graham Williams stepped down as *Doctor Who* producer in late 1979, feeling exhausted by the workload. On Williams' recommendation, his production unit manager John Nathan-Turner was appointed as new producer, initially with Barry Letts acting as executive producer. Letts was the very successful *Doctor Who* producer from 1970 to 1975 and was considered an experienced pair of hands to help Nathan-Turner as a first-time producer. John Nathan-Turner was a gregarious, larger than life character who would usually be found wearing brightly coloured Hawaiian style shirts which seemed to reflect his flamboyant personality. He would become the longest serving producer of the programme – holding the role throughout the 1980s – as well as its most recognisable and high-profile to date. He was also a 'BBC man', however, having spent most of his career with the organisation and risen through the ranks.

Nathan-Turner was keen to shake up the programme which, he felt, had become too comedic and light-hearted. This had been a partly deliberate response by the previous producer to criticisms (from the likes of Mary Whitehouse) that mid-1970s *Doctor Who* was too violent and frightening for children, despite it being more popular than ever. Nathan-Turner felt this sea change had gone too far, however, affecting the programme's style and reputation. He wanted to make *Doctor Who* more serious, whilst also refreshing the style to reflect the tone of the new decade. This was partly to make his own mark on the programme, but also because he felt it was right for the organisation. "Getting the best out of your staff and out of the BBC system, was important to me". [1]

Nathan-Turner commissioned a new logo and titles sequence for the programme, designed by Sid Sutton, replacing the kaleidoscopic tunnel effect visuals used throughout the 1970s with a computer graphic star field. Peter Howell, from the BBC Radiophonic Workshop, was also asked to create a new version of Ron Grainer's main theme. It was an extremely risky decision to amend such an iconic theme, one which had barely changed since the programme's debut in November 1963, but Howell's reworking was excellent, and its dramatic energy and quicker pace fitted the new tone and era.

Nathan-Turner also asked the BBC Radiophonic Workshop to create the incidental music for the show, replacing long standing incidental music composer Dudley Sutton. He felt the electronic synthesiser sound offered greater flexibility for incidental music and was more typical of the era, but he also wanted to distinguish *Doctor Who*'s music stylistically from the BBC's other science fiction programme *Blake's 7*, for which Dudley Sutton also composed. Sutton had worked on *Doctor Who* since the 60s but was unceremoniously dumped over a lunch with Nathan-Turner at the Balzac restaurant in Shepherd's Bush. The news came as a complete shock to Sutton, so it must have made for a tense meal between the two.

There were further changes too. Costume designer June Hudson was asked to create a new look for Tom Baker's Doctor, as Nathan-Turner was keen to update the image. Hudson wisely decided that the silhouette of floppy hat, scarf and long coat should remain as it was intertwined with Baker's portrayal, but changed the texture of the materials and used a single, more sober, burgundy colour. She also introduced question marks on the Doctor's shirt collar in response to Nathan-Turner's request for a shirt that might be marketable.

Nathan-Turner also decided to replace Romana and K-9 as the Doctor's companions. For Lalla Ward, who played Romana, it was a mutual decision for her to leave part way through the next series. The removal of K-9 was highly controversial, however, and resulted in an outcry from young fans who loved the Doctor's robot dog. It led to a brief tabloid "Save K-9" campaign and caused BBC executives to invite Nathan-Turner to rethink his decision. He refused, feeling the character was overshadowing the Doctor and provided an easy 'cop out' solution in stories. Instead, Nathan-Turner suggested K-9 be given his own programme which eventually resulted in the one-off *K-9 and Company* which also starred Elisabeth Sladen returning as the beloved former companion, Sarah-Jane Smith. Broadcast in December 1981, this odd and quirky hour-long show attracted highly respectable viewing figures of 8.4 million, but was not critically well received and never commissioned as a series.

Nathan-Turner appointed Christopher H Bidmead as new *Doctor Who* script editor, replacing Douglas Adams who had also left a few months earlier. Bidmead was a writer and computer magazine editor with a passionate interest in science. He was recommended by previous *Doctor Who* writer Robert Banks Stewart who created hit the detective programmes *Shoestring* and *Bergerac*. In subsequent interviews Bidmead comes across as strong-minded and sometimes self-deprecatingly arrogant, but he was also extremely creative and industrious and shared Nathan-Turner's vision for a more serious and scientifically literate approach to the programme, feeling that it had become too fantastic. His immediate priority was to find stories for the eighteenth season, airing in August 1980, as no scripts had been inherited from the previous production team.

The first two stories were unremarkable and did not reflect any major shift in programme style. *The Leisure Hive* was mainly notable for the return in a guest role of Jacqueline Hill, who had previously played Barbara, a member of the original Tardis crew with William Hartnell. To this day it is the only occurrence of a *Doctor Who* regular cast member coming back to the show as a different character (though there are plenty of examples of the reverse, where different guest actors appear as the same regular characters). *Meglos* introduced a new video effects technique called Scene-Sync which electronically synchronised two cameras to track movements so that a composite image could be maintained in movement. This was a development from the previous Computer Separation Overlay (CSO) technique widely used by TV in the 70s.

A week after the final episode of *Meglos* was broadcast, the biggest demonstration of a new era for the show was unveiled as a hurriedly assembled press conference, in October 1980, announced that Tom Baker was to leave the show at the end of this series. Baker was so firmly established in the role of The Doctor that this news created front page headlines and caused considerable shock. Many young viewers had never known another Doctor. Some felt Baker's departure was the final piece of Nathan-Turner's mission to change *Doctor Who*, though it seems that this was very much a mutual decision and he and Baker enjoyed a good personal and professional relationship. Baker had threatened to leave the role in previous years, but with all the other changes he must have felt it was finally time to move on – even though he would much later comment that it was a decision he regretted.

The next six stories reflected a clearer tonal change and formed two loose trilogies of tales, the second of which would span into the next series. The first trilogy was set in the separate universe of E-space as devised by Bidmead. *Full Circle* introduced the new companion, the youthful Adric played by relative newcomer Matthew Waterhouse and created by Nathan-Turner and Bidmead, seemingly to appeal to a teenage audience. The second story, *State of Decay*, was a gothic vampire tale, whilst the third, *Warriors Gate*, was an imaginative, visually impressive but thoroughly confusing story which saw the departure of K-9 and Romana who decides to stay in E-Space to embark on her own adventures, rather than return with the Tardis to the normal universe.

The second trilogy began with *The Keeper of Traken*, an ingenious and intriguing tale which introduced another new companion, Nyssa, played by Sarah Sutton. Originally the character was intended to only feature in this story, but Sarah Sutton so impressed the production team that they decided to keep her as a regular cast member. This late addition did mean that Nyssa's character was undeveloped for the next few stories. *The Keeper of Traken* also features the unannounced return of the Doctor's nemesis The Master – who had become an emaciated skeletal figure. In a further twist, at the end of the story, The Master subsumes the body of Nyssa's father Tremas, played by Anthony Ainley, in order to rejuvenate. Although, in hindsight, viewers may have realised that Tremas is an anagram of Master, this twist came as a complete surprise in those spoiler-free days and was the first of a number of surprise twists that feature in early 1980s stories.

The next twist came in *Logopolis,* written by Bidmead; the final story of the season and of Baker's era. The story is archetypal of the inventive scientific concept story Bidmead wanted to develop, and introduced the final new member of the Tardis team, Tegan Jovanka, an Australian air stewardess. Played by Janet Fielding, Tegan would prove to be one of the most popular cast regulars from 1980s *Doctor Who*, due in no small part to Fielding's personality and skill in transforming a sketchy idea for a companion into a strong and fully rounded individual. A mysterious silent white figure known as The Watcher also appears enigmatically at various points throughout the four episodes.

Logopolis is a planet of mathematicians who use their calculations to maintain the fabric of the Universe. The Master attempts to use the power of the Logopolitans for his own evil ends, but in killing some of them terminates their calculations which inadvertently threatens to destroy the Universe itself. The Doctor and The Master are forced to work together to save the Universe, using a giant radio telescope to transmit a copy of the Logopilatans' programme of calculations. The Master betrays The Doctor and uses the situation as an opportunity to hold the Universe to ransom. In a climactic scene reminiscent of Holmes and Moriarty in *The Final Problem*, The Doctor foils The Master but falls from the radio telescope to the ground. In his final words, Baker's Fourth Doctor reassures his companions that "It's the end – but the moment has been prepared for", at which point The Watcher reappears and is revealed to have been "The Doctor all along". In one of the most memorable regeneration sequences, The Watcher merges with The Doctor's body to become the fifth incarnation.

That fifth incarnation was played by Peter Davison, already a household name thanks to his popular portrayal of Tristran Farnon in BBC's hugely successful *All Creatures Great and Small* series. Nathan-Turner had worked on this programme and felt Davison would bring a similar youthful charm and energy to the role of The Doctor and would be an effective contrast to Baker. This approach was consistent with the tradition of choosing an actor for the role who differed considerably from their predecessor. He also thought Davison's existing fame would help audiences adjust to the transition from Baker and potentially attract new viewers. Throughout his tenure, Nathan-Turner would regularly cast famous actors and personalities as guest cast members, another means of promoting the programme to old and new viewers alike. He has been criticised for this tactic, but it was an effective way of maintaining the programme's profile in an increasingly competitive 80s television market, when viewing habits were changing and when the show could no longer rely on strong support from BBC bosses. A similar approach has been successfully adopted by producers of post-2005 *Doctor Who*.

Davison was a long time *Doctor Who* fan, but was initially reluctant to take on the part, feeling that, at only 29, he was too young for the role. In the end, however, he reasoned he would regret turning down the opportunity and accepted the part. Davison was given very little steer on how to portray 'his Doctor' and drew inspiration from his predecessors, particularly William Hartnell and Patrick Troughton, the first and second Doctors respectively. Consequently, although he did successfully bring a younger enthusiasm and dynamism to the role, there was also an older, curious, professorial quality about his portrayal, even down to his need to use half-rimmed glasses to read. Davison's Doctor was simultaneously heroic yet vulnerable. He would often make mistakes but was fearless and courageous.

In his office, Nathan-Turner had an array of photographs related to previous productions on which he had worked, one of which was of Peter Davison playing in a charity cricket during his time in *All Creatures Great and Small*. This perhaps inspired the choice of the fifth Doctor's outfit: a summery Edwardian outfit comprising long coat, striped pyjama-like trousers and a cricket sweater. Bizarrely, Nathan-Turner also decided Davison's Doctor should wear a stick of celery in his lapel. Like the question marks on the shirt collar, the idea was to give the Doctor an eccentric identifiable 'hook' (akin to Columbo's raincoat or Kojak's lollipops), but it was an odd choice that was only explained – and rather unsatisfactorily – in Davison's final adventure.

Davison's first series, season 19, commenced on 4th January 1982 and in another huge shake up the programme was moved from its traditional Saturday night teatime slot, for the first time in its history. The series was scheduled for a weekday early evening slot, and two episodes per week were transmitted, in a style reminiscent of soap operas. This change seems to have been initiated by Alan Hart, then controller of BBC 1, as an experiment possibly to boost viewing figures in the face of Saturday evening competition from glossy imports such as *Buck Rogers in the 25th Century*, or possibly to trial the viability of running a twice weekly early evening BBC drama serial...an idea later realised with *EastEnders*. Whatever the reasons, it was an early taster of the influence of BBC management on the programme which would become a theme throughout the decade. The experiment proved successful as viewing figures increased by more than 2 million and it helped establish Davison's popularity in the role from the outset. Along with the reduction from 28 to 26 episodes, it did mean, however, that *Doctor Who*'s run was reduced to 13 weeks from its previous 28 week schedule.

Christopher H Bidmead had stepped down from the script editor role, although he had commissioned most of the stories of Davison's first season. He wrote the series opener, *Castrovalva,* the final part of the loose trilogy which had begun with *The Keeper of Traken.* Inspired the works of artist M C Escher, *Castrovalva* was another intriguingly complex story which focused on a post-regeneration Doctor struggling to settle into his new identity and seeking sanctuary in the peaceful world of Castrovalva which turns out to be a paradoxical illusion created by The Master to trap the Doctor. Anthony Ainley initially appears heavily disguised as a character called The Portreeve to welcome The Doctor and his companions, before being revealed as The Master, a plot twist which would be used in several subsequent stories including *Time-Flight,* the final story of the season. Bidmead wrote the story before Davison had been cast and so the concept of a new Doctor struggling to establish his new identity was almost art imitating life.

Anthony Root took on the script editor role temporarily, before Eric Saward was appointed as permanent successor, having impressed Nathan-Turner with his scripts for two other stories in Davison's first series, *The Visitation* and *Earthshock.* The first was an entertaining historical story set in 17th century London where The Doctor encounters three alien creatures called Terileptals who have escaped from a crashed spaceship and plan to destroy all life on Earth by releasing an enhanced strain of the plague. The Doctor foils their plot but in doing so causes The Great Fire of London. During the story, the Doctor's famous sonic screwdriver – regularly used by the character from Patrick Troughton onwards – is destroyed, marking its final appearance until the series returned in 2005. It is also notable for the first example of animatronics in

Doctor Who, used to provide movement for the Terileptal leader's mask.

Saward's second contribution was *Earthshock,* one of the strongest stories from the Davison era. The story featured the surprise return of the Cybermen, the most famous Doctor Who 'monster' after the Daleks. Once again Nathan-Turner decided to keep this a secret, even turning down the opportunity of a *Radio Times* cover, and the gamble worked brilliantly. The appearance of the Cybermen in the final seconds of episode one was a genuine shock and remains one of the most memorable twists in the programme's history.

Earthshock is also famous for the death of Adric at the end of the story, having bravely but vainly tried to prevent a spaceship crashing to Earth (which it transpires causes the global devastation that wiped out the dinosaurs). Only two of the Doctor's companions had been previously killed off – Sarah Kingdom and Katarina – both in the William Hartnell story *The Dalek Master Plan*, but both of these had only appeared in a few episodes, whereas Adric had featured in eleven stories. Nathan-Turner had felt that three companions was not working. It was difficult to incorporate them all into stories and often at least one would make a limited appearance.

Adric had not proved a particularly popular or well-developed character, often coming across as a sulky teenager. This may have partly reflected Matthew Waterhouse's lack of experience as an actor and – perhaps because of his inexperience – he also unknowingly annoyed fellow cast and crew members. In subsequent interviews, Waterhouse is described as being patronising, not very good, possessing "absolute zero humility" [2] and "a little brat" [3] amongst other reflections. Nevertheless, Waterhouse's performance in *Earthshock* is strong and Adric's death is shocking and emotional. The last image of him, staring into camera clutching his dead brother's belt, is moving, as is The Doctor's realisation that he cannot save Adric and the effect it has on him and the other companions. The impact of the finale was re-enforced by the brilliantly dramatic decision to roll the credits without music over the image of Adric's broken badge.

Earthshock – and the appointment of Saward as script editor – marked another tonal shift. Under Nathan-Turner's tenure, the programme's style had already become pacier with more action, but this increased further, whilst stories also became darker and violent, a trend that would attract some criticism. Davison's Doctor kills a Cyberman in *Earthshock* and in future stories is more frequently involved in action scenes, even seen holding a weapon on occasions, though he continues to primarily resolve problems though his intelligence and ingenuity.

Davison's second season marked *Doctor Who*'s 20th anniversary and the choice of stories was designed to reflect this by including some returning characters and themes, as well as new ones. The first story, *Arc of Infinity*, was partly set on Gallifrey (The Doctor's home planet) and featured the return of Omega the legendary rogue Time Lord seen in 1973's *The Three Doctors* produced to celebrate the 10th anniversary of the show. The story was also partly set in Amsterdam, the first of several occasions where Nathan-Turner included overseas location filming for no obvious dramatic reason other than to spend some time abroad and generate publicity – which was successfully achieved with photos of Davison riding a bicycle around Amsterdam's canals featuring in several newspapers.

The second story, *Snakedance*, was a sequel to *Kinda* from the previous season and this was followed by another loose trilogy of stories featuring The Black Guardian and The White Guardian, omnipotent beings first introduced in Tom Baker's eras and who (as the names imply) reflect a cosmic battle between the forces of good and evil. The first story, *Mawdryn Undead*, is set in 1977 and 1983 and introduces a new companion, Turlough (played by Mark Strickson), a mysterious alien boy who is living as a boarding school pupil on Earth and who is initially tricked by The Black Guardian to kill The Doctor. Whilst there are some obvious similarities with the original concept for Adric, Turlough is a much more interesting and developed character, thanks in no small part to Strickson's nuanced performance.

Mawdryn Undead also features the return of Brigadier Alexander Gordon Lethbridge-Stewart (Nicholas Courtenay), of UNIT (United Nations Intelligence Taskforce). Somewhat bizarrely, the character has now retired and is working as a maths teacher at Turlough's school in 1977. This creates a major continuity challenge for *Doctor Who* fans. According to previously established timelines, Jon Pertwee's Third Doctor worked with The Brigadier and UNIT in the late 1970s and into the 1980s which, according to *Mawdryn Undead*, is after The Brigadier has seemingly retired. Of course, there have been numerous continuity issues throughout the sixty plus years of *Doctor Who* – it is often best to ignore them – but this was a particularly significant one and also seemed an odd development for the character. The reason was that the story was originally due to feature William Russell returning as Ian Chesterton, teacher and original companion of William Hartnell's First Doctor. This would have made much more sense but, unfortunately, Russell was unavailable. The plot required the inclusion of a long established and familiar friend of The Doctor, hence the choice of Lethbridge-Stewart. Bizarre or not, it was still a delight to see the return of The Brigadier, one of the most popular characters in *Doctor Who*'s history.

The second story of the trilogy, *Terminus,* saw the departure of Nyssa. Industrial action by BBC electricians impacted on recording for this story, requiring the need to reschedule studio time. This subsequently impacted on the production schedules for *Enlightenment,* the final part of the trilogy and the two-part historical story *The King's Demons* featuring the unannounced return of The Master, initially disguised as Sir Gilles Estram (a fairly obvious anagram of Master). Although it is an entertaining story which features an impressive cast including Gerald Flood, Frank Windsor and Isla Blair, the inclusion of the Master is somewhat contrived. The Master uses a shape changing android – known as

Kamelion – to replace King John and stop the signing of the Magna Carta, although why the Master would be interested in doing this is not really explained.

A consequence of the industrial action which forced rescheduled production for these stories was that there was no studio availability to record the final planned story of the season. *The Return* – written by Eric Saward – was to have featured The Daleks and was intended to be a major element of the 20th year celebrations. The forced cancellation of the story deeply upset Saward and created tensions with Nathan-Turner which were to grow and impact on their relationship (and ultimately the series) for the next few years. It also meant that the season officially finished with Kamelion joining the Tardis team at the end of *The King's Demons*.

This seems to have been another of Nathan-Turner's whims. He and Saward had been hugely impressed by a demonstration of the Kamelion 'android' by the company that had designed it and felt there was great potential for it as a character and also for potential marketing and merchandise. Unfortunately, the Kamelion prop proved to be very limited in its use and completely unreliable, frequently not working. Consequently, it could not be used much and was hardly ever seen on screen again until the character was written out in the next series.

From the outset, Nathan-Turner had sought to connect with *Doctor Who* fans more than any previous producer, both because it was something he enjoyed but also he saw it as important to galvanise fan support in the context of a BBC that seemed to be increasingly taking the programme for granted. By 1983, he had become a frequent attendee of conventions in the US and UK. Whilst UK conventions were usually small-scale fan organised events, where guests attended out of good will with little or no financial reward, the US equivalents were larger, slicker, more professional, and more financially lucrative. They were also an important way of promoting the show to a US audience, something Nathan-Turner considered important to strengthen the show's global reach.

Whilst keen to maintain a relationship with all fans, not unsurprisingly Nathan-Turner started to prioritise participation in the US events and would also help secure the involvement of past and present *Doctor Who* luminaries, meaning they were less likely to be available for UK events. This began to create resentment with Nathan-Turner from some UK fan groups such as DWAS (the *Doctor Who* Appreciation Society), a situation which would develop over the coming years. Even in the age before social media, it was an example of how co-ordinated fandom could be, a blessing and a curse to television programme makers, even if such groups were not necessarily representative of the totality of fans and casual viewers.

For the 20th Anniversary milestone, Nathan-Turner and the BBC decided to organise an official *Doctor Who* Celebration event held at Longleat on Easter Sunday and Monday 3rd and 4th April 1983. It was, by far, the biggest event of its kind in the UK to that date, and featured numerous guests along with sets, props, costumes and screenings of old episodes, all held in various marquees across the grounds. Longleat had been the home of a *Doctor Who* exhibition for many years and it offered a perfect location for something on this scale. The event was extremely slick and professional, but organisers had completely underestimated the popularity, expecting around 10,000 visitors over the weekend whereas over 40,000 attended. This apparently included a young Russell T Davies, as well as (very definitely) a 20-year-old me experiencing my first convention and my first attempt at camping! (I still have the ticket, programme, photographs, and autographs along with some amazing memories.) Queues were huge and everywhere, but it was all good natured, tremendous fun and a treat to see and hear from so many famous and favourite cast members, past and present, as well as designers, members of the radiophonic workshop, people involved in various elements of production and John Nathan-Turner himself.

Many of the guests and displays from the Longleat event featured in the main anniversary television celebration, a 90-minute special called *The Five Doctors*, written by former *Doctor Who* scriptwriter Terrance Dicks, filmed in March (a month before Longleat) but broadcast later that year on 25th November 1983. The episode featured all five Doctors, numerous current and ex companions, The Master, Time Lords and assorted monsters including the Cybermen, a Yeti and a Dalek. Patrick Troughton and Jon Pertwee reprised their roles as the Second and Third Doctors respectively, whilst well-known character actor Richard Hurndall brilliantly recreated the part of the First Doctor, as William Hartnell had died eight years previously. Very sadly it was one of Hurndall's final roles as he would also pass away in April 1984. Whilst the task of packing so much into 90 minutes meant that, inevitably perhaps, the story was uneven, it was enormously entertaining, a nostalgic treat and a fitting tribute for the 20th anniversary.

Robert Holmes, another legendary *Doctor Who* writer, had originally been asked to write the episode and devised an outline story called *The Six Doctors*, but he struggled to turn this into a workable script which incorporated so many favourite characters and monsters. Dicks, a master at quickly turning out even the most challenging stories, was therefore asked to take on the task. This was made even more difficult because of continual changes in the availability of actors due to appear in the episode. Most significantly, this included Tom Baker who had originally accepted the opportunity to return, only to change his mind as filming approached. Consequently, Dicks had to make major last-minute changes to the script and a few clips from *Shada,* the Baker story, which was never completed, were instead incorporated.

In addition to producing a whole series, an anniversary special and helping organise the Longleat event, Nathan-Turner was facing increasing pressures from his new Head of Department, David Reid, who it seems was more critical of the producer and the programme than previous bosses. This was very much a taste of things to come. Nathan-Turner was also attracting some criticism for the time he spent attending conventions and also producing annual pantomimes. These often featured stars from *Doctor Who*. Nathan-Turner was a showman at heart and loved the theatre and the fun of pantos, but he also felt it was another way of highlighting the *Doctor Who* brand to a wider audience, especially children. Even though there is no evidence that any of this interfered with his work on *Doctor Who*, it raised concerns from bosses and critical fans that it was a distraction.

Furthermore, Peter Davison decided to step down from the role of The Doctor at the end of his next series. Davison felt his second season had not been as strong as his first, and also reflected on the advice he had originally been given by Patrick Troughton that three years in the part was about right. Although tempted to stay for a fourth year, by June 1983 he had informed Nathan-Turner that his mind was made up and so began the task of looking for a replacement. After initially considering several possibilities, Nathan-Turner's choice was Colin Baker, who had previously appeared as the guest character of Commander Maxil of the Gallifrey Chancellery Guard in *Arc of Infinity* when, rather ironically, he shoots Peter Davison's Doctor! Nathan-Turner and Baker met again at a mutual friend's wedding where Baker had been on sparkling form, entertaining guests with humorous anecdotes. Nathan-Turner was impressed with Baker's personality and thought he would be perfect for The Doctor.

Davison's final season began transmission on 5th January 1984, continuing in its twice weekly evening slot, premiering with *Warriors of the Deep* which saw the eagerly awaited return of fan favourite 'monsters' from Jon Pertwee's era, the Silurians and the Sea Devils. It was an ambitious story but severely hampered by budget limitations (a perennial challenge for the programme's makers) and enforced scheduling problems. Margaret Thatcher had decided to call a snap election in June 1983, smack in the middle of the story's production schedule. The BBC had to hastily rearrange resources and studio facility availability to organise election coverage which severely impacted on *Doctor Who* and other programmes. The *Warriors of the Deep* production schedule had to be significantly rearranged to avoid cancellation altogether. Recording time, along with preparation/operational rehearsal time for a range of visual effects and a large sea creature costume called the Myrka (operated by two people akin to a pantomime horse) was slashed. Consequently, much of the intentional impact of the model effects was lost and the Myrka, in particular, looked crude and clumsy.

Season 21 continued with *The Awakening* a two-part historical story followed by *Frontios,* about a human colony set on a far-flung planet, written by ex-script editor Christopher H Bidmead. The actor Peter Arne was tragically killed only hours after attending a costume fitting for a guest part in the story and was replaced by William Lucas. At the end of *Frontios,* the Tardis becomes trapped in a 'time corridor', a segway into the next story *Resurrection of the Daleks* written by Eric Saward. Originally intended for transmission over four standard length episodes, the story was re-edited and broadcast in two 45-minute episodes to make more slots available for the BBC's coverage of the Winter Olympics.

The convoluted plot involves The Daleks rescuing their creator Davros from a prison spaceship and trying to replace The Doctor and his companions with duplicate replicants in order to assassinate the High Council of the Time Lords. In keeping with Saward's style, the story is fast paced, full of action, with a high death count! There is also a noticeable increase in violence and onscreen gore, particularly in the scenes where the Daleks attack the spaceship. This more adult style attracted praise and criticism in equal measures. The story saw the departure of Tegan who, weary of the number of killings, tearfully decides to leave the Tardis and stay on Earth. Although the explanation may be reasonable, given the scale of slaughter in the story, it is a sudden and unsatisfactory conclusion for such a successful character.

The following story, *Planet of Fire*, saw the departure of Kamelion and Turlough and the arrival of a new companion, a young

American girl called Peri, played by Nicola Bryant. Although British, Bryant had won the role having pretended to be from the United States and had a very convincing accent. Bryant was young and very attractive, and her introductory scenes see her dressed in a bikini. Perhaps unsurprisingly for the decade, the production team used this to promote the programme, arranging a photoshoot of a bikini-clad Bryant accompanied by Peter Davison dressed in a tuxedo holding a gun *a la* James Bond. Filming took place in Lanzarote, which was the setting for part of the story but this time the foreign location made sense as it also doubled for a volcanic alien planet.

Davison's final story, *The Caves of Androzani*, is not only his best but is considered by many to be one of the greatest ever *Doctor Who* stories. Written by Robert Holmes, it references *The Phantom of the Opera* featuring a disfigured masked madman, Sharaz Jek, who hides in the shadows too (in this case the said caves of the planet Androzani) and becomes infatuated by Peri and her beauty. Jek controls production of a life extending drug refined from a substance called spectrox. He is an anti-hero, fighting government troops sent into the caves by the villainous Morgus who wants to seize control of the drug production. The Doctor and Peri become infected by contact with raw spectrox and are captured, initially by government troops, and then by Jek.

Dancer/actor Christopher Gable is magnificent as Jek, portraying the dark madness and pitiful loneliness of the character purely through voice and body movement, being without the aid of any facial expression. John Normington is equally superb as Morgus and a wonderful cast also includes Maurice Roeves, Robert Glenister and Roy Holder. The direction, by Graham Harper, is also stunning. Everything is played dead straight in a dramatic, almost operatic, style including Morgus looking into the camera to deliver certain lines like a Shakesperean aside.

The exciting conclusion sees The Doctor escape Morgus' hired gun runners and rush to find an antidote to the infection. As Jek, Morgus and the soldiers die in a climactic battle, he carries a sick

Peri to the Tardis but there is only enough antidote for her. She instantly recovers but The Doctor collapses. He sees images of previous companions encouraging him to live – whilst The Master encourages him to die – and then regenerates…into Colin Baker.

Nathan-Turner had decided to end season 21 with Colin Baker's first story, the intention being to give viewers the opportunity to grow used to the new lead actor before his first full series. This would have been a good idea had the first story been strong. Unfortunately, The *Twin Dilemma* is dire, its negative impact made worse by the stark contrast with the quality of the preceding *The Caves of Androzani*. Baker's debut as the Sixth Doctor also suffered from other creative decisions. Historically, the Doctor's behaviour is eccentric in his first post-regeneration story as he adjusts to his new identity; it is often an important plot device. In this story, The Doctor's emotional mood swings were particularly extreme, however, with him being downright unpleasant to Peri, even trying to strangle her at one point. It was only towards the end of the story that his personality starts to settle. Had this been the first story of the season, this might have been fine, but with a gap of ten months before the next season it left many viewers unsure whether or not they liked this new Doctor. Not perhaps the best hook to attract audiences the following year.

Another huge error was made in the choice of outfit for the Sixth Doctor. Nathan-Turner wanted a garish outfit comprising hideously clashing colours which emphasised the Doctor's brash and slightly contradictory personality. It was too extreme, however, and unfairly saddled Baker with an image that became a distraction and talking point for the wrong reasons. The actor himself disliked it, wanting something more subtle. Russell T Davies has since called it "one of the single worst decisions in television history" [4]. Nathan-Turner, it seems, was just about the only person who liked it.

It could be said that 1983 and 1984 were watershed years for *Doctor Who*. Not only did it mark a change of lead and regular cast members, but also the appointment of Jonathan Powell as Head of

Drama in 1983 and Michael Grade as Controller of BBC1 the following year. Both men made it clear they did not like *Doctor Who* – although Powell's initial memos to Nathan-Turner were constructively critical. The attitude of BBC management shifted from indifference to open hostility. The programme had long struggled with a lack of financial backing from the BBC, but now it suffered from a lack of love too. Nathan-Turner must have felt under greater pressure and his continued participation in overseas conventions and pantomime production, in addition to use of budget for overseas locations, attracted further scrutiny from fans and BBC management alike. This context may explain why from this point it sometimes felt that the show was less confident, unclear of its direction and generally bleaker. Another issue may have been the decision reportedly made by outgoing BBC1 controller Alan Hart to change the length of the episodes to 45 minutes, which suddenly meant the production team were adjusting to a different format.

Certainly Season 22 (Colin Baker's first full season) was a mixed bag of stories and quality, with an over-reliance on classic *Doctor Who* themes, monsters and villains featuring in four of the six stories. The style was also notably darker and nastier. This contrasted with the other imposed change which saw the programme return to its Saturday night transmission, but at a 5.20pm slot, not 6.20pm as originally planned.

The tone was set in the first story, *Attack of the Cybermen*, a slickly directed but highly derivative tale which featured the eponymous monsters along with other familiar characters and settings in a disjointed story where some of this seems to have been thrown in for effect rather than plot relevance. There is plenty of violence and a scene where a character's hand is crushed by the Cyberman is particularly gruesome. The subsequent *Vengeance on Varos* is also extremely violent and grim, but it is a much stronger, darkly satirical story, written by Philip Martin (writer/creator of the BBC 1970s series *Gangsters*). Inhabitants of an authoritarian society are kept entertained by broadcasts of public torture and execution. The story is a commentary on the contemporary popularity of video nasties and snuff movies as entertainment and the dangers of a desensitised society. On broadcast, it attracted both praise for its exploration of these topics but also considerable criticism for its violent content, including scenes of torture, hanging and human experimentation.

Mark of the Rani was a much more traditional and entertaining story, set in England during the Industrial Revolution, featuring the return of The Master and introducing a new female Time Lord villainess, wonderfully played by Kate O'Mara. The interplay between the Master, The Rani and The Doctor is especially fun. This was followed by *The Two Doctors* where the Sixth Doctor and Peri meet the Second Doctor (Patrick Troughton) and his companion, Jamie (Frazer Hines), along with another classic monster, The Sontarans (last seen in the Tom Baker era). A fine cast also included Laurence Payne, Jacqueline Pearce and John Stratton. What should have been a series highlight is, however, a disappointing mess of a weak and over-long story, nonsensical continuity and elements which serve little purpose. Troughton is wonderful, but completely underused, as are The Sontarans, whilst the use of Seville for the setting (and subsequent costly location shooting) adds nothing and seems pointless. Worst of all, although the story contains plenty of dark humour, it is also deeply unpleasant, with themes of cannibalism, biological augmentation and scenes that are gratuitously gory – including vicious killings, a character murdering and eating an old woman and also eating a rat, and Sontarans being mutilated with acid. All of this being shown on Saturday at teatime.

The penultimate story, *Timelash* was very poor – arguably the worst of Colin Baker's era although it does feature a gloriously over-the-top performance by Paul Darrow as the chief villain played in the manner of Laurence Oliver's Richard III. Darrow even suggested the character should have a hump! The final story, *Revelation of the Daleks*, was the best of the season, although it is sometimes too frantic and confusing and, once again, contains considerable violence, horror and unsettling themes and scenes. Set on the planet Necros, the facility of Tranquil Repose supposedly offers the opportunity for wealthy dead clients to be cryogenically frozen until a time that developments in science mean they can be resuscitated. In a theme similar to the movie *Soylent Green*, it transpires that the bodies are actually turned into synthetic food for export and as raw materials for a new race of Daleks being created by Davros. The story benefits from an excellent guest cast, including Eleanor Bron, Alexei Sayle, Clive Swift and (in particular) William Gaunt brilliant as the mercenary, Orsini, a superb character who deserved his own series.

One major success of the season was the consistent excellence of Colin Baker and Nicola Bryant. The intention for Baker's Doctor was that he would continue to be unpredictable, and his character would evolve more slowly over time. This idea was repeated with Peter Capaldi's Twelfth Doctor debuting in 2013. Nonetheless, Baker's Sixth Doctor had already become much more stable and, as the season unfolded, the relationship with Peri, whilst continuing to be occasionally abrasive, became much warmer; their growing on-screen chemistry reflected Baker's and Bryant's off-screen friendship too. Their performances compensated for a season of stories that was decidedly variable in quality, and with a tone of increased horror and violence which made some people uneasy, although others pointed out that they had been features of the programme since its inception.

Off-screen, however, momentous events were occurring. On 21st February 1985, Nathan-Turner received a phone call from record producer and *Doctor Who* 'super-fan' Ian Levine relaying a rumour that the programme was to be cancelled by the BBC. Around the same time, writer Robert Holmes called Eric Saward with the same news. This was a complete shock to Nathan-Turner who dismissed the rumour as he had had no contact from the BBC on the matter and there had been no discussion about such a decision. He then flew to the US to attend another convention. On 25th February, on his return, Nathan-Turner was summoned to a meeting with Jonathan Powell who told him that *Doctor Who* was being cancelled with immediate effect and planned work on the next series was to be shelved.

Multiple conflicting explanations have been given for this decision, and for what happened next. In a recent interview, Michael Grade proudly claimed that it was his decision to end the programme at that point; however, he was surprised to be reminded that it ran for another four years. Subsequent events also suggest that Grade's thinking, responsibility, and power were not always what he claimed. At different times, Michael Grade has variously stated that the cancellation was because *Doctor Who* had become too violent, had lost its way, was past its sell by date, that there was dissatisfaction with the production team, the programme was no longer attracting viewers against US imports, and that as a studio-based drama shot on video it looked cheap and less relevant to audiences in a post *Star Wars* world. Although some of these points have merit, they do not stand up to full scrutiny.

If the main issue had been the programme's tone and violence, or its production team, it would have been easy for BBC bosses to force changes – and there is little evidence that they had tried. Whilst the move back to Saturday night had seen a drop in viewing figures, they were still reasonable for a BBC family programme. There is no doubt that *Doctor Who* looked cheap compared to other TV series and movies, but this had been the case from day one and *Star Wars* and subsequent high budget movies and US TV series had been around a long time, during which period *Doctor Who* had maintained its popularity. It is certainly the case that the 1970s saw a gradual shift away from studio-based drama, but if this was the BBC's primary issue with *Doctor Who* it seems contrary to its refusal to increase the show's budget, which was lower than other BBC dramas. Furthermore, continued high international sales, including growing popularity in the US, brought significant income to the BBC and was not suggestive of a programme that had lost its appeal.

The primary reason for cancellation seems to have been money and the influence of increasing government criticism. The BBC was facing considerable financial pressures, due to key management decisions. The cost of producing new flagship soap opera *EastEnders* had been a huge commitment and required cuts to other areas of the series and serials budget. Meanwhile, it had been decided to bring forward the launch of the BBC's new daytime service to steal a march on ITV, but this had created a hole in BBC finances. Furthermore, the BBC was operating in the context of licence fee restraints and a very hostile Government. This was not new; governments of all shades of political opinion had attacked or tried to control the BBC when it suited, and its most effective way of doing this was through setting the licence fee, the BBC's primary income source. With spiralling inflation, Jim Callaghan's 1970s Labour Government had fixed a punitively low BBC licence fee, resulting in a real term loss of income which had a major effect on the BBC's finances into the 1980s.

However, with Margaret Thatcher hostilities became visceral. She saw the organisation as the antithesis of the privatised, free market society she championed, but feelings reached a crescendo with her unhappiness over the corporation's coverage of the Falklands conflict. Mindful of its requirement for impartiality, the BBC sought to delicately reflect a wide range of views including those that were opposed to the war. This resulted in ministers, Conservative MPs and newspapers with vested interests (such as Murdoch's *The Sun*) accusing the BBC of treachery. The attacks continued. Thatcher had already packed the BBC governors with 'her own men' and by early 1985, as difficult current licence fee negotiations were concluding, she initiated The Peacock Committee, an ultimately unsuccessful attempt to scrap the licence fee and reduce the size of the BBC.

This scenario must have influenced BBC management decisions, and some fans suggested that cancelling an institution like *Doctor Who* was a way of showing the consequences of BBC funding cuts, although Grade has denied this. It seems more likely that Grade and Powell's personal dislike of the show would have done it no favours in budget decisions. If Grade thought this would be an easy decision, however, he was in for a shock. A wounded Nathan-Turner, who must have felt betrayed by an organisation he had spent his career with, enlisted the support of Ian Levine to ensure the news of the cancellation was leaked. This caused a furore with fans and in the tabloids. Journalists pursued Grade whilst on a skiing holiday. Several papers, including the *Daily Star*, launched 'Save Doctor Who' campaigns. Angry fans jammed switchboards, and even second Doctor Patrick Troughton helped with the campaign.

The reaction caused consternation amongst the BBC Board of Governors. Just a few days later, on 1st March 1985, a press release reported a phone call BBC Managing Director Bill Cotton had made to the coordinator of the DWAS (Doctor Who Appreciation Society) confirming that *Doctor Who* would return 18 months later, starting in Autumn 1986, and back to the familiar 25-minute episodes so it could run for more weeks, concluding, "I am confident that *Doctor Who* has a great future on BBC1". [5] Grade's reaction was once again contradictory. At the time he stated that the next season was just being delayed for a year and that *Doctor Who* would be back – "That's a promise. And it will be better than ever". Whether the real aim was cancellation, or delay, it is clear that Grade and Powell had significantly underestimated the affection for the programme and lost control of the situation, resulting in some furious back peddling. BBC managers considered it another misstep by Grade, who had faced a similar outcry when he initially cancelled *Dallas*.

In spite of the BBC's reassurance, Nathan-Turner and Saward were left in limbo, unsure how and whether to plan for the next season, while fans were still frustrated with an eighteen-month delay. The media campaigns continued, and the most bizarre episode was the recording of a charity record *Doctor in Distress*, written and produced by Levine. A promised A-list celebrity 'supergroup' did not materialise, but the record did feature cast members Colin Baker, Nicola Bryant, Anthony Ainley and Nicholas Courtney, along with an eclectic mix of performers who happened to be around and available on the day, including singers Jona Lewie, Hazell Dean, Phyliss Nelson, comedienne Faith Brown, actress Sally Thomsett, members of groups Bucks Fizz, The Moody Blues, Dollar and the cast of Starlight Express. Interestingly, it also featured a young Hans Zimmer on keyboards. As a *Doctor Who* fan, I naturally bought the record and can confirm it is truly awful. The lyrics, which reference characters and creatures from the series, are gut-wrenchingly dire and give the impression of being written on the back seat of a bus on the way to the recording studio. Unsurprisingly, it failed to trouble the charts and the BBC banned it, either because of its implied criticism of management or simply out of good taste.

Rumours quickly circulated that, on its return, the programme would be reduced to just fourteen 25-minute episodes. This was strenuously denied by Nathan-Turner (who had not been told this), but once again fan and media rumours turned out to be true. Season 22 debuted on 6th September and comprised a single overarching 14-part story called *The Trial of a Time Lord;* the longest single *Doctor Who* story ever made. The Tardis is taken out of time and the Doctor is brought before a Time Lord court to stand trial for his 'crimes' of interference with the events on other worlds. The court is presided over by The Inquisitor (judge), played by Lynda Bellingham, and the Doctor must defend himself against the prosecuting counsel, The Valeyard, played by Michael Jayston.

Devised by Nathan-Turner and Saward, the story was clearly art imitating life mirroring the feeling that the programme was on trial with BBC management. The trial was an overarching theme, incorporating three distinct but linked segments which feature as evidence presented to the trial. Consciously referencing Dickens' *A Christmas Carol*, the first segment is set in the past, the second in the present and the third in the future. The final two episodes form the story's conclusion. In these, The Master appears on the court screens and reveals the Valeyard to be a distillation of the dark elements of The Doctor's persona, somehow turned into a future evil incarnation who has corrupted The Matrix (the repository of all Time Lord knowledge) to distort the evidence and take over The

Doctor's remaining lives. The Doctor enters The Matrix to defeat both The Master and The Valeyard.

Dominic Glynn was commissioned to write a new version of the *Doctor Who* theme, and the series style was less violent than the previous season, although there was still plenty of action and death! The second segment saw the return of the character Sil, previously seen in *Vengeance on Varos,* and the departure of Peri (by mutual consent with Nicola Bryant). She is apparently killed after being victim of yet another biological experiment, but at the end of story it is revealed that this has been faked and she is alive and well. The third segment featured the introduction of new companion Mel, played by Bonnie Langford whose casting seemed to be another whim on Nathan-Turner's part. As this segment is set in the future, we meet Mel having already apparently become an established companion. The lack of a backstory or explanation is confusing and reflects a hastily created character who was never really developed much further through the rest of the time on the programme, and too often was reduced to a caricatured screaming assistant. This was a waste of a famous and talented actress who was capable of bringing much more to the show.

Tensions between Nathan-Turner and Saward had been bubbling for some time but came to a head during the making of *The Trial of a Time Lord.* Robert Holmes was commissioned to write the concluding episodes 13 and 14 but fell ill and sadly passed away before he could complete them. Saward finished the scripts, but Nathan-Turner did not like his ideas for the final episode which ended on a cliff-hanger with The Doctor and The Valeyard locked in mortal combat in the time vortex (another allusion to Holmes and Moriarty in *The Final Problem).* Nathan-Turner felt the ending was too downbeat; perhaps he was also concerned it might encourage a further cancellation of the series. A furious and already frustrated Saward quit as script editor and refused permission for his final episode script to be used in any way. With the clock ticking on production, Nathan-Turner asked stalwart writers Pip and Jane Baker to come up with a new version of the final episode in a few days. He sent them the episode 13 script to read and met them with a lawyer present to ensure they were given no information on Saward's episode 14 script. The result, particularly given the circumstances, was a surprisingly entertaining and satisfactory finale. The Doctor is victorious, but the final scene reveals The Valeyard to have escaped, potentially to return again.

The Trial of a Time Lord has received a mixed response, with some feeling the overall story was too long, confusing and that it did not really hang together. The trial linking the stories together was an interesting concept, but some felt that it slowed down and interrupted the action. It is certainly the case that some segments felt stronger than others. Personally, I find it more enjoyable, interesting and entertaining than Baker's previous season. There are no real dud episodes, and the final two episodes are particularly imaginative, especially given the context of how they were put together. The courtroom setting works well and the verbal jousting between The Doctor and The Valeyard is great fun. Michael Jayston is a superb actor and brings real colour and presence to the role, whilst Lynda Bellingham is also excellent as the arched but ultimately fair Inquisitor. Colin Baker seems much more settled in the role. He has several moments which show off the best qualities of The Sixth Doctor and his brash over-confident persona is very suited to the concept of defending himself in a Time Lord court.

Sadly, however, BBC managers felt it was time for a change. Once again, there are contradictory explanations for what happened next. For some time, Nathan-Turner had expressed a desire to leave *Doctor Who* and had been proposing other projects to produce, all of which had been rejected. His diaries indicate that at the end of 1986 he had been told he could leave, but that he first had to inform Colin Baker that his contract was not being renewed. There are different versions, as to whether this was an instruction by Michael Grade or Jonathan Powell. Nevertheless, someone instructed Nathan-Turner and despite his protestations, he was forced to break the bad news to Baker. It has been suggested that BBC management really wanted to force Nathan-Turner to leave, so this instruction was a bluff to force his hand. If true, it backfired, and Baker was unhappy that he felt his producer had not really stood up for him. When news broke that Baker was leaving, there was huge sympathy from fans and sections of the media who felt he had been treated badly and not had the support or the quality of scripts enjoyed by his predecessors. It must have been especially awkward as shortly afterwards Nathan-Turner started rehearsals on another pantomime, starring Colin Baker!

Around this time, Michael Grade approached Sydney Newman, the man who had devised *Doctor Who* back in 1963, for ideas to revitalise the programme. Newman proposed setting more stories on Earth and bringing back Patrick Troughton as The Doctor, with two young companions. At a later stage, Troughton would regenerate into a female Doctor, demonstrating that this was not a 21st century idea at all. These discussions contradict Grade's subsequent confident assertions that he was intent on killing the programme at that point. Jonathan Powell rejected the ideas, and in late November told Nathan-Turner to produce the next season and find a new Doctor. Nathan-Turner was deeply unhappy, having been reassured he could finally leave the show, but was given no choice and was not going to throw away his BBC career by refusing.

Sylvester McCoy was chosen to be the seventh Doctor, which initially provoked a lukewarm response as although he had considerable theatrical experience many recognised McCoy as an entertainer, from programmes such as *Tiswas* and *Vision-On*. This did nothing to improve Nathan-Turner's image with many fans. Many fan groups were openly critical, causing Nathan-Turner to reduce contact with fans and stop attending UK conventions. Another new titles sequence and version of the theme (by Keff McCulloch) was produced for the new era. Andrew Cartmel, who up until then was relatively inexperienced, was appointed as new script editor and, once again, the immediate challenge was to quickly find suitable scripts with production rapidly approaching. The haste goes some way to explain a lacklustre first season for McCoy which comprised four stories over 14 episodes, but which nevertheless, once again, attracted an array of star names in guest parts.

Colin Baker turned down the opportunity to make one more story, at the end of which The Doctor would regenerate. Baker was, understandably, feeling bruised and felt that if he was being removed, he needed to get on with his career. A pre-title sequence for the first story *Time and the Rani* therefore used video effects to blur Sylvester McCoy in a rather unconvincing 'Colin Baker wig' as he is transformed into the new Doctor. At first, and with very little guidance, McCoy was unsure how to approach the role and, drawing on his background, was too comedic in much of his first series, even playing the spoons in the opening episode! Whether it was under direction from the BBC or due to the limited time to properly plan the new season, the overall style was considerably lighter, frothier and (literally) brighter, re-enforced by loud synth-based incidental music and a switch to using video for location shooting, resulting in a cleaner, less grainy feel.

The second story, *Paradise Towers,* had a darker satirical undertone which was not effectively realised on screen. Based on a JG Ballard book, a range of bizarre characters on an alien world live in a dilapidated tower block managed by authoritarian bureaucratic caretakers serving a mysterious evil disembodied 'architect'. It is both a fantasy about an alien society gone crazy, but also can be seen as extreme metaphor for 1980s inner city decay and social decline. It features a terrific guest cast, including Richard Briers, who shamelessly hams up the comedic role of the Hitler-like Chief Caretaker.

Highlight of the series was the inventive and entertaining *Delta and the Bannermen.* A group of evil humanoids (Bannermen) pursuing Delta, the last surviving member of her species, land in a Welsh holiday camp in the late 1950s, very much referencing *Hi-Di-Hi.* It is full of pace, humour and 1950s music. A super guest cast includes Don Henderson, Hugh Lloyd, Stubby Kaye and Ken Dodd as The Tollmaster who is killed by the wicked Bannermen. Nathan-Turner had to respond to numerous letters from viewers upset that the beloved Doddy had been murdered on TV!

The final story of the season was *Dragonfire* which saw the departure of Mel and the debut of new companion, Ace, played by Sophie Aldred. Sophie and Sylvester had a wonderful chemistry off and on screen and their partnership would last for the remainder of the decade. Bonnie Langford's exit was as sudden, inexplicable, and disappointing as her entrance. Her character suddenly decides to leave the Tardis and go travelling with the shady, but loveable rogue, Sabalom Glitz (Tony Selby), first seen in *The Trial of a Timelord.* The story features a famous horrific scene where the ice skinned chief villain's face melts under the intense light from the sun. The special effects team realised this by creating a model skull head covered in wax skin layers which were melted by a heat gun.

Season 24 was transmitted at 7.35pm on Wednesday evenings, scheduled opposite the television behemoth *Coronation Street*, a national institution and one of the few programmes to have been running longer than *Doctor Who*. This move ensured viewing figures would not improve and suggested that the BBC no longer cared about the programme. On the plus side, the working relationship between producer and script editor was much happier, Sylvester McCoy had now settled into the role and Nathan-Tuner was content to remain as producer. Furthermore, they had more time to plan for the next season – the 25th, *Doctor Who's* Silver Jubilee – so there was a renewed energy and confidence about the future.

Nathan-Turner and Cartmel felt they should adjust the programme's tone to be less whimsical and more dramatic. He and McCoy also felt The Doctor should be played more seriously: an enigmatic, mysterious, and manipulative character. These changes were first seen in the season opener, *Remembrance of the Daleks,* by Ben Aaronovitch, which has become renowned as a stone-cold classic and was the perfect start to an anniversary season. A pre-titles sequence shows a spaceship approaching Earth, picking up a jumble of satellite broadcasts from the world including the sound of a speech from John F Kennedy. The Doctor and Ace have mysteriously landed near Coal Hill School in 1963, the school where we first met the Doctor's granddaughter, Susan Foreman, and her teachers Ian and Barbara, way back in the opening episode 25 years previously. They encounter a group of scientists and soldiers, led by the Brigadier-like Group Captain Gilmore (Simon Williams) investigating strange signals who battle a lone Dalek which The Doctor destroys with some Nitro 9 stored in Ace's backpack.

As the story unfolds, it is revealed The Doctor has set a trap for his old adversary, The Daleks, by luring them to capture the Hand of Omega, a powerful Time Lord weapon. He had not anticipated there would be two Dalek factions, however; a small group of rebel traditional grey Daleks led by the black Dalek Supreme, and a larger force of white Daleks led by The Dalek Emperor who are using Coal Hill School as a location of a transmat for scout Daleks to seek out the rebels in advance of a full landing party. The Doctor's task is to keep the humans out of harm's way whilst his plan is realised. After a titanic battle between the Dalek factions, the Emperor's Daleks seize the Hand of Omega. The Doctor contacts the Dalek mother ship, and the shock reveal is that The Emperor is Davros who has re-established his authority over his creations. The Doctor tricks Davros into using the Hand of Omega weapon to apparently destroy Earth, but instead it has been programmed to seek out and destroy Skaro.

The story is full of delightful moments. A Dalek hovers up the stairs to pursue The Doctor (the very first time this was seen on screen). A television is switched off just as the announcer is introducing the brand-new Saturday teatime science fiction series. The rebel Daleks are hiding in a scrapyard, reminiscent of the Totters Lane junkyard where The Doctor 'lived' in 1963. In the school laboratory, Ace picks up the same book that Susan Foreman had been reading in that very first episode. It is also intriguing. We do not know how long The Doctor has been working on his plan, whether he stole The Hand of Omega, or if the fact that he possesses it suggests that he is either acting with the authority of The Time Lords or that he is a more powerful figure than we had previously suspected. The story also comments on racism, not just through the inclusion of The Daleks themselves but also through the motivations of some human characters and references such as a note in a guesthouse window making it clear that people of 'colour' were not welcome.

The second story, *The Happiness* Patrol, is a curiosity: inventive, interesting, but not entirely satisfying. The Tardis materialises in an alien society where sadness is illegal and can be punished by death. Although a fantasy, the story is also a subtle allegory to 80s Britain and another excellent guest cast is headed by Sheila Hancock who plays the planet's ruler and expertly channels elements of Margaret Thatcher in her performance. One of the real 'marmite' aspects is the Kandy Man monster which looks like a life-sized Bertie Bassett. It is simultaneously a brilliant and completely absurd character which attracted criticism and ridicule.

This was followed by *Silver Nemesis* which, as the title implies, can be seen as the celebration story for The Doctor's silver jubilee and, in fact, its first episode was broadcast 25 years to the day from when *Doctor Who* began. It is a complex, confusing, but not unexciting story featuring the return of the Cybermen, a mysterious time-travelling 16th century alchemist who it seems has previously encountered the Doctor, a small group of modern-day Nazis and host of other eclectic characters. It feels extremely rushed and there are too many characters for it to make any sense, but it is still an enjoyable romp. Once again, the sense is that The Doctor is manipulating the whole situation and ultimately tricks everyone to prevail.

The season's final story, *The Greatest Show in the Galaxy*, preys on the common distrust of clowns, that many people fear. The Tardis lands on a planet and encounters a 'psychic circus' performing to a single family who turn out to be the Gods of Ragnarok who constantly crave entertainment. The main villains are the sinister Chief Clown and his group of robot clowns but there are also other odd and mysterious characters. Production almost had to be cancelled due to asbestos being found in the BBC studios, but Nathan-Turner ingeniously arranged for a large circus tent marquee to be erected in the BBC car park which allowed shooting to be completed. Ultimately, this made it a visually stylish and innovative story, but not the strongest on which to end the season.

Although Nathan-Turner had been happy to stay on for the anniversary season he once again asked to be released to work on other projects, only for this to be refused again. There must have been a sense that the programme was living on borrowed time with the BBC. It continued to be scheduled opposite *Coronation Street*, budgets remained restricted, and both its studio set and video recorded format increasingly contrasted with the trend for dramas series shot on film. Furthermore, the drive from the new BBC Director General, John Birt, was to buy in programmes from independent production companies, reducing the need for established BBC production departments and so many contracted staff producers.

Season 26 launched with very little publicity. The collection of stories would largely focus on Ace and see The Doctor being increasingly shadowy and manipulative, even to the point of appearing to 'use' Ace on occasions. There was also a suggestion that The Doctor was sadder, weary of the violence and suffering he had seen. McCoy now wore a brown jacket which emphasised The Doctor's increasingly darker and brooding character.

The opening story *Battlefield* was an action packed and enjoyable story, drawing on Arthurian Legend, featuring the return of The Brigadier and a modern UNIT. The suspended animated body of Arthur is discovered under the sea in a long-crashed spaceship from a different dimension. UNIT must battle with Morgaine and other dimension travelling knights to prevent them taking the Excalibur, which is a powerful weapon, and to save The Earth. Enigmatically, Morgaine recognises The Doctor as Merlin (possibly from The Doctor's future). The subsequent story *GhostLight* is a densely complex story set in an old house in Perivale in 1883 which (we learn) Ace would subsequently burn down in her 20th century childhood. It is a highly original and imaginative but baffling tale, featuring an array of mysterious characters, none of whom are who they appear, including the alien Light who is prevented from destroying the Earth by The Doctor.

The Curse of Fenric has become a fan favourite and weaves together a traditional monster story with themes including Norse mythology, vampirism, the power of faith and the morality of warfare. The Tardis materialises near a naval base towards the end of the Second World War where Fenric (an evil creature defeated and trapped by The Doctor centuries before) is released. A wonderful guest cast includes Nicholas Parsons, superb as the local vicar. In a poignant scene he is killed by haemovores (humans transformed into vampires), his vulnerability exposed because his experiences of the war have caused him to question his faith. Ace helps a mother and baby who it turns out will grow up to be her mother with whom she clashed so much as a child.

By now it was increasingly clear that *Doctor Who*'s days were numbered, so it is ironic that the final story is called *Survival*. Another imaginative and unusual story, but not the strongest on which to end a run of twenty-six years. The Doctor takes Ace to her home in Perivale where she discovers that her friends have been curiously transported to another planet whose inhabitants are transformed into Cheetah people. The Doctor meets The Master who is, himself, falling victim to this influence. It is a bizarre tale which combines both drama and offbeat humour and features possibly Anthony Ainley's best performance as The Master as he comes across as an evil but also tragic figure.

In September 1989, Nathan-Turner advised Sylvester McCoy and Sophie Aldred that the BBC would not be taking up their contracts for a 1990 season. At that point it was still not clear whether the programme was being rested or cancelled. Perhaps mindful of the previous furore, it seems as if the BBC was unsure itself and half-heartedly explored the possibility of independent production companies taking over the programme, possibly to return in 1991. Nathan-Turner was clearly in doubt, however, and arranged for McCoy to record a new post-synched voiceover speech for the final scene of *Survival* which would be a more fitting finale. Ironically, the recording took place on 23rd November 1989, twenty-six years to the day that *Doctor Who* was first broadcast:

"There are worlds out there where the sky is burning, where the sea's asleep and the rivers dream. People made of smoke, and cities made of song. Somewhere there's danger, somewhere there's injustice and somewhere else the tea's getting cold. Come on Ace, we've got work to do".

And with that, on 6th December 1989 *Doctor Who* ended. Not with a loud fanfare, protest, or argument, or even any certainty of what would happen next. After twenty-six years, it just stopped. A few months later, and with no further projects to work on, John Nathan-Turner was made redundant, discarded by the organisation in which he had spent his entire career. He would never work for the BBC again. On his final day, 31st August 1990, he packed up his office, preserving as many photographs, scripts, and documents as he could because anything that was left was to be junked. Friends and cast members did surprise him with a drink to wish him well, but the gregarious, flamboyant character decided against a farewell party, preferring to leave more quietly.

So, was the BBC right to pull the plug? There is no doubt that part way through the 80s the programme had taken a dip. This is not a reflection of the lead cast members who were excellent, but it seemed the production team had lost direction, resulting in some poor decisions on style and stories. Undeniably a lack of love and support from the BBC was largely to blame for this. It cannot have been easy to feel constantly threatened, under pressure and under-resourced, and see the programme shifted mercilessly around the schedules as if the Corporation was slightly embarrassed by its existence. In many ways, Nathan-Turner was remarkably successful in fighting for the continuation of the programme when so many of his BBC superiors clearly did not care.

The irony is that towards the end of the decade, the programme had felt re-invigorated. Stories were still inconsistent, but there was more creativity, variety, and less reliance on past glories. The Doctor had become a more interesting, enigmatic character and the character of Ace – whilst too dominant in some stories – was fresh and modern. Indeed, there were many similarities to their relationship as that between The Doctor and his/her companions in the post 2005 era. Cancellation also resulted in a burst of creativity. Passionate fans who had become professionals wrote original *Doctor Who* novels, produced videos, and audio plays, keeping the flame burning brightly. Many of these would go on to play a big part in its enormously successful future revival.

Whether or not the programme should have been axed, there is a strong argument that 1980s *Doctor Who* lay the foundations for the continuing interest in the show, long after its initial cancellation, and ultimately led to its triumphant 21st century return.

© Trevor Knight

1. John Nathan-Turner, *Doctor Who Magazine* special edition, 'In Their Own Words' Volume 3, p. 67.
2. Janet Fielding, *Doctor Who Magazine* special edition, 'In Their Own Words' Volume 4, p. 12.
3. Lalla Ward, *Doctor Who Magazine* special edition, 'In Their Own Words' Volume 3, p. 74.
4. Cited in *Who Do We Think We Are? Doctor Who's Britain* by Daniel Martin (2014) on the BFI website.
5. *Doctor Who: The Eighties*, (Virgin, 1996), p. 82.

RUMPOLE OF THE BAILEY – AN APPRECIATION

Horace Rumpole: "I often think that knowledge of the law is a bit of a handicap to a barrister."

There are few television series that, over the decades, I watched live when broadcast for the first time, then recorded episodes on to VHS video cassettes as that technology became widely available and affordable, then – as a completist wanting every episode advert-free – bought on official videos after waiting what seemed like an eternity for their release while copyright owners and distributors decided if the show was too niche, and then individual series DVD releases before, finally, in an all-in-one DVD box set. *Rumpole of the Bailey* is one of those rare series, alongside a few others including *Hill Street Blues* and *To the Manor Born*.

There are even fewer series that I instantly recall having sat as a young child and watched with my mother, while my father was out at a local council meeting, Masonic event or some such, or so he claimed. He was out a lot and that suited me just fine. My mother had taken me to the theatre as a child, to the Royal Festival Hall to see the Nutcracker Suite, to a 2,000-seater cinema to see Peter Ustinov as Hercule Poirot in the original and (for me) best adaptation of *Death on the Nile* and then at home on our three seat sofa we watched television dramas. These visits and viewings brought out in me a passion for live productions, film and television which has stayed with me throughout my life, a passion which still rages deep inside me as I take my children to the theatre and cinema. It is a passion which endured and sustained me while I served as Chairman of Elstree Studios for sixteen years from 2007 to 2023, as a continuing proud member of Bafta, a writer, documentary producer and broadcast journalist. It really is down to Mum. And two brilliant English teachers, one at primary school and one at secondary school who pushed and encouraged me into the Arts.

I was a mere fledgling when John Mortimer's witty and wily defence barrister Horace Rumpole first appeared on our small screens in the BBC's much-admired and award-winning series *Play for Today* which presented one-off works of drama, comedy and fantasy, for fourteen years between 1970 and 1984. *Rumpole of the Bailey* was one such one-off drama broadcast on the 16th of December 1975 and starring Leo McKern in the lead role. Whilst it is quite impossible now to imagine anyone in the titular role other than Leo McKern, it was rumoured at the time that the role had been pencilled in for the lugubrious Scottish actor Alistair Sim, but according to Mortimer "he turned out to be dead so he couldn't take it on!"

Rumpole of the Bailey was written by John Mortimer, a British barrister, dramatist, screenwriter, and author, born on 21 April 1923. During World War II, Oxford educated Mortimer was classified as medically unfit for military service due to poor eyesight and weak lungs. He was sent to work at the Crown Film Unit – an arm of the Government's Ministry of Information – which was tasked with making flag waving and jingoistic films to lift British spirits at home and abroad. Mortimer was assigned to work with poet, novelist, and screenwriter Laurie Lee, in the CFU's documentary department. As Mortimer recalled in his autobiography *Clinging to the Wreckage*: "I lived in London and went on journeys in blacked-out trains to factories and coal-mines and military and air force installations. For the first and, in fact, the only time in my life I was, thanks to Laurie Lee, earning my living entirely as a writer. If I have knocked the documentary ideal, I would not wish to sound ungrateful to the Crown Film Unit. I was given great and welcome opportunities to write dialogue, construct scenes and try and turn ideas into some kind of visual drama."

After the war, Mortimer was called to the Bar aged just 25, his early years taken up primarily with divorce work, which paid the bills. It was when he became Queen's Counsel in 1966 that Mortimer became firmly entrenched in criminal law, the early seeds for the character of Horace Rumpole being sown as the number of cases he fought grew, and his experience of the system with it.

Reginald 'Leo' McKern was born on 16th March 1920 in Sydney, New South Wales. He left school at just 15 and it was while working in a factory that he was the victim of a tragic accident which resulted in him losing his left eye. McKern took to acting, performing the first of hundreds of stage roles, in Sydney in 1944. He fell deeply in love with Australian actress Jane Holland and moved to England so he could be with her. They married in 1946 and McKern quickly established himself as an accomplished actor, a stint at the Old Vic lifting his reputation, transforming Shakespearean characters with a depth of understanding and aplomb not often seen in an actor of his young age and certainly not letting a glass eye and an Australian accent get in the way of notable performances.

McKern was in demand for film too, with roles in a diverse array of movies including cheap but thrilling *X the Unknown* (1956), Val Guest's groundbreaking end-of-the-planet drama *The Day The Earth Caught Fire* (1961), Oscar-winning and multi award-winning films *A Man for All Seasons* (1966) and *Ryan's Daughter* (1970). On the small screen he remains fondly remembered as one of the several different actors to play Number Two in the iconic late-60s series *The Prisoner*. McKern found the experience arduous, suffering a breakdown from the intensity the role demanded. No one could ever accuse Leo McKern of not throwing himself fully in to every role he took on and he became a much relied upon staple of stage and screen.

When cast as Horace Rumpole, McKern, a jobbing actor, believed, as indeed did creator and writer John Mortimer, that this was to be just another one-off job. The original play was set in the year 1974 and defence barrister Horace Rumpole is 64 and approaching the latter years of his vocation. He has not progressed far up the legal ladder, much to the dismay and constant embarrassment of his wife Hilda, whose father was C H Wystan, Head of Rumpole's Chambers. Hilda cannot for the life of her fathom why it is that Rumpole has not made it higher up the legal ladder as her dear daddy did. If not head of Chambers, perhaps a Judgeship. She is not in denial. Hilda is aware of the ire and disapproval that his behaviour and the clients and causes he chooses to represent causes among fellow barristers and judges. Yet Hilda still holds out hope that her husband will one day, even after many decades at the Bar making very little upwardly mobile progress, finally do the family name proud. Horace seeks to placate her, he wants a quiet life, while in turn and out of ear shot refers to Hilda as 'She Who Must Be Obeyed', a nod to the strong-willed defiant Queen in H Rider Haggard's novel *She*. It is an irony in that Rumpole mostly fails to obey her, choosing his own path at every available opportunity.

Rumpole sees himself purely and simply, in his own words, as an Old Bailey Hack. He will take on any job so long as it is defending. The legal mantra he lives by is "Never plead guilty!" Rumpole always ensures that a client is made aware that if they declare their guilt to him he is unable and unwilling to defend them in court, for he is a man of principle and while he may hold his own private views as to the guilt or otherwise of a client, as long as the client himself has not confessed to the crime, he will ensure the client has their days in court with him leading the charge at the defensive helm; Rumpole always gives it his best shot. He is a firm believer in the presumption of innocence, the golden thread of British justice.

In the BBC *Play for Today*, *Rumpole of the Bailey*, we are introduced to the irreverent sixty-something defence barrister whose court style displeases his prosecution counterparts and sitting judges in equal measure. Horace Rumpole has been married to wife Hilda for more years than either of them care to remember, a union which produced just one off-spring, son Nick, who has always felt second place to the criminals his father spends most of his waking hours preparing to and then defending. Indeed, with Nick imminently leaving to study in America, Rumpole instead of spending what little time he has left with Nick before the trip - which may or may not see his son return to England - is in court defending a Jamaican teenager who claims to have been coerced in to confessing to carrying out the random stabbing of a pedestrian waiting at a bus stop after a cricket match. En route to the airport, Nick stops off at the Bailey to have lunch with his father and they part on speaking terms. It is clear that the Old Bailey is Rumpole's home, certainly where he feels at his happiest, and he needs to defend the prosecuted as much as they need him to defend them. It is a perfect symbiotic relationship giving Rumpole short-lived highs he craves and affection too from those found not guilty - affection and respect so clearly deficient in almost every other aspect of his personal and working life.

The one off *Rumpole of the Bailey* was produced by Irene Shubik who began her working career at ABC TV, as well as working as a story editor on *Armchair Theatre*. Shubik co-produced *The Wednesday Play* for the BBC, overseeing its morphosis in to *Play for Today*. It was Shubik who insisted on the casting of Leo McKern, when Michael Hordern was seriously mooted to take on the lead role. McKern and Shubik hit it off from the word go. McKern found the production deeply satisfying, along with John Mortimer's clever pithy script. With McKern's enthusiasm to return to the role (if ever called upon to do so), it was only a matter of time before he would be donning Rumpole's battered wig and gown once again.

Irene Shubik, buoyed by the positive audience reaction and, most importantly, BBC Executive feedback to the play, believed that there was a deep vein of courtroom drama to be mined. As producer, she set about commissioning six new scripts from John Mortimer for a series of one hour dramas for the BBC. Her enthusiasm was frustrated by a change of senior personnel at the Beeb which saw the project put on ice for a year until, at the invitation of the head of drama at Thames Television, Verity Lambert, Shubik packed her bags and, with her six *Rumpole* scripts under her arm, made the move across to 'the other side'.

Looking back now, it still seems impossible to believe that the BBC would have turned down the opportunity to have made what would turn out for Thames TV to be several series across 14 years of the increasingly successful and popular exploits of Horace Rumpole. But television history is littered with passed over projects, shows that almost did not get made, and some abandoned by one channel after a series or so only to be picked up by another and run with. Massive BBC comedy hit *Gavin and Stacey* was turned down by ITV, according to its former Head of Comedy, because it was largely set in Wales! Writer Jed Mercurio said publicly that the Beeb turned down his first pitch for *Line of Duty*. *Men Behaving Badly* began its life on ITV who ditched it only for the BBC to turn it in to a comedy viewership juggernaut for the next five years. And let us not even go to *Fawlty Towers* or *Dad's Army* and the now well documented views of those doubting Thomas BBC executives at the time. "I wouldn't say the BBC threw away a pearl richer than all its tribe, but it has mislaid a tasty box of kippers", wrote Nancy Banks-Smith in *The Guardian*. Ah, isn't hindsight a marvellous talent to possess?

The 50th Academy Awards took place on Monday 3rd April 1978. Woody Allen's *Annie Hall* won four awards including Best Picture, and Best Actress for Diane Keaton. *Star Wars*, made at Elstree Studios, took home six Oscars, *Julia* starring Venessa Redgrave and Jason Robards won three including Best Supporting Actress and Actor, and Richard Dreyfuss won Best Actor for *The Goodbye Girl*.

On that same date the first of what would turn out to be six series and a two-hour special of *Rumpole of the Bailey* finally made it to UK television screens. All six episodes were written by John Mortimer. John Gorrie, who had directed the 1975 *Play for Today* one off Rumpole drama, was replaced by Herbert Wise, a television drama big hitter who began his career in the mid-1950s and would go on, as well as *Rumpole*, to direct classics including *I, Claudius* and Alan Ayckbourn's play cycle *The Norman Conquests*. On the big screen, Wise had directed one of the still much-adored *Edgar Wallace Mysteries* B-features, *To Have and To Hold*, and the big screen version of the small screen sitcom hit, *The Lovers*, written by Jack Rosenthal and starring Richard Beckinsale and Paula Wilcox.

In the first episode of the run, entitled *Rumpole and the Younger Generation*, Rumpole is called upon by the Timson clan, a well-established south London family, overtly moral yet with covert criminal tendencies. Rumpole is to defend the boss' son who appears to have inherited the light-fingered genetics of his elders. The Timson family would appear regularly across all the six series of *Rumpole of the Bailey*. As *Doctor Who* has his regular foes, be they Daleks or Cybermen, so too would the London courts have theirs across Rumpole's 14-year run, particularly the Timsons – Fred, Dennis, Cyril, Jim, Percy, Hugh, Nigel, Tony and Cary - and Rumpole was always on call to defend them all.

Horace Rumpole: "I find your restaurant pretentious and your portions skimpy. Your customers regale themselves in a dim religious atmosphere more fitting to evensong than a good night out. I find you an opinionated and self-satisfied bully. However, unlike you, I am on hire to even the most unattractive customer."

The television series gave writer John Mortimer screen time to draw out the main characters, add further layers of depth, give them more life and with as much of the drama taking place outside the courtroom as inside, whether it be Horace and Hilda's home at 25b Froxbury Mansions on the Gloucester Road, London SW7, Rumpole's Chambers at Number 3 Equity Court, or at the end of a hard day advocating for often the pettiest of criminals, joining him in a glass of Chateau Thames Embankment, the much maligned but even more drank house red at Fleet Street Wine bar, Pomeroy's, where Rumpole is allowed to sit, without criticism, to puff away on his cheap cheroots, his inexpensive billowing cigars, often the subject of critical debate at Chambers and liked even less by long-suffering wife Hilda. Forty years on, Rumpole's favourite smoke would most likely be banned in London as a major contributor to the city's pollution problems. Terrible things they were. And then it was back home to 'She Who Must Be Obeyed'.

Along the way, we get to hear either by his character voice over off-screen, or Rumpole on screen, (often in a whisper), his mind's workings along with his passion for poetry...Wordsworth in particular. Horace is well educated, well read and in another world perhaps might have fancied his chances of treading the theatrical boards as a classical actor. The performances of a barrister and an actor on stage have much in common, believability to the jury or audience at their core. It is not lost on any fans of the drama that Leo McKern was just that, a classical actor, and so able to bring a depth of understanding to that aspect of Rumpole's character that never allows for his courtroom mannerisms, gesticulations, or outbursts - however theatrical Rumpole's intends them - to be anything less than convincing within the confines of the character himself. Watching McKern as Rumpole acting up is very clever and always truthful. Joyous even. One never feels Rumpole is behaving this way because he wants to be the one in the limelight, or wishing to be fawned at, with people saying how great he is. No. Rumpole behaves like this simply to get through life and, more importantly to him, to get his defendants found not guilty and saved a term inside. It is a cigar smoke and mirrors trick, an act of deflection as well as act of defiance, often Horace's only way to get through the day. The audience never feels Rumpole is venal or arrogant for his own ends. It is clear that he takes the business of being a defence barrister very seriously indeed. The wig-and-gown is his costume and, once donned, he can place to one side most of the drudgery that this man in his mid-60s is beginning to feel; downtrodden after forty year's marriage to 'She' and to the service of the great accused of London.

After two highly successful and critically acclaimed series of *Rumpole of the Bailey*, Horace retires and along with Hilda goes to live in Florida to be with his son Nick who has now become a sociology professor and head of department at the University of Miami. The last episode of the second series was broadcast on 3 July 1979.

Hilda Rumpole: "You don't want to die in harness, do you? Poor old Daddy died in harness, didn't he?"
Horace Rumpole: "Oh really? I thought he died in the Tunbridge General Hospital."

And that was that. Except of course, it wasn't. Horace and Hilda were back for a one-off feature length special: *Rumpole's Return*, broadcast on ITV over the festive fortnight on 30 December 1980. The premise for the plot was quite simple: Rumpole is clearly bored living in retirement in Florida and when contacted by a member of Chambers, is quick to pack his cases and return to Froxbury Mansions and the British weather.

Viewers thought that really was the last we were to see of Horace Rumpole, and it was almost three years before the next series broadcast in October and November 1983 and a further three years before series four came along in January 1987. Writer John Mortimer was as busy as ever, with his legal work, his writing and his flamboyant lifestyle away from court and typewriter. All the *Rumpole* stories were also published in literary form, and I so enjoyed reading the books, each more than once so indelibly printed in my mind were the characters brought to life on screen that I could envisage them all and hear their voices when reading the words off the written page.

Indeed, it is right and fitting to give credit not just to Leo McKern for his delicious performance as Horace Rumpole but also the wonderful array of accompanying actors playing recurring characters, some in almost all episodes, some from time to time, that help lift John Mortimer's legal drama to even greater heights.

Of the many recurring characters, some who had lots to do and others just the odd line, I will choose just a few personal favourites, the ones who brought me the most on-screen joy, the ones with whom Rumpole's character and theirs melded so beautifully so as to cause not just moments of high drama but high comedy too. In no particular order, there was Horace Rumpole's long suffering wife Hilda, played originally in the BBC *Play for Today* by Joyce Heron, then Peggy Thorpe Bates for the first three series and *Rumpole's Return* and then Marion Mathie for series 4-7 when Peggy became too unwell to continue. Horace and Hilda Rumpole were indeed a marriage made in comedic drama heaven. Their tribulations brought us much viewing joy.

Hilda Rumpole: "Is that you, Rumpole?"
Horace Rumpole: "No, it's the Lord High Chancellor popped in to read the gas meter."

Guthrie Featherstone QC, soon to be knighted and become Sir Guthrie Featherstone, the head of Rumpole's Chambers, played by Peter Bowles as a regular across the first two series and then - as his own acting career skyrocketed following three viewing ratings breaking series of *To the Manor Born* for the BBC - appearing occasionally as a guest star until the end of the series in 1992. Guthrie is everything that Rumpole is not: tall, handsome, suave, well-groomed, a bit of a brown noser and well connected, knows how to play the game. He becomes a Member of Parliament during the series' run and then a High Court judge where he must sit in judgement on cases where Rumpole is leading for the defence. Their badinage, sometimes faux hostility, and at times happy camaraderie makes this odd couple such fun to watch.

Phyllida (nee Trant) Erskine-Brown was also a staple of the first two series and then a guest character across the rest of the series.

Played throughout by Patricia Hodge, Rumpole would refer to her as the "Portia of our Chambers". Phyllida bring some feminine grace into the very male and stale Chambers environment. She often supports Rumpole, but is not a pushover, has strong views of her own and advances in her career, becoming a Queen's Counsel, Recorder, and High Court Judge. She is married, not particularly happily, to fellow Chamber QC and would-be philanderer but in reality, rather dull – with everyone knowing it but himself - Claude Erksine-Brown. Phyllida EB allows the series a strong young female lead, emphasising how difficult it was for women to get such positions within the world of law. This was at a time when a woman had, for the first time, become Prime Minister of the United Kingdom and Phyllida's appointment to Chambers at 3 Equity Court reflected a wider and much overdue societal shift towards women achieving on merit, roles they were always able to take on, but often obstructed from doing so by male elders. Indeed, there was in her portrayal of Phyllida Erskine-Brown a touch of Margaret Thatcher, not in her politics, but in her determination to be heard and respected for her ability and not to allow the legal system in general and some of the fuddy-duddies in Chambers in particular, to get in her way. It was more than just about her. It was for all her sex.

Of all the judges that Rumpole came into combative contact with, none could have been more bullish than His Honour Judge Roger Bullingham who appeared with much grandeur and pomposity across the first four series before the actor who played him, Bill Fraser, passed away. It was a fittingly over-the-top swansong role for one of the country's great comedy character actors: a judge who could not abide defence barristers, whose automatic default view was that a defendant must be guilty or why were they in his court. He liked Rumpole even less than those he was defending. Their courtroom battles were renowned in legal circles and made great viewing.

Horace Rumpole (to himself): A fair judge, an upright judge – always a terrible danger to the defence!"

And an honourable mention in dispatches for the oldest member of Chambers, T C Rowley, referred to by all as Uncle Tom. Played across six series by the great comedy actor who became a household name from the 1940s, Richard 'Stinker' Murdoch. Uncle Tom has not had a legal brief for as long as anyone can remember, but no one has the heart to let him go. Rumpole clerked for him when just a junior some four decades earlier. Uncle Tom, now fast approaching 80, still attends Chambers every day, practising his golf putting and unintentionally making very un-PC and inappropriate comments while wating for a brief to arrive, any brief, which of course they don't. He is loved and adored by all. The last vestiges of a bygone era at Chambers. As indeed was Richard Murdoch for fans of old school comedy. Uncle Tom was the last role Old Stinker Murdoch played in his 50+ year stage, radio, film and television career; he had made his first film appearance in 1937. He evoked a smile from the viewer in even the shortest of scenes, often with just a line to deliver, which he always did with aplomb and relish, the old professional that he was.

Rumpole of the Bailey returned for a sixth series in the autumn of 1991 and a seventh and final series of six episodes a year later in late 1992. The show had straddled three decades, primarily the tumultuous 1980s. After a one-off BBC play, 42 one-hour episodes and a two-hour special, it really was time for Horace Rumpole to hang up his wig and gown and retire. The very last episode – *Rumpole on Trial* – sees Rumpole charged with contempt of court and where he must be defended by fellow barrister Sam Ballard as Horace faces disbarment.

Sam Ballard: "Rumpole as a client! God give me strength!"
Hilda Rumpole: "Oh don't worry Sam. If God doesn't, I certainly will!"

The final episode of *Rumpole of the Bailey* saw original 1975 *Play for Today* director John Gorrie taking helm of the production proceedings back, some 17 years later, one last time, to ensure Horace made it safely through with his reputation intact.

As Horace Rumpole had by now hit his 70s, so too had Leo McKern, who while no longer able to work at the breakneck speed of decades before, continued to act, making his last film appearance in 1999. He died on 23 July 2002 aged 82.

Horace Rumpole: "Birth and death! They silence us all in the end."

Although nominated three times as Best Actor on television by BAFTA for his portrayal of Horace Rumpole, he never won the award. To fans of *Rumpole of the Bailey* across the world, there was no doubt Leo McKern was a winner. And after an almost six decade acting career, yet ultimately tending to be remembered for one role, McKern himself commented: "With Rumpole, one comes to be reconciled to the fact that it isn't half a bad thing to be stuck with." A view that perhaps even Hilda Rumpole came to hold in the end.

© Morris Bright MBE

ENDPIECE: THE DECADE WHEN TELEVISION BEGAN TO UNRAVEL

The television of the 1980s has always occupied the area akin to the 'decline and fall' of an empire in my mind, a decade which started badly and got worse. It was, I had long contended, the mirror image of the 1960s, which saw the medium go from strength to strength, producing some of the most imaginative and memorable work we have ever seen. The 1970s kept the momentum going to begin with, but ultimately suffered from the pressure to keep coming up with something new and exciting, and struggling to do so in the shadow of the previous decade. Even the wider roll out of colour television wasn't quite enough to compete with the magic, although it certainly had an impact for those viewers who could afford it. By the middle of the next decade, 18.5 million people tuned in to see the conclusion of the snooker world championships *beyond midnight,* although I was still watching TV in black-and-white. While I retain the view that TV's greatest decade was the 1960s and we have had diminishing returns ever since, I was nonetheless pleasantly surprised, as I began considering this 1980s journey, to be reminded that it wasn't as bad as I remembered. In fact, although by 1990 we had witnessed the slow beginnings of what was to become – in my eyes – the total disintegration of television as a creative medium, the 1980s did produce several classic series, which are every bit as good as anything from the swinging 60s era.

To provide some context, previous essays I have written on 1960s and 1970s television have looked at how what we were seeing on our screens went hand-in-hand with societal events and the development of fashion, popular music and culture. These things are inseparable. Television does and must reflect the world around it – and the best creative television will probe the society it comes from and satirise it. It will ask questions and present alternative viewpoints. It will debunk outdated theories and it will push the boundaries of what entertainment is. It will amuse, delight and shock... but above all, it will make viewers *think* for themselves. When television fails to do this, for several reasons – as we shall see – the result is a churning, hamster wheel of mind-numbing content. If you're not questioning the status quo all the time, you are, in effect, submitting to it and television, because of its relative ubiquitousness, was the perfect instrument with which to do either. It still is, of course, but these days the method of delivery is much wider, across other media platforms.

The beginning of the decade in the UK was also the start of a new government, with a new Prime Minister, who would – for better or worse – occupy the office for the entirety of the next 10 years. Whatever your opinion of Margaret Thatcher, she was there in Downing Street all through the decade, unlike the 2020s where we have seen three different Prime Ministers from the same party in the space of three months. But I digress, the point I'm making is that, at least cosmetically, there was some continuity in politics, unlike in the previous two decades. The effects of it or the damage being done to British society during that time is largely a matter for a political thesis, but it does have some relevance both to the creative output of the era and to the decade which succeeded it, the 1990s...more on that later. For now, as the 1970s drew to a close, with American-made television firmly ensconced with both feet under the table of British consumption, we were about to experience a particularly bleak moment in British pop culture.

Paul McCartney began 1980 flying into Japan with Wings to play gigs there, much to the excitement of his Japanese fanbase. The now legendary rocker in his own right had spent the 1970s shaping his own career away from the band he was in during the 1960s. Not even the musical material which filled the void left by The Beatles – hard rock, metal, glam, disco, punk, new wave, reggae – had been enough to suppress McCartney, so he ended up doing it to himself. The Japanese authorities found marijuana in a suitcase, and he was thrown in jail, where he spent nine nights before being deported.

That was it effectively for Wings. The band was over, and McCartney was rudderless again. Never one to be kept down for long though, he fell back on some home recordings he'd made the previous year and hey presto – he had a hit album with them: *McCartney II*! Meanwhile his ex-writing partner John Lennon, possibly inspired by the way McCartney had managed to turn things around, decided it was time for him to emerge from his self-imposed exile from the music business and release new material too. What we got was typically autobiographical and written by a more-mellow Lennon, enjoying life as a family man and settling nicely into telling the world about it all until...

One of the darkest days in the history of rock'n'roll and possibly wider western pop culture was arguably 8th December 1980. John Lennon, founding member of the music group that changed it all, loved by millions the world over, was murdered in New York City by someone seemingly fixated on attaining infamy. Lennon was gone. The possibility of a full reunion of the band was also lost. The world was in shock. Symbolically, the 1980s had begun with the senseless removal of one of the figures who helped to bring it all alive in the 1960s. What on earth was the 1980s going to bring next?

I mention these Beatles-related events because they are significant in the progression of popular culture in the UK (and the wider world) and would haunt the rest of the decade as an example of the influence of the once indestructible positive energy of a previous generation sinking to an all-time low, only to unexpectedly be resurrected by the next one in the 1990s. I don't mean to suggest that the 1980s didn't have the right to follow its own path in terms of culture and creativity. I'm simply observing that the era was, unfortunately, ushered in with an act of despicable narcissism in the spotlight, a quality which would pervade all aspects of popular media and politics thereafter to varying degrees, right up to the present day. Fame is dangerous. And so are people who control the mediums which enable it.

On the small screen, we began the decade with the hangovers from the previous one, many American shows riding high in the ratings. The US had spent much of the 1970s subconsciously examining its own place in the world, through the medium of television especially. How ironic then that the show which most mercilessly exposed the hollowness at the heart of the American Dream was also the one which drew the biggest audiences on both sides of the Atlantic and ensured the ongoing success of the soap opera format by propelling itself into the next decade with such unstoppable force that the basic format is still being copied today. Yes, *Dallas* (1978-91) was everywhere and in 1980 it mesmerised the viewing public in a way never quite seen before. The "Who shot JR?" storyline seemingly garnered enough goodwill to sustain the show for another incredible 11 years, no matter how absurd the storylines became. It wasn't long before we saw spin-offs and inevitable similar-styled soaps, most notably *Dynasty* (1981-89), in which Joan Collins made a name for herself all over again and the storylines became even more implausible than the ones in *Dallas*. The gross excesses and dysfunctional antics of the Ewings, Carringtons, Colbys et al were to become arguably the most obvious example of television mirroring society in this decade, where money was power and big business was about to trample all over the ordinary working person.

In the UK, that is exactly what was happening. This is the decade which saw the collapse of the unions, the rise of the City, the closure of the mines and the emergence of the media moguls, one of whom in particular would make the leap from print to screen and in doing so cause television to be splintered into unending fractals. The wave of 'patriotism' caused by Thatcher's response to the Falkland Islands crisis was both fuelled by elements of the media and fed back into it, creating a society where the press now had a stronger grip on governing the land than the government did.

Getting back to the subject of US television on UK screens for a moment, while *Dallas* was doing a lot of heavy lifting in 1980/81, we also had two other shows of note from across the Atlantic, continuing the exploration of a theme which, besides money and power, was still very much an open wound for American society – Vietnam. *M*A*S*H* (1972-83) had been making thinly veiled observations about the conflict for years and *Magnum, P.I.* (1980-88) was about to explore the subject in a new direct way, at last offering a more rounded sensitivity to the effects that the war had on those sent into the frontline. *Magnum, P.I.* is clearly a great vehicle for Tom Selleck, who serendipitously was contracted to make the show instead of starring as Indiana Jones in *Raiders of the Lost Ark*. [1] Despite its surface layer of 'another US detective show' and breathtakingly beautiful Hawaiian setting (effectively taking over from *Hawaii Five-O* 1968-80 in this regard, which had just ended its 12-year run), *Magnum, P.I.* is also one of the cleverest shows in US history. Many of its storylines do explore Vietnam and its social impact as already mentioned, but they also deal with the running question of "Who is Robin Masters?", adding a delicious layer of surrealism to the whole narrative, which is reminiscent of *The Prisoner*. The dynamic between Magnum and Higgins is also one of the show's unique selling points. It really is an 'onion' of a presentation, revealing new layers as it moves along and inviting the viewer to consider different perspectives and possibilities, without sacrificing any of the action or entertainment value audiences had come to expect from the genre it is associated with. [2]

Vietnam provided the basis for another television series later in the decade, *The A-Team* (1983-87), another phenomenal success for Stephen J Cannell, having previously co-created *The Rockford Files* (1974-80). *The A-Team* possesses little or none of the subtlety of the multi-layered *Magnum, P.I.* and is essentially a cartoon being acted out. However, the show was incredibly popular, with its catchphrases and sanitised violence making it a huge hit with younger audiences and rejuvenating the career of George Peppard while sending that of Mr. T stratospheric. When a TV show imprints itself indelibly in the minds of a whole generation, it can legitimately be referred to a 'classic', even if it is relatively uncomplicated in its approach. For me, the best part of every episode is the initial confrontation between the team and the antagonist. It is a formulaic device which had previously been used in *The Incredible Hulk* (1977-82) and would go on to be used in other shows, most notably *The Equalizer* (1985-89). In a wider sense though, there is always that paradoxical attitude to violence, perhaps reflected in American society as a whole (and others). Mr. T might be advocating kindness and understanding, as B.A. Baracus, but was equally ready to trash the place and beat the living daylights out of the 'baddies'. Widen that out on a geopolitical scale and you can see how television both mirrors and shapes the world. The problem is, of course, that in the real world, the bullets and the pain are real too.

The A-Team did not have the monopoly on comic-book violence. Another show, which would also catapult its main protagonist into TV legend, was also captivating younger audiences around this time. *Knight Rider* (1982-86) is perhaps the most '80s' show of them all, with the Hasselhoff hair, open shirt and leather jacket accompanied by KITT – the car co-star. Like *The A-Team*, *Knight Rider* burst onto the screen with an instantly memorable theme tune, like all the best TV shows, setting the standard for the pantheon of (largely male-dominated) superheroes who would strut across our screens for the rest of the decade, projecting that goodies v baddies chestnut which TV drama loved to champion. *The Incredible Hulk* had provided the allegory for the duality of the US society in the late 1970s. Now *Knight Rider* was doing it too – pitting a good and evil version of both Knight (Michael v Garthe) and near-indestructible cars against each other. *Superman* was also doing it on the big screen. So, while the US carried on wrestling with its own identity, mirroring the world whilst at the same time inviting us to participate in its own delusion, UK audiences were more than willing to do just that.

Perhaps the biggest and most influential piece of comic-book violence from the era manifested itself in precisely that form. When Filmation unleashed *He-Man and the Masters of the Universe* in 1983, based on the Mattel toy, they could never have known what the impact was going to be. The phenomenon that He-Man became opened the doors to endless similar animated features and also pushed the boundaries of on-screen violence for younger viewers again, in the name of good. Cartoons had always featured violence in one form or another, but in He-Man we have the US flexing its muscles again, making subtle political points with a prince who changes his form to fight the "evil forces of Skeletor" (note that 'form-shifting' trope again). He-Man is not only strong, he's "the most powerful man in the universe", but only when he needs to be. The rest of the time he's the carefree Prince Adam. Mattel sales of the He-Man toys peaked in the mid-80s, but dropped off rapidly when the cartoon's production was halted in 1985, indicating once again how powerful television was at this time. Other cartoons followed, with similar dualistic lead characters – *ThunderCats* (1985-89), drawing on a mystical sword to transform or boost their abilities to fight evil. Perhaps the most unsubtle example of all was *Transformers* (1984-87), the clue being in the name, where everyday vehicles would change into robot warriors. Nevertheless, by the middle of the 1980s, the US' obsession with split-personality heroes was at its absolute zenith, in both grown-up and children's entertainment, as if it was subconsciously psycho-analysing and reflecting itself simultaneously. While conversations were held at the time about levels of violence in children's shows, many more were taking place in relation to the same thing on home videos.

The home video market took off in the 1980s, with people suddenly having access to a vast amount of material, either officially in terms of film releases or unofficially with bootleg copies. Films, in particular low-budget horror, the so called 'video nasties', were being made specifically for video. Initially a pricey hobby (video recorders were expensive, as were the cassettes), by the end of the decade it was big business. If you had a television (preferably colour) and a video recorder, you could record broadcasts and rewatch them over and over again. In one sense, this opened up an exciting world, yet in another respect it was the first nail in the coffin of new creative TV. Production companies suddenly did not need to rely on television to be the broadcast receiver, only the apparatus through which to view the video. Also, there was less of a requirement to produce new material because people were starting to clamour for videos of old shows.

Before we explore the UK's own television output, I want to mention *The Equalizer* once more, tying in with the subject of violence. Set in New York City for the most part, the show reflects levels of violence, especially gun crime – brought into sharp focus by the murder of John Lennon there in 1980 – something which the city had built up an unenviable reputation for. *The Equalizer* mixes the spy genre with elements of the popular vigilante or maverick style films most notoriously presented in the *Death Wish* franchise, a body of work which has debatable artistic merits, especially in its later entries, but which is infamous for its portrayal of violence. *The Equalizer* is undeniably a violent show. It seeks to portray the dangers of New York in the 1980s, with darkened alleyways and graffiti-covered subways, the suggestion being that malevolence is lurking there constantly, overwhelming the authorities and being fought against by our hero, one Robert McCall. The show was immensely popular because, once again, it partly mirrored reality. People could relate to it and bought into the fantasy element of the indestructible McCall, "the most dangerous man in North America", being the avenging (or in this case 'equalizing') angel. Except that Robert McCall was most definitely not an angel. He was a tormented 'agent' with a cold talent for assassination and a past riddled with dark secrets of a morally ambiguous nature. He was now attempting to make amends for this mysterious backstory by helping people in trouble for nothing in return. A self-sustaining adventurer in a similar style to *The Saint*, he drives a luxury car and has access to seemingly limitless financial resources, weaponry and professional assistance. He will front up any adversary and ends up completely deconstructing whatever villainy they are perpetrating. This must surely be America presenting itself again, except there is a twist this time. Robert McCall, though he may be American, is more 'transatlantic' because he is portrayed on screen by Edward

Woodward, giving us, essentially, a revamped version of Callan, but with the same intense hatred of authority. So convincing was Woodward's portrayal that he would regularly have people approach him directly and ask for help, as if he actually was Robert McCall in real life. He said that he used to carry leaflets with information about citizens advice to hand out. That is the power of television right there.

In the UK, this power was about to be harnessed in a way not seen before by audiences. To some, it would be used as a tool to play on society's conscience, while to others it was about to be used in a way that had genuine impact on people's lives. While some areas of the country were to profit hugely from the Thatcherite approach to the economy, others inevitably suffered and by the end of the decade unemployment was soaring, as was homelessness. The gap between the rich and the poor, which has always existed, seemed to be on an irreversible course of widening by the day. [3] The Establishment's response? Highlight the destitution it had caused in TV specials and get the viewers to dip into their pockets to raise money, so the cynical might say. Broadcast charity events were not new, but in the 1980s they went into overdrive on UK television. The BBC's *Children In Need* in 1980 essentially opened the floodgates for this format. Images of the disadvantaged being broadcast into people's living rooms, followed by a number to call to pledge money was the standard approach. Big-name presenters and other famous faces would get onboard with it and soon these shows would become national events, with *Children In Need* occurring every year since. Other similar shows would follow. ITV's first *Telethon* was broadcast in 1988, consisting of 27 hours non-stop fundraising, fronted by Michael Aspel, their Terry Wogan equivalent at the time. Possibly the most monumental shift in using television as a vehicle for charity came in 1984 when the BBC News report by Michael Buerk in Ethiopia was broadcast, revealing the scale of famine there and what he referred to as "hell on Earth". Pictures of starving and dying men, women and children in the news report were genuinely shocking to a large portion of the viewing public, many of whom responded by donating to relief charities. Later, we would see *Comic Relief* being set up in response, another charitable venture for television, involving the sale of red noses, firstly for people, then later for vehicles, as well as a whole host of memorable TV moments involving the cream of Britain's comedy performers. The UK, while continuing to aggressively pursue its capitalist agenda both internally and globally, was at the same time entering its golden age for broadcast charity events. In a way, comedy was the perfect way to explore this awkward relationship between capitalism and charity, the gross excesses of the 1980s typified in Harry Enfield's obnoxious Loadsamoney character, waving wads of cash around and then being 'run over' on his way out of the studio. We've seen how television was used as a platform in the US to explore some of the contradictions in the culture there and now the UK was following suit, taking away with one hand and giving with the other, all made possible by television.

The Ethiopia crisis in 1984, initially brought into our homes by television, would rekindle and effectively boost into hitherto unthought-of proportions, another social phenomenon, facilitated in huge part, by television. When Band Aid put out the charity single *Do They Know It's Christmas?* in 1984 to raise money for the starving in Africa, it touched a nerve with the record-buying public, who quickly rallied to make it the fastest selling 45rpm disc up to that point. The accompanying video showing the plethora of pop and rock acts who had come together to record the song was given plenty of TV airtime. But this was just the beginning. Bob Geldof, who had first conceived the idea of the charity record, was about to instigate an even more logistically Herculean process in the form of *Live Aid*. This was to be a largely transatlantic event, with two main concerts taking place in London and Philadelphia, involving some of the biggest names in music and broadcast into as many homes as possible on television. The fund-raising concert idea was not new either, with George Harrison having organised the *Concert For Bangladesh* over a decade earlier, but this time the scale of the event was much larger and more complex, using the Bangladesh event as a basic template. It has been estimated that around 40% of the world's population at the time saw the broadcast, totalling 1.9 billion people in 150 countries. The concerts, though plagued by some technical issues here and there, were largely successful and entertaining at the same time, illustrating the power of television once again – this time on a massive scale and motivated by the desire to achieve something for the betterment of the human race. The medium had indeed come a long way since Logie Baird's demonstration of the first working television in 1926.

So, while television as a medium clearly had a firm grip on society by the 1980s, thanks in part to technical advances and thanks also in part to the quality of the material being broadcast over the previous 25 years, it was also, in many respects, at a crossroads. No longer a vehicle for pure entertainment, art for art's sake or escapism, TV had the power to control, to manipulate and to *scare*. Arguably, this had been the case since day one, but now we were starting to see it in full swing. Frank Zappa had lampooned the power of television and society's willingness to lap it up in the early 1970s, calling it "the tool of the government and industry". The public health campaign in relation to HIV/AIDS which appeared on our screens in the middle of the decade in the form of adverts voiced by John Hurt was immensely dark in tone, featuring volcanoes and tombstones – imagery which was seared into the minds of a whole generation. You can debate forever the fine line between informing the public of a danger and fuelling anxiety. There is no doubt that this particular campaign walked that line and achieved both, with long-lasting ramifications. The British government at the time claimed that it did alter people's behaviour and so in essence saved lives. Exactly to what extent this is true can obviously never be proven, but the campaign certainly had an impact.

I have hinted that television was fragmenting. The 1980s saw the launch of Channel 4, meaning that terrestrial viewers now had four channels to choose from. Here we begin to see the phenomenon of more choice not necessarily translating into more quality. By the end of the decade, yet more choice was available as traditional broadcasters began to receive more and more competition. Satellite or cable television was rapidly threatening the status quo, as was the advent of 24-hour news and programming. [4] In the 1960s, content had to be good to get airtime. Now, by the end of the 1980s, there was more airtime and TV schedules to fill than you could shake the proverbial stick at; the home video market was booming and gaming was also starting to get its tentacles into the market. What happened to the creative side of UK television in the 1980s? Where did it go right, and where did it go wrong?

The Professionals had begun in the 1970s and carried on into the 80s, beaming larger-than-life macho escapades into our living rooms until 1983. Although I enjoyed the series, I always thought of it as a more comic-book version of *The Sweeney* in style. There was violence, certainly, and the three main protagonists always brought the highest of professional standards to the screen (pun intended). Storylines dealt with plenty of prescient topics – terrorism, kidnappings, Cold War espionage, corruption and political intrigue were the regular themes – but the show is most definitely a 70s creation. It would take the arrival of *Dempsey and Makepeace* (1985-86) to begin to challenge or question the 'male-centred' attitudes which had prevailed since the action genre began. *The Avengers* had made some progress in the 1960s in this regard, but I would argue that its own descent into silliness took the edge off that. Its revival as *The New Avengers* rowed back a bit on the slapstick, but strong – genuinely strong – female leads were still relatively rare. [5] The US had provided us with *Cagney and Lacey* (1982-88) which made big steps towards a female-led crime series and *Dempsey and Makepeace* picked up on that. Now one of the co-leads was a woman and just as involved in the main – dangerous – action as the man. It was a relatively short-lived show in the grand scheme of things, running to only 30 episodes, but certainly helped introduce the idea of a female lead in a serious action/drama role, rather than the lighter-toned shows that had done so previously.

There was also more compelling and great thought-provoking drama on offer if you knew where to look for it. I'm thinking specifically of BBC2's broadcast of *Edge of Darkness* right in the middle of the decade, drawing specifically on another major source of societal and political anxiety - nuclear warfare. Television as a medium was now regularly being used as means of speaking to or about existential issues in its main features as well as its advertising. No matter where you went on television, you couldn't avoid famine, disease or the threat of death. Another one-off dramatic presentation I always think of from the 80s was broadcast on ITV in 1988 and was a 100% Cold War thriller called *Codename: Kyril*, featuring a host of big names, including Edward Woodward again, painting an intensely bleak picture of world affairs.

As a generalisation, the BBC had major success in the 1980s in two areas of entertainment: soaps and comedy, while ITV tended to play host to major drama series. The TV soap had long been a winning formula for the BBC's competitor, with *Coronation Street* dominating the ratings since 1960 and *Crossroads* also enjoying success since the mid-60s. This monopoly was about to change as the BBC introduced *EastEnders* to its schedule, finally providing some serious competition for *Coronation Street*, a rivalry which continues to this day. [6] It is hard to pinpoint exactly what the popularity of these shows is founded upon, but it is undeniably the case that millions of people love them. We have discussed how television mirrors people's lives to varying degrees, and this must surely be at the heart of what makes a soap successful. It takes everyday life and exaggerates it slightly – sometimes a lot – and uses familiar characters as a means of exploring all kinds of real-life dramas. In the early 1980s, the TV ratings battle was all about the 'big two', with Christmas storylines becoming particularly melodramatic in a bid to snare the coveted top spot. Excluding special events, the three highest-viewed TV broadcasts in the UK are all from the 1980s, and all are soaps, with the 'Angie and Den divorce papers' episodes of *EastEnders* in slots one and two (30.15 and 28 million), and Hilda Ogden's exit from *Coronation Street* in third place (26.65 million). [7] While to some in the 1980s the soap opera may have represented the lowest form of television entertainment – in an era before reality TV took over – it was also by far the most popular statistically. Not only that, the BBC, on a roll with *EastEnders*, also hit the jackpot with a total punt of an import from Australia later in the decade, creating another TV phenomenon which, at its zenith, would rival the big two. Australian soaps were already on our screens in the UK in the 1980s, *Sons and Daughters* and *The Young Doctors* being two reasonably successful examples, but nothing could have prepared us for the juggernaut of *Neighbours*. The show became so popular, especially with younger audiences, that the BBC had to reschedule its regular broadcast time so that children could watch it after school. It also made international superstars out of several of its cast, some of whom branched out into music and/or film careers.

In the meantime, while soap operas were king on British television, comedy was also experiencing something of a resurgence, especially on the BBC, which had a great back catalogue in the genre, particularly situation comedy. *Hancock's Half Hour* (1956-60), *Steptoe And Son* (1962-74), *Monty Python's Flying Circus* (1969-74), *Porridge* (1974-77), *Dad's Army* (1968-77), and *Fawlty Towers* (1975 and 79) are among a few of their classic shows in a popular genre in terms of peak viewing timeslots from the late 1950s onwards. The 1980s were about to yield a fresh crop of new cutting-edge comics and writers who would move the form on again just as their predecessors had. While the BBC by no means had the monopoly on comedy, or the performers, many of the shows which have now engrained themselves in the nation's psyche were first viewed on the channel. It is interesting that the term 'alternative comedy' was applied to this crop of new talent until, of course, it became completely mainstream and, in some cases, flagship. [8]

The cult surrealism of *The Young Ones* (1982 and 1984) and biting satire of *Not the Nine O'Clock News* (1979-82) soon developed into the era-defining, ever-evolving show that we know now as *Blackadder*. Encompassing the talents of Richard Curtis, Ben Elton,

Rowan Atkinson, Stephen Fry, Hugh Laurie, Tony Robinson and Tim McInnerny, the series grew in popularity from initially modest beginnings. The second series saw a major uptick in quality and the establishment of a winning formula which was sustained through the third and into the fourth and final regular iterations of the show. The last episode of *Blackadder Goes Forth* (*Goodbyeee* 1989) is considered by many to be one of the finest ever in situation comedy, crossing over as it does successfully with historical drama of the utmost poignancy. As a piece of historical comedy commenting on war it has arguably never been bettered. Yes, *Blackadder* was formulaic, but it was also brilliantly witty and insightful in terms of lampooning the Establishment, which – I would suggest – all the best comedy should do. This era also is notable for the rise of female writers and comediennes, with Victoria Wood, Dawn French and Jennifer Saunders gaining prominence and enjoying great success in a field hitherto dominated by men. [9] The other phenomenal success for the BBC during this time was *Only Fools and Horses* (1981-2003), which grew and grew in terms of popularity as the decade progressed, crossing successfully into the 1990s and hitting an all-time audience peak in 1996 with the festive episode *Time on Our Hands* (24.35 million). It was a show which tapped into society's conscience as much as *Blackadder* did, but probably appealed to a wider demographic because it was set in a time and place to which most people could immediately relate – Tory Britain – with Del Boy's constant refrain about becoming 'millionaires' chiming with the dream/fantasy being sold to the public by the government.

On ITV, we were introduced to the world of *Spitting Image* (1984-96), a puppet-show like no other. To say the series took no prisoners in terms of its satire would be an understatement, with pretty much anyone and everyone in the public eye being lampooned at one point or another. Margaret Thatcher and the royal family were frequent targets, as were many others from the world of politics, music, entertainment and beyond. It was crude at times, and sometimes disproportionately so, but it still performed a function which society desperately needs and that is to be free to laugh at itself. It also serves as a good litmus test for fame – a 'celebrity' would certainly know they had hit the big time when the puppeteers immortalised them. Despite the (at times) savage nature of the satire, because it was under the auspices of comedy somehow it was deemed acceptable. I can remember watching the 1987 General Election Special and loving it, while also wondering how on earth they were getting away with it. The antics of politicians in particular were singled out and magnified in amusing, though unsubtle, ways. Political comedy of a far more nuanced, yet immensely popular nature was rumbling along on the BBC in the form of *Yes Minister* (1980-84) and later *Yes, Prime Minister* (1986-88), with the loquacious Sir Humphrey Appleby (Nigel Hawthorne) brilliantly exposing the preposterous nature of bureaucracy at the heart of the Establishment.

On ITV, the 1980s would give us Granada's *Sherlock Holmes* (1984-94). On the face of it, revisiting a character which had already been portrayed numerous times for decades might seem like a backward step. The only way to make it work and make it significant, would be to employ a totally dedicated production team and first-rate cast. Fortunately for us, that is exactly what happened. Initially at least, the TV screenplays were faithful to the source material and the portrayal of Holmes by Jeremy Brett soon became definitive for many, me included. The 1980s saw the production of *The Adventures of Sherlock Holmes*, *The Return of Sherlock Holmes* and two feature-length presentations, *The Sign of Four* and *The Hound of the Baskervilles*. All of these are excellent. Towards the end of the decade, Jeremy Brett's health problems were beginning to show on screen in terms of his appearance, but his absolute grasp of the role is enough to compensate for this and, indeed, some of the later shows are among the best.

Towards the end of the 1980s, we were, somewhat unexpectedly, presented with another instant classic rendering of a hero from detective fiction. *Agatha Christie's Poirot* (1989-2013), as it was known, first appeared in the final year of the 80s, but soon established itself as one of the greatest dramatic presentations of the decade, and the 1990s would see the production go from strength to strength. Liberties were taken with the source material more so than with the early *Sherlock Holmes* shows, but David Suchet's portrayal soon became as synonymous with the Belgian sleuth as Brett's had with Holmes. Unlike with the Holmes shows, versions of every Agatha Christie story featuring Poirot were eventually made, giving the series a wonderful beginning, middle and end which few often get. The earlier ones are the best, in my opinion, as the later productions go significantly darker in tone, possibly playing to the perceived demands of the audience. However, the 1980s had given us two of the greatest classic detective series ever on British television and ones which it will be very, very difficult to ever better.

At around this time, the US flung in a curveball as well, but certainly a welcome one...It brought back *Columbo*. Initially marketed as 'new Columbo', the show soon settled into an irregular production pattern until the early 2000s when it finally ended. Peter Falk's portrayal this time around is generally more benevolent, and the overall standard is not as good as the 1970s show, but there are one or two gems in there. ITV also brought us John Thaw's second signature role in the form of *Inspector Morse*, which started in 1987 and became hugely successful. The Channel Islands would be brought into focus in the 1980s as well, as the setting for yet another detective caper, *Bergerac* (1981-91) which drew on some elements from its creator's earlier show, *Shoestring* (1979-80), to create an interesting 'hero'. Jim Bergerac, our protagonist, is a recovering alcoholic and as such is portrayed by John Nettles as a man with vulnerabilities. Aside from the main character's depth, there are interesting societal frictions reflected in the series, with a lot of rich versus poor undercurrents and also occasionally hints of the supernatural. The show was a success and ran for a decade. Add to this *Taggart* (1985-2010), *The Ruth Rendell Mysteries* (1987-2000) and any number of other shows of a similar vein which graced the screens during these ten years, and it is plain to see that audiences in the 1980s loved their detective stories.

Although it began in 1979, there is one show which is quintessentially 80s and which walks a fine line between drama and comedy in a rare and effective way. Originally intended as a vehicle for Dennis Waterman, *Minder* (1979-94) drew on similar inspirations as *Only Fools and Horses* and created a character every bit as memorable as Del Boy, possibly even more so. Like *Dallas*, which was initially supposed to be about Bobby and Pam and ended up being the Larry Hagman show, *Minder*'s popularity began to be founded on George Cole's timeless, superb portrayal of Arthur Daley. The creation of television's ultimate 'wide boy' was a masterclass from the actor who had been 'Flash Harry' on the big screen. Cole had been heavily influenced by Alastair Sim earlier in his career and you can clearly see this in Arthur Daley. Every mannerism, facial expression and reaction is straight from the Sim school of observational comedy. Arthur Daley became popular with viewers because we all knew him, or someone like him, especially in the 1980s, when aspiration and rip-off seemed to go hand-in-hand. When Waterman decided to leave the series, it is fair to say it did begin to drop off in quality, so it wasn't all about Cole. Their on-screen chemistry was magical, and the writing was also razor-sharp, two factors which helped make pretty much every episode from the Waterman-Cole era a winner.

Viewers seemed to enjoy lighter drama, as demonstrated by the success of *Minder*, another bullseye for Euston Films, while the BBC had been running *All Creatures Great and Small* since 1978 and this also became a mainstay of 80s television. Once again, the world being presented here is almost soap opera, but with enough comedic elements to make it something else entirely. Like *Minder*, the ratio is probably 40:60 in favour of drama, although some may argue it is more equal than that. This is an important distinction from a show like *Only Fools and Horses* or *Blackadder*, where the emphasis throughout is clearly on comedy, despite both those shows being notable for their serious messages too. It is, therefore, no surprise that *Lovejoy*, which first appeared in 1986 on the BBC, was ripe for success. Ian McShane brings us yet another 'lovable rogue' in the form of the eponymous hero, the fourth-wall breaking antiques expert and gallivanting chancer, in a series which pushes the comedy ratio the other way. This is light entertainment at its best, once again tapping into the public's thirst for salt-of-the-earth protagonists – the 1980s revelling in the adventures of Del Boy, Arthur Daley and Lovejoy. As every great comedy writer knows, there is something connectable about a character who strives all the time to succeed and we love it when they do it against the odds, at the expense of the Establishment. It's that fantasy again, that delusion, which television provides us with continuously. [10]

One show which hit the rocks in the 1980s was *Doctor Who*. The sci-fi classic, which had started in the 1960s and flourished through the 1970s with Jon Pertwee and Tom Baker in the lead role, limped into the 1980s with a newish production team and seemingly even less ideas than money. Production values had always been a challenge for the series, made as it was on a shoestring budget and having to compete with the glitz of big-screen science fiction. For whatever reason, the show soon moved into the crosshairs of the BBC bosses and its days were numbered from about 1984 onwards. Initially the show faced a hiatus, then cancellation in 1989. To be fair to the programme, it did significantly improve in the last two years of production and was on an upward trajectory when the axe was brought down. It has always amused me that, having rinsed the video market for the show for the next fifteen or so years, the BBC then regenerated it with flagship status, which it retains to this day. Such are the ups and downs of a long-running TV show, with an obsessive fanbase. *Tales Of The Unexpected* (1979-88) lasted almost ten years, making it a mainstay of 1980s television. The anthology show would genre hop and attract top talent and, as a result, has gained cult status. One week you would get a straightforward crime thriller, the next a sci-fi caper, then a historical drama, horror, comedy...it was all in there. It was similar to *The Twilight Zone* in some respects and so, in a decade when retro was suddenly beginning to become fashionable again, it was curious to see Rod Serling's show resurrected as well. Although the venerated creator himself had died ten years earlier, his image appeared at the start of every new episode, now in colour of course.

If the 1960s was the party, the 1970s the hangover, then the 1980s was surely the "What the hell do we do next?" decade. In popular music, when New Wave crashed onto the sands, artists then began actively looking back to the 60s for their inspiration, having (mostly) actively shunned it 10 years earlier. The surviving members of The Beatles suddenly became hugely popular again, enjoying chart success and/or massive-grossing live tours. By 1989, the seeds of what would be referred to as Britpop in the 90s were being sown by acts like The Stone Roses and the Happy Mondays, although Britpop as a term is meaningless and the bands certainly had no agenda for creating a movement based on the past. They were simply drawing inspiration. By the mid-1990s, any attempt to disguise the influence of the 1960s, with the music press pretending they had found a new groove, subsided completely when Oasis started steering the ship. The 60s were in again and it was party time once more. The geo-political landscape was changing too. Towards the end of the 1980s, the Cold War was becoming less immediately relevant, the Berlin Wall eventually came down and then the Soviet Union collapsed as the 90s began. Tensions in the Middle East had always been high, but with the USSR fading from existence, America needed a new enemy, who duly stepped forward in the person of Saddam Hussein, ushering in a new era of constant needling and antagonism in the region which would cast its dark shadow way beyond the next decade, into the next millennium. Television would be there for all of it, replaying every second over and over again into the clobbered minds of each new generation, until the medium itself would be challenged.

The era of reality TV threatens to erase any creative energy from the airwaves and other platforms offer a constant flow of information, much of which has no basis in truth. Now – to borrow from Frank Zappa – the slime oozes out from your phone or device as well, [11] but will the human race be clever enough to consolidate what is beneficial from our rapidly advancing technology and use it to end wars, prevent pandemics, stabilise climate and restrain artificial intelligence? Or will we simply continue to watch it all on television and now the internet, buying into the delusion and pretending none of it is really happening? You decide. Or, if you prefer, watch someone claiming to be famous stick their head into a box of kookaburra excrement.

© Mike Pegler

1. Editor: ironically, a Screen Actors' Guild strike delayed production on the first season of *Magnum, P.I.* from March to December 1908 which meant that Selleck could have made *Raiders of the Lost Ark* after all.
2. Editor: I share Mike's love of *Magnum, PI* and would simply add here that the series frequently defies viewers' expectations of the detective genre, in terms of mood, style and theme: ranging from truly dark plots and killers to almost slapstick storylines and guest characters. The series continually throws us curveballs such as dream narratives, ghost stories, time travel, crossovers, film spoofs...
3. "In 1980, a man in the top 10% of earners would, on average, have been on 2.5 times the weekly income of a man in the bottom 10%, after income tax. By 1990, it was more than 3.5 times. This was achieved partly through tax reductions and deregulation, which allowed net incomes to rise at the top end of the pay scale. Further down, restrictive laws to curb trade unions kept a check on wages." Andy McSmith, *No Such Thing As Society: A History of Britain in the 1980s*, p. 6.
4. Editor: we could add the emergence of 'breakfast television' into this TV saturation, I guess.
5. Editor: genres and subgenres are obviously fluid. While one might argue that both *The Gentle Touch* and *Juliet Bravo* are

police procedurals rather than 'action' series, there is no question in my mind that they had both made inroads in terms of gender stereotyping, long before the SI 10 pairing of Harriet Makepeace and James Dempsey.

6. Editor: the rival soaps did join forces in 2010 to make a crossover episode – *East Street* – for *Children in Need*.

7. Editor: the Adalyser website breaks the ratings into two categories: TV Special Events – such as royal weddings, state funerals, World Cup Finals – and regular TV Broadcasts. Bizarrely, it considers Live Aid (24.5 million) as a broadcast rather than a special event.

8. Editor: 'alternative comedy' is often used as a term to define "comedy that makes a conscious break with the mainstream comedic style of an era". There are alternative – no pun intended – definitions though, as in the concept of "anti-establishment comedy: containing a political component and offering an alternative, dissident voice". Ben Elton, for me, would be a comedian who fits either definition.

9. Editor: I would throw in Channel 4's *The Comic Strip Presents...* (1982-88) as both an example of pioneering 'alternative comedy' and a great showcase for French and Saunders.

10. Editor: Yes, for me Del Boy and Arthur Daley are the 80s most powerful satirical figures, in the sense of their significant influence on popular culture. Despite both characters obviously buying into the concept of 'entrepreneurial Britain', as I observed in my Preface you can have affection for their roguish characters whilst still acknowledging the satire lurking beneath.

11. Frank Zappa: "I am the slime oozing out from your TV set. You will obey me while I lead you, and eat the garbage while I feed you."

CONTRIBUTORS

Morris Bright MBE has worked as a writer and broadcast journalist for more than 30 years. He has written and co-authored many books, including the definitive histories of Pinewood, Shepperton and Elstree Studios, of which he was the Chairman from 2007-2023. He remains a director at Elstree, the historical home to the first *Star Wars* and *Indiana Jones* trilogies. He has written biographies on Dame Thora Hird, *Carry On* producer Peter Rogers and books for the BBC on *Fawlty Towers* and *Last of the Summer Wine*.

JZ Ferguson is a British popular culture enthusiast with a particular affinity for television series of the 1960s and 70s. She contributed chapters to all five volumes in *The Avengers on film* series. She has also written for the *Classic British Television Drama* book series. She contributed chapters to *Tis Magic! Our Memories of Catweazle*, *Swinging TV*, and *Survival TV*. She has also written for the website *The Avengers Declassified*. She lives in Canada.

Edward Kellett is a TV historian and the author of *Reaching a Verdict: Reviewing The Bill* (1983-1989), published in 2023 by devonfirebooks.com.

Trevor Knight stumbled into a career as a senior manager at Staffordshire and Aston Universities but has always wanted to be a writer. He has a lifelong love of 'classic' television, films and popular culture, especially from the 1950s (though he is not *that* old) to the end of the 20th century after which it all went a bit blank, as well as music of various genres including film and TV scores. He lives in Worcestershire with his wife, son and an excitable Jack Russell. He contributed two chapters to *Survival TV*.

Joanne Knowles is a Senior Lecturer in Media, Culture, Communication at Liverpool John Moores University.

Andrew Lane is a novelist and audio script writer who has also written non-fiction books about Aardman Animations, sci-fi series *Babylon 5*, the BBC version of *Randall and Hopkirk (Deceased)* and James Bond in books, films, animation, comics and computer games, the latter co-written with Paul Simpson.

Madeleine Langham has worked in both radio and in library services. She is a child of the 1990s who fell in love with older films and television series at an early age. She can be found writing predominately about classic era film and television at her website classicfilmandtvcorner.wordpress.com.

Rodney Marshall is the son of television and film script writer Roger Marshall. He has written and edited books on a range of subjects including Scottish Noir crime fiction, Oradour the WW2 'martyr village', football and British television drama in the 60s, 70s and 80s. He is a co-host of the *ITC Entertained the World* podcast.

Tomas Marshall is the grandson of television and film script writer Roger Marshall. He has a life-long passion for animation which he studied at Nottingham Trent University. He is currently working in the field of video game animation.

Richard Marson joined the BBC from university and spent many years as a TV director, producer and executive. He spent ten years on *Blue Peter* (with four of them as Editor) during which he won a BAFTA. He also produced and directed the 90-minute documentary *Tales of Television Centre*. He is the author of several books, including biographies of John Nathan-Turner, Verity Lambert and Biddy Baxter and a history of the series *Upstairs, Downstairs*. He lives in the wilds of West Yorkshire and enjoys good conversation, walking, reading, history, and all kinds of TV, from 'trash' to all-time classics.

Ian Payn works in the legal sector. He owns many antiques, none of them bought from a man in a leather jacket with a dodgy mullet.

Mike Pegler is a writer and blogger on subjects including TV, music, film, cooking, gardening, astronomy and the exploration of the natural world. He contributed chapters to both *Swinging TV* and *Survival TV*.

Al Samujh is a co-host of the *ITC Entertained the World* podcasts and an occasional essayist, having written studies on both *Man in a Suitcase* and *Catweazle*. A lifelong cinephile, TV addict and researcher, you will find his name peppered amongst several volumes of film and television studies, sometimes as a complete surprise to him. He contributes to books and magazines on classic horror films and, back in the days of old technology, wrote Teletext notes on vintage television for a satellite TV company. He contributed chapters to both *Swinging TV* and *Survival TV*.

Lucy Smith enjoys classic television, from being fascinated by the Thames ident at the start of *Rainbow* repeats as a child, to getting to write about British television whilst studying history at university, during every appropriate module.

Cailin Thomas runs the popular and humorous *Sweeney Archive* Twitter/X feed and is a "major car buff", with a passion for restoring old classics. She contributed a chapter to *Survival TV*.

Paul Watts is the author of *Above the Law – The Unofficiial Guide to Star Cops*, and has also written about *Doctor Who*. When not working as a Learning Disabilities carer he is an illustrator, contributing to several horror-themed publications.

Chris Wood trained in film and animation at St Martin's, was poached from the rigours of BBC Open University graphic design to spend four wonderful years Playing Away on BBC's Children television. The glamour of celluloid called, and in 1980 he joined National Screen to become Creative Director, initially designing and producing movie and TV title and presentation sequences, before forming W3KTS Ltd and specialising in Promos - most notably for

Bravo TV. He is currently resting between pictures (i.e. sleeping on a bench in an art gallery) in York.

SELECT BIBLIOGRAPHY

Baker, S and P Hoey, P, 'The picaro and the prole, the spiv and the honest Tommy in Leon Griffith's *Minder*', *Journal of British Cinema and Television*, (2018)

Bakhtin, M, *Rabelais and his world*, (Indiana University Press, 1984)

Brassett, James, *The Ironic State: British Comedy and the Everyday Politics of Globalization* (Bristol University Press, 2021)

Carpenter, Humphrey, *That Was Satire That Was*, (Orion, 2000)

Clement, D and I La Frenais, *More Than Likely: A Memoir* (Weidenfield and Nicholson, 2019)

Cooke, Lez, *British television drama: a history* (2003, BFI 2015 2nd edition)

Cooke, Lez, *A sense of place: regional British television drama, 1965-1982* (Manchester University Press, 2012)

Curran, J. and V Porter, (eds) *British Cinema History* (Weidenfield and Nicholson, 1983)

Evans, Jeff (ed), *Demystifying Social Statistics*, (Pluto, 1989)

Goodwin, Andrew (ed), *Understanding Television* (Routledge, 1990)

Gray, Ann, *Video playtime: the gendering of a leisure technology* (Routledge, 1992)

Hendy, David, *The BBC: A People's History* (Profile Books Ltd, 2022)

Hirschkop, K and D Shepherd, (eds.), *Bakhtin and Cultural Theory* (Manchester University Press, 1989)

Howe, David J, Mark Stammers, Stephen James Walker, *Doctor Who: The Eighties*, (Virgin Publishing Ltd, 1996)

Howe, David J and Stephen James Walker, *Doctor Who: The Television Companion* (BBC Worldwide Ltd, 1999)

Jackson, B and R Saunders, eds. *Making Thatcher's Britain* (Cambridge University Press, 2012)

James, Peter, *Travelling Man* TV tie-in (WH Allen, 1984)

Jürgen, Kamm & Birgit Neumann, *British TV Comedies: Cultural Concepts, Contexts and Controversies* (Palgrave Macmillan, 2016)

Kay, Peter, *T.V.: Big Adventures on the Small Screen* (HarperCollins)

Kellett, Edward, *Reaching A Verdict: Reviewing The Bill (1983-1989)* (Devonfire Books, 2023)

Mark, Roger (Anthony Fowles), *Floodtide* TV tie-in (Javelin, 1987)

Mark, Roger (Anthony Fowles), *Floodtide 2* TV tie-in (Javelin, 1988)

McSmith, Andy, *No Such Thing As Society: A History of Britain in the 1980s* (Constable, 2011)

Meikle, Denis, *A History of Horrors: The Rise and Fall of the House of Hammer* (Scarecrow, 2009)

Molesworth, Richard, *The John Nathan-Turner Production Diary 1979-1990,* (Telos Publishing Ltd, 2022)

Morgenstern, Matthew: 'The Marshall Chronicles', *Primetime* magazine, 1987

Morley, D (1986) *Family television: cultural power and domestic leisure* (Commedia, 1986)

Mortimer, John, *Clinging to the Wreckage* (Penguin, 1986)

Roddam, F and D Waddell, *The Auf Wiedersehen, Pet Story: That's Living Alright* (BBC Books, 2003)

Rosengard, Peter & Roger Wilmut, *Didn't You Kill My Mother-In-Law?* (Methuen, 1989)

Sandbrook, Dominic, *Who Dares Wins: Britain, 1979-82* (Penguin, 2019)

Schlesinger, P, et al. *Televising Terrorism: political violence in popular media* (Commedia Publishing (1983)

Smart, Billy, *Spaces of Television*, University of Reading Weblogs, 2012.

Stern, B, 'Historical and personal nostalgia in advertising text: the fin de siècle effect', *Journal of Advertising,* 1992

Stewart, Graham, *Bang! A History of the 1980s* (Atlantic Books, 2012)

Strinati, Dominic, An Introduction to Studying Popular Culture (Routledge, 2000)

Tolley, Gail, The hidden history of homesickness. Wellcome Collection: The Heart of Homesickness, part 2, 2020

Turner, Alwyn W, *Rejoice! Rejoice! Britain in the 1980s* (Aurum, 2010)

Wickham P, *The Likely Lads* (Palgrave Macmillan for BFI Books, 2008)

Wyles, Lilian, *A Woman At Scotland Yard: Reflections on the Struggles and Achievements of Thirty Years in the Metropolitan Police* (Faber and Faber, 1952)

Printed in Great Britain
by Amazon

37114770R00218